A Grandmother's Legacy

A Memoir of Five Generations who lived through the Days of the Raj

Jenny Mallin

About the Author

Jenny Mallin's earliest memories are of her mother in the kitchen, tapping a wooden spoon against the side of the metal dekshi and then tasting her curry sauce, checking the seasoning. From that moment, Jenny was hooked and her mother continued to nurture her love of cooking throughout her childhood. The kitchen, a wonderfully warm and intoxicating environment, became an indoor playground filled with new experiences, the end result - something delicious on a plate. She took such a pride in helping her mother that it wasn't seen as a chore, but as a special time together. Consequently, that love of cooking coupled with a desire to please someone with her food has never left her.

With her passions for cooking, India, research and writing, the outcome has been a labour of love – a memoir that mingles the history of her family when they lived in India, with her grandmothers' recipes that were prudently passed down through the generations. Each recipe has been lovingly researched, leading Jenny on a road of discovery about her ancestors, with her grandmothers' legacy continuing to assist in providing clues to their rich and eventful past.

Now a writer, Jenny has worked in the past as a PA, a Travel Buyer and in a number of television production roles for the BBC. Now living in Kingsclere with Stewart, her husband of over 30 years, and their three cats, any spare time is devoted to cooking, painting, and enjoying the outdoors.

https://agrandmotherslegacy.co.uk/

Wilhelmina
born 1828
in Madras,
India

Ophelia
born 1855
in Mylapore,
India

Maud
born 1879
in Madras,
India

Irene
born 1899
in Madras,
India

Cynthia
born 1927
in Calcutta,
India

I dedicate this book to all my grandmothers, but especially to my darling mother who gave me life and taught me how to believe in myself, my principles and most importantly inspired me to go after my dreams…

Acknowledgements

The Internet – the virtual world we all live in now, without which this book simply would never have got off the ground...

I would also like to thank the following people:

Amy Wiley who did much of the excellent editing work from all the way across the pond on the West Coast of America. To Rowena Hensman for her most helpful proofreading in the initial stages. A very special mention must go to Louise Sharma, who not only became my close friend whilst I was touring India, but was instrumental in providing the essential network to my frame, when I was in need of connecting with the right people in India, Louise proved to be a most valuable and indispensable source for me.

For this beautifully designed book cover, I would like to show my appreciation to the incredibly talented Dheeraj Devgun for his creative skills in providing such amazing artwork for me - he truly is a genius.

There are two special ladies who have supported me in my marketing activities: Barbara Payne of Digital House and Claire Sutton of Minerva Marketing both of whom continue to support me through strategic marketing planning on all aspects of my book through events. My sincere thanks to them both.

My book would not have been written if it wasn't for Bulent Akkaya who saw right from the early days (soon after losing my father) that I needed to write "my project" into a book - my grateful thanks therefore must go to a lovely couple and dear friends of mine, Bulent and Dilek Akkaya for their encouragement and support along the way, but also for Bulent's foresight in recognising that there was a "book" waiting to be written here...

Lastly, to my other half Stewart for being my rock in so many ways, and someone who has never stopped believing in me.

Foreword

Often as Indians we think about the fabulous foods we ate in the home prepared by several aunts, grannies, our mums and we yearn as we grow older for those foods. The memories never go away; they may fade a bit and then all of a sudden we realise the loss as the older generations pass away one by one and we grapple for the recipes, the tastes, the feeling, the sensations and the aromas.

At once a familiar aroma or scent transports us in a millionth of a second to those days around the dining table and immediately memories of the food and its taste and the people around that table spring up. That's when you think I have to get hold of those recipes and treasure them for posterity to share with our kids and keep them as family heirlooms and so on and so forth.

Some manage and some do not and then some are left perhaps with just faded long jaded memories of great memories of yesteryears. Personally, I managed to salvage some from my family and now with both my parents having departed I struggle and feel the pain of not having made enough time to get as much noted as was possible.

Then out of the blue, the daughter of a pupil who was Head Boy at my old boarding school approached me for help in getting her book published. Jenny Mallin was struggling to find someone to publish her book and asked if I could help; sadly we hit several dead ends, but having seen the effort and the passion and love put into the book it is my honour and privilege to write the foreword to this amazing book; a collection of stories, recipes and above all fond memories.

The passion with which the book is written is amazing and can only come from someone who actually deeply and passionately loves food as much as I do and, that runs right throughout the book. Deep passion evokes deep memories and transports people to childhood memories often bringing several smiles to your face. The grandmothers here play the vital roles of matriarchs and cooks extraordinaire. But here above all is a cuisine quite not known so much and yet quite what the British Public at least ought to know about. Here is a cuisine that was created as a result of mixed marriages between two cultures, One Indian and One British at some stage. These marriages were much encouraged by the then Empirical Governors as a means of integration or at times to have off shoot that could think differently and be more aligned to British thinking. BUT what it did not realise or understand that in that marriage of cultures a cuisine would be born that would for several years remain treasured and much appreciated in India and also remain unique to that great country, never leaving its borders.

However since my career began in India and since having grown up amongst a very close knit and widespread Anglo Indian community, my experiences of Anglo Indian cuisine goes way back into my own childhood and the many friends I grew up with and my family interacted with.

In this book, Jenny manages to bring her grandmothers to life, as though they are still there standing with their hands on their hips giving orders and directions to get things right and the perfection of preparing food for the patriarchs of the family is all so familiar to us who grew up in India.

As soon as one starts reading you wish to experience the food at once and the palate is in a battle to trace back the flavours you knew so well. The readers' tastebuds are sure to be set alight with these recipes. It is easy to understand the reason behind the book and why it is so important to launch and release it, readers will from the start get an idea of what awaits within it from chapter to chapter. A collection of authentic recipes, which are truly Anglo Indian, different, and flavours that are so adaptable and, acceptable to all palates. The book is bound to hold the reader's interest and attention throughout.

This is indeed a charming, funny and moving memoir accompanied by some great dishes, many of which I hope can be featured on my menus in time to come. This is as I would expect a fascinating culinary journey with family sepia photographs evoking a bygone time that can never be rekindled. The Anglo Indians have spread far and wide and have never been understood properly as a people born of India and yet so different. I have some amazing friends and it will be no surprise to me that many will want this book. Many shall weep and many shall treasure it forever and hand it down to their progeny. It is not just evocative it is a page-turner and one has no option but to get drawn into a family's Rich Heritage.

Enjoy and Have fun

Cyrus Rustom Todiwala OBE DL DBA

Definition of Anglo-Indian

"Historically, it refers to people who were of British descent but were born and raised in India, usually because their parents were serving in the colonial administration or armed forces. However, this definition has become looser in recent decades, and can now denote any mixed British-Indian parentage, but for many its primary meaning refers to people of longstanding mixed lineage, dating back up to 300 years into India's colonial past.

They dress like the British, their mother tongue is English and they are Christian. They began leaving India in droves in the 1950s and 60s, dispersing throughout the Commonwealth countries of Canada, Australia and New Zealand, and their 'motherland', the UK. They have a distinct cuisine - Jalfrezi was a staple, and Country Captain Chicken and Railway Lamb Curry a throwback to India's railway on which many Anglo-Indians worked. But the younger generations are no longer cooking these dishes, the unique hybrid culture overarching Anglo-Indian identity is expiring, diluted through intermarriage."

"Old recipes can be one of the most valuable items you have in your kitchen. Written on scraps of paper or yellowed recipe cards in handwriting from family members that may no longer be with us, they bring back treasured memories of days gone by…"

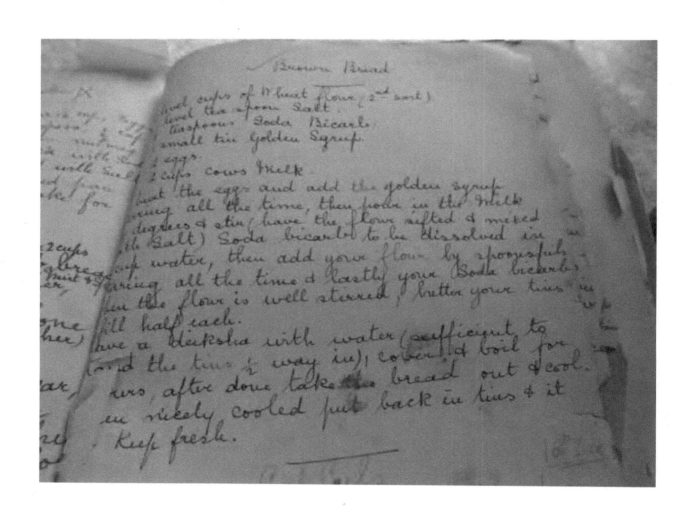

Contents

Introduction

"Just go stand and watch your mother whilst she's cooking...."

(This is a picture of my mother, taken in Bombay in 1952; she's on the left holding my brother).

I was only five at the time, but those words and its importance were drummed into me at an early age by my father. To be honest, I really enjoyed watching my mother cooking - in a small London kitchen she would produce such wonderful dishes, whilst listening to Housewives' Choice on the radio (a very popular BBC record request programme specifically to appeal to housewives at home during the day).

It was Great Britain in the fifties, not long out of food rationing, a young Queen Elizabeth is crowned, a six day working week, with Tupperware and supermarkets just around the next corner.

"Rai, jeera, haldi.." she would whisper under her breath whilst counting out the ingredients on her fingers - cooking came naturally to my mother but occasionally she would open the pantry door and out would come this huge ledger book, whereupon she would leaf through the pages until she found the recipe she was looking for.

With no title on the cover to distinguish it from the other cookbooks, the only distinctive thing I can recall is that each page was so delicate and fragile that it would snap like a poppadom therefore it was out of bounds for us children to open – set high on a shelf my mother could see at that time that this book was just too precious to lose.

Hidden high in the pantry, this dull and most unglamorous book with its ochre, faded pages bespattered with sundry sauces and flavourings revealed copperplate recipes handwritten by my great, great, great grandmother Wilhelmina dating back to 1850.

Turning the pages of the book, the handwriting style changes over time. One can see evidence of how over five generations, each one of my grandmothers have passed this on to their next generation, with the result of offering a glimpse into a fascinating time in history known as "the days of the Raj" when India was under British rule.

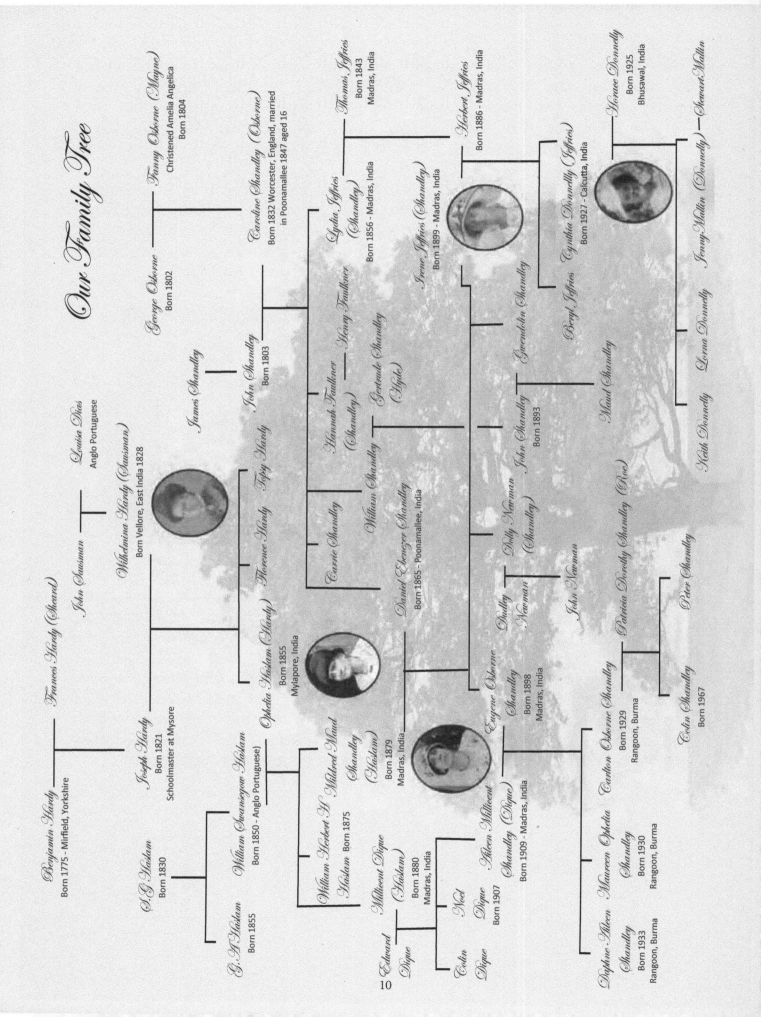

Our Family Tree

Our Family Tree

Let's take a look at my family tree and concentrate on Maud and Daniel's four children: Eugene, Irene, Gwendolin and Dolly (clockwise)...

You will see that Eugene married his first cousin Aileen (his mother Maud was sister to Millicent, Aileen's mother). In Irene's case, her father Daniel Shandley was brother to Lydia Shandley, her husband's mother. With Gwendolin, her husband John Shandley was a brother to Daniel Shandley – so Gwendolin was born a Shandley and remained a Shandley the rest of her life, so she didn't need to change name in marriage. Now see how they kept their maternal link to the family name of George Osborne right down to Eugene and his first born son Carlton with both of them carrying Osborne, the maiden name of their grandmother and great grandmother, Caroline Osborne. Additionally they kept their other great grandmother's name by christening Eugene's first daughter as Maureen Ophelia Shandley.

Family Gallery

Wilhelmina Sausman

Joseph Hardy

Ophelia Hardy

Millicent Haslam

Mildred (Maud) Haslam

Daniel Shandley

Dudley Newman

Dolly Shandley

John Shandley

Daphne Aileen Shandley

Maureen Ophelia Shandley

Carlton Osborne Shandley

Florence Hardy

Topsy Hardy

Edward Dique

Noel Dique

Aileen Millicent Dique

Eugene Osborne Shandley

Gwendolin Shandley

Irene Shandley

Herbert Jeffries

Beryl Jeffries

Cynthia Jeffries

Horace Donnelly

13

Wilhelmina

To begin my family's story of their connection to India, we need to go back seven generations to 1775, and to Yorkshire in England.

Benjamin Hardy was born into a weaving family who lived in Mirfield, a small but important industrial town with a population of two thousand people, this was an area known as the Heavy Woollen District of West Yorkshire. With a third of its population involved in the cloth making industry, over four hundred of those worked out of their tiny cottages, each member having a role from carding (which is a procedure of combing to separate the wool fibres), to spinning and finally weaving the wool to make into cloth.

It is thought there were over 100 pairs of looms in the homes of Mirfield at that time – a real cottage industry one could say.

In 1794, Britain declared war on France and a nineteen year old Benjamin Hardy enrolled as Private No. 77 with the newly formed 1st Battalion of the 84th Foot regiment of the British Army. His battalion, which was raised in York went on to become known as "The York and Lancasters" and were part of the Duke of York's ill-fated expedition to Walcheren in the Netherlands. One year later, his regiment sailed to the Cape of Good Hope - that same year Benjamin had married Frances Sheard back home in Mirfield.

Sailing to India in 1798, Benjamin and his regiment would stay for the next twenty five years there with such diverse postings as Madras, Bombay, Goa, Kattiawar (now Baroda) and Kutch, there were also detachments sent to the island of Perim in the Red Sea, Aden and Mauritius where they participated in the capture of the island from the French.

Benjamin's last posting was to be Bangalore, his regiment was stationed there for four years and during that time it's feasible that he decided then to bring wife Frances over from England as in 1816 she bore him a son. Three years later, his regiment disbanded and about to return home to England, Benjamin chose to stay in India and be discharged from the British Army due to ill health. He was forty four now and with chronic rheumatism, had spent the larger part of his life in a hot dry climate and probably decided that the warmer conditions would help his rheumatics. So with his wife and young son Joseph, Benjamin settled down to live the rest of his life out in India. In fact he lived only for another four years, passing away on 23rd December 1823.

Frances and her son Joseph stayed in India and continued to live in Bangalore. We know that Joseph became a schoolmaster by profession in Mysore. In 1833, an English-medium school was opened for the first time in Mysore and by 1881 there were over 2,000 English-medium schools in the state of Mysore. An 1835 Charter Act on the New Education Policy would further determine that English be made the official language of the courts, diplomacy and administration, prior to that date the official language had been Persian. From that moment on, only those with Western style education and a knowledge of English were eligible for government employment, or for a career in public life.

This all ties in nicely with Joseph's living in Mysore at a time when English education and the existence of English-medium schools was on the rise.

In 1844, at the age of twenty eight, Joseph married fifteen year old Wilhelmina Sausman in St. Mark's Church in Bangalore.

St. Mark's Church, Bangalore.

Born on the 12th September 1829, records suggest that Wilhelmina was Anglo-Portuguese as her mother's name was Louisa Dias, a common Portuguese name used in the Portuguese colonies of Goa and the west coast of India. Her family came from Vellore, a city one hundred and thirty miles east of Bangalore.

During their marriage, Wilhelmina gave birth to eight children, only three survived, sadly the other children died as babies and infants to the widespread pandemic of cholera. Their three daughters were named Ophelia, Florence and Topsy. Ophelia, their eldest child was born in 1855 and is my great, great grandmother.

Here is the oldest photograph in my family collection, it shows schoolmaster Joseph and his wife Wilhelmina who are now in their mid-forties/early thirties respectively.

This fascinating photograph of my ancestors (note how Wilhelmina is holding an elegant fan) would have been taken around 1860 by studio photographers Orr & Barton, who were based in South Parade in Bangalore. Orr & Barton were also a reputable and trusted jewellers and silversmiths. The company is still in business today, on the same road which is now known as M.G. Road (South Parade was renamed as Mahatma Gandhi Road in 1948).

Image source: courtesy of DiscoverBangalore (owner unknown)

It was thanks to Wilhelmina's foresight that we now have this book which is over one hundred and seventy years old. For a memsahib, running a household was an overwhelming experience, thwarted with all sorts of difficulties. Aside from the unrelenting heat, the major problem would be in the hiring of servants, and in finding a cook who would be willing to touch the different meats that wouldn't conflict with their religious beliefs. A Muslim servant would not touch pork, nor serve wine, remove dirty plates from the table or wash them. Hiring a Hindu could also be fraught with problems, they would not handle beef, fish, poultry, eggs or alcohol and the very strict practitioners would also refrain from onions and garlic. At about the same time, Mrs Beeton had just written her bestselling guide covering all aspects of running a household, another publication gave detailed instructions to European women on effective household management in India.

It's quite possible that Wilhelmina felt it good sense to write all her recipes in one book which could then be given to the cook to follow...

Wilhelmina's Kedgeree (serves 6-8)

This dish became popular during Colonial India, and stayed firmly on the breakfast menus in Anglo-Indian kitchens thereafter.

Ingredients

700g smoked haddock fish
2 bay leaves
170g basmati rice
350ml water
Knob of butter
15ml rapeseed oil
1 medium onion, finely chopped
1 green chilli, finely chopped
2.5cm piece of ginger, peeled and finely chopped
1 clove of garlic, finely chopped
2 tablespoons of Madras curry powder
2 tablespoons of chopped coriander
2 hard-boiled eggs

Method

In a shallow pan put the fish and bay leaves with enough water to cover, bring to the boil and then simmer for 5 minutes. Flake the fish into chunk size pieces.

In a large pan, throw the rice into enough salted water to cover the rice (about two fingers of water above), or to be precise 350ml of water. Bring to the boil, lower to a simmer for exactly 5 minutes and then drain. Add a knob of butter and then cover the rice with a piece of kitchen towel and allow to cool.

In another pan, heat the oil and fry over a moderate heat the onion, chilli, ginger and garlic for 3-4 minutes until softened. Toss in the curry powder and cook for 2 minutes. Add the flaked fish and cooled rice to the pan and gently warm through.

Place in a serving dish and garnish with quartered eggs.

Pekin coy Sambol (Salt fish Sambal)   (serves 4)

Ingredients

2 large pieces of salted cod
15 ml rapeseed oil
2 large onions, chopped
½ tsp mustard seeds
1 tsp ground turmeric
1 tsp ground coriander
3 garlic cloves, finely minced
2.5cm piece of fresh ginger, peeled
 and finely chopped
1 birds eye red chilli, finely chopped
1 tin of tomatoes
Juice of half a lime
200ml coconut milk
¼ tsp coarse black pepper
Salt if necessary (according to taste)

Method

In a large wide pan, heat the oil and fry the onions until translucent, add the mustard seeds and fry for one minute, now add the turmeric, coriander and a splash of water. Now add the garlic, ginger, chilli and tomatoes, and allow to cook for five minutes. Add the salted cod, lime, coconut milk and black pepper and allow it all to simmer slowly until the fish is perfectly cooked.

Before serving, check for seasoning and add salt if needed.

Wilhelmina's Matheekie Barge   *(serves 2-3)*

So, here we have a recipe from Wilhelmina for Methi Bhurji with eggs. In other words, a version of scrambled eggs using fenugreek leaves as the herb.

Matheeki Barge... Just the name of this recipe stumped me for ages, I hadn't come across this recipe in our family before and my mother certainly hadn't heard of it either. Then it suddenly occurred to me that one of the main ingredients, ventheum greens is the name for fenugreek which is also known as methi (and when pronounced phonetically it becomes mathee). The rest came fairly quickly after that once I put a different emphasis on the sound of the word Barge, and then read it out as Bhurji (which in Hindi means scrambled).

Ingredients

1 bunch of methi leaves, roughly chopped
2 large onions, finely chopped
2 medium tomatoes, diced
2-3 green chillies
2 garlic cloves, finely chopped
2.5cm piece of fresh ginger, finely chopped
¼ tsp ground turmeric
Salt to taste
6 eggs, beaten
Handful of chopped coriander
Milk (optional)

Method

Wash the leaves really well and keep to one side. In a large frying pan, heat some oil and fry the onions until transparent. Toss in the tomatoes, methi leaves, chillies, garlic, ginger and turmeric and fry for a few minutes, then add salt and give it all a good stir. Lower to a really gentle heat, the lower the better, and add the beaten eggs stirring the whole time until the eggs are cooked through. If the mixture becomes too dry, add a small amount of milk. Finally add some chopped coriander and serve.

Vudaes   (serves 6-8)

Vudaes, better known as vadas, are to this day a very popular roadside snack in India. They can also be made with mashed potato which has been seasoned with mustard seeds, turmeric, coriander and green chillies formed into large doughnut shapes, coated in a thick batter made from chick pea (gram) flour and then deep fried. Vada pavs are these savoury fritters served piping hot and crunchy sandwiched between a soft bread roll (pav) with either a coconut chutney or sambar (spicy dhall) dip. Absolutely delicious!

Ingredients

2 large potatoes, boiled and lightly mashed
15ml rapeseed oil
1 onion, finely chopped
Handful of curry leaves
½ tsp mustard seeds
½ tsp cumin seeds
1-2 green chillies, finely chopped
1" fresh ginger, peeled and finely chopped
¼ tsp ground turmeric
1 tbs lemon juice
Salt to taste
Handful of chopped coriander

Batter:
140g chickpea (gram) flour
Pinch of baking powder
Water

Method

In a large pan, heat the oil and fry the onions until translucent. Throw in the curry leaves, mustard seeds, cumin seeds and allow them to brown slightly. Add the green chillies, ginger, turmeric and the mashed potatoes and keeping it on the heat cook for a further minute.

Turn off the heat and stir in the lemon juice, salt and coriander. Leave to one side to cool.

In a large bowl combine the flour and baking powder and slowly add water to make a thick batter with a dropping consistency. Form the mashed potato mixture into small balls roughly the size of a billiard ball.

Deep fry until golden brown.

Vudaes

1 lb Lu

Plum & Cor: chopped 1 doz: potatoes, 6 Chillies
6 onions & ginger & a little sugar & baking powder
a handful of 'Kudalee dhatt' powder to thicken
Chop the D.C, onions, ginger & mix all
together form thick like a vudae & make a
hole in the middle & fry in boiling oil, mix a
little saffron also. When you are ready to fry
have a piece of wet Cloth, put it on the palm
of your hand, form your vudae on it & it slips
off easily ready to be fried.

Sambar (Spicy Dhall)   (serves 4)

Ingredients

250g red or brown lentils
15ml rapeseed oil
1 large onion, thinly sliced
2.5cm piece of fresh ginger,
 peeled and finely chopped
2 garlic cloves, finely minced
½ tsp ground turmeric
1 tsp cumin seeds
½ tsp methi seeds
1 tsp mustard seeds
½ tsp garam masala
1 ½ tsp tamarind extract
1-3 red chillies, split in half
3 tomatoes, roughly chopped
½ tsp sugar
1 tsp salt
Handful of fresh coriander, finely chopped

Method

Wash lentils and soak for an hour. In a large pan, add the drained lentils and enough water to cover the mixture. Allow to cook for 25 minutes then cover and simmer until the lentils are soft.

In a large saucepan, heat the oil and fry the onions until golden brown. Toss in the ginger, garlic, turmeric, cumin, methi, mustard, garam masala, tamarind and chillies and fry for a further 3 minutes adding a little water to avoid catching.

Add the cooked lentils to the onion mixture and the tomatoes, sugar and salt. Without covering with a lid, allow the dhall to cook for a further 20 minutes or so until the mixture becomes creamy.

Jalfrezi *(serves 4)*

This dish appeared on the menus of the British Raj as a way of using up leftovers as it was cooked with chilli and onion which preserved it a little longer. The name Jalfrezi comes from two words, jhal meaning spicy food in Bengali and parhezi which in Urdu/Persian means suitable for a diet.

Ingredients

4 chicken breasts, cut into 3cm pieces
Marinade
1 tsp ground turmeric
1 tsp ground cumin
1 tsp ground coriander

15ml rapeseed oil
1 large onion, finely chopped
2 garlic cloves, finely chopped
1 green chilli, finely chopped
1 tin of tomatoes, chopped
1 tsp sugar
300ml water
1 tbls ground turmeric
1 tbls ground cumin
1 tbls ground coriander
2 red chillies, finely chopped
A handful of chopped coriander

Method

In a large bowl marinate the chicken with the turmeric, cumin and coriander mix and leave for at least 3 hours in the fridge so that the flavours are absorbed in the chicken.

In a large pan, heat the oil and fry the onion until a golden brown, add the garlic and chilli and fry for a further 3 minutes, adding a splash of water to avoid it catching. Now add the tomatoes, sugar, water, turmeric, cumin, coriander and bring it all to the boil and then reduce the heat and simmer for a further 20 minutes.

Add the marinated chicken breasts to the gravy and allow the mixture to cook for a further 25 minutes, until the chicken is cooked.

Just before serving stir in the chopped coriander.

Coconut Rice (serves 4)

Ingredients

15ml rapeseed oil
1 onion, sliced thinly
2.5cm piece of fresh ginger,
peeled and minced
2 garlic cloves, finely chopped
½ tsp ground turmeric
1 cinnamon stick
3 cardamom pods, crushed
2 cloves
1 cup Basmati Rice
Salt to taste
2 cups of coconut milk

Method

In a large pan, heat the oil and fry the onions until translucent.

Now add the ginger, garlic, turmeric, cinnamon, cardamom and cloves and give it all a good stir.

Add the rice, salt and coconut milk and bring the whole thing to a boil, stir and then lower the heat and cook for 15-20 minutes until the rice is cooked.

Drain and cover with a piece of kitchen towel. After 5 minutes, fluff up the rice with a fork and serve.

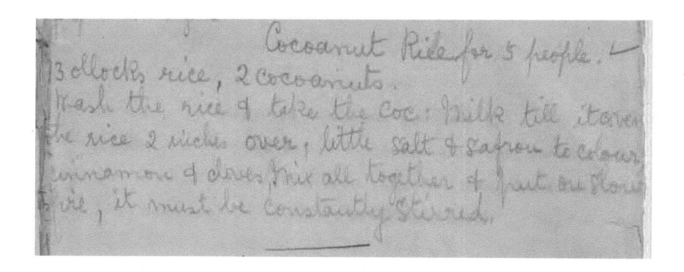

Cocoanut Rice for 5 people.
3 ollocks rice, 2 cocoanuts.
Wash the rice & take the coc: milk till it covers
the rice 2 inches over, little salt & safron te colour,
cinnamon & cloves, mix all together & put on slow
fire, it must be constantly stirred.

Salt Beef

Ingredients

3kg brisket of beef

<u>Brine</u>
Juice of 5 limes
55g saltpetre
350g sea salt
275g muscovado sugar
2 tsp black peppercorns
4 cloves
4 bay leaves
2 ½ litres of boiling water

Method

In a large saucepan, add all the ingredients bar the beef and bring it all to the boil, stirring to dissolve the sugar and salt. Let it bubble away for 2 minutes, then turn off the heat and allow the liquid to cool.

Prick the meat all over with a fork, then in either a large sterilized plastic box or bucket (it must be something non-reactive) place the meat and the brine mixture in the receptacle ensuring that the beef gets a good old rub all over with the mixture. Make sure that the beef is totally immersed. Cover with cling film and keep in the fridge for one week. Several times each day, turn the meat over and repeat the process again, rubbing the mixture into the beef well.

After a week, in a large saucepan or pressure cooker, add the beef and the juices and enough water to cover the beef and on a low heat cook the beef for exactly three hours.

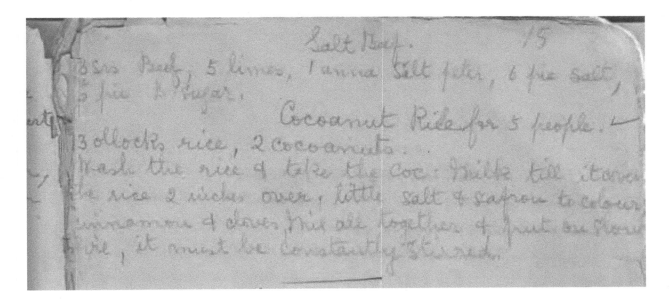

Oxtail Vinthal (Vindaloo)   (serves 4)

Ingredients

1kg oxtail, cut into 5 cm pieces
15ml rapeseed oil
3 onions, finely chopped
2.5cm piece of fresh ginger,
 peeled and finely chopped
3 garlic cloves, finely chopped
1 tsp ground turmeric
1-2 red chillies, finely chopped
3 cloves
1 tsp cumin seeds
1 tsp black pepper
1 cinnamon stick
6 medium tomatoes, roughly chopped
3 tbsp vinegar

Method

In a large pan fry each oxtail piece until browned all over and place in a large ovenproof dish that has a lid.   Using the same pan, fry the onions until a golden brown. Now throw in the ginger, garlic, turmeric, chillies, cloves, cumin, pepper and cinnamon and a splash of water and fry for 3 minutes. Add the tomatoes and continue frying until the oil separates from the spice paste, and add the vinegar. Bring the mixture to a boil then pour over the oxtails adding enough water to cover them.

Cover the dish and bake at 200c gas mark 6 for 30 minutes. Remove dish from oven and turn the oxtails over adding a little water if necessary, and cook for a further 1 ½ hours until the oxtails are tender and soft and the meat falls off the bone.

Almond Rock

Similar to peanut brittle, this confection remains very popular in India...

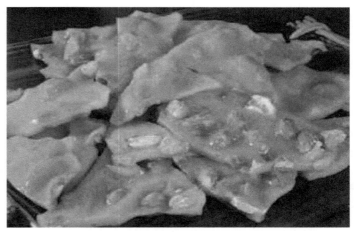

Ingredients

170g whole almonds, blanched
1 tsp lemon juice
150g granulated sugar

A buttered tray or shallow dish

Image source: MSPhotographic/Shutterstock.com

Method

In a large saucepan boil the sugar and lemon juice in 60ml of water. As soon as it starts boiling turn off the heat and add the almonds.

Transfer to the buttered tray or dish. Cut into pieces when cool.

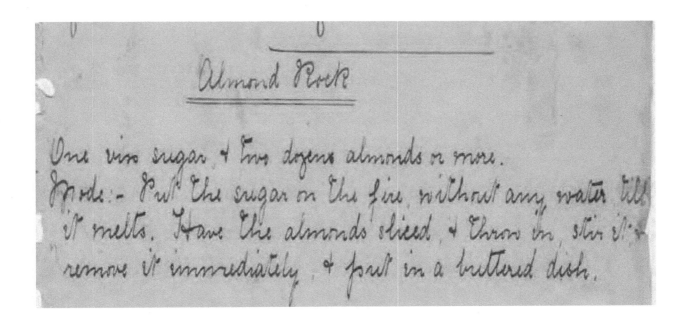

Cajure (Cashew Burfi)

My grandmothers made several versions of their own kind of burfi (an Indian sweetmeat), here's one made with cashew nuts and coconut.

Ingredients

200g roasted cashew nuts,
 roughly chopped
300g granulated sugar
60ml water
½ tsp ground cardamom
Shaved coconut (for sprinkling)
Pistachios (for sprinkling)

1 buttered tray or shallow dish

Method

In a large saucepan bring the sugar and water to a fast boil, remove from heat. Stir in the ground cardamom and nuts and whilst the mixture is hot spread it onto your tray or dish. Cut the burfi into squares or diamond shapes whilst warm and sprinkle over the coconut and pistachio nuts.

Allow the burfi to cool.

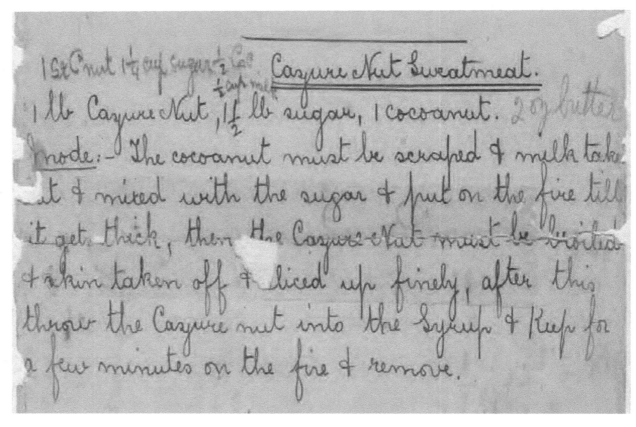

Wilhelmina's Christmas cake Recipe

Wilhelmina's well-thumbed and well-loved 19th century recipe has had all kinds of additions and changes made to it since her original version! Her ingredients would have taken much longer to prepare compared to nowadays - her currants needed to be "cleaned, stoned, picked and dried" and she would have made her own butter which had to be "perfectly free of water". It must have been quite a rich cake as she used 40 eggs, with 1 ½ lbs of flour, ½ lb semolina and 2 wine glassfuls of the best Brandy available. Over the years, her daughters, and also their cooks would have made a little change here and there to both the ingredients and proportions, according to their liking and in the introduction of a new ingredient. Prunes and plums (raisins) were eventually added by her granddaughter, Maud to the recipe, butter was replaced with ghee (clarified butter) and baking powder added to give the cake a lighter feel. Irene, Wilhelmina's great granddaughter has written across the side of the page "This quantity will make a 16 lb cake". (signifying good fortune),

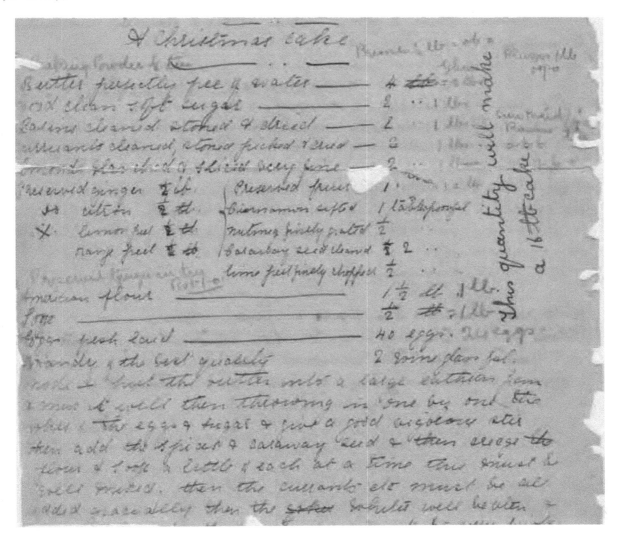

One of my grandmothers definitely had a Hindu cook, as a quarter of the way down the left side of the page are two recognisable Hindu symbols. The first one is "Om" a symbol of the Absolute – as the cross is to Christians, and the second is a Hindu swastika – an ancient symbol of good luck and auspiciousness.

Doctor Vegetable

In her recipe book, Wilhelmina lists the benefits of vegetables. *They knew the answers then...and of course now modern day affirmations agree!*

If you suffer from sleeplessness the veg cure is lettuce, you should eat at every meal. *Lettuce contains opiate-like chemicals that help relax and sedate the body.*

To keep your liver in good condition, eat tomatoes. *Tomato has a detoxification effect in the body due to the presence of chlorine and sulfur.*

For nerves, onions to banish the odour and taste – nibble a small piece of parsley. *Onions contain Vitamin C and B6, excellent for the nervous system.*

For an anaemic, there is nothing better than spinach. *An amazing superfood, rich in iron and known to prevent anaemia.*

For the rheumatic, eat rhubarb or celery, you can stew this and drink the water. *A diet rich in both these foods can help due to their anti-inflammatory properties.*

If you want to put on flesh, eat beetroot. *Beetroot has a high sugar content.*

Broad beans and peas are excellent brain food. *Studies have shown that both broad beans and peas assist in the prevention and treatment of Alzheimer's.*

If you suffer from indigestion, eat parsley all year round – the effect is magical. *Parsley stimulates both digestion and the kidneys.*

Those past middle life and who begin to feel a failure of physical and mental progress should eat pumpkin. *Pumpkin can help with lowering of bad cholesterol and promote a regular, healthy heart.*

Carrots too will cleanse the blood, and are good for the heart. *Rich in alkaline, carrots purify and revitalise the blood.*

Dieter Vegetables +

If you suffer from sleeplessness the veg
... is lettuce. You should eat at every
meal.

To keep your liver in order & in good condition
eat tomatoes.

For nerves, onions, to banish the odour &
taste of onions nibble a small piece of
parsley.

For an anaemic there is nothing better
than spinach. For the rheumatic
eat rhubarb or ~~the~~ celery. You can
stew them & drink the water.

If you want to put on flesh eat chestnut
Broad beans & peas are excellent brain food
If you suffer from indigestion eat parsley
the year round. The effect is magical
... past middle life & who begin their
... failure of their physical & ...
... should eat pumpkin.
... wants to build ...

Analysis of the handwriting of Wilhelmina

The way Wilhelmina has written her capitals signifies a single-mindedness, a tenacious character with a persistent nature.

If you look at the way she crosses her t's they are frequently long which shows determination, verging on stubbornness and in letting things go. Staying with her t's if we look at where she positions them, they're usually right at the top of her stroke which shows she is optimistic, ambitious and enthusiastic in her approach to life. She dots her i's to the right showing both impatience and an eagerness to move on, someone who is seen as being in a rush almost all of the time. The writing shows speed and a desire to finish tasks quickly without paying attention to precise details. The central zone of her characters have a stretched appearance showing a need for room, a desire for freedom from supervision and someone who works best on their own. Her sharp angular writing denotes ambition with an inquisitive nature.

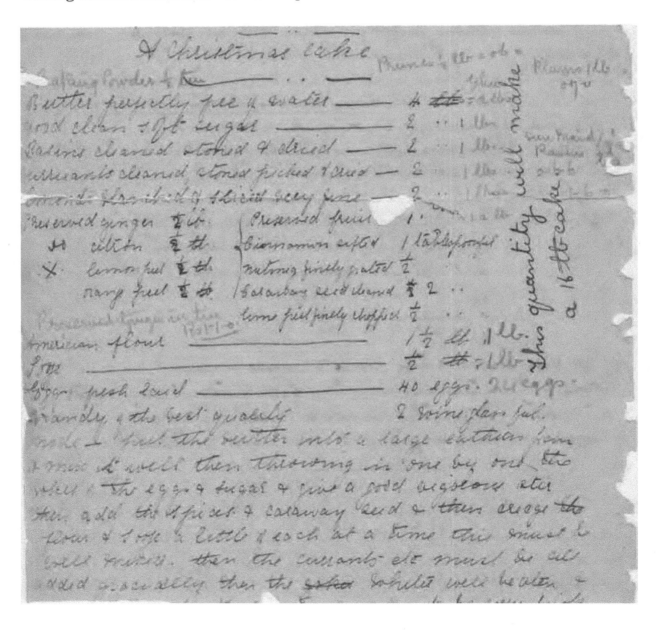

Ophelia

Joseph and Wilhelmina's daughter, Ophelia was born on the 1st August 1855 and baptised shortly afterwards on the 20th August that same year - an indication of their concerns over the possibility of their infant dying before she was baptized - they had after all, lost five of their babies to cholera. Ophelia surpassed all expectations and lived to a grand old age of eighty nine.

Family records show that Ophelia was brought up in Mylapore, a well to do suburb of Madras during the 19th century. Once an ancient port in the early 6th century, it fell into decline until the 16th century when the Portuguese established a settlement there. It is thought that the origin of the name Madras comes from the Portuguese name Madre de Deus. This old photograph shows Madras Harbour during Ophelia's time in 1890.

Parry's Corner - Madras 1890

Born into a decade of rapid change, when the British government took control of India from the East India Company and became officially a British colony, Ophelia and her family would have benefited directly by these positive changes. A new road network was constructed, and the building of dams, bridges, and irrigation canals meant that sanitation and public health improved. A railway line created during the East Indian Company days between Bombay and Thane of 21 miles long, was significantly expanded together with the telephone and telegraphic network further enabling India to modernise its infrastructure.

By 1880, India had created a vast railway network covering over 9,000 miles, branching out from the three presidency towns of Bombay, Madras and Calcutta. Railroads transported raw products from the interior to the ports and manufactured goods back again. Most of the raw materials were agricultural products produced on plantations. Plantation crops included tea, indigo, coffee, cotton, and jute.

At the age of nineteen, Ophelia married William Haslam, who was Anglo-Portuguese by birth. William was a Permanent Way Inspector with the South Indian Railway. They were living in Poonamallee, a suburb of Madras where the South Indian Railway company still has its headquarters. In this early map you will see that Poonamallee Rd is just above Egmore and Mylapore is south of the town.

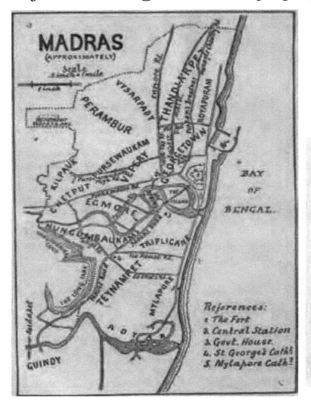

Primarily an engineering role, a Permanent Way Inspector had ultimate responsibility for the condition of the railway track and embankments in his area of jurisdiction.

He would make physical inspections of the track on a push trolley and have a team of maintenance staff working alongside him to ensure that the tracks were kept in good order and the safety of the railway was not compromised. Rigid checks would entail the thorough inspection of all bridges every year, all level crossings would be scrutinised every six months, the checking of curves on the track and their effect would be addressed every quarter, and an inspection of all points were undertaken annually.

In addition to all the above, there would be the daily review that maintenance of both track and structures were being carried out in a satisfactory and safe manner. The entire inspection would have been carried out by trolley.

This photograph was taken on one of the tracks owned by the South Indian Railway in the 1870s, you will see a Permanent Way Inspector on his trolley inspecting the track with his team. The next is a Magic Lantern image taken in British India circa 1895. This was an early type of image projector which was developed in the 17th century.

Ophelia and William's marriage produced three children, a son named William born in 1875, followed by two daughters, my great grandmother Maud born in 1879 followed by Millicent in 1880.

In the next photograph we have a family wedding, it's Boxing Day on 26th December 1927 and we are at Maud's house (Ophelia's daughter) on Pettigrew Street, St John's Hill in Bangalore. Ophelia is in the centre row far right, her daughter, Millicent (the bride's mother) is to her right. Behind Millicent is her husband, Edward. Ophelia's eldest daughter, Maud (the bridegroom's mother) is in the same row, second left. Maud's husband, Daniel is standing behind her and to Maud's right is Ophelia's sister, Topsy. It is the wedding of Maud's first born son, Eugene to his first cousin Aileen whose mother is Millicent and sister to Maud. A joyful day for Ophelia as she is witnessing the wedding of her two daughter's offspring on the very same day, although her smile is not necessarily present!

Now, for whatever reason, it is this generation of family that have made a very conscious decision to keep the family blood ties close, resulting in cousins marrying cousins. Three of Ophelia's four grandchildren chose to marry their first cousins, only one flatly refused to do so! That was Dolly, who is also present in the above wedding picture – as a 12 year old, she's sitting on the rug, far right...

Bringing this now into some sort of reality, my mother as a child remembers watching, in her words, her three maiden aunts, who were of course Ophelia, Florence and Topsy.

"The three sisters were sitting on the family porch in their rocking chairs wearing high necked Edwardian dresses, their white hair piled up into a bun. They were obviously enjoying a lively gossip which was promptly interrupted by their discovery of seeing me in close proximity and suddenly the animated chat was dropped and kept for a more appropriate time!"

Here is Ophelia at 85, with her six great grandchildren around her, the photograph was taken in 1940. My mother is third from the right.

Mulligatawny soup *(serves 6)*

The history of this recipe goes back to the 18th century and the East India Company who were based in Madras at that time. When the British first arrived in India they insisted on soup being served as a course at dinner – however, soups were not part of the Indian menu, so their Indian cooks served a mixture of spices boiled in water.

Incidentally, the word Mulligatawny comes from the Tamil word for "milagu" meaning pepper and "tunni" meaning water.

Ingredients

1 large onion, diced
2 garlic cloves, minced
3 tsp black mustard seeds
3 tsp coriander seeds
3 tsp cumin seeds
2 tsp garam masala
1-2 tsp red chilli powder
1 ½ litres of vegetable stock
1 tin of coconut milk
55g fresh spinach
6 medium sized tomatoes, chopped
Small handful fresh coriander, chopped

Image source: Maraze/Shutterstock.com

Method

In a large pan, fry the onion until golden brown.

In a spice blender or a pestal and mortar grind the seeds to a powder, then add them to the large pan together with the garam masala, chilli powder and fry for one minute.

Throw in the stock and coconut milk and give it all a good stir, finally add the spinach and tomatoes and bring to a boil, reduce and simmer for 15 minutes.

Sprinkle coriander over the soup just before serving.

Potato Chops

A family favourite, we always seemed to be asking for this as children. Best described as a stuffed potato croquette which has been filled with tasty mince...yum!

Ingredients

500g cooked mince (lamb or beef)
500g mashed potatoes
1 large onion, finely chopped
1 green chilli, finely chopped
1 tsp cumin seeds
Salt and pepper to taste
2 eggs, beaten
Box of panko or fine golden breadcrumbs
2 large bowls
2 smaller bowls
Rapeseed oil

Method

In one large bowl have the cooked mince, onion, chilli and cumin seeds, seasoning mixed together, the other large bowl your mashed potatoes.

Rub a little oil onto your palms and then take a tablespoon of mashed potato and knead it into a small ball and flatten with your palm.

Fill this with a tablespoon of mince, flatten slightly and add a further tablespoon of mashed potato on top of this, patting down gently to form a patty shape.

Continue until all the cutlets have been shaped and formed.

In a smaller bowl, add the beaten egg mixture and dip each cutlet into this mix and then coat each cutlet firmly in the breadcrumbs.

Refrigerate the cutlets for at least 30 minutes. Shallow fry until golden brown.

Kitchedy Rice   (serves 4)

Not to be confused with Kedgeree, this dish of rice and lentils comes from South India and later became the inspiration for Kedgeree. It comes from the Hindu word "kitcheri" which means jumbled up.

Ingredients

225g yellow split pea lentils
600ml water
225g basmati rice
½ tsp salt
15ml rapeseed oil
2 bay leaves
3 green cardamom pods, crushed

Method

Have two large bowls ready. The first bowl soak the lentils in 600ml of water and the other bowl soak the rice also in 600ml of water – both for an hour. Then in a large saucepan add the drained lentils and put enough fresh water to cover the lentils and cook for 30 minutes or until soft. Remove the cooked lentils and keep to one side. Using the same pan, toss in the rice, salt, bay leaves, cardamom and enough water to cover the rice. Bring to the boil and reduce to a gentle simmer for 5 minutes or until cooked. Drain off excess water and cover the rice with a piece of kitchen roll, this will allow the rice to dry off so that each grain separates. Add the lentils to the rice.

Pilau   (serves 4)

Ingredients

30ml rapeseed oil
1 large onion, thinly sliced
2 cloves
3 green cardamom pods,
crushed
2 sticks of cassia bark
1 bay leaf
2 tsp ground turmeric
150g basmati rice
300ml water

Method

In a large pan, heat the oil and fry the onions until almost burnt – keep to one side.   In the same pan, fry off the cloves, cardamom, cinnamon and the bayleaf for 2 minutes. Toss in the rice and turmeric and fry for a further minute.

Add the water and bring to the boil and stir, then cover with a lid and leave to cook over a low heat for 10 minutes.   Remove from heat and drain.   Before serving scatter the fried onions over the rice.

My grandmother used cassia bark in all her recipes, which is a member of the cinnamon family. Cassia bark, native to Burma at that time, has a much stronger flavour so less is required in recipes. It's best used for savoury dishes rather than in desserts and for baking.   I tend to use cinnamon sticks for both curries and sweet dishes - they are shaped like quills and as they are thinner than the cassia bark look more inviting and appetising in a glass of mulled wine.

à la differénce !

Prawn Coconut Curry   (serves 4)

A wonderfully aromatic prawn curry...

Ingredients

30ml rapeseed oil
1 onion, finely chopped
3 garlic cloves, crushed
5cm piece of fresh ginger,
 peeled and finely chopped
2-3 green chillies, finely
chopped
4 green cardamom pods,
crushed
3 cloves
1 tsp cumin seeds
1 tsp ground coriander
½ tsp turmeric
140ml water
500ml coconut milk
100g ground almonds
Juice of half a lemon
Handful of chopped coriander
500g prawns, shelled

Image source: Travellight/Shutterstock.com

Method

In a large pan, heat the oil and fry the onions until translucent.

Toss in the garlic, ginger, chillies and a splash of water and cook for 2 minutes. Now add the cumin, coriander and turmeric and continue to fry for a further 3 minutes. Add in the coconut milk and ground almonds and bring to the boil, then add in the lemon juice and cook for 2 minutes.

Finally toss in the prawns and cook for 3 minutes or as soon as the prawns turn a pale pink, then turn off the heat and add the chopped coriander, the prawns will finish cooking in the residual heat of the gravy.

Fragrant Chicken Curry   (serves 4)

Ingredients

4 chicken breasts, cut into 5cm
cubes
15ml rapeseed oil
2 large onions, finely chopped
3 garlic cloves, finely chopped
5cm piece of fresh ginger,
 peeled and finely chopped
2 tbsp garam masala
½ tsp ground turmeric
1-2 red chillies, finely chopped
500ml chicken stock
1 small pot of yoghurt
Handful of fresh coriander,
 chopped

Method

In a large pan fry the chicken pieces until golden brown and leave to one side.

In the same pan, add some oil and fry the onions until golden brown and then toss in the garlic, ginger, masala, turmeric and chillies and a splash of water and fry for a further 3 minutes.

Add the chicken and stock and bring to the boil, then simmer gently until the chicken is cooked.

Stir in the yoghurt and sprinkle the coriander over the chicken.

Beef Madras Curry (hot)   (serves 4)

Ingredients

700g stewing beef, cubed into
 2.5cm pieces
15ml rapeseed oil
2 large onions, finely chopped
1 tsp fenugreek seeds
1 tsp mustard seeds
5cm piece of fresh ginger,
 peeled and finely chopped
3 garlic cloves finely chopped
1-3 red chillies, finely chopped
1 tsp ground turmeric
2 tsp ground coriander
1 tsp cumin seeds
½ tsp ground black pepper
1 tsp red chilli powder
½ can tinned tomatoes
1 tsp tomato puree
1 tsp salt
450ml water

Method

Heat the oil in a large pan and fry the onions until a golden brown.

Fry the seeds for a few minutes and now add the ginger, garlic and chillies, turmeric, coriander, cumin, black pepper and chilli powder, and a good splash of water and allow to fry for 5 minutes.

Toss in the tomatoes, tomato puree and salt and cook for 2 minutes and finally add the meat and 450ml water, bring to a boil and then simmer for 1 hour stirring every 10 minutes.

Mahratta Curry

A hot, rich and spicy curry made in the Mahratta mode. By the middle of the 18th century the Maratha Empire was the leading power in India with their capital in Pune. This fierce Hindu warrior caste known as The Mahrattas were well respected by the British military. They had a reputation it is said for enjoying their food with plenty of chilli in it to match their fiery temperament, hence any recipe made in the Mahratta mode would be hot and fiery too! My grandmothers would make a masala, which is the method of roasting the seeds first, then grinding them and mixing with a little liquid, in this case coconut milk.

Ingredients

750g chicken thighs
1 tsp cumin seeds
1 tsp aniseeds
1 tsp coriander seeds
6 peppercorns
1 cinnamon stick
4 cardamom pods, crushed
3 cloves
2 medium onions, finely sliced
15ml rapeseed oil
1 tin coconut milk
1 tsp ground turmeric
2.5cm piece of fresh ginger,
peeled and finely chopped
3 garlic cloves, finely chopped
2-4 birds eye chillies, finely chopped
1 tsp salt
250ml water
Bunch of fresh coriander, roughly chopped

Method

In a large pan, dry fry the seeds, peppercorns, cinnamon, cardamom, cloves for a few minutes and then in a spice blender or using a pestle and mortar grind them finely. Now fry the onions in the oil until golden brown, now add the blended mix, coconut milk, turmeric, ginger, garlic, chillies and salt.

Give it all a good stir and then add the chicken pieces and continue cooking for 5 minutes stirring regularly. Pour in the water and bring to the boil and cook on high heat for 3 minutes, then reduce the heat, and allow to simmer gently for 15 minutes or until the chicken is cooked. Stir in the chopped coriander.

Mahratta Curry   X

heap teaspoon of Ghee. ¼ Coc. 1 large onion, 1
tea spoon Commine Seed, 1 tea spoon Soiling, 6 p[...]
long, 2 inch Cinnamon, 2 Cardamom, 3 clove[...]
or 5 dry chillies, 1 table spoon of roasted Coriander
the Coc: must be cut up in thin slices. All the[...]
must be boiled up the Ghee sreat the[...]
[...]seeds of Coriander, leaves, ginger, 2 g. chilli[...]
[...]nicely Saffron, all this to be ground, cut up[...]
[...] onions, Cut up & the Coc: Put in your Ghee[...]
[...] some onions & sliced Garlic, then throw[...]
[...] and the masala & fry, then throw in [...]
[...] & fry well & cover up with sufficient water.

Mahratta Curry   X

dry Chillies, Garlic, C. Seed, Mustard & Saffron
¼ pie Coc: 3 large Onions. Coc: & Onions mu[...]
be boiled & ground, cut up Coc: in small pieces [...]
slice onions, 3 pie Brinjals & Venthenum.
Slice some more onions, boil the oil then
throw in Onions & Venthenum & fry well, then
put in the C. Stuff & fry after the ground Onion
& Coc: & fry then put in the sliced Brinjal
& fry a little while, put in the water & co[...]
up, after the Brinj: is boiled, squeeze a little
tamarind juice & cover it up, when leaving
in the dum put a little sugar.

Hot Chilli Vegetable Curry   (serves 4)

Ingredients

15ml rapeseed oil
½ tsp cumin seeds
½ tsp black mustard seeds
1-2 green chillies finely chopped
2 garlic cloves finely chopped
2.5cm piece of fresh ginger,
 peeled and finely chopped
340g potatoes, diced into 2.5cm cubes
Half a cauliflower, cut into
 small florets
170g green beans
4 medium tomatoes, roughly chopped
100g peas
1 yellow pepper, roughly chopped
1 red pepper, roughly chopped
½ ground turmeric
1 ½ tsp salt
1 tsp sugar
Fresh coriander, chopped

Method

Heat the oil in a large pan, toss in the seeds and fry for a few seconds, toss in the chillies, garlic and ginger and fry for a further 3 minutes.

Put in the vegetables, turmeric, salt and sugar with enough water to cover them. Bring to the boil and then gently simmer for 20-30 minutes until the vegetables are tender.

Sprinkle chopped coriander over dish before serving.

Ophelia's Coconut Pepperwater   *(serves 6)*

Ophelia's recipes are faithful to the days of the Raj – here she gives us a recipe which has evolved down through the generations in my family with various adaptations along the way, but we came to know it simply as "Coconut Pepperwater", a side dish served alongside curry and rice.

Ingredients

2 large onions, thinly sliced
15ml rapeseed oil
200ml coconut milk
1-2 red chillies, finely chopped
1 tsp ground turmeric
3 garlic cloves, finely chopped
2.5cm piece of fresh ginger,
 peeled and finely chopped
Juice of half a lemon
Salt to taste

Method

In a large saucepan, heat the oil and fry the onions until golden brown. Add the coconut milk, chillies, turmeric, garlic and tamarind or lime juice and salt and cook for 15 minutes, adding water if necessary. The consistency needs to be that of a thin gravy.

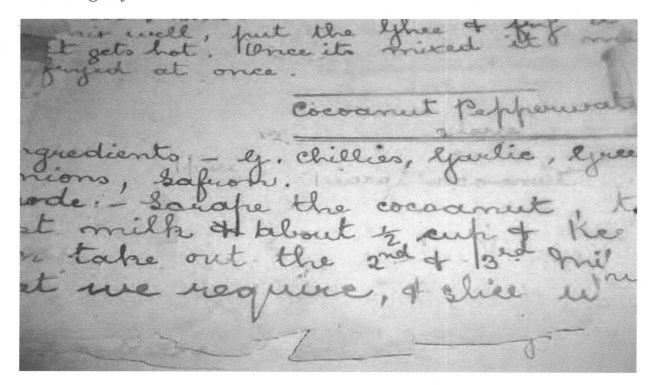

3 pieces Dhall + 1 piece g... ulinthu, take a little ... chillies, 1 Seed Mustard, garlic to be ground
1 Onion to be roasted & ground, 1 piece tur... 1 dessert spoon brown sugar ... to be ground
little of leaf & coriander green, to be tied toge... all this & put water according to the pepper wa... needed & allow to boil a little, take down but tamarind put on 2nd boiled, take down ... soon piled fry onion ... Ventheum & throw ... 3 ... whole ... 1½ quantity of ... Dhall to be boiled & mixed with the water of ...

Plain Omelet.

Breast Pepperwater

little coriander, common seed, mustard, garlic & safron, chillies & onions, lime. Grind all curry stuff, cut the mutton in pieces, wash it & put in a chatty. Put the curry stuff in & mix with 8½ half cups of water, with ½ coconut milk taken, 2nd & 3rd milk mixe. Put some sliced ginger, onions, green chillies & salt ... all & allow to boil. After well boiled squeeze the tamarind ... up again for a little while, then take it down. ... little onion + boil it in & put in 1st milk & take down.

Ventheum Pepperwater.

chillies, mustard, garlic, common seed, & a little ventheum, onions & safron, & tamarind. Broil the curry stuff except ventheum, put it on the stone & bruise it. Put it in a chatty with sufficient water, squeeze the tamarind in & put sufficient salt & allow to boil. When boiled take it down, fry some onions & ventheum & pour in after its strained. 3 cups of water for 3

Tapps Sauce

In 1838, Lea & Perrin's launched their famous Worcestershire Sauce, a recipe with its origins in India. Soon alternatives followed, namely The Empress of India, British Lion and Tapps Sauce. Although the Worcestershire Sauce recipe remains a closely guarded secret, it is thought to contain vinegar, sugar, soy sauce, molasses, mushroom ketchup, tamarind, shallots, anchovies, ginger, chillies, cloves, nutmeg and cardamom. Here is a version of Tapps Sauce from Ophelia.

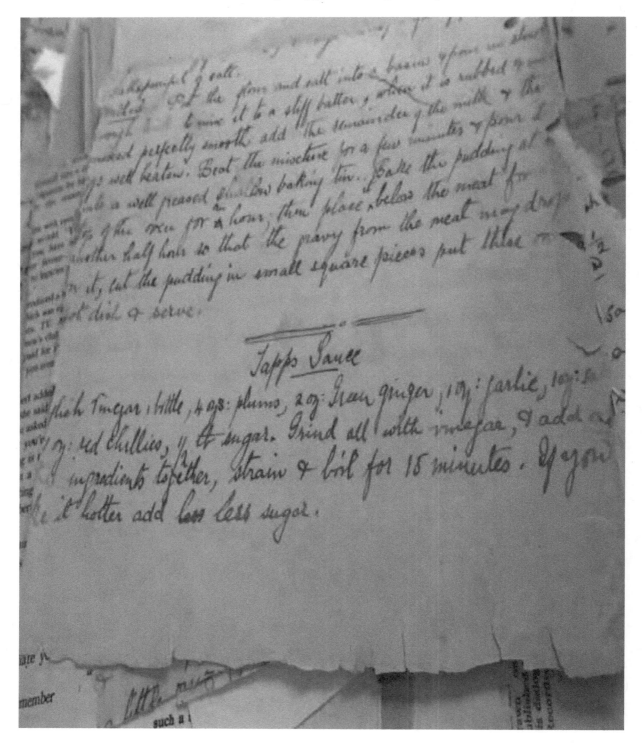

Ophelia has noted down two popular tea time treats – a Telegram Cake and a Victoria Sandwich. The Telegram Cake may well have been so called as it was a quick cake to bake (and telegrams were a fast method of communicating), note how Ophelia suggests the Victoria Sandwich is baked in a quick oven too!

The Victoria Sandwich was created when one of Queen Victoria's ladies-in-waiting suggested an afternoon tea service which could consist of small cakes, bread and butter sandwiches, assorted sweets and, of course, tea in order to avoid "that sinking feeling" at about four o'clock in the afternoon.

Telegram Cake.

Weigh 3 eggs in butter, sugar, & flour, 2 oz: desiccated cocoanut, ½ teaspoonful baking powder, & a few drops cochineal. Beat butter & sugar to a cream, then add the eggs (well beaten). Stir mixture thoroughly, adding, by degrees, flour — cocoanut, &, lastly, the baking powder and cochineal. Beat all for 10 minutes, then sprinkle over the cake a little cocoanut. Bake in shallow tin from 25 to 30 minutes in a moderate oven.

Victoria Sandwich

Take the weight of 3 eggs in flour, butter, and castor sugar. Beat butter & sugar with a wooden spoon till they are like a cream. Then beat the eggs well in (one by one). Gradually & lightly stir in the flour. Grate the rind of half a lemon into it, and lastly, add 1 teaspoonful of baking powder, & 1 tablespoonful of milk. Grease a shallow baking tin. Line it with greased paper, & turn the mixture in. Smooth it over & bake in a quick oven till pale brown (for 10 minutes) When done, turn on to a piece of sugared paper, & leave till cool. Spread with rasp or any other stoneless jam, & cut in neat pieces.

Ophelia's Christmas cake   (makes an 8" cake)

Ophelia's recipe is the closest version to my own recipe which I've been using with great success for the past 35 years. The cake is delicious, rich and moist and with just the right mix of fruit, nuts and cherries. The only difference between her recipe and mine is that I omitted the black treacle and instead of using caster sugar, I use muscovado sugar which gives it a wonderful taste of treacle.

Ingredients

225g sultanas
225g raisins
225g currants
100g glace cherries, chopped
150g mixed peel, chopped
50g flaked almonds
50g cashew nuts, chopped
50g pistachio nuts, chopped
150ml sherry
2 tsp mixed spice
2 tsp freshly grated nutmeg
250g butter
250g caster sugar
5 large eggs
250g plain flour
2 tbsp black treacle

8" cake tin lined with baking parchment and brown paper round the tin

Method

In a large bowl soak the dried fruit, nuts and spices in the sherry and cover. This can be left for up to a week but make sure you stir the mixture daily. In a mixing bowl, cream together the butter and sugar until pale. Add each egg alternately with the flour then toss in the fruit and mix well. Add the black treacle and stir well.

Spoon the mixture into the baking tin and bake the cake at 120c/Gas mark 1 for approximately four hours. It is cooked when a skewer inserted comes out clean. Let it cool in the tin for an hour, then transfer to a wire rack. Make tiny holes with a skewer on the surface of the cake and once a week, add a few drops of sherry into the holes.

Keep in airtight tin or foil wrapped until use.

Analysis of the handwriting of Ophelia

The first thing that strikes you is Ophelia's long tall characters on a right hand slant. This shows an assertive person who is confident, but also someone who can be insensitive. She writes stretching her characters out between the upper and lower zone leaving a small middle zone i.e. if you look at the way she has written "tablespoonful" you can see how she devotes the largest portion of each letter between the upper zone and lower zone leaving the middle zone with proportionally a much smaller size. This is a sign of intelligence, an ability to concentrate, someone who is modest and would prefer to work in a non-spotlight job. She pushes her strokes fully and utilises the upper zone for her characters. Each of her capital letters are written with curved elaborate detail and they flatten out at the base of her stroke which signifies someone who deliberates before making up their mind, this slow and deliberate action is a form of cautious control and self-preservation. The overall impression is a person possessing a certain dignity and formality about themselves.

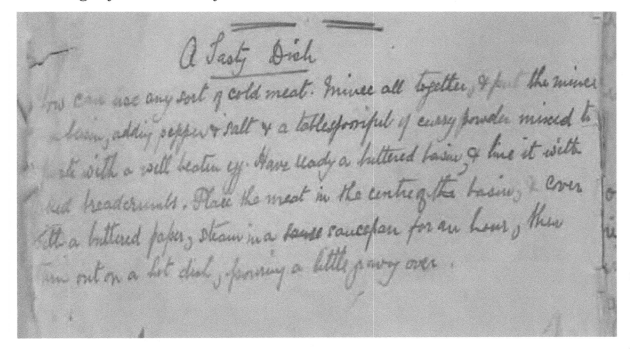

Maud

On the 14th October 1896, sixteen year old Maud Haslam (Ophelia and William's eldest daughter) marries Daniel Shandley at St. Matthias Church, Vepery which is a suburb north of Madras.

In the late nineteenth century, Madras had several pockets or close neighbourhoods (sometimes they were containing just two or three roads). My family lived in a district called Chinglepet which had the following neighbourhoods in them: Vepery, Egmore, Poonamallee and Pursewaukum.

Below is a photograph taken at C.H. Doveton, studio photographers who were on the Poonamallee Road (they are still in existence as photographers on the same road which is now called Purusavakkam High Road). The year is 1920, and Maud is seated far right with her four children and Ophelia, now in her sixties is also there.

Interestingly Daniel, Maud's husband is not present – this is most likely due to the First World War which probably accounts for the fact also that there is a large age gap between Maud's first two children: Eugene and Irene and her next two, Gwen and Dolly.

Just like Maud's father, Daniel was also a Permanent Way Inspector by profession. With the opening up of the railway network, Maud and her family were the first generation to experience the excitement and delight of train travel in India, where it became possible for the first time to explore the country in relative comfort and ease. Furthermore, Daniel's position as a Permanent Way Inspector allowed his family the entitlement to travel in their own railway carriage.

Here is another photograph, it is 1940 now and Maud is sixty one, she is third from the right. Daniel, Maud's husband has now passed on but we can see their two youngest children, who are now adults. Gwen is second left with her first cousin, John Hector Shandley (who she married) and he is standing to her right. Dolly is far right with husband, Dudley who is standing to her right (and true to her word when she saw all her other siblings marrying their first cousins she flatly refused and did marry someone outside of the family!) Maud's granddaughter, Beryl (my mother's sister) is in the centre of the photograph and to her left is her father, my grandfather.

The opportunity for Maud and her family to travel now by train and discover the different regional dishes around the whole of India must have made their journeys all the more interesting. Not only that, it must have been hard to contain themselves seeing all the different varieties of ingredients, spices and cooking styles that they surely came across. So with Maud's recipes we are treated to a wider scope of ingredients – with more use of fish, coconut, chillies, lime and particularly tamarind – and for the first time in the book we have recipes for fish moley, prawn curry and fresh coconut in curries.

Maud's recipes are a fascinating read, she describes so many of them using different types of measurement terms, that I must admit to being distracted by the actual words she chooses when describing the quantity of ingredients required instead of the actual ingredients.

Her first entry in the book is for "Mrs Hemley's Plum Sauce" and under the ingredients she writes "5 pollum plums (raisins), 5 pollum dry chillies, 2 ½ ginger, 1 pollum garlic". Hours of research later I was still nowhere near finding out what a pollum was. Google Internet service told me that a pollum was hashish – surely not, Maud!

It would be months later when I happened to mention this word to a chef friend of mine, Rui Madre Deus from Goa and through making enquiries himself he eventually found out that a pollum was a very old word which was no longer in use. It was a word to describe the actual weighing scale dish found in all the markets and bazaars!

From as early as the 14th century right through to the 19th century, Edam cheese was the world's most popular cheese. It was shipped to all the colonies as it not only matured beautifully but also kept well during its long sea passage from Holland. The cheeses were encased in brass cylindrical containers, and local tradesmen would cut the brass container in half and re-use them as brass dishes that would sit on their weighing scales in the markets and bazaars.

Recognised as a "pollum", this was a unique, informal measurement known most likely only between the market seller and their customers.

Mrs Hemley's Plum Sauce

I would say that Mrs Hemley was a good friend or neighbour of Grandma Maud's. This is a good standby recipe for a sticky sweet and sour sauce and keeps very well for a long time in the fridge. A very useful jar to keep handy as when mixed with a little soy sauce, a little hoisin sauce and some garlic you have a good dip, sauce or marinade. Alternatively, add equal amounts of tomato passata with the sauce and it makes an excellent sauce to serve with slow roasted pork belly, duck, fish or even chicken...

Ingredients

450g plums, stoned
200g sugar
200g white distilled vinegar
2.5cm piece of fresh ginger,
peeled and finely chopped
3 garlic cloves, finely chopped
2-3 red chillies, finely chopped

Method

In a large pan with a heavy bottom base, throw in all the ingredients and bring to the boil, stirring regularly.

Reduce the heat to a moderate heat and allow to gently boil for 30-40 minutes until the liquid has almost evaporated.

Pour into warmed sterilised jar(s) topped with greaseproof paper before closing the lid.

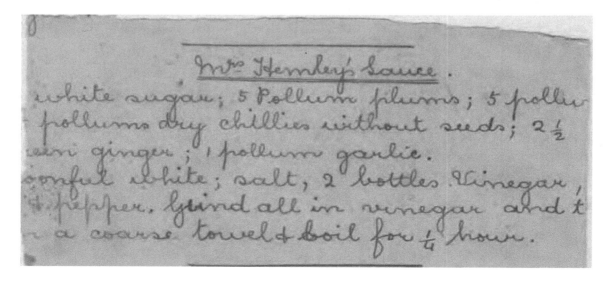

"Rumble-tumble" Scrambled eggs   (serves 3-4)

Known affectionately as "Rumble-tumble" within Anglo-Indian circles, this is my grandma Maud's recipe.   My mother tweaked it a bit and included bacon or sometimes ham and used Carnation milk which made it rich and creamy.   Any leftovers can be made into sandwiches the next day or heated with a little more milk as it keeps well and the flavour just improves.

Ingredients

6 eggs
1 large onion, finely chopped
1 tomato, chopped
1-2 green chillies, finely chopped
Salt and pepper to taste
140ml milk

Method

Heat a little oil in a frying pan and fry the onions until golden brown and caramelised, making sure not to burn them.

Fry the chillies for minute, then add the eggs and tomato and cook on a very low heat for the next 10-15 minutes, stirring often to make sure that the mixture does not catch, adding milk gradually when required.

Ding Ding Fry Curry   (serves 4)

Ding Ding Fry was originally a recipe for using sun dried meat, similar to Biltong, pieces of meat would be marinated in a mixture of vinegar, salts and spices and hung up in the sun to dry.   In our family, we came to enjoy Ding Ding Fry as a recipe for using up leftover roasted meats.

Ingredients

15ml rapeseed oil
450g beef or lamb, into 2.5cm cubes
2.5cm piece of fresh ginger,
 peeled and finely chopped
½ tsp ground coriander
¼ tsp cumin seeds
2 garlic cloves, finely chopped
1-2 green chillies, finely chopped
½ tsp ground turmeric
¼ tsp mustard powder
3-5 tbsp malt vinegar

Method

In a large pan, heat the oil and toss in the ingredients except the meat and the vinegar and fry for 3 minutes.   Throw in the meat and stir frequently for 10 minutes, add a little water if necessary to avoid it catching.

Add the vinegar and cover and simmer checking regularly to see how the mixture is until the meat is cooked – your aim is to end up with a dish that has a coating of the curry around each piece of meat.   This is a dry meat dish with no gravy.

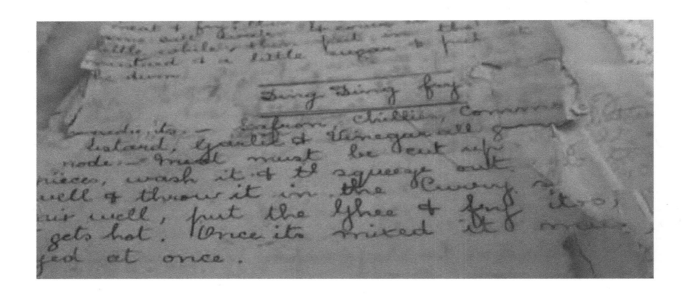

So began a fascinating journey of exploration for me on Maud's choices of measurements throughout the book. Maud uses measurement terms introduced by the British India presidency of Madras in 1833 for her recipes. She lists her quantities for measuring grain using a term known back then as an ollock, sometimes abbreviating the word to oll: i.e. "Five oll: table rice, 1 ½ oll: Mysore dhall". In other recipes she uses the term "viss" and "seer" for sugar and dried fruit weight, one viss was equal to just over 3lbs and one seer was roughly 2lbs.

A popular way of describing measurement in the 19th century was to use the proportion of your hand. Maud describes her method of cooking rice, "put two cups of rice into a pan with two fingers of water covering the rice." Two fingers breadth would be equal to the length of the first joint of the thumb. Four fingers breadth would be equal to the size of the palm. Three palms would equal a span, and three spans would equal a cubit. Four cubits would equal the distance between the tips of the middle fingers when the arms outstretched.

Maud also lists her ingredients by their monetary cost, for example, she would describe an amount of say chillies required in a recipe, by how many "pie" it would cost in the bazaar. So we come across recipes which are written with ingredients stating "1 pie cuscus (poppy seeds), 4 pie coriander greens and 1 pie ginger. A "pie" was the smallest denomination of coin at that time (like our old halfpenny).

It makes absolute sense to do it this way – so that when her cook went out to the bazaars shopping for the ingredients, the list would give the exact amount to ask for, and having the correct amount of money, no mistakes were made...that doesn't mean to say that the cook probably made a little profit on the side by only purchasing a ¾ of a pie and keeping the rest of the money for himself – it was the perks of the trade after all!

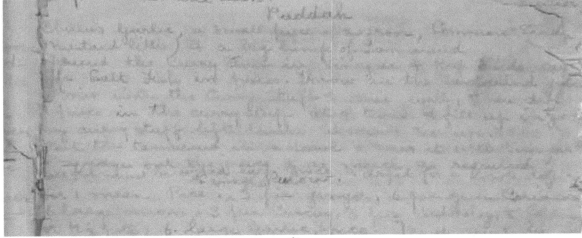

At that time, a rupee coin was broken down into seven smaller divisions, artharupee, pavala, beda, anna, paraka, kani and finally a pie which would be 1/192 of a rupee.   Here are some of the coins that my ancestors kept which were used during the period of the

British Raj. We have a close up of a pie coin (which is 1/12th of an anna) from 1926, and a 1 anna coin from 1920. The large silver coin is a rupee.

Out of all of my grandmothers' recipes, it is my grandma Maud's recipes which have proved to be so interesting and given me the most amount of pleasure in researching. She gives us a generous amount of recipes, yet her dishes are both inventive and yet you also gain a real sense that she was inspired by the old English recipes.

Maud seems to indulge herself in a love of baking and has an obvious love for puddings, and she starts a wonderful collection of recipes for old English puddings from the early part of the nineteenth century. Inside my grandmother's book, we see recipes for Cabinet Pudding, Chester Pudding, Transparent Pudding, Yomandry (Yeomanry) Pudding and a delightfully named Fair Rosamund Pudding – all hailing from good old Blighty! Most of them are early versions of our popular puddings nowadays such as Lemon Meringue Pie, Bakewell Tart and Bread and Butter Pudding.

Bombay Beveca

Also known as Bebinca, this traditional dessert cake is served on festive occasions and comes from Goa originally. It's a multi-layered cake made from flour, eggs, coconut milk, sugar and nutmeg and takes a long time to prepare as a thin layer is baked each time until golden brown and then another layer is repeated and so on until you end up with seven layers. The number of layers is said to represent the seven hills of Lisbon and Old Goa.

Apples à la Portugaise

Ingredients :- Two pounds of apples, a little jam,
cherries, sugar. Method :- Peel and core the app[les]
without dividing them, and cook them in
syrup till tender, but not broken. Put the
apples in a glass dish, fill the centres with
Strawberry jam, and decorate them with gr[een]
cherries. Boil the syrup till thick, add a littl[e]
of the juice of the jam in it, and colour w[ith]
cochineal to a pretty pink, then pour it rou[nd]
the apples, and serve them cold.

Green Gage or Gooseberry Pudding.

1 bottle tart fruit stewed, with 2 large slic[es]
of bread & sugar to taste, add 3 oz butter, an[d]
when it is melted the yokes and whites of 5
well beaten, Bake gently. Mode :- Stew the fr[uit]
with sugar to taste (without water), place
2 slices in a buttered dish & throw the stew
over. Then beat the eggs up well with the
butter & put over the stew & baked.

Yeomanry Pudding   (serves 6)

Created in Staffordshire in 1838, this pudding is an earlier version of the Bakewell Pudding.

Ingredients

Filling:
2 large eggs
2 egg yolks
3 tbsp raspberry jam
2 tbsp ground almonds
225g butter
225g caster sugar

Pastry:
175g plain flour
¼ tsp salt
100g butter
1 egg yolk
3 tbsp cold water

Method

Sift the flour and salt into a large bowl. Toss in the butter until it resembles breadcrumbs. Add the egg yolk and water and bring the dough quickly together using minimum handling. Roll out the dough and line a greased 8 inch pie dish and chill in the fridge.

Preheat the oven to 220c/Gas mark 7.

Spread the jam over the chilled pastry. In a large bowl cream the butter and sugar until pale, toss in the almonds and the beaten eggs.

Pour this mixture over the jam/pastry and bake for 10 minutes then reduce the heat to 180c/Gas mark 4 and bake for a further 50 minutes or until golden brown.

...it all together about 2 teacups, if more ...more should be taken; Mix Sugar & ...our with a little salt together 1st. Then the... the eggs & while throwing in mix. Then ...the milk & be careful not to allow the flour ...become lumpy. Put a lot of Ghee on the fire ...place the mould in the Ghee till it gets hot ...take out the mould dip it in the Flour half ...and put its in the Ghee to fry. After every ...phoky is fried remove it & place the mould ...the Ghee till warmed again & dip i... ...flour, & or so on till finished. To test the ...mould dip the mould in the Flour, if it ...well, that shows its warm enough.

Yomandry.

...yolk...
...p of Butter; glaze of three eggs; one viss of
...monds; 1 tin of jam; and sugar to taste
...beat the glaze to a nice froth, butter to b...
...eaten up well and Almonds to be ground;
...all together with sugar; spread the Ja...
...a soup plate and the paste to be spread
...the jam thickly & baked in a slow oven
...well browned.

Rolong Ulva.

ingreidients :— ½ seer Rolong or ½ meas; ½ viss sug...
...Almonds; ¼ viss Ghee.
...k the Rolong over night, then in the morni...
...the song well, then pour a cup of wat...
...it & ...ze well till the milk comes out...
...3 times the milk must be taken out &
...ed through a cloth. After the milk...

Cabinet Pudding.

... thin slices of bread with the crusts
... off, butter each slice on both sides,
... put two slices together in a pie dish,
... slices one upon the other at the bottom,
... put a layer of jam on top, then
... the other six slices on top of the
... Make a custard with 3 eggs and
a ... pint of milk using some essence, then
... the cream on top of the slices,
... it all absorbs and after ½ an hour
... it in a moderate oven.

Transparent Pudding.

... eggs well beaten; ¼ lb of white sugar; ¼ lb ...
2 large spoons of marmalade; Stir over the ...
till it thickens; when cooled, pour into a ...
dish; and bake in a moderate oven.

Carrot Pudding.

... bread crumbs, 4 oz finely chopped suet;
... lb stoned raisins; ¼ lb carrot; ¼ lb currants
... sugar; 3 eggs; milk; ¼ nutmeg. Boil the
... carrots till tender enough to mash to a pulp
... the remaining ingredients and moisten
... sufficient milk to make the mixture
... consistency of thick batter; pour into
... buttered basin; wet a piece of cloth &
... it over with a little flour & tie on
... & boil for 2½ hours.

Chester Pudding (serves 6)

Grandma Maud has written down an absolute classic Victorian recipe from England – Chester Pudding was an early version of the Lemon Meringue Pie but instead of a lemony filling it has a tasty almond filling...

Ingredients

Pastry:
200g plain flour
110g butter, softened
2-3 tbsp very cold water

Filling:
6 eggs (yolks and whites separated)
60g sugar
Juice and zest of a lemon
100g butter
50g ground almonds

Method

In a large bowl, sieve the flour and toss in the softened butter and rub between your fingers until the flour resembles breadcrumbs. Add the water a little at a time until it all comes cleanly into a dough. Chill in fridge for 30 minutes.

Roll out and line a pastry tin. Mix the yolks with the sugar, butter and lemon juice and zest and whisk until creamy.

Have a small pan with 200ml of water on to boil. Place the bowl with the yolks mixture over the pan to allow to steam and gently whisk for a few minutes until it thickens. Pour this mixture into the pastry case and bake for 20-25 minutes at 200c/Gas mark 6.

While this is baking, whisk the egg whites gradually adding the ground almonds until the mixture is stiff. After 25 minutes, take out the pastry tin and cover the top with the egg white and almond mixture and return to the oven for a further 10-15 minutes until the top is golden brown.

Chester Pudding

... butter; ¼ lb white sugar; 1½ oz Almonds; ... lemon; 4 eggs; .

... the butter beat it well, sugar pounded, ... Almonds blanched & pounded, the juice ... the lemon, and the peel grated & the ... of 4 eggs well beaten; put all this in ... saucepan over the fire, and stir till near ... then pour into a pie dish lined with ... pt pastry, & bake it, the whites of the ... eggs to be beaten up into snow, and ... over the pudding just before it is ... out of the oven; strew a little ... powdered sugar over it.

Burnt Custard.

... lock of milk; 2 eggs; 6 Almonds, burnt with ... little brown sugar; bruise it up & mix with ... the custard & baked.

Fair Rosamond Pudding.

... bread crumb (inside of bread). ½ pint of ... milk, 3 oz of butter, 2 yokes, 4 whites of eggs, ... of sugar; 1 lime-peel chopped or grated. ... the bread & milk, & add the other ingredients ... the bread & milk is cooled. Put a layer of Apricot ... in the dish, pour the mixture in, & sift ... sugar over before baking.

Maud's Fair Rosamund Pudding

I became very intrigued with the name of Maud's recipe for Fair Rosamund Pudding, especially as my mother had not come across this dessert in the family before.

Researching on the Internet gave me no further clues to a pudding. But what it did explain was who this lady was and why she was linked to the history pages of England.

Fair Rosamund was the much adored Royal mistress of Henry II, King of England in the 12th century and its written that she lived in a bower (a country retreat) called Freemantle Park in Kingsclere.

Just what makes this rather interesting is that Freemantle Park happens to be in my village where we have lived for more than 20 years. I was totally unaware of this legend as I am sure most of our residents will be. Even more bizarre than that is that I only have one view from my house (as we are surrounded by meadows) and that is of Cottington's Hill, the exact location of Freemantle Park.

A recipe from India with origins at my doorstep... Serendipity!

As we head towards the 1940s, I have a personal recollection from Maud's granddaughter, Daphne of her childhood memories of the time she spent in India at her grandmother Maud's house.

"The milkman came to the home with his cow and went round to the back of the house. As children, we had to take it in turns to be there to see that he didn't add water to the milk! - it was all in a day's routine. The dhobi man (household and personal laundry) would arrive on his donkey to deliver the clean laundry (which I must say was spotlessly clean and well ironed (and starched if necessary) and, of course, to take the next batch. Every item was spread on the floor and grandma made a note of each item as he collected the soiled linen. What faithful and honest service we received. I must add that our faithful servants walked barefoot from their village homes to get the list of ingredients to be purchased at the market, and then to cook on mud stoves in a tiny room in the back yard. Only to serve delicious meals - every day – lunch which was usually a curry and rice. Dinner was a tasty meal (no rice) with soup, a side dish and dessert. Tea was at 4pm and we always had a treat and a cup of tea."

We have four generations here, it's now 1948 and we have Maud who is now approaching her seventies and has her great granddaughter, Wendy on her knee with her daughter Irene to her right and Irene's daughter Beryl to her left.

Further delving into the book we gain an insight into some necessary culinary changes for Maud. Maud's mother, Ophelia is now approaching her 90th year and her appetite has lessened so Maud is

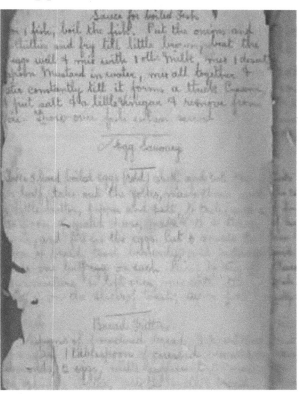

now producing lighter but tasty suppers for her mother so we see recipes for Baked Eggs, Fishcakes, Cheese Soufflés, Crepes (Pan Roll) and Egg Custard. Note in her Pan Roll recipe she writes "the glare of the eggs", this is a very old Middle English/French/Latin term "glair" meaning egg whites from the 14th century.

This marvellous book provides us with so many clues as to my family's lifestyle that it can almost be considered a time capsule. Generations have not only chronicled events but inadvertently thrown hints to us without them realizing... We can see the family favourites simply by the amount of times the recipe is repeated in the book, it's as if they don't want to forget that particular recipe so it's noted down by the next generation of daughter. So we've got several versions of Guava Cheese, Halva, Seed Cake, Pilau Rice and Pepperwater. Their recipes charmingly reveal to us their genuine love of good hospitality. Where doors are thrown open for family, friends and neighbours throughout the year, it may be for a special birthday event or an elegant tea party complete with cut sandwiches made from Grandma's Brown Bread recipe to Afternoon Teacakes, Hot Scones and Lemon Cake, with the most important celebration, of all Christmas...

Christmas cakes would be made at least six weeks ahead in order to improve their flavour and other seasonal delights were made such as Beveca, Fudge, Rose Cookies and Kul Kuls, a biscuit like crunchy treat coated with an opaque sugar frosting. Members of the family would sit round the kitchen table and help with the rolling out and shaping of them into a butter curl. Christmas day would come and homes would be opened to all your family, friends and neighbours inviting them to share in the delights of your hospitality – a slice of Christmas cake, some Kul Kuls, and a couple of grandma's Christmas pies, a sing song or two around the piano all washed down with perhaps a glass of home-made punch, cordial or ginger wine.

Brown Bread

1. 5 level cups of Wheat flour (2nd sort).
2. 1 level tea spoon Salt.
3. 3 teaspoons Soda Bicarb.
4. 1 small tin Golden Syrup.
5. 2 eggs.
6. 2 cups cows Milk.

1st beat the eggs and add the golden syrup stirring all the time, then pour in the Milk by degrees & stir (have the flour sifted & mixed with Salt) Soda bicarb to be dissolved in ½ cup water, then add your flour by spoonsfuls stirring all the time & lastly your Soda bicarb when the flour is well stirred, butter your tins fill half each.

have a bicksha with water (sufficient to stand the tins ½ way in), cover & boil for 3 hours, after done take the bread out & cool. when nicely cooled put back in tins & it will Keep fresh.

Note how grandma Maud has produced her Brown Bread by boiling the mixture in hot water, it is said that this method has its origins with the New England early settlers who would made them with jars or tin cans. Both grandma's recipe and the New England early settler's recipe for boiled bread required either molasses sugar, honey or in grandma's case, golden syrup. The bread remained remarkably fresh for some time too.

Grandma Maud shares her recipe for Christmas cake with an engaging insight into the actual cost of her ingredients. This is more than an insight into her methods, now this is of historical interest too as it gives us a unique understanding of the individual costs of produce at that time! Quite amazing, particularly when you see how expensive candied peel was then, and very interesting that it was the same price as almonds. Nowadays the cost of candied peel has dropped dramatically, and when I'm baking my Christmas cake, the most expensive item to purchase are always the almonds. Note also how Maud must have produced many batches of her cake in different sizes, as she writes at the very bottom, "…..six cakes, lbs, 1 3/4lb, 2 1/2lb, 2 1/4lb, 3lbs"

On the subject of Christmas cakes, whilst conducting through social media my own research on the large quantities my grandmothers appeared to use for their cakes, I came across others who were able to share their own memories of the way their family prepared and baked their enormous batches of fruit cake. This all came about as a result of a post I sent out on my grandmother Irene's Christmas cake recipe where she describes her ingredients as 2 measures of rolong which was 16 ollocks in weight of semolina, 150 egg yolks, 2 viss of almonds (7lbs), 1 viss plums (3 ½ lbs), 2 ½ viss of sugar (7lbs) and so on with a painstaking 3 hours of kneading!

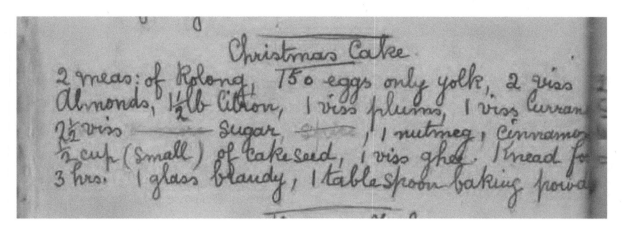

Cecil D'Souza

Jenny, my late Grand Uncle and my Dad used to make 40 kilos of fruit cake every year in Madras for Christmas. My GU worked in the railway and usually bought the butter from Erode and all the other fruit from some places that he would travel to on work. Cashew nuts came from Mangalore. We had a lot of work churning butter and granulated sugar to a smoothie and beating a lot of eggs to such an extent that it would be turned down if it was not approved. It was quite tiring because we used the fork. There were no mixers in those days in India. Most of the vessels for churning were brought from the railway kitchens. I will try to find out the recipe that was followed but since both have passed away, I wonder if anybody else would be able to let out the secret.

Lorraine Moniz

Yes my dad used to do a similar quantity but take it to our local bakery for them to mix and bake. We kids had to chop and dice huge quantities of fruit and nuts and he would probably get about 60 cakes which we distributed to friends and family at Christmas time. He would put a little slip of baking paper with his name on it so they would not get mixed up as all the locals did this in Calcutta. Our bakers name was Abdul.

Patti Peters

If you note there are 2 measures of semolina which means 16 ollocks (in those days. It was 8 ollocks to one measure) so it could be right with the eggs. I remember helping my grandmother as a little girl - we used to take a huge dekshi and all the kids had to have turns to stir the ingredients in. The cake with semolina was delicious. We used to pour the mixture after done into many trays which were lined with brown paper and ghee - one for the family doctor, one for each teacher, even the tailor got one - that was such fun really. You have got me going down memory lane now Jenny. Thanks.

Fay Adolphus

I wouldn't be surprised at 150 egg yolks because my gran used to make a HUGE amount of cake mix - enough for several cakes. She would book her time at the bakery and the cakes would go into the baker's (not her) oven a good few weeks before Christmas. Then she would poke the cakes with a knitting needle periodically and pour a little brandy in. By Christmas they were well and truly sozzled and very popular. Everyone has their own recipe. Semolina or suji was a major ingredient but I know from my family recipe that flour also was added.

Bridget Kumar White

As we presumed, the quantities mentioned in your grandmum's recipe should be for a number of cakes. Since they couldn't possibly bake so many cakes at home, they had to bake it in a huge bakery oven. I guess the local baker gave each family a specific date for baking their cakes in his oven, so they would have had to mix this huge quantity of the cake dough then carry it in a large dekshi to the bakery where the baker and his boys would pour it in greased and papered cake tins (as I'm sure our ancestors didn't possess more than a couple of cake tins themselves!) and bake it for them. Then again in the evening, the family would go and collect the baked cakes from the baker most probably in a huge black trunk!

Melissa Arulappan

I've been pouring over my grandmother's (Angela Abreu) handwritten recipe books too as am trying to build something around them and she has the most fascinating side recipes - her christmas cake and wine recipes have costs written in the margins and yes, all in large amounts too. My mum still makes my grandmum's recipe.

Anita Mawdsley

Eggs in those days used to be smaller - none of our tasteless ones we get nowadays. So the 150 yolks would have been about right. But many people made cake with rolong instead of maida + semolina. This was to ensure that it would stay longer and be easier to slice in slabs. The amount of fruit/almonds etc are also a lot, so the egg yolks would have been that many. Cakes were stirred so long only because of the rolong. Modern day Christmas cakes made with maida do not need this and in fact after any liquid is added in any cake (not Christmas cake of course), you shouldn't stir it much. Will give you a rubbery cake.

Yasmeen Ali

Lol that's how they rolled in those days. My grandma's recipe for egg halwa asked for something like twelve dozen eggs! The halwa was made in a huge lagan (a flat metal pot with shallow sides) and baked over coal with coal placed on the lid too.

Analysis of the handwriting of Maud

Maud's handwriting is perfectly spaced which indicates mental clarity and a sense of order. A person who is good at analysing situations and concepts and is able to plan ahead and organise her life and time effectively. She knows the importance of contingency planning—that is, leaving enough time and space in which to handle the various emergencies of daily life without leaving herself in the lurch. She's not afraid to use her environment to her advantage and this implies self-assurance. The writer is objective when dealing with a situation or problem, and considers a variety of potential responses and how they might affect the outcome. She reasons well and uses good old-fashioned horse sense to help her make decisions. Her tastes tend to be elegant and refined with a strong sense of aesthetics, and a love of beauty, someone who is happy in her home environment.

French Chocolate Biscuits

Ingreidients :— ½ lb sugar; ½ lb Almonds; ¼ lb Chocolates (pounded), 1 egg, spice to taste. Mode :— Grind the Almonds to a paste, add the sugar and Chocolate with the spices + mix with the e Roll out the paste + add a little flour while rolling so as not to allow it to stick. Shape biscuits + allow it to remain for some hou baking! Finish them on a slow fire or ove

Brinjal Pickle.

1 viss good Brinjals, 10 foll: ry. chillies, 5 foll: ly ginger + 1 foll: garlic, 3 foll: Mustard, 1½ tablespoon Salt, ½ bottle Gingelly oil, 1½ bottle Vinegar, 2 large pieces safron, 3 tablespoons brown sugar. Cut the brinjals up in pieces + throw in half a bottle of Vinegar, wa + wipe the ly. chillies + slit half way. Skin the garlic ginger + grind fine in Vinegar, also the saffron + must Put the oil on the fire + boil with a few curry leaves till crisp. Then put in the Saffron + garlic + fry a little while, then add ginger + mustard. Mix the sugar + salt in half a bottle of Vinegar, strain + in. Then add ly. Chillies + brinjals, throwing in he remainder of the Vinegar + boil till the brinjals are tender, bottle when cold.

Irene

My grandmother, Irene Shandley, was born at the turn of the century in India in 1899. From a comfortable middle class background, Irene was one of four children, she had an older brother, Eugene who was a year older than Irene, and her two younger sisters, Gwen and Dolly. There was a gap of thirteen years between Irene and her sisters. Here she is aged 14 with her baby sister, Gwen and her brother Eugene aged 15 and at a later stage when Irene is aged 19 with her baby sister Dolly, then aged 4.

As a young woman, Irene became quite well known in her circles for her excellent game of tennis – she played a tough game, slugging her best shots from the base line.

She would regularly play tennis tournaments at the Bowring Institute in Bangalore, an elite social club to this day, and had quite a hectic social life centred on numerous tea parties, galas and balls.

On the 3rd of May 1920, Irene has married her first cousin, Herbert John Jeffries. The wedding, attended by both sets of family was witnessed by Patrick Delaney (Herbert's brother in law) and Maud Shandley (Irene's younger sister). Irene was just twenty and Herbert, thirteen years older at thirty three. It appears that it was entirely expected for men to wait until their thirties to marry, in order to build up a proper career and to hold a respectable income and this has been true for all my family, the brides were as young as fifteen, no more than twenty yet their husbands were all in their thirties when they married. In this wedding photograph we can see the bride's mother, Maud and her baby sister, Dolly.

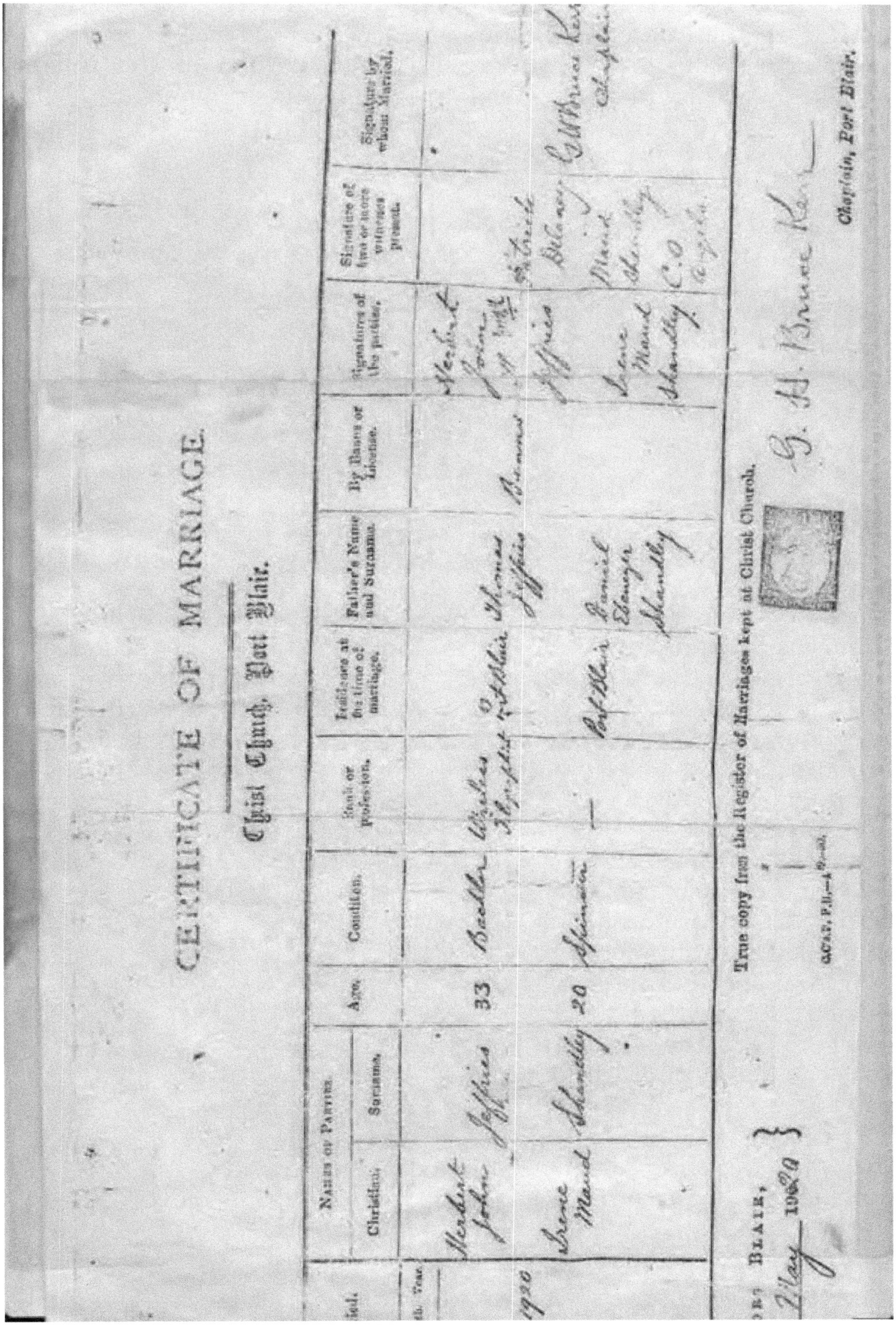

CERTIFICATE OF MARRIAGE.

Christ Church, Port Blair.

When Married	Names of Parties — Christian	Names of Parties — Surname	Age	Condition	Rank or profession	Residence at the time of marriage	Father's Name and Surname	By Banns or Licence	Signature of the parties	Signature of two or more witnesses present	Signature by whom Married.
1920	Herbert John	Jeffries	33	Bachelor	Works Inspector	Ross Island	Thomas Jeffries	Banns	Herbert John Jeffries	Patrick Delaney, C.M. Bruce Ker, Chaplain	C.M. Bruce Ker, Chaplain
	Irene Maud	Shanley	20	Spinster	—	Port Blair	Daniel Edwin Shanley		Irene Maud Shanley	Maud Shanley, C.O.	

True copy from the Register of Marriages kept at Christ Church.

BLAIR,
2 May 1920

G. A. Bruce Ker,

Chaplain, Port Blair.

QRT. P.B.—4 No.25.

Their wedding has taken place over five hundred miles away from Madras on the Andaman Islands at Port Blair, as Irene is starting off her married life as the wife of a Prison Warden at the infamous cellular jail, living in close quarters to notorious criminals...

A colonial high security prison used by the British to exile political prisoners, the name "Cellular Jail" derived from the solitary cells which prevented any prisoner from communicating with any other. It was so designed that the end wall in one cell faced in another direction to the adjacent cell, making communication between the prisoners impossible - therefore complete solitary confinement.

My grandfather is shown here on the right and again on the left standing just behind his brother in law, Patrick Delaney, who was Chief Jailer at the Cellular Jail when this photograph was taken.

They are standing at the entrance to the prison.

From there, my grandmother Irene went to live in many parts of India, from the Andaman Islands which is as east as you can possibly go, to the north east in Calcutta, to Pondicherry and Madras in the south of India and right up to the very north of India in Rawalpindi, which is now Pakistan, where she was to become governess to a young wayward sixteen year old Benazir Bhutto.

What a contrast of location, cultures, food and way of life she must have come across! In the north of India she would have discovered the Kashmiri curries which were fiery hot with chillies, and sampled the kofta meatballs in Delhi and the creamy Mughlai korma dishes. She would have been introduced to the abundant vegetarian dishes in the Gujarat region and noted how the strict Jain cuisine meant that curries were always made without onions and garlic for religious reasons. Whilst living in Calcutta she would have also come across Panch Puran, a whole spice blend of five different seeds (panch in Hindi means five): cumin, fennel, fenugreek, mustard seed and nigella seed. In the very south of India in Kerala, she would have tried a masala dosa – a huge crispy crepe like pancake filled with spiced potato curry and would have been inspired by all the fresh spices: cinnamon, ginger, cardamom, nutmeg and black pepper. Whilst in Bombay she would have been tempted to try the delicious pomfret and red snapper, two very popular fish from that area and tried the Portuguese-influenced vindaloo, prawn balchao and pork sorpotel.

With all these opportunities of living in many different regions of India and experiencing first hand their local ingredients and dishes, Irene ended up being an accomplished and confident cook. She would entertain and cook for large parties without ever getting flustered.

Always fascinated with food, my grandmother would correspond with my mother describing her long and exhausting journeys but the main part of the letter would be describing all the exciting dishes she had come across! She showed a keen interest in discovering different ways of cooking and their ingredients.

Whilst living in Pondicherry, Irene became influenced by dishes reflecting a French flavour to them. Within her pages we come across recipes for Chicken Fricassée, Consommé, French Toast and Spinach Gratin. Pondicherry was the largest French colony in India, and although small, it has still managed to retain its unique French Quarter with leafy boulevards and 18th century French colonial buildings, many streets still retaining their French names to this day.

Lamb Almode   (serves 6)

Ingredients

750g middle neck of lamb
15ml rapeseed oil
2 large onions, finely chopped
2 medium potatoes diced into 5cm
cubes
3 carrots, cut thickly
1 tbsp tomato puree
1-2 green chillies, finely chopped
8 cloves
2 garlic cloves, finely chopped
1 tsp black peppercorns
2 sticks of cinnamon
5 green cardamom pods, crushed
2 bay leaves
1 tsp mixed herbs
500ml beef stock
Dash of Worcestershire Sauce
2 tbsp plain flour
3 tbsp water

Dumplings:
125g self raising flour
60g butter
1 tbsp dried parsley
Pinch of salt
100ml cold water

Method

In a large pan, fry off the lamb pieces until brown on all sides and keep to one side. In a large bowl mix the flour, butter, salt and parsley, gradually adding small amounts of water to form a sticky dough. Flour your hands and then roll the dough into 12 little balls. Place on a plate and keep in the fridge to chill.

Heat the oil in a large pan and fry the onions until golden brown. Toss in the chillies, cloves, garlic, peppercorns, cinnamon, cardamom and bay leaves and fry for a further 3 minutes. Now throw in the meat, potatoes and carrots, tomato puree and herbs and fry for a further 5 minutes, adding a little stock at a time in order to avoid it catching. Add all of the stock and the Worcestershire Sauce stir, and bring to the boil, then simmer slowly for 1 1/2 hours or until the lamb is really tender and almost falls off the bone. Remove the meat, potatoes and carrots and place temporarily in a large bowl. Then blend 2 tbsp of flour with 3 tbsp of water and stir into the stew, cook until the mixture begins to boil, reduce the heat and place the dumplings into the stew and cook slowly over a low heat for 10 minutes, uncovered. Return the meat, potatoes and carrots to the stew.

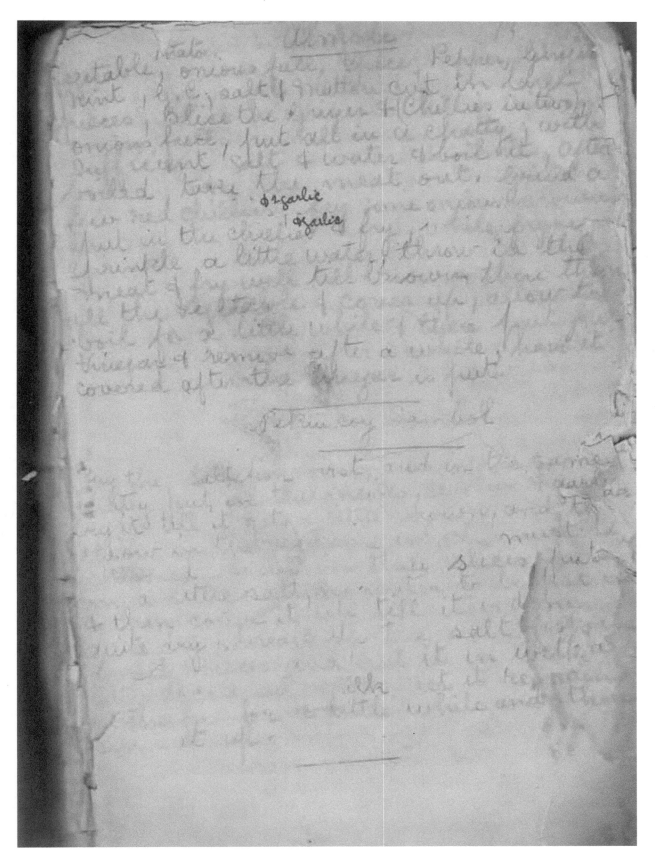

Dhall   (serves 4)

Ingredients

250g yellow split pea lentils
15ml rapeseed oil
1 large onion, thinly sliced
2.5cm piece of fresh ginger,
 peeled and finely chopped
2 garlic cloves, finely minced
½ tsp ground turmeric
1 tsp cumin seeds
½ tsp garam masala
1 tsp black mustard seeds
1-2 green chillies, finely chopped
1 tsp salt
Handful of fresh coriander, finely chopped

Method

Wash lentils and soak for an hour. In a large pan, add the drained lentils and enough water to cover the mixture. Allow to cook for 25 minutes then cover and simmer until the lentils are soft.

In a large saucepan, heat the oil and fry the onions until golden brown. Toss in the ginger, garlic, turmeric, cumin, garam masala, black mustard, green chillies and salt and fry for a further 3 minutes adding a little water to avoid catching.
Add the cooked lentils to the onion mixture and without a lid, keep cooking stirring occasionally for a further 20 minutes or so until the mixture becomes creamy.

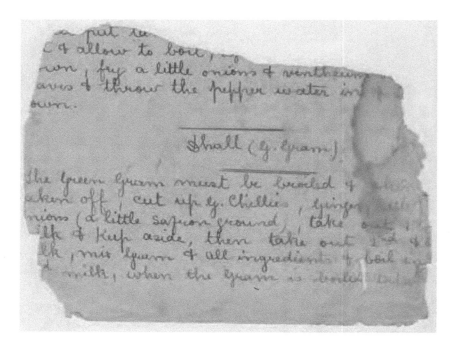

Green Masala Chicken (serves 4)

A wonderful thick green paste curry using fresh spices – if you wish you can add two more chillies for a real fiery taste.

Ingredients

15ml rapeseed oil
1 medium onion, finely chopped
1 kg chicken joints, skinned
200ml water
1 tbsp butter
Salt and pepper to taste

Paste
150g fresh coriander
1 medium onion, peeled and chopped
1-2 green chillies, finely chopped
5 garlic cloves, finely chopped
2.5cm piece of ginger,
 peeled and roughly chopped
10 black peppercorns
3 cloves
5 green cardamom pods, crushed
1 stick of cassia bark or cinnamon stick
1 tsp cumin seeds
1 tsp coriander seeds

Method

Blend the ingredients for the paste.

Fry onion until soft and caramelised, add the paste and cook on a moderate heat for 10 minutes, stir in the seasoned chicken, water, butter and bring to a boil. Cover and cook on a low heat for 30 minutes or until the chicken is cooked.

Hoppers

Hoppers originate from Kerala, South India. They are thin rice pancakes made from fermented rice flour. The batter comprises of rice, yeast, salt and sugar and this mixture is allowed to stand for a couple of hours. They can be made sweet using jaggery, which is unrefined sugar, or savoury when served with a chutney or chickpea curry. Their soft spongey centres are perfect for soaking up the delicious gravies from curries. As they would be eaten at breakfast time, my father (an interloper as he was from Bombay) would always jest and say "hoppers at h'past eight".

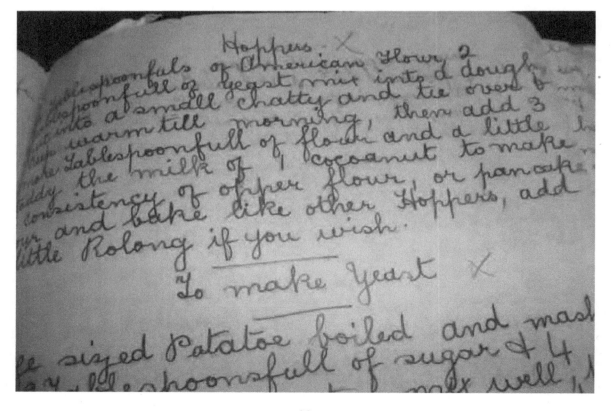

Here is Irene outside her house, 13 Jeremiah Road, Bangalore with her little dog, Laddie. It's the early forties which makes Irene also in her early forties and she is by now building quite a reputation for her great chutneys and pickles selling them to friends and neighbours. Meanwhile, her husband, Herbert Jeffries by now of a fragile nature, would live to only fifty nine leaving Irene a widow at just forty seven.

We know Irene was particularly good at making chutneys and pickles as she gives us recipes in the book for Lime Pickle, Tomato Chutney, Brinjal Pickle and a wonderful Green Coconut Chutney.

Green Coconut Chutney   *(makes 250g)*

Delicately cut sandwiches filled with this delicious chutney were always popular at our family picnics. It can also be used as a cooling agent when tackling a hot curry or just treat it as a dip and serve with warmed pitta bread or better still serve alongside Wilhelmina's vudaes (see earlier recipe).

Ingredients

250g grated
coconut
1 bunch coriander
1 bunch mint
1-2 green chillies
6 garlic cloves
1 tsp cumin seeds
1 tbsp sugar
juice of a lemon

Method

Blend all the ingredients into a blender adding a little water if necessary – the consistency needs to be like thick porridge.

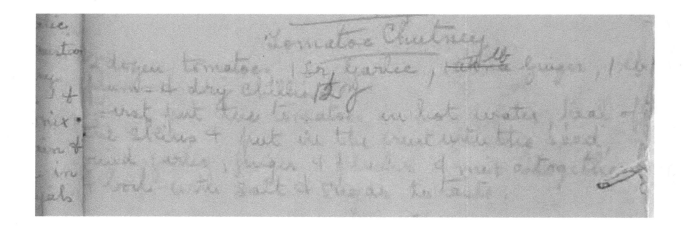

Brinjal Pickle (good)

...s Brinjals, small 1½ table-spoons salt
...ed chillies, 2½ oz/s garlic, ¾ oz saff...
ginger, ½ tea-cup white sugar, ½ Bo...
..., 1 oz garlic extra, ½ tea-spoon
...um seed, ½ desert spoon mustard so...
...ble-spoon cummun seed (jeera), ½ oz
...illies, some curry pillay leaves, ¾ Pl...
...ew pepper corns,
...ections - Slice the brinjals in two,
...te in salt, grind the red chillies,
...ngredients in vinegar. Clean the 1 oz
...lic, pound the rest required, render...
...stard, & cummun seed. Boil the on...
...curry pillay leaves, garlic etc, & boil...
...ll the brinjals & vinegar. Cook w...
...d ... looks like a curry, remo...

Mango Chutney

...il gently 3 lbs raw mangoes cu...
...mall pieces in the same weight
...ugar till of the consistency of jam
...s garlic & ginger 6 oz/s, 2 oz/s pow...
...d chillies. 1 lb of rasins, ½ pint
...negar, 2 oz/s salt, mix thorough...
...il gently to a good consistency...
...ttle when cool.

95

Hot Mangoe Pickle

25 mangoes. 26 garlic, Dry Chillies
seeds must be taken off & soak in vinegar
_____ C. Seed, Mustard, 1 ½ bottle
gingelly oil, 8 table spoons Sugar, Salt to taste
ground ¾ garlic & remainder put in fully, 6 pie
green chillies split on top, & ___ ____ ground
Where the oil __ ____ take it down & put
in the Curry stuff little by little, so the oil
will ____ deliver, with the oil just _____
___ cumin seed & C, leaves & boil.

Devil Chutney

Chillies (Dry): Ginger: 5 Flakes of Garlic;
____ind; Small Onion; Salt (for taste): (Small
_antity of Sugar)

Curry Leaves Chutney

____ ___ must be ____ ____ it to a brown
colour ____ ____ ____ then the Chillies ____
to be thrown in & broil a little more, ____
____ ___ must be ground with garlic
put oil on fire till its boiled, throw in two
tea spoons Mustard & fry, then throw in
all the ground ingredients & fry well.

Grandma also enjoyed making homemade punches, non-alcoholic drinks, and spiced tea. A family favourite was her version of a popular non-alcoholic drink that was known as O.T.

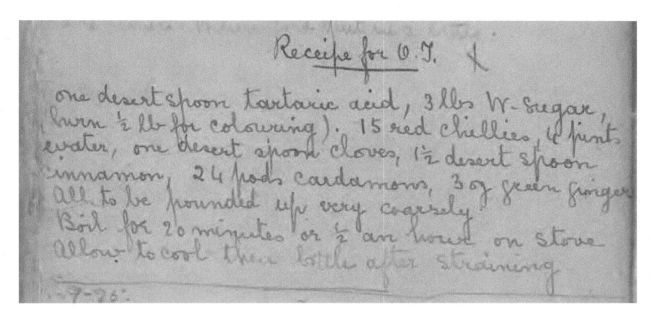

This was a spicy hot chilli punch made with ginger, red chillies and spices, which could also be mixed with whisky, brandy, beer, or alternatively, with aerated water or even milk. This recipe was originally invented by an Indian Maharajah in the early 1900s. In 1948 prohibition enforced banning of both the sale of alcohol and its consumption in many states in India. This caused a few problems for my parents, who were married in Bombay in 1951 and were caught in a bit of a predicament as to what drink should be offered to their wedding guests to toast the bride and groom. Irene stepped in and saved the day making, according to my mother, a wonderful non-alcoholic O.T. punch which proved to be an excellent alternative to champagne – it obviously "packed a punch" and was a real hit with all their guests!

Ginger Cordial

1 Drachm is = to a teaspoon

½ oz Tartaric Acid, one Drachm essence of Cayenne, 3 Drachms essence of Ginger, 2 table spoons sugar burnt, 1½ lbs sugar
Directions. ~~Pour~~ Put 4 tumblers water & boil well, when its boiled well put in 1½ Sugar & allow to dissolve, then put all ingredients & mix, then burn sugar & pour in & mix well.

Jellabies

Jellabies are a type of Indian sweetmeat – bright orange in colour and served in a sugar syrup – they are made using a fermented batter of wheat flour and yoghurt, formed into a circular coil like shape and deep fried. Note how Irene suggests using an empty tin with a hole in the bottom and that by filling the can with the runny batter will make easy work of forming the coil shapes quickly into the hot oil in a fast and safe way.

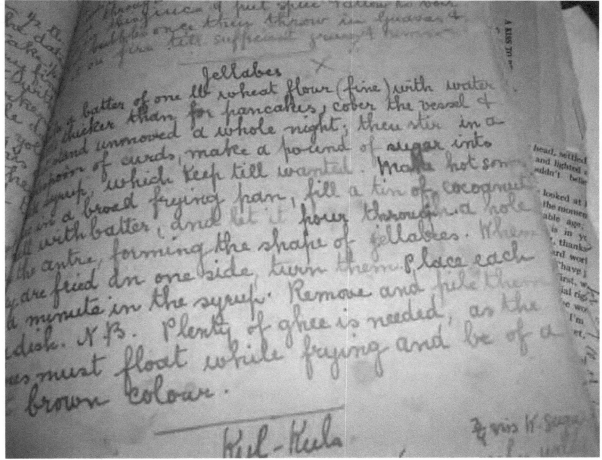

like cream, then put the flour in quick
and mix it till it gets thick and then k...

Rich Fruit Cake
8 lbs.

2 lbs butter, tin, 2 lbs plums, 2 lbs currants,
1 lb candied peel, 2 lbs flour, 2 lbs su...
40 eggs, ½ a nutmeg grated, 2 glasses brandy
mode. First butter to be kneaded well, the
the sugar till it disolves it must be pou...
& put, then the flour, yokes of the eggs,
spice well smashed, last of all put t
brandy. The ____ clare must be put
the fruit, well wisked, it must not b
watery & too thick.

Siones.

Plum Cake.

1½ lb Flour; 1 lb Butter; ½ lb sug...a'0 eggs;
½ lb Marmalade; ¼ lb Almonds; ½ ... Plums
a nutmeg scraped; 1 spoon (desert) spices;

Analysis of the handwriting of Irene

Irene's large handwriting suggests a person who loves being the centre of attention and someone who demands attention. Since the largest proportion of her writing is in the middle zone, this tells us she is needing elbow room. Perhaps indicative of her great tennis playing days, she writes using a very firm pressure which shows a person with high emotional energy, who is very outgoing with great vitality and good health. Her large generous lower loops in her g's show again physical activity and a need for plenty of physical space. The rest of her letters are straight up and down which suggests a person who rules by the head not the heart. The erratic slant moving between left, middle and right tells us she lacks flexibility.

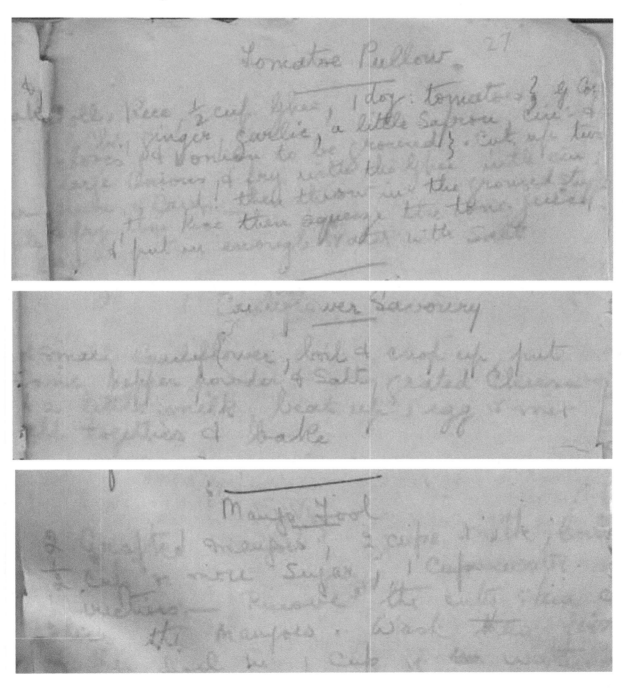

I feel blessed that I had two wonderful parents, they obviously loved each other very much and were looking forward to celebrating their 60 years of married life together with their diamond wedding anniversary on the 6th January 2011. On the 19th November 2010, just seven weeks before their special anniversary, my father died, it was a sudden and immediate shock to the whole family, as just the day before he had gone out as usual to do some shopping, carrying all his shopping bags home (the way he always used to without accepting any offer of a lift from neighbours) "Pop, jump in let me drive you home..." "No, that's fine," my father would say "I consider this my daily exercise, but thanks all the same". "Your father won't change..." my mother would say to me when he would come back from shopping at 8 o'clock at night "he's still on Indian time!" as he would go out to the shops at 5 o'clock (just as they were closing here in England) but of course it would have been the prime time for shopping if you're in India...best time to go out when the shops were open through the evening, when the heat of the day made the experience a little easier!

They first met each other on a blind date, it was 1947, mother was just 20 and my father 22. Their date was all arranged through a mutual friend of theirs Jean, who earlier in the week had bumped into my father and asked him if he was going to the dance on Saturday?

My father shook his head saying that he wasn't planning to as he didn't have a partner to take. Jean retorted, "Don't worry about that, I'll arrange for you to have a partner for the night, just turn up and meet me there Saturday night okay?"

On entering the dance hall, my father's immediate thoughts were "I wonder what my date will look like, will she be pretty, I hope she's tall." My father glanced around the dancefloor for signs of Jean. When suddenly his eyes fell upon a pretty young girl who was wearing a gorgeous green dress sat at one of the tables – green was his favourite colour! On the dance floor, Jean caught sight of my father and whisked him over to her table and introduced him to his date for the night. It was my mother, the lovely girl in the green dress. She stood up and they shook hands. To my father's mind there was a problem right away, she was 5'1" tall, two out of three – not bad my father reasoned in his mind. During the course of the evening, the two of them got on like a house on fire, they found they had similar likings, similar backgrounds and upbringing (a very important detail for both of them) and more to the point, they shared a love of dancing!

Despite my father's attempts that night to keep any suitor at bay, he was sometimes forced to cede her to other dancing partners. One such moment came in the cloakroom when my father was fetching my mother's coat, one suitor who was my mother's childhood friend said to my father, "Don't worry I'll walk Cynthia home tonight". This was just too much for my father, who then decided that the fairest thing would be to toss a coin and the winner gets to walk "the little lady" home! Of course, my father won the toss...and it's amazing to think that I'm only here because of the toss of a coin.

My parents were engaged for four years, and as a child I would often ask them about how they met and I would be whisked off in my mind to another time, another place in the world. They would regularly enjoy telling me their own version of "Dad's little black book" which my father kept during his engagement to my mother. This book was kept secretly by my father who would, wait for this...instigate an argument with my mother just to see how she would react. It was father's way of ensuring that his partner for life would be someone who can cope with everything that came her way! Father would deliberately start an argument and then, mark my mother out of 10 as to how she performed and reacted. Apparently, according to my father she faired extremely well. Mother was unaware of all of this.

Years later my father confessed to my mother all of this and considering everything I think she took it all very well – she always loved telling me about "your father's little black book" and would have a little wink in her eye, giving me one of her wry smiles. I believe mother made sure that father got rid of his little black book before they left for England, she wasn't having this throughout her marriage after all.

I often wonder what life must have been like for my parents who had no choice but to adapt to a new country, finding employment and having to learn quickly how to run a household completely different from the lifestyle they experienced in India. My parents, along with others, left India in 1953 for Britain after Partition.

Leaving all those loved ones, family and friends in India must have been an enormous wrench for them. Here's a photograph of their "send off" party, my parents are in the middle, father at the back mother to his right and my brother is at my mother's side.

My father was particularly saddened about having to say goodbye to his little chokra boy servant who had given him years of loyal service whilst he was in the Royal Navy as an officer and was absolutely dedicated to my father. On leaving, the little boy threw himself at my father and begged him to take him with him...

Any feelings of doubt would have been smoothed over with the knowledge that my father's sister and her husband would be there to meet them when they arrived off their P&O boat in England.

Arriving at Tilbury Docks on one of the coldest January days on record, the whole of Great Britain was experiencing the worst floods in 500 years and furthermore, due to the severe cold snap, all the household water pipes had frozen up. What a difficult start for them.

Just the everyday activity of ablutions entailed a trip to the Public Baths due to their frozen water pipes at home. Armed with their soap, towel and a saucepan they all walked down to the Public Baths. The saucepan was necessary to bring with them so they could on their return fill up with drinking water from the standpipe in the road. Mother's memory of her first week in England was how fast everyone seemed to walk (and with such purpose)! In India, where the weather dictates your pace, most people strolled along to their destination and would gently nod to a passerby or stop for a chat.

In some ways, it was a perfectly natural instinct for them to return to their Motherland, it was the home of their forefathers, and a lot of their traditions had come from England after all. My father would recall to us how his whole school would, at morning assembly stand to attention and salute the Union Jack flag. Having been taught by only English schoolmasters, my father was proud that later on in life he was able to quote from many a Shakespeare sonnet or fully recite a poem from Wordsworth or Byron. My father sat and passed his final year school exams which were known as Senior Cambridge. The examination papers were written, assessed and marked by Cambridge University. The year my father took his Senior Cambridge exams, the papers were, for the first time ever, produced with a carbon copy set so as to guarantee their arrival. Both sets of examination papers were shipped back to England but on different ships as it was during World War Two and there was a very good chance of ships being destroyed.

In fifties Britain, further challenges lay ahead for my mother, this time at the High Street. She really struggled to find her usual spices and condiments which were found so easily in the markets and bazaars back home in India. The food and variety of dishes appeared really bland to her. She learnt to adapt her cooking and turned to Mustard, Vinegar, Worcestershire Sauce, Soy Sauce and Tomato Ketchup to provide a little taste... A trip to the butcher's shop also highlighted just another problem - trays of cut meat had their own bewildering names which were completely unknown to my mother, who in the end would just point and ask for a pound of that one and take pot luck on what she had purchased.

This next family photograph, was taken in 1956 shows my parents now settled in England.

They're visiting my mother's auntie Aileen (second on the left) and her three children (my mother's cousins) in their north London home. You will remember a younger Aileen from the chapter in Maud's section, which shows her as the bride on her wedding day when she married her first cousin, Eugene.

Meanwhile, here are all the cousins grown up since we last saw them in the studio photograph of them with their great grandmother Ophelia when they were children. My mother is third left and my father is far right, standing next to him is his sister (who was there to meet them on their arrival into the country). The children are of course my brother and sister (I wasn't born yet).

My mother never actually wrote in the book, perhaps a reflection of her busy life. A mother of three, she worked all of her life as a secretary in a busy office environment, and I guess for convenience she produced typed up versions of her recipes whenever anyone asked for a certain dish.

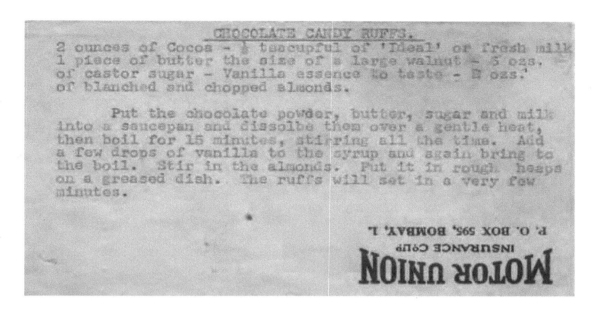

CHOCOLATE CANDY RUFFS.

2 ounces of Cocoa - ½ teacupful of 'Ideal' or fresh milk
1 piece of butter the size of a large walnut - 5 ozs.
of castor sugar - Vanilla essence to taste - 2 ozs.
of blanched and chopped almonds.

Put the chocolate powder, butter, sugar and milk
into a saucepan and dissolve them over a gentle heat,
then boil for 15 minutes, stirring all the time. Add
a few drops of vanilla to the syrup and again bring to
the boil. Stir in the almonds. Put it in rough heaps
on a greased dish. The ruffs will set in a very few
minutes.

Thanks to the recipes she typed up and gave to us, my mother provided her three children with years of solid, reliable and tasty dishes that would ensure we would never run out of ideas of what meals to make.

It's a totally different way of following a recipe because my mother condensed the way she listed her recipes (i.e. she would write "for a 1lb of meat or fish" and then would detail the measurements of spices required). By doing it this way, it gave you greater flexibility of being able to choose your own choice of meat, fish or whatever so that you were much more spontaneous with the dish you were creating and this allowed you to think outside the box. It was especially useful as it meant you just had to open the fridge and see what meat you happened to have, and then just decide on the kind of dish you felt like cooking, so with chicken it was just a simple choice of whether you felt like a Korma, Vindaloo, Country Captain or Jalfrezi. It certainly made things easy.

Rather than try and convert each of my mother's typed up recipes I have decided to deliberately leave it exactly the way she wrote them, without offering further guidance (as opposed to the rest of the recipes here in this book). What will be interesting is that hopefully you will also "find" your way through each of them and discover for yourself your own mode of cooking!

So, I hope you enjoy these well used, typed up recipes with their curry splodges all over them...!!

BROWN KHORMA

CHILLIE POWDER
GARLICK
JEERA
CINNAMON (1" stick)
CLOVES (3-4)
Ground mixed spice ($\frac{1}{2}$ teaspoon)

Fry onion, with cinnamon, cloves. When nice and brown add
the rest of the powders and about 1 tablespoon vinegar and
fry well adding a little water to prevent it burning. After
about five mins. the masalla is ready. To this you can add
meat, chicken and cook till tender. Adding salt towards
the end.

COUNTRY CAPTAIN

Chillie powder
Saffron (huldi)
garlick
Little vinegar

MUM'S FISH FINGER FRY

Fry a large onion with 2 green chillies
(cut fine) then add your fish fingers
cut in 1" pieces and fry a little.
Scrumptious !!

You can do this with more or less
anything viz. cold lamb or any leftovers.

FISH PIE

2 cod steaks
6 sticks macaroni
1 potato
Little cauliflower

Fry onions, (add the rest - all previously cooked). Add
pepper and salt. Then add a few peas for colouring. Place
this in a pie dish alternating with grated cheese, finishing
with cheese on the top. Beat an egg add to $\frac{1}{2}$ cup milk and
cover the top of pie. Sprinkle with bread crumbs and dot
with butter and place in mid. shmf No. 4 for about twenty mins.

MOLEE (This masalla can be used for Fish, Mutton - in fact anything)

Onion   Fried golden brown
Saffron   1 teaspoon
Garlic   "
Ginger   3/4 teaspoon
Green Chillies about 4, sliced and fried with your onions
Coconut Cream 1/4 packet. You can also use dessicated - pour boiling water
and leave to stand. Then extract milk and use.

DHALL

Lentils   1 cup
Onions   2
Saffron   1/4 teaspoon
Garlic   1 teaspoon
Coconut Cream   1/4 packet

MODE: Fry one onion (sliced long). Add saffron, garlic and salt and fry.
Then add lentils, coconut cream and second onion (chopped in squares), and 2
cups water, ADD MORE IF LENTILS ARE STILL HARD.

You can have this with rice, as a secondary dish, or just dhall, rice and a
nice omelette.

You can also make a Dhall curry (using the Curry Masalla) and add hard boiled
eggs (sliced in half lengthways) or make a Dhall and Meat Curry (Lovely).

You can also make Mutton curry and add 1/2 cup of split peas. The mutton and
split peas usually take the same time to cook - so you can put them both in
together.

MEAT BALL OR MUTTON GLACE

Onion   1
Mixed Spice   1 teaspoon
Mixed Herbs   1 teaspoon
Oxo cube   1
Ginger   1/2 teaspoon
Worcester Sauce 1 tablespoon
Tomato Sauce
Bread   1 slice)soaked in water

TO MAKE MEAT BALLS: Mix since with onion (chopped fine), and the same amount
of mixed spice, herbs and ginger. Mix in bread which has been extracted from
the water. Add salt and mix well. Grill. Add balls to the prepared fried
onions etc, and cook slowly for about 5 - 10 mins. Adding about 1/2 to 3/4
cup of water so that you have a gravy. Thicken with 1 teaspoon cornflour. At
end, add potatoes.

FOOGARTH

Cabbage
MODE: Fry onions, garlic, and add 2 green chillies. Then add chopped cabbage
and salt. ONLY USE A LITTLE WATER.

THIS IS THE BASIC SAUCE FOR ANY CURRY viz. meat, poultry or fish.
For 1lb of meat, poultry etc. the following curry mix should be ample.
Increase accordingly when using more meat.

3/4 teaspoon   Mustard
2   "   Cummin Seed (Jeera)
1   "   Huldi (Saffron)
1   "   Chillie Powder
1   "   Ground Garlic (or 2/3 pods chopped)
3   "   Corriander (Dhanniah)
3/4   "   Ground Ginger
1 small tin Tomato Puree or soft tomato.
SALT - to taste
(for a change you can add 1/2 teaspoon ground mixed spice and 1/2" slice of
coconut cream.

MODE: Mix the above ingredients with a little water. Fry a large onion in a
little oil and lard till nice and brown (BUT DO NOT BURN). Then add the curry
paste and fry slowly adding a little water at a time (about 2 teaspoons) to
keep it from burning and catching. After about 2 mins. or so when the oil
appears on the top of the paste add the meat or whatever and fry for a
further two mins, adding water to prevent it catching. Then add a cup of
water and cook till soft. Add a little more water if it is getting too dry.
(If you are using a whole tomato, mash this in after the curry paste is fried)

VINDALOO (Meat, Poultry, Fish or Prawns)

Mustard
Cummin Seed
Huldi
Chillie Powder
Garlic

MODE: Mix the above with salt and vinegar (about 2-4 teaspoons) and add to
the fried onions.

JAL FRAZI (Delicious made with cold meat left over. (mutton joint)

Onion   (sliced thin)
Garlic   1 teaspoon
Ginger   3/4 teaspoon
Saffron   1 teaspoon
Red Chillie   1 teaspoon
Green Chillies (Optional) 2 small sliced right down
Vinegar   about 1 tablespoon
Tomato Sauce   (Optional) 1 tablespoon

MODE: Fry onion with green chillies till a golden brown - then add all the
ingredients and carry on using the same method. Since you are using cooked
meat this does not need much cooking.

Methe Mince:

Fry the methe seeds with
the onions and then use
the basic masalla adding
the tomato puree. Add the
mince and fry well and cook
for ¼ hour with a little water. Potatoes can be added half
way and if desired spinach can be added at the end (fresh or
frozen).

- Teaspoon methe seeds (if poss)
- Onion
- Teaspoon tomato puree
- Potatoes if desired
- Spinach   "   "

Country Captain :

2 Large Onions
Chillie
Saffron
Garlic
Ginger

Fry 2 large onions (Half of the very brown ones to be placed
over the dish at end) Into the onions put chillies, saffron,
garlic and ginger, salt. Fry well adding a bit more oil and
water. This dish is not so runny as a curry. Can be made out
of leftover lamb roast, or fresh chicken. Cover and simmer
for 10 mins.

Fish or Prawn or Vegetable Molee :

Using the same method as for Pepperwater adding fish & pieces
of potato (about ¾hour's cooking) To thicken gravey (if needed)
add a little cornflour.

Burmese Curry:

DO NOT FRY ONIONS - slow cooking/little water.

Onions
Huldi
Ginger
Fresh red chillie powder
tomato puree

Put all together with meat and cook slowly till oil appears
(like pickle)

Masalla Steaks:
Marinate in vindaloo paste and fry.

Potato & Mince Cutlets:

Potatoes
Mince
Mixed herbs
Mixed spice
Little Mint
Garlic (1 pinch)
Ginger ("   )

form into shapes & put into fridge till needed. Then fry as
...

Here is a rough guide as to the ratio of each 'masala' (with
the exception of vindaloo where 3 of Jeera is needed and not
1 teaspoon). Each dish is started off by frying the onions.

For one pound of meat/chicken:

Huldi (Tumeric)	½ teaspoon
Jeera (Cummin Seed)	1 teaspoon
Chillie Powder	½ teaspoon (according to taste)
Ground Garlic	½ teaspoon
Ground Ginger	½ teaspoon
Dhanniah (Corriander)	2 teaspoons

Mince Curry Puff - using same as chapatee dough

Filling: Vindaloo Mince :

½ teaspoon	Mustard
2 "	Jeera
½ "	Huldi
½ "	Chillie Powder
½ "	Garlic

You can either make
square or round shapes.
Damp one edge with water
put mince in and fold over.   Add vinegar to taste
Outline edge with fork &   (about 2 teaspoons)
deep fry for a few secs.

Chapatees

1lb Self raising flour
1 teaspoon oil (added to flour)
boiling water (with 1 tsp salt

Add the salt to the boiling water and pour straight onto the
flour little by little - using a wooden spoon to bring all the
flour together. Then as soon as the dough cools gently knead
for a little while. Keep aside in a cool place till needed.

Frying:

Take each ball (billiard ball size) and roll out. Place in
and on hot greased heavy frying pan and put a few drops of oil
& prick - when bottom is getting a light brown us our turn over.
It should take about ½ a minute each side.

Coconut Pepperwater:

1 Onion
3 Pods Cloves and Garlic cut finely
Fry the onion (keeping as-   ½" Piece Ginger
side little for garnish)   1 Green Chillie
Add tip of tsp. of huldi   Lemon juice to taste
(enough to colour) and salt   ½" Coconut cream
Bring to boil and simmer   2 Cups of water
for about ½ to 3/4 hour.

Often my mother would list the ingredients starting off with rai (mustard), cumin (jeera) and turmeric (haldi). So for me, "Rai, jeera, haldi" – is as familiar sequence of words I heard as a child as hearing "1, 2, 3". Mother would open the store cupboard and whisper under her breath these ingredients as she was reaching for her spices, and to this day it still continues to hold a special place in my memory of those magical moments of cooking with my mother.

My mother had an incredible imagination who allowed me into her world of cooking, I was her little helper and I felt really special. My tasks in the kitchen were sorting through the rice grains on a big plate and picking out any gravel or pieces of husk, snapping rounds of uncooked poppadoms into quarters ready for mother to fry, shaking the flour onto her wooden board, and finding the right utensil from the table. My mother would lay out all her utensils she would need in the way a surgeon would expect their instruments laid out for an operation, and she would ask her nurse, "a teaspoon please". Everything she touched and handled was with loving care and she would tenderly stir her ingredients, blowing on the wooden spoon and when it was cool enough - lean forward and say "here try this, how does it taste?"

It is entirely down to my mother's creativeness and her unfailing desire to please everyone who ate her food, which gave me a real passion for cooking and set me on a road of tastebud discovery.

Happy memories...

Meanwhile, the following pages have recipes which are ones that reflect the many happy hours my mother and I would spend cooking these dishes together in her kitchen. Mother quite often adapted a few of her recipes for other meals, her Methi Mince would also double up as the filling for her wonderful Curry Puffs. Her sausagemeat stuffing mixture would also be the main ingredient for her puff pastry sausagemeat pie.

Curry Puffs (Mince Patties)   (makes 18-25)

At any family gathering we had, these snacks were always the first to go...

Ingredients

1 large onion, finely chopped
½ tsp mustard seeds
½ tsp ground cumin
½ tsp ground turmeric
1 green chilli, finely chopped
2 garlic cloves, finely chopped
450g minced beef
1 tsp salt
2 tsp tomato puree
1 tsp sugar
2 tsp vinegar
2 cups frozen peas
1 packet ready to roll puff pastry
1 beaten egg

Method

Heat the oil in a large pan and fry the onions until golden brown, toss in the mustard seeds, cumin, turmeric, chilli and garlic and fry for a further 3 minutes. Toss in the mince, salt, tomato puree, sugar and vinegar and give it all a good stir then reduce the heat slightly and fry for 20 minutes, adding a little water if necessary to avoid the mixture catching. The mixture needs to be a dry mixture with hardly no liquid. Toss in the frozen peas.

Roll out the pastry thinly and using a teacup saucer plate as a template cut circles. Add 2-3 tablespoons of the mince mixture to the centre of the circle and wet the outer edges of the pastry, sealing up the mixture so that it resembles a half moon. Press the joined edges with a fork and prick the patties with a fork 2–3 times to allow the steam to release.

Brush each patty with a beaten egg and bake in oven 180C/Gas mark 4) for 20-30 minutes.

Chapattis (serves 6-8)

There are three key stages to achieving a successful soft chapatti. The first is in the kneading of the dough which must be done for at least 15 minutes, the second is in very slowly adding the boiling salted water to the mixture and the third point is in the lighthanded use of flour on your board.

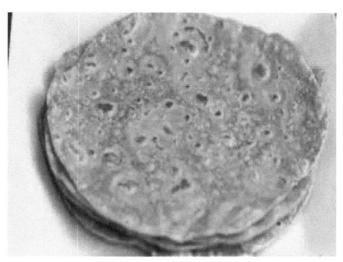

Ingredients

500g self raising flour
1tsp rapeseed oil
210ml water, just boiled
1tsp salt
30ml rapeseed oil (for shallow frying)

Method

Add the salt to the boiling water and pour straight on to the flour little by little – using a wooden spoon to bring all the flour together. Then as soon as the dough cools gently knead for a little while. Keep aside in a cool place until needed.

Frying: Take each ball (billiard ball size) and roll out. Place in medium hot greased heavy frying pan and put a few drops of oil & prick – when bottom is getting a light brown colour turn over. It should take about ½ a minute each side.

You can make a stack of them by buttering each side and serve them piping hot. They can also be stored in a closed container for 24 hours. The other totally unhealthy but delicious option is to fry them in a little oil and watch the bubbles come up on each chapatti – then any that are left over can be rewarmed the next day and spread with butter and Marmite ! A childhood delight...

Tomato Curry (serves 4)

A delicious curry – which can also be eaten cold the next day on toast (like a chutney). My mother always added a couple of pieces of dried Bombay Duck when frying off the masala, which absolutely gives it a unique flavour all of its own. If you decide to add the Bombay pieces, remember to remove them before serving! Do try and get the curry leaves though...it makes all the difference to the dish.

Ingredients

1 large onion, finely chopped
15ml rapeseed oil
2 tsp coriander seeds
2 tsp cumin seeds
6 cardamom pods, crushed
2 tsp fennel seeds
½ tsp black mustard seeds
4 cloves
10 curry leaves
2 garlic cloves, minced
½ tsp ground turmeric
1 tsp garam masala
2 tins of tomatoes
1 tsp sugar

Method

In a large saucepan, fry the onions until a golden brown and put aside on a plate. In the same pan, fry the coriander, cumin, cardamom, fennel, mustard, cloves and curry leaves and dry fry for 2 minutes. Add the minced garlic and give it all a good stir. Fry for a further minute.

In a small bowl mix the turmeric and garam masala with a little water to a smooth paste and add to the pan as well as the onions. Fry for 2 minutes, and now add the tomatoes and sugar and if you have the Bombay Duck pieces add them now and cook for a further 10-15 minutes.

Serve with plain boiled white rice.

Brinjal Curry (serves 4)

This aubergine curry has a wonderful flavour, and the addition of a little sugar makes all the difference...

Ingredients

1 large aubergine, cut into 2cm cubes
2 large onions, finely chopped
60ml rapeseed oil
1 tsp cumin seeds
½ tsp fenugreek seeds
½ tsp mustard seeds
2 tsp tomato puree
½ tsp ground turmeric
1 tsp garam masala
2 tsp sugar
Salt to taste
90ml water

Method

In a large saucepan, fry the onions until golden brown, toss in the cumin, fenugreek and mustard seeds and fry for one minute. Add the tomato puree and aubergine pieces and cook for 2 minutes.

In a small bowl, mix the turmeric, garam masala to a smooth paste with a little water and add to the pan and give it all a good stir. Now add the sugar and salt check for seasoning.

Add 90ml of water and bring to mixture to the boil and then lower the heat and simmer gently for 30-35 minutes, stirring regularly to avoid the vegetables catching.

Served with plain boiled white rice.

Foogath (Spicy Cabbage dish)   (serves 4)

A lovely side dish which can be served with any curry but is also useful as a different vegetable dish to serve with sausages, chops or even a roast chicken.

This can also be made without using coconut milk – just replace with 175ml of water instead.

Ingredients

1 large onion, finely chopped
15ml rapeseed oil
1-3 green chillies, finely chopped
1 tsp mustard seeds
1 garlic clove, finely chopped
Handful of curry leaves
1 large white cabbage, finely shredded
175ml coconut milk or water

Method

In a large saucepan, fry the onions until golden brown, add the chillies, mustard seeds, garlic and curry leaves and fry for a further 2 minutes.   Add the cabbage the coconut milk or water and bring to the boil, lower to a gentle heat and simmer for 5 minutes, checking on the water and if necessary add a little more to avoid it drying out completely.

The liquid will be absorbed by the cabbage and you should have a dish which is just a little moist with hardly any juices.

Prawn Bhuna   *(serves 4)*

A medium hot dry curry originating in Bengal. The uniqueness of this dish is that the recipe requires no extra water, the curry cooks in its own juices.

Ingredients

30ml rapeseed oil
½ tsp black mustard seeds
1 tsp cumin seeds
2 large onions finely chopped
1-2 green chillies, finely chopped
3 cloves
2 garlic cloves, finely minced
2 medium tomatoes roughly chopped
1 tsp salt
1 tsp ground turmeric
½ tsp ground ginger
2 tsp ground coriander
½ tsp ground cinnamon
500g fresh shelled prawns
Handful of curry leaves, chopped

120ml water

Method

In a large pan, heat the oil and fry the seeds until popping, toss in the onions and fry until golden brown.   Add the chillies, cloves and garlic and fry for 2 minutes.

Throw in the tomatoes and salt and cook for a few minutes. In a small bowl mix the cumin, ginger, coriander, cinnamon in a little water to a smooth paste and add this to the dish and cook for a further 2 minutes.

Toss in the prawns and the curry leaves add 200ml of water and mix well, cover the pan and lower the heat and simmer for 3 minutes or so until the prawns are cooked.

Meatball Curry

The Sunday lunch favourite. Meatball Curry was always accompanied by Yellow Rice and Coconut Pepperwater...

Ingredients

Paste
1 medium onion, finely
chopped
3 tbsp rapeseed oil
1 tsp garam masala
1-2 green chillies, finely
chopped
3 garlic cloves, finely chopped
5cm piece of fresh ginger,
 peeled and finely chopped
1 tsp tomato puree
Salt, to taste
800ml water

Meatballs
400g beef mince
½ medium onion, finely
chopped
1 tsp garam masala
2.5cm piece of fresh ginger,
 peeled and finely chopped
4 garlic cloves, finely chopped
1 large egg
¼ tsp black pepper
½ tsp salt

Method

In a large pan heat the oil and fry the onions until golden brown, toss in the rest of the paste ingredients and fry for 10 minutes adding a little water to keep it from sticking until it forms a soft smooth paste. Add 800ml water and bring to boil for 5 minutes.

Meanwhile make up your meatballs by mixing all the ingredients together and forming them into walnut-sized balls. Add to the curry and simmer for 20-25 minutes until the meatballs are cooked through.

Chicken Country Captain   (serves 4)

This dish has its origins with the British Raj in the 1800s when the British trade ships were called Country Ships and their Captains were known as 'Country Captains'.

Ingredients

750g chicken joints
6 whole peppercorns
1-2 red chillies, finely chopped
1 cinnamon stick
3 cloves
2 green cardamom pods, crushed
1 tsp ground turmeric
2 garlic cloves, finely chopped
1 tbls tomato puree
1 tsp salt

Method

In a large pan, fry off the chicken pieces until golden brown on all sides. Keep to one side.

Fry the rest of the ingredients for 5-8 minutes and then add the chicken adding a little water if necessary. Lower the heat and cook gently until the chicken pieces are cooked.

Lamb Devil Fry　　　　(serves 4)

This is a lovely quick curry, with a kick of fiery hotness...! My mother would use her left over roast lamb to make this dish, and depending on the joint either cubed it or sliced it.

Ingredients

450g roast lamb cubed or sliced
15ml rapeseed oil
2 large onions, finely chopped
3 red chillies, finely chopped
1 tsp red chilli powder (optional)
2 tsp ground cumin
2 garlic cloves, finely chopped
1 tsp mustard powder
1 tsp ground turmeric
1 tbsp vinegar
1 tbsp Worcestershire Sauce
1 tsp salt
1 tsp sugar

Method

In a large pan, heat the oil and fry the onions until golden brown.

Toss in the chillies, cumin, garlic, mustard, turmeric, vinegar, Worcestershire Sauce and fry for 5 minutes. Stir in the sliced meat and a little water in order to avoid it catching.

Add the salt and sugar and cook for a few minutes more.

Meatball Glassy *(serves 4)*

Ingredients

Gravy
15ml rapeseed oil
1 large onion, finely chopped
2 tsp ground cumin
2 tsp ground coriander
2 tbsp vinegar
2 tbsp Worcestershire Sauce
2 garlic cloves, finely chopped
1-2 chillies, finely chopped
1 tin of tomatoes
2 tsp sugar

Meatballs
450g beef mince
½ medium onion, finely chopped
1 tsp garam masala
2.5cm piece of fresh ginger,
 peeled and finely chopped
4 garlic cloves, finely chopped
1 large egg
¼ tsp black pepper
½ tsp salt

Method

In a large saucepan, heat the oil and fry the onions until golden brown. Now add the cumin, coriander, vinegar, Worcestershire Sauce, garlic and chillies and allow to cook for a few minutes. Add the tomatoes and sugar and cook for 10 minutes.

Meanwhile make up your meatballs by mixing all the ingredients together and forming them into walnut-sized balls. Add to the curry and simmer for 20-25 minutes adding a little water if necessary to avoid it catching.

Methi Mince

Ingredients

450g beef mince
15ml rapeseed oil
½ medium onion, finely
 chopped
1 tsp methi seeds
¾ tsp mustard powder
2 tsp ground cumin
1 tsp ground turmeric
3 tsp ground coriander
1-2 chillies, finely chopped
2 garlic cloves, finely chopped
30ml tomato puree
1 tsp sugar
1 bag of washed spinach (optional)

Method

In a large pan, heat the oil and fry the onions, until translucent. Now add the methi, mustard, cumin, turmeric, coriander, chillies and garlic and a splash of water allow to fry for a few minutes, adding more water if necessary.

Add the mince and 250ml of water and allow to cook for 20 minutes. Include the spinach at this stage and cook for a further 5 minutes.

Sausagemeat Stuffing (for Christmas Day turkey)

This recipe is my mother's, her magnificent stuffing was valued more than the actual turkey on the day and because of this, my mother would always make twice the amount and use the same mixture for her own "sausage rolls" during Christmas – fabulous!

Ingredients

15ml rapeseed oil
2 large onions, finely chopped
2-3 green chillies, finely chopped
4 garlic cloves, finely chopped
4 rashers smoky bacon
Turkey giblets (heart, liver etc)
  boiled and very finely chopped
1 tbsp tomato puree
1 tsp mixed spice
½ tsp ground ginger
½ tsp cumin seeds
½ tsp mixed herbs
450g pork sausagemeat
Salt and pepper
340g sage & onion stuffing mix

Method

In a saucepan boil the giblets in water and cook until softened. Allow to cool.

In a large pan, heat the oil and fry the onions until a golden brown. Toss in the chillies, garlic, bacon and giblets and fry for 3-4 minutes. Mix in the tomato puree, mixed spice, ginger, cumin, mixed herbs and give it a good stir.

Now add the sausagemeat and season with salt and pepper. Gently cook for 15 minutes stirring all the time to ensure that the mixture does not catch.
Make up the sage & onion stuffing mix in the usual way and add this to the sausagemeat stuffing.

This mixture can be now be used to stuff the neck part of the bird which is recommended as the flavours then permeate throughout the bird when it is cooking otherwise bake in a greased dish for 20 minutes at 180c/Gas mark 4.

Great aunt Constance (my grandfather Herbert's sister) was born during the height of the British Raj in Madras in the year 1888. After the Indian Mutiny in 1857, there was a need to create a distinctive culture for the women of the British Raj.

Anglo Indian domesticity was very much based on Victorian values, with a strict etiquette of dress code. Despite the discomfort of living in tropical weather, it was incredibly important how one should dress, indeed hold themselves, stand, sit or even how one should enter a room. With high standards in dress code, there was certainly no room for sloppiness of dress. Formal dress was therefore required at every social engagement, whether it be at the gymkhana, a garden party, the tombola or simply drinks at The Club. Ladies required cooler, lighter clothing which was made of thin serge, nun's veiling or even silk. In addition, it was also necessary to "dress" for dinner every night, warranting a complete set of freshly laundered clothes.

As a young woman, Constance would fill her days with coffee mornings and tennis parties, whist drives and games of bridge or mahjong, tea parties, fancy dress costume parties and dances, all held at the Club. It was, for them, a way of life...

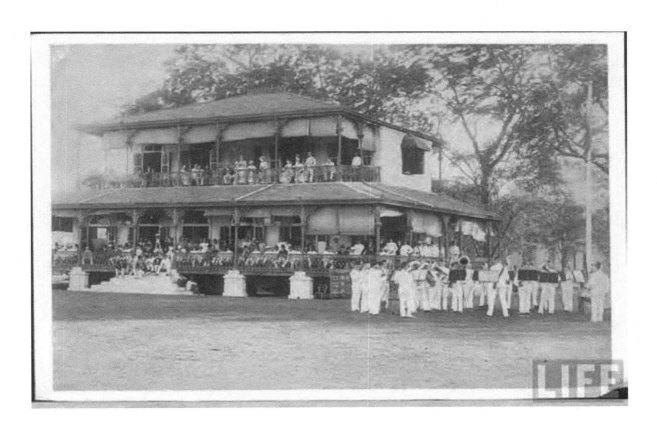

Constance, now in her late twenties with a young family of her own made the choice to move to Burma with her husband. Burma was still under Indian rule and part of the British Colonial Empire which at that time had over 14,000 people working in the Indian Civil Service (or ICS as it was better known) in the Police, Telegraph and Railway, many of those came from the Anglo-Indian community. By the late 1930s Rangoon, the capital of Burma had grown from a population of 200,000 in 1900 to that of almost 500,000.

By December 1941 Constance was still in Rangoon when the Second World War had spread to Asia, Singapore had fallen to the Japanese and it was only a matter of time for Burma to be attacked.

On the 23rd December Rangoon started off the same way it always had, people were out and about doing their Christmas shopping, visiting family and friends, some were returning from church, when suddenly a heavy Japanese air attack filled the skies with bombs raining down all around Rangoon. In twenty minutes more than 2,000 people were killed, more fatalities than the heaviest all night air raid experienced over London.

Hastily made evacuation plans were issued by the government for Europeans to leave en masse and arrangements were made for their departure by plane, boat and overland by lorry and jeep. Panic and chaos ensued with the looting of shops and gang violence broke out. All trading ceased immediately. Food became scarce and law and order broke down. Government civil servants then dismantled institutions designed for social control, with custodians and attendants at the central jail deserting their posts, 5,000 prisoners were released into the community. Similarly, the government mental hospital released its "criminally insane" patients. The man who gave this order was so disturbed at the chaos that resulted that he committed suicide the next day.

As Japanese forces advanced further into the country, the situation became increasingly hopeless and soon most of Burma's infrastructure, the railway lines, the river boats and airfields were destroyed. With the initial exodus of thousands of government administrators others stayed at their posts and continued to run the telegraph and phone operations and other infrastructure systems until sadly for those who were left behind, there was no other option now but to walk to India. There were two routes: an easterly one which went over the Arakan Hills into Chittagong, a relatively short passage, but very dangerous. The other way was in a northerly direction following the course of two rivers, the Irrawaddy and then the Chindwin river, it was several hundred miles long with the final assault over completely unchartered terrain, the impenetrable and forbidding Naga Mountains and finally into India.

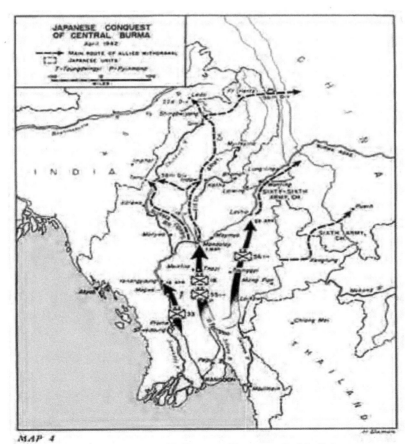

Image source: H. Damon/Dartmouth Medicine

Caught up in this harrowing situation, Constance and her family made the decision to take the Chindwin River passage, and so closed the door on their house, leaving behind all their possessions, pets and cherished belongings joining a convoy of thousands of people making their way towards the Irrawaddy with just the clothes on their back.

With its pre-monsoon rainfall, the dense tropical jungle path turned swamp-like, bodies started disappearing into the thick mud. Wading through ditches waist deep in contaminated water, dysentery soon became rife and malaria picked off the weaker travellers. People would just collapse from exhaustion unable to move any further. Families were left with harrowing decisions to make, to walk on and save themselves or stay. At the Chindwin River improvised rafts would be made from tree branches tied with anything that could hold them together. An extremely wide river with a strong current made it very difficult to navigate added to that the monsoon would have broken properly causing the river to swell considerably higher, making this part of the journey also treacherous. Heading closer north, the fast flowing river now included ice melt water from the snow on the high mountains, making the water extremely cold.

On reaching Kalewa and on foot once more, this path became known as the "Black Route" as thousands died here of cholera, typhoid and dysentery. Deep gorges and thickly covered jungle paths would make it another difficult terrain to cross with very steep climbs and drops which appeared to be less than half a mile apart and yet would take days to climb each one. It would take a further 300 gruelling miles to reach the foothills to the Naga Mountains and despite help from the Naga people along the way, the challenging jungle trek and climb over 12,000 foot mountains proved too much, many died of exhaustion.

By the summer of 1942, New Delhi reported that 500,000 refugees had arrived into India from Burma. Of those, 70,000 evacuees had left Burma by boat, a further 200,000 individuals by land and then steamer and 12,000 by plane. The less fortunate ones were the 125,000 individuals who had no other choice available to them but to trek all the way to the Indian border (which could be anything up to 1,000 miles) across some of the most treacherous terrain. Tragically, a further 100,000 perished along the way.

Great aunt Constance and her family did make it to the Indian border. They, with thousands of others had walked the entire journey from Rangoon to Tamu. So the family story goes, Constance and her family arrived very late one night on the doorstep of a relative's house looking extremely dishevelled with only the clothes on their back, they were barefoot, emaciated and beyond any recognition to those who previously knew them well...

Uncle Johnnie

This is my father's uncle Johnnie, here as a young man on the left and then later in his life at his home in Poona, a military hill station.

My father was extremely fond of him and spoke of the time when he was in his teens and at boarding school, how uncle Johnnie helped his nephew build up a bit of muscle on his skinny frame by giving him a body building manual (here is my father's original copy)...!

Following Joe's manual to the tee and doing his exercises daily meant my father getting up an hour earlier than the rest of the school did at 5am in order to work on his physique and it obviously did the trick for, at the age of 16, my father whilst still a schoolboy, knocked clean out a regular soldier in a boxing bout which was held between the Military Encampment at Deolali and my father's school...

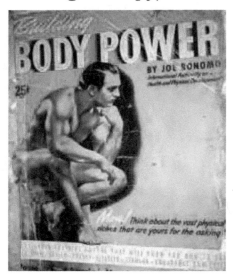

Great Uncle Eugene

My mother's uncle Eugene was the last living relative on her side who was still living in India. Born in 1898, he was now aged a spritely ninety-three and lived in the charming Eventide Rest Home (a sunset retirement home for senior Anglo-Indian citizens).

As we were in Bangalore, we decided to pay a visit to uncle Eugene. I was looking forward to seeing him again as the last time must have been over twenty years ago when he flew over to see his family in England.

Tucked away just off Residency Road, the retirement home was a delight to visit. You could feel the warmth and love in the atmosphere. The staff made us feel very welcome and guided us into their lounge, as it was Sunday morning and the Morning Prayers service was in full swing...

Soon uncle Eugene emerged. He was an extremely dapper, good-looking gentleman in a smart fawn-coloured suit and was wearing a cravat; he invited us into his room.

We were immediately taken with its charm, adorning his bedroom door hung a pin up calendar from 1953 with Marilyn Monroe resplendent in her swimsuit, and on his wooden dresser were fascinating items of a bygone age including a lovely old tin of Black Magic Chocolates.

As a child, I always remembered the cards we received from uncle Eugene each Christmas, as well as his unique card-giving method. For without fail, his Christmas card to us was in fact the very card we had sent to him the previous Christmas.

The front of the card remained intact, the inside greetings page was then covered up with another piece of card onto which uncle Eugene wrote his own message of greetings. The original envelope too was revamped in that it was carefully opened up flat, and then reshaped with the inside now becoming the outside, and cleverly reused. Surely a prime example of recycling at its best!

Sadly, we were the last family members to see uncle Eugene for a couple of months later he passed away peacefully.

Gerald Donnelly

My paternal grandfather, Gerald Herbert Donnelly was born in 1887, in Jubbulpore. He was, by all accounts, quite a character. Here he is seated with some of his children, my father was one of ten.

My father would recount stories that he heard as a child from his father whilst sitting on his knee. Jaw dropping stories of tiger hunting with the emphasis of the story aimed not at bagging a tiger - which they probably never experienced - but in the potential build up and excitement of packing their guns, walking off into the forest and finding a good place to sleep up in the trees that night and then describing vividly all the disturbing sounds of the forest.

But by far his happiest days were those spent as a train driver. A natural communicator, he was able to speak and be understood in most of the Indian languages at that time, including their dialects. He was known to be a fun person to be around with a wicked sense of humour, and for his playing of pranks and tricks on his colleagues.

This was the only railway photograph in my father's collection and it seems reasonable that the tall gentleman in the centre of this photograph is my grandfather as he was well over 6 feet tall.

During WW1 my grandfather served in the British Army with the Royal Garrison Artillery in Mesopotamia. It was a campaign represented by the British Empire with most of its troops from India.

Conditions in Mesopotamia were extreme, with an arid desert, regular flooding, temperatures of 120 degrees, flies, mosquitoes and other vermin - this all led to appalling levels of sickness and death through disease.

Units fell short of officers and men, and often reinforcements were half-trained and ill-equipped. These factors, together with the determined Turkish resistance, contributed to high casualty rates.

It was whilst there that a light-hearted send up of the days spent in that inhospitable climate came about (writer unknown) but within my family this parody of grammatical nonsense would be reflected upon by my grandfather and subsequently my father on such occasions that would allow this now very un p.c. to be read out...

Experience in Mesopotamia

Good evening, ladies and gentlemen; my name is Mr Ramchandra. I am hailing from Madras University, I am B.A. failed.

This evening I am giving you some of my experiences in the Mesopotamia. Mesopotamia from the early Scriptures is one land flowing with milk and honey, but upon my arrival honey bees consuming all honey, and flies and bees they are terrible. I am joining British Army. One day we are ordered to take up advance on Turkish rascals. At this stage I am somewhat nervous. I am explaining to Colonel Brown, but Colonel Brown is telling me, "Mr Ramchandra, do not afright" but what say I? Am I one prawn in the hand of the great prawn broker?

Suddenly while I am talking, one bomb is bursting in my amidst. I am becoming affixiated. After one long serious illness in the British Military Hospital I am obtaining a discharge and convalescent in the London.

Upon another one occasion, Colonel Brown an old friend of mine from India, invited me with the object of taking a ride on his European horse. This European horse is one very fierce creature, but Colonel Brown is explaining to me, "Mr Ramchandra, do not afright, all you have to do is to sit on back of European horse, touch rein, turn toe, apply spur". Complicitly I am following to his direction. I am sitting on back of European horse, I am touching rein, turn toe, apply spur, but horse behaving in most obstreperous manner. While forward portion is elevated, hind portion is deferate. While hind portion is elevate, forward portion is deferate. Yup and down, yup and down "what is it this stupid creature animal?" Suddenly, he is going galloping, galloping and I am falling fatang on pavement!

But in India, we are having one very safe conveyance, what you are calling donkey. This animal is going jolty, jolty, jut pat jut pat, then jut pat jut pat, jolty, jolty. Foot is touching this side, foot is touching that side, no fear of fall off.

But European horse? Ari babri!!

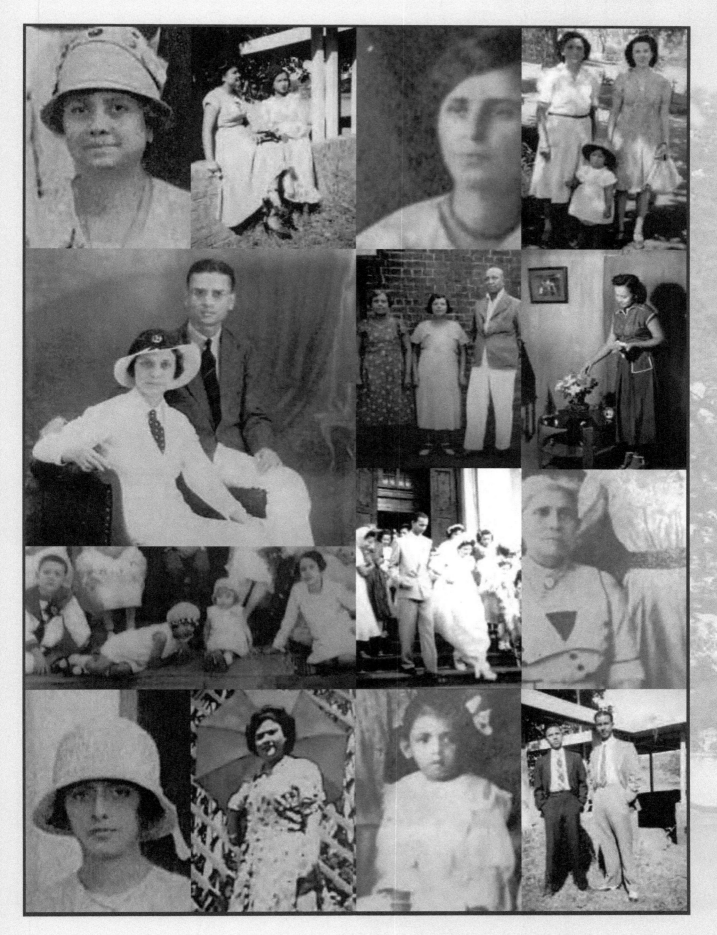

Travel snippets

These snippets of travel stories happened to me whilst I was travelling in India with my husband. We finish with a story which happened to my father in 1944 whilst travelling on a bus in Bombay...and a last minute "stop the press" addition that just has to go into my book – an account of a day spent here in England whilst a group of people from Bangalore responded so kindly to my urgent request for help in establishing whether my grandmother's house still stands in Bangalore.

<u>Visnum and the red silk jacket – February 1991</u>

It was nearing the end of our second trip to India, armed with my shopping list, I headed for the market in search of some spices: nutmeg, cinnamon, cloves and some razor blades (they're so cheap here). Not forgetting of course the most important item, which was underlined twice on my list so as not to forget, my new silk jacket which was being made by the tailor at the silk shop.

As I entered the silk merchant's shop, I noticed a crowd around a young backpacker who was in a bit of a quandary as he had just had his wallet stolen. Within moments, a local Goan man had offered his help to this guy, and furthermore given him some emergency cash and proffered his business card. He said that if he needed further help to just show that card to... (I guess the bank or travel agents) "...and just mention Babu sent you". Babu is a generic term used in India for a bureaucrat or government official. After watching this philanthropic gesture, I quietly went over to the counter and collected a bag which contained both my original jacket, which was from England and a new jacket which was being copied from my own jacket, and left the shop.

I was looking out for a taxi when the Goan business man reappeared and I commended to him that I thought his act of kindness given to a complete stranger was an extremely refreshing sight to behold. He appeared a little embarrassed and shy and then asked me if I was enjoying my holiday. After some more exchanges, he continued on his way, but not before passing me his business card, saying that if I ever needed help to make sure I called him. I kept the card safe and noted to myself that it was fortuitous that I should meet this person. India, whilst being a fascinating and incredible country to visit and explore, can turn on you in the blink of an eye and throw all kinds of dilemmas and frustrating obstacles in your path.

On returning to England and unpacking my suitcase, I noticed that my original jacket was not with the new silk jacket from the merchant's shop. It was a great favourite of mine and I can only think that the design might have been of interest to the tailor for his future clients who may need guidance on design possibilities. Numerous phone calls to the shop were to no avail – each call fell on deaf ears, I just couldn't be understood. Furthermore, I had also written to the shop outlining everything, but either the letter didn't arrive or it was just ignored.

In desperation, I contacted the Goan businessman, Visnum.

It transpired that he was leaving for Canada that night and would not be returning to Goa for another six months. However, he reassured me that he would give the job of getting my jacket back from the shopkeeper, to a clerk from the Dutch Embassy who worked for his friend. He assured me that the clerk would not leave the shop until he got the jacket back for me. A few weeks passed and I received an update from Visnum. The clerk, a very persistent man, gave it his all but finally, after a long period, left the shop empty-handed. "But don't worry," Visnum retorted. "I have another person in mind who is extremely good in this kind of situation. He'll get your jacket back for you, no problem at all." The second in reserve had an equally difficult job on his hands, apparently arguing with the shopkeeper and goodness knows what other exchanges were made, but he also came back minus the jacket. "Do not worry, I am going back in three months' time and the first thing I will do is to go straight to the shop and without fail, I shall get your jacket back from the shopkeeper."

I sat back and the months rolled by, until I received another call from Visnum. This time he had good news for me. He had the jacket. Excitedly, I asked what happened. "Well, just as before, the owner denied all knowledge of having the jacket, but I insisted he should go and check everything behind the shop and the shopkeeper came back saying he had turned his shop over and the jacket just wasn't there. I wasn't going to leave the shop until he gave me the jacket, and I continued challenging him, until finally, the shopkeeper broke with, 'I don't know why you are bothering with this person, she was, after all, just a hippy." An indignant Visnum exclaimed, "She's no hippy – she's John Major's sister in law." And, with that, the owner went straight to the back of the shop and handed Visnum my jacket.

Gouri

I first met Gouri outside our hotel, she was selling little necklaces. Her stall wasn't exactly a table but two wooden boxes and a rough old plank, she must have been all of 6 or 7 years of age. She didn't come over as a child at all, for she had experienced life the hard way and had no choice but to grow up fast. And what a hardworking and industrious saleswoman she was, managing to draw customers in with her good command of English, she was a marvel to watch – a real master at work. She just oozed charm and had her band of loyal hotel customers who were regular tourists coming back year after year and who made a point of seeking her out as her "shop" would not doubt "shift" each year when she would often have to pack up her stock at a moment's notice due to the presence of the police. It was impossible to walk past her table and not buy anything, she impressed you so much with her skills in "talking the talk" that you were soon admiring her confidence and flair and I soon became one of her customers who wanted to help improve her lifestyle. She would set up her shop each morning by 7am and close up at sunset.

It was five years later when I caught up with Gouri, she was in a different beach resort thirty miles from where I had first seen her. This time round I learnt a little more about her life. Originally from Karnataka, she was orphaned at an early age and was taken in by her mother's sister who already had a family of her own. Although hardworking, (the rest of her family worked the land back in Karnataka growing sunflowers and then harvesting them) none of them displayed any sign of Gouri's entrepreneurial skills in Goa. In fact, it was Gouri who made the decision to start selling the little necklaces.

Yet, in five years she had developed her business and was now selling all kinds of items ranging from t-shirts, beach towels and sunglasses even. She had an impressive stand with two aisles of simple beachwear clothing, and another table neatly laid out displaying her sunglasses and thoughtfully arranged second hand books that her customers no doubt gave to her before they returned home.

It was 1996 now and Nokia were the first company to introduce mobile phones into India. It was to prove to be a massive hit with everyone, from the corporate business individual to the kid on the street, but it would take time to filter through to all parts of India. Subscriptions in the first five years were still relatively low at just five million subscribers in whole of India. However, mobile phone providers could see the potential here for everyone, and four years later mobile phones with a Hindi menu were on sale...

Gouri, the little entrepreneur at heart, took an immediate shine to my new mobile phone. Taking it from me, she confidently strutted up and down her shop imagining a conversation was taking place with her supplier – she walked up and down the street pretending she was in full conversation and indeed looked every inch the businesswoman she was, and became fully at ease with using the mobile as if she had been using one for years!

One afternoon Gouri asked me to come back in an hour as her auntie wanted to meet me. This time, her whole family turned up, auntie had produced two more children since I last saw her and there was another baby on the way. I was treated to a head massage with jasmine oil, then we all had our toes painted, my hair was then plaited and finally a rose was placed behind my ear.

Trying to think up a suitable game in which all the children could play, I decided on Boxes (where you each draw a line and the person who closes the box as a square wins that point). Using the back of a discarded old shoe box, I had a group of maybe seven or eight children, all wanting to join me in this little game. With very little explanation they all sat down crosslegged and quietly joined in, adding their box with their initial to show they had "secured" their box.

What was amazing to me was how soon these children mastered this popular childhood game, which was so recognisable to me as noughts and crosses is, yet totally unknown to each of them. Their concentration and purpose of mind really was a joy to watch...

It was to be another four years later that I bumped into one of Gouri's cousins, Lalita. She was now just 16, newly wed and expecting her first child. She suddenly stopped in mid flow of our conversation and opened her handbag. Out came her mobile phone and soon she was speaking to someone. It was Gouri, who on hearing of my return insisted on meeting up with me the next day.

It is interesting to see how quickly India has come along. It's still very much a third world country, but one which has seen the widespread infiltration of mobile phones into every house, every village, town and city since 1995 and this essential must-have accessory can now be found with aunties, children and even the odd stall holder...

Buying a train ticket – January 1992

In India, fourteen million passengers travel by train each day...

Considering how many passengers are stuffed into railway carriages as well as hanging on the outside of the train on the windows, doors and the roof, we decided that the journey itself was going to be the adventure rather than the destination. The booking hall at Bangalore Railway Station was filled to the gunnels with people, reminiscent of an airport delay at Gatwick. We stood in the shortest line of eight different queues.

Unaware of the Foreign Tourist Quota where a small number of seats are kept aside for foreign tourists on certain trains, we stood patiently in line. Two hours later, we had got to the front counter and with our rupee notes in hand we asked for two tickets on the next train to Mysore. The clerk pointed to a sign above his counter which was written in Hindi and then below that to another smaller sign marked "D-F" and advised us that since we were needing tickets for Mysore, that we needed to join the even longer queue marked "L-P".

We were halfway down this new queue when the gentleman in front of us enquired if we had completed our travel form. We were directed to another counter where blank forms needed completion before joining any queue. Skimming down the form, we were amazed at the amount of questions: not only names, but age and gender, where we had come from, how much money we were travelling with and where we were staying in our next destination. The one thing we had learnt from our travels in India was that it was no good to show your impatience, as it was never going to change anything by far the best way to embrace India and all of its challenges was to simply go with the flow. So we took a deep breath, completed our form and joined the masses.

On reaching the front of the line, which by now must have taken hours (who knows and furthermore, who cares), we handed over our form, our rupee notes and excitedly waited for our tickets. With a nod of the head, our ticket clerk told us that all we needed to do next was to come back here tomorrow morning at 6 am and check on their huge reservation board to see if our names were on the list...

Oh what joy and pleasure can be gained by tearing up a tiny receipt into a million pieces!

Tigers in Ooty – January 1992

We were looking forward to visiting Ooty, a hill station known as the Queen of the Hill Stations in India, set deep in the Nilgiri Hills in the Indian state of Tamil Nadu.

Our taxi journey turned out to be spectacular. We were soon climbing up the hairpin bends of the forest floor, which was home to both tigers and elephants, until we reached a plateau which offered a stunning tapestry of green patchwork squares of tea and coffee plantations. Dotted around the lakes were the odd shed or two complete with bar stools. Here refreshments were provided for passing tourists, as well as the chance to sample their estate's own tea served in dainty china cups and saucers, and a pineapple cream biscuit for dunking. All very civilised...

We ascended the winding road toward a smoky blue haze, which turned out to be a thickly forested canopy of eucalyptus trees. We were now 7,000 ft above sea level.

On reaching Ooty, with its colonial British mansions, manicured lawns and even a boating lake, we took the decision to enjoy the hot sunshine in the Botanical Gardens as it was mid-afternoon, and basked ourselves on the lush green lawn under the sun's hot rays.

Having fallen asleep for several hours we awoke to find people walking around in thick coats and woolly hats and even balaclavas. How bizarre we thought. We soon realised why – the sun had gone down and the temperature had dropped 15 degrees. Now we were the ones with odd clothing, as with only shorts and t-shirts, we checked into our hotel and settled into our freezing bed straight after a hot dinner.

In the middle of the night a loud commotion outside our door sharply awoke us. It was our driver, encased in a full-length fur coat with only his eyes peeking out from his black balaclava. He was frantically advising us to get quickly dressed! He explained that the Tamil Tigers (a high profile militant organisation from Sri Lanka, who remain the only militant group to have assassinated two world leaders) were in town and had just overturned a bus. It was not safe for us to stay here.

In the dark night, a convoy of three taxis with tourists aboard, crept their way close together through the freezing fog inching their way along narrow stretches of a sloping mountainous road with a treacherous drop on one side. After only a short distance, we found we couldn't go any farther as the road had been blocked.

Our lead driver gestured to the other two drivers that a three point turn would be necessary, and it couldn't have been at a more dangerous point in the road. We could see the front car undertaking its three point turn and saw how close to the edge of the road the back of his taxi was, complete with passengers, and we were about to do the same...

"On the Road to Udaipur"

It was a chance of a lifetime, we had secured a VIP reservation at the stylish luxury Lake Palace Hotel, which normally held a two year waiting list.

A vision of shimmering white marble, floating on the lake and set against the backdrop of the Aravali mountains, this exotic Indian palace is recognised as the most romantic hotel in the world.

We were to fly from Goa the next morning directly to Udaipur and fingers crossed would arrive just in time for afternoon tea on the terrace! However, on arriving at the airport we were advised that most of the internal flights around India were being cancelled due to airline losses because of the Gulf War.

With a 1,000 mile journey ahead of us, the prospect of getting to Udaipur was looking grim. Luckily, our friend the assistant manager from our hotel was with us and by pulling a few strings, managed to get us confirmed flights to Ahmedabad, Udaipur's nearby state in Gujarat. Our friend reassured us that this would be the best route and then we would need to find our own way to Udaipur which was a further 200 miles away.

On the flight, I took advantage of reading up on Ahmedabad, which is not known for its tourism. My guide book stated that it was the sixth largest city in India, and was nicknamed the "Manchester of India" due to its cotton and textile industry. I relaxed back in my seat and drew some comfort from knowing that there would probably be good transport facilities available. However, it was 8pm by the time our flight had landed and as we walked through the airport terminal, there were few signs for tourists to find information. It was a bit like arriving in the financial district in London on a weekend when everyone had gone home.

We stood outside the airport, fully expecting to see taxis, but there were none. No traffic, no bicycles, no-one walking by, no nothing. It was a bizarre feeling to be in India and yet feel so alone.

"Hello, hello...my friends, my name is Mr Moni, can I help you with anything?" I took one look at this gentleman and thought immediately of two things: he can either rob us or he can help us. I always like to see the best in people, and I decided that we should ask for his help in finding us a car and a driver. "Why, no problem at all, stay right here and I'll have a driver and car in ten minutes for you." We stood firmly rooted to the spot and sure enough within fifteen minutes a car and a driver turned up. Mr Moni wasn't with him so we were unable to thank him properly for his kindness.

Soon we were on our way through this large sprawling city, where the landscape soon changed to open barren land and rickshaws gave way to the "vehicles of the desert" - camels pulling carts laden with sugar cane. It had a distinct medieval atmosphere.

The roads became extremely rough with large deep pot holes and with clouds of dust and small stones flying in all directions, it felt as if we were driving through a building site. My interest then turned away from the road and instead concentrated on the embankment which appeared to be littered with burnt out lorries. Naively, I decided to start counting the number of lorries we had passed which must have had collided with another lorry, overturned and then rolled down the embankment.

After 34 lorries in a short space of time, I seriously started praying, especially since our driver was now dropping off to sleep at the wheel! Keeping a close eye now on the driver, I kept a constant check on him in the rear mirror for any signs of his head falling. I then remembered my packet of glucose tablets which we had bought ahead of the journey, for our trip in the desert. The next six hours were spent either prodding our driver in the back or feeding him with my supply of glucose tablets! The irony here was that for Stewart and I the journey was so fraughtful, filled with nervous energy that it was just impossible to be anything <u>but</u> wide awake, unlike our driver...

It was 2.30am when we arrived at our destination. Amazingly, our driver just turned round and made his way back to Ahmedabad like he had just been on a short little trip. Incredible. To his credit, our driver had dropped us off at exactly the right place, a jetty at the City Palace Gardens, for our hotel was only accessible by boat. Waiting for us at the jetty was a boatman with a sumptuous Venetian style boat with large comfortable cushions to sit on ready to take us to the middle of the lake.

At the entrance to the hotel stood the manager, who warmly greeted us. He had been advised of his VIP clients arriving late, and knowing that internal flights had been cancelled, was curious as to how we had got there. He immediately recognised how exhausting our long journey had been and suggested we relaxed a little, took our time to enjoy a hot shower and change of clothes and that he would be delighted to give us a personal tour of his hotel when we came down followed by dinner also. (He had kept his chef and bearer up that night). "Choose anything you wish from the menu, the chef will be delighted to cook it for you."

It felt like we were in a dream...

Pushpa

Waking up the next morning at the Lake Palace Hotel, we had slept really well, and feeling refreshed with the past experiences of yesterday far from our minds, we were ready to explore this most romantic city of Udaipur.

We had seen the City Palace with its eleven individual palaces, marvelled at the Amar Vilas with its beautiful hanging gardens complete with fountains, towers and terraces. Admired the wonderful collection of royal paintings, antique furniture, and even seen the crystal and porcelain figures at the Ruby Palace. We had visited the Palace of Mirrors famous for its breathtaking mirror work, and as if that wasn't enough sightseeing for the day had taken a rickshaw up to the top of the hill to see the Monsoon Palace, the home of Kamal Khan, the principal villain featured in James Bond's Octopussy movie.

Back down on terrafirma once more, we were just ambling along with no particular agenda in mind, when a crowd of children rushed up to us and clearly were agitated and wanted to talk. One boy piped up, "Let me take you on a tour of Udaipur" when suddenly a little girl took my hand and smiled saying "Miss, don't listen to that boy, let me show you round".

I was very taken with Pushpa, she was charming to listen to, her command of English was excellent and you could see that she was being protective, wanting to make sure that we didn't get drawn into any further conversation with this "terrible" boy! So despite our initial reluctance, we were given a personal tour by little Pushpa of the local zoo (if I'm honest which we didn't enjoy at all because of the state of the animals in their cages) and after a short visit around the surrounding park, we said our goodbyes to this little girl. I tried to give her some money for her trouble, but she was insistent that we don't pay her.

The next day, as we were strolling around Udaipur enjoying all the beautiful scenery and just taking things in, we came across Pushpa who was on her own, she asked if we would like to visit her family for a cup of tea. We agreed to this, knowing inside ourselves that there might just be a motive behind this. We were so glad we did, as on entering the family's room we discovered all her family were hard at work producing souvenirs that we had come across in the shops.

There were several children painting black clay pots with various designs on them and her parents were skilfully painting on little patches of silk small, intricate designs of an elephant procession complete with mahout wearing a traditional costume.

Our eyes turned to the corner of the room where we noticed a huddled figure of a small boy with a grey blanket covering him. He looked very ill, he was trembling. We decided there and then to purchase all their pictures and small clay pots which we could then give away as souvenirs to our family and friends, but more importantly, we knew the money needed to go straight to this family.

After our cup of tea and meeting all of Pushpa's family, we said our goodbyes. As I was leaving, Pushpa stopped me and told me to squat down and she started to paint my hand with a henna design. She told me this would bring me good luck and we waved goodbye.

A few months later back home in England, we received quite unexpectedly an airmail letter from India. It was written by Pushpa's school teacher advising us that the money had been spent on the little boy's medication that wasn't available at the free hospital and that Pushpa had asked her to write to us as she wanted to say thank you from her family.

Superstition, Indian folklore and Faith healing

Superstition, so deeply rooted in India that it is considered unwise by most to ignore. We had by now witnessed first-hand instances where a particular sight or a harmless few words spoken would completely change someone's mindset to one of agitated urgency.

We had a taxi driver in Delhi once ask us to leave his cab (we had only seconds before got in), we later found out from our next taxi driver that this was because a widow had crossed the road in front of the taxi driver just as we got in, and that was considered bad luck.

On another occasion we set off in a taxi when suddenly through our open window a sadhu holy man thrust his head into our cab and asked us where we were going.

Once more we were asked by the taxi driver to leave the taxi as being asked this question was tantamount to bad luck, as it foretold you that your journey would not be fulfilled. A sadhu is a wandering holy man who has renounced his worldly life, walked away for good from his family and possessions, social position and standing. With his matted hair, and his naked body covered in ashes, he leads a life of celibacy, ascetic yoga and a search for enlightenment.

Even the sight of an empty basket has warranted odd behaviour. Visiting a very good friend of ours in Goa, the three of us were about to leave the house for the day. We had taken only two steps away from the front door when our host swiftly returned to the house. Had we forgotten something, I wondered. No, our host was simply taking precautions as he had noticed just as we were leaving the house that a woman was passing by with an empty basket – a sure sign that you would have bad luck all day.

So we stayed inside the house and luckily India being India it was only five minutes before we saw another person walking past this time with a full basket of dekshis, plates and tiffin boxes in her basket...

On another occasion, at the same friend's house a crow landed on the window ledge and starting cawing. Our friend jumped up and announced that someone would be coming to visit us. Sure enough, within minutes a visitor appeared at the same window and then knocked on the door. My friend was not in the least bit surprised by the arrival of his visitor.

Indian folklore

Whilst travelling up in the north of India, we had met a fellow traveller who was telling us about his recent experience in having his palm read. Totally fascinated with palm reading, I pressed the traveller for details of where he had his reading. As he started to write down the address of the palmreader, he suddenly stopped in his tracks and said there was a better way to do this which would mean that I did not need to travel the sixty miles in order to see him. If I posted a photocopy of my palm to the palmreader, enclosing my name and home address and include a fifty rupee note inside the envelope, the palmreader would provide a full reading and analysis report and post it back to my home address in England. Great idea, I thought particularly when travelling around India is not that easy to do.

The next day, standing in the local Xerox copy shop with my palm facing down on the photocopier glass, I noticed the shopkeeper's full attention on me. He was beyond curious seeing someone photocopy their hand of all things! Once I explained why I was doing it, he just nodded and then proceeded to read my palm himself...

The most bizarre thing was that he was uncannily accurate with not only his description of my past, but of the kind of work I was doing at that time, with his future predictions, and particularly on the timing of them...and all of this for only fifteen paisa!

Faith healing

The day had started off well. We were to join our Goan friends for a family picnic by the riverbank. Our jeep with just four of us, soon grew in capacity, collecting grandmas, aunties and cousins along the way. Each one of them were clambering on board carrying items, until we finally ended up with eleven family members in the back of our jeep, plus enormous hot aluminium deskhis of various curries and steaming rice, homemade Goan patties, and various others snacks in boxes were slid were under our seats, together with bottles of lemonade and cashew feni (a very popular Goan local drink which is a triple distilled spirit made from the cashew apple) – with all these ingredients, we were ready for one amazing picnic...

Stewart had been feeling "off colour" for a couple of days, but we had decided we didn't want to spoil the planned event by not going, but further into the day, Stewart's condition worsened considerably, until his breathing became irregular panting and his body started shaking uncontrollably. The previous day we had visited the doctor and he was given a huge injection of antibiotics and pills to take – but they just didn't seem to be helping. Our friends decided that there was nothing for it but to take Stewart immediately to grandmother.

Living on a little island not far from the picnic area, grandmother didn't speak any English, just Konkani (the Goan mother tongue). Stewart was quickly directed into grandmother's house and without any delay, the grandmother started to put red chillies on the crease of Stewart's elbow, behind his knee, the back of his neck, the top of his shoulders and then ran another chilli down his spine, at which point she thumped his lumbar region.

Our friend said, "Stewart, my grandmother wants to know whether you felt anything when she ran the chillies down your spine?" Stewart, who normally resists medicine and going to the doctor, said that he definitely felt something! The grandmother nodded and we were told that Stewart would be okay now, as the evil spirit had left his body. An hour later, Stewart who had been quite seriously ill for days, had completely recovered.

1001 Arabian Nights

It was straight out of a childhood adventure book – a fairy tale medieval city majestically rising from the sands of the Great Thar Desert.

Jaisalmer, with its impressive fortification of castellated walls and bastions must have looked like a mirage in the desert haze to those silk and spice traders 800 years ago when they were making their way to Egypt, Arabia and Persia. We had decided to try a three night camel safari with local guides taking us out into the desert, sleeping under the stars on a simple bedroll and no tent. With introductions and exchanges we met our three nomadic guides who were going to be our only companions for the next four days - Shadrach, Meshach, and Abednego.

Of course, that wasn't really their names, just something that came to mind and was only used between Stewart and myself. Shadrach, who was the eldest of the three spoke and understood a little English, certainly enough for us to communicate with him on a very basic level.

The challenge would be how on earth we were going to mount our camels. It was actually a lot easier than we first thought as camels conveniently lower themselves to the ground and then it's just a case of swinging your leg over the top of the camel's back, however it was with a sudden thrust forward when they straightened their back legs to stand up, that we found ourselves having to hang on tight! We were now 10 feet off the ground sitting astride a wooden saddle which was laden with thick cotton blankets and with no stirrups our legs were left dangling by the side of the camel.

We made our way out into the desert, and occasionally Shadrach would turn and check on his charge and ask "Good? Double good?" to which we would reply: "Yes, double good". Two hours into the trek we had reached the Sam Sand Dunes, where we stopped for a welcome rest under the shade of an acacia tree, after that we never rode for more than one and a half hours at any one time. During these rests, water would be drawn from the wells and a large canopy was laid out on the ground to mix the camel food.

A camp fire of dry sticks was soon put together followed shortly by hot refreshments of chai (tea), and a lunch consisting of rice, dal, vegetable curry and chapattis.

The nomadic villages gave us a fascinating insight into a world far removed from ours, elderly women sat spinning wool whilst the younger womenfolk chose to watch the spectacle of strangers passing through their village.

Traversing further into the sand dunes, we arrived at our first stop for the night and the guides set about making a campfire and preparing dinner. Watching the incredible colours of the sky change at sunset whilst running up and down the sand dunes is a memory I shall never forget.

Over dinner a livelier conversation took place with our guide Shadrach, who told us that he married his wife when she was only twelve years of age and he talked about his family. Suddenly, he jumped up asking if we would like to hear some local music and with that Abednego left the campfire and started walking out into the silent darkness. Fifteen minutes or so must have passed when we heard Abednego shout at the top of his voice something and he calmly returned back to us and sat quietly by the fire once more.

As if from nowhere another man appeared with two flutes. Meshach took up an empty plastic water container and started strumming with his fingers a catchy rhythm - the stranger now placed the two flutes in his mouth, and suddenly we had music!

Later that night as we settled down to sleep on the desert sand with just our thick cotton blankets and a pillowcase filled with seeds, Shadrach came to tuck us in, and with a wagging finger he instructed us that "These blankets are the borders between India and Pakistan – no crossing."

Edna and her family

I wish you all could have met Edna and her family. Well actually I heard Edna first – it was 12.15am and Edna was shouting at the top of her voice, "Hello-o-o-o-o-o-o" to wake up the reception/hotel staff. Worn out and travel weary from a lengthy and arduous journey they were surprised to find their hotel had closed up for the night. Finally, the night porter, who had awoken with all the commotion outside slowly stirred himself to open the gates.

Meeting them for the first time at breakfast the next morning, the whole family were remarkably buoyant and upbeat – ready to enjoy their holiday in Goa. Yesterday's bad journey was a thing of the past and they were all refreshed and revitalised.

Despite being seasoned travellers themselves, they admitted they were worn down and totally frustrated at the difficult journey they had just experienced. True travellers to India soon learn to accept these frustrations as they're all part of the "experience" of India.

Edna (a Chinese surgeon) with her husband (a Californian physicist) had taken their children from an early age on some of the most exciting trips across the globe to places that most people never get a chance to see in their lifetime. All of them had an adventurous spirit and were very keen to explore new places, experience cultures and meet people from all walks of life.

Mature, well-adjusted individuals each of their three children were in their own way animated, fun loving and a joy to be around. Five year old Kelvin told me how they had recently met some Irish backpackers in Delhi who hadn't been to India before and during the conversation the children asked where the backpackers were going to visit. Looking very "cool" the backpackers proceeded to tell the children "...yeah we're planning on doing Varanasi, Agra and Jaipur and seeing the few odd temples along the way..." When Kelvin suddenly interjected with "Have you been to the Base Camp at Mount Everest all at? It's just incredible, and have you ever been to Mongolia it's amazing?" I can just imagine the backpackers trying to remain composed on hearing the five year old's adventures!

Edna's surgical skills had almost immediately come into play as the day before I had managed to scrape my knee badly and the wound had become infected. With her breakfast knife she deftly cut away the infection and recommended I go straight into the sea for a swim. The salty water helped. Each morning over breakfast, Edna would examine my knee and provide the necessary treatment until the infection cleared. Meanwhile, her physicist husband gave lively and fascinating discussions on the subject of waves and energy, and how if you take a clock and travel with it, time actually goes slower...that kind of thing – it would leave me thinking, "Hang on, okay I got it, no just repeat that bit again...oh no, I've lost it again!" I took the opportunity to mention something that happened to me over twenty years ago, but one which has remained a total enigma to me.

I was about to cross the International Date Line, a flight which would take me from Hawaii to Auckland. Just before boarding my flight, I rang my husband, Stewart who was back in England, and we discussed his plans for the day. It was Good Friday and he planned to take his mother to Church. In closing, I said I would give him a quick call when I arrived in Auckland and that my flight would take 8 hours and 35 minutes.

Now I completely embraced the fact that I would be losing a whole day by flying westwards across the International Date Line, but it was the following incident which would leave me in a state of perplexity...

Landing at Auckland, I rang my husband to let him know we landed safely, and his response was just like out of the film "Groundhog Day" where the same event gets repeated, he was saying that he would be taking his mother to Church that morning. Utterly confused and jet lagged, I decided that I must have got the wrong end of it in our previous call. But no, Stewart re-emphasised to me that he had already been to Church with his mother on Good Friday morning, which was two days ago – and now he was about to take his mother to Church for the Easter Sunday service.

Whilst I completely get the principles here of losing 24 hours, what I cannot get my head around is that in reality just 9 hours or so of real time had passed between our telephone conversations, and yet in that short time Stewart had managed not just one visit to Church - but two! How can it possibly be that Stewart experienced two Easter services whilst I was on a 9 hour flight? Explain that one...

Poona

I'm now settled into Auntie and Uncle's colonial house in Poona. What a special place it is – a little oasis, nestling amidst the hurly burly of a modern city. It stands alone, defying the onset of the twenty first century.

This lovely heritage house sits quietly smiling around a fast hectic environment, like an old grandfather clock that ticks along happily to its own tune, this place has charm.

With its verandah overlooking a lush garden full of colourful plants, scented honeysuckle and bougainvillea, you can sit and simply watch the world go by.

A boy travels past on a bicycle with two steel milk churns filled to the brim, a very distinguished gentleman walks along with his dog, the Times of India strapped under his arm. Cars honk, a temple bell sounds in the background, and a big black crow sits under Auntie's magnolia tree, and I see the bottle brush tree in full bloom, with a purple wisteria just opening out. The sun is full out and it's a beautiful morning. Close your eyes, do you feel like you're with me now?

There's a lovely swing in their garden with passion fruit growing over it and it suddenly reminds me of a family photograph I have, it's a photo which was taken around 1930 with my father as a five year old boy sitting cross legged on the ground whilst his parents and family are sitting on a garden swing... I wonder, could it be the same swing?

As soon as you arrive at their home, you get an incredibly warm feeling rush over you as both auntie and uncle are very relaxed and just want to make you feel "at home". Auntie's car plays a tune when she reverses it – out of nowhere melodic strings start playing "There's no place like home, there's no place like home". Uncle also has one in his car, only it plays "Oh when the Saints, coming marching in, when the Saints come marching in". Both auntie and uncle are such a sweet couple, wonderful hosts and an absolute delight to be around.

Much later now, and I'm woken to the sound of talking, it's auntie's voice I can hear and she's chatting in Hindi to one of her servants. My bed has mosquito netting on all four sides and I'm tucked in nicely. I sit up in bed and feeling totally refreshed, I wash and get dressed. Breakfast is all laid out on the table, there's a boiled egg with buttered soldiers, a delicious cup of good Indian tea together with a scrummy piece of shortbread, made locally by a firm of bakers.

Auntie's doing the cooking, and she's rustling up a family favourite of spicy scrambled eggs with peppers, chillies and onion called Rumble Tumble, these are to go into sandwiches for our picnic auntie tells me we're having today. She also advises me that she and uncle are taking me away for the weekend. How lovely! Uncle has taken time out from his busy workload and agenda to spend time with his niece auntie advises me, and he will be doing the driving as we are heading out from Poona along the Western Ghats to a hill station called Mahalabeshwar, about 60 miles from Poona. Famous for its pleasant climate, during the summer this was a popular choice by the British Raj as a suitable resort for wives and children who would otherwise suffer from the hot dry arid plains. It's also famous for being the backdrop for the *Jewel in the Crown* and *Passage to India* stories.

Soon we were ascending up from the foothills of the Western Ghats. The Western Ghats is a chain of mountain ranges running parallel to Indian's western coast. The forests have some of the best representatives of non-equatorial tropical evergreen forests in the world, it is a UNESCO World Heritage site, and is one of the eight "hottest hotspots" of biological diversity in the world.

One hour into our travelling, we broke journey arriving at a beauty spot, just the place for a picnic. We're at the top of a dry and dusty plateau, and the area around looks every inch like a baby version of the Grand Canyon.

The scenery is spectacular with views on all sides with mountains which seem to go on for miles. We settled down to our picnic, spreading out a blanket and arranging all the various foodstuffs and plates, when something else caught my uncle's eye. Unknown to us several of the cars that were parked alongside us, had now gone and we were now the only ones left... and in close distance was a whirlwind of dust, twisting and twirling in fast motion and it was heading straight for us! As fast as we could, we gathered up our picnic and belongings and made a run for the car and within minutes the whole car was engulfed with ginger particles of fine dust.

Our cottage for the next two days was Frederick's Hotel, a wonderful heritage family establishment with an olde world charm harking back to those bygone days. The resort had a series of bungalows overlooking lush green mountains, exotic plants and beautiful scented flowers which filled the air. Being the highest point of the Western Ghats (at over 1372 metres) it is also subject to extraordinary weather. At the start of monsoon weather in June, heavy mists arrive and bring a dramatic drop in temperature followed by a deluge of biblical proportions – up to seven metres of rain can fall in two months. At sunset, we drove to Bombay Point and saw a large gathering of holidaymakers waiting to see the sun go down. There were horses and ponies with children galloping fast through the crowds. There was a wonderful carnival atmosphere about this place, with even a small funfair complete with helter-skelter, coconut shy and an Aunt Sally! Whiffs of familiar childhood smells came to me and drew me closer to the candy floss man and the vendor selling his charcoaled maize. A wonderful unexpected end to the day!

The next morning before breakfast, we were woken by somebody knocking on our front door. It was a man selling some chuppels (leather sandals) which he had in his big carpet bag, hundreds of them! We decided to try some on. Soon another man appeared at the open doorway...he was selling artefacts, so whilst we were still waiting for our breakfast we passed the time admiring his stock! Another knock on the door, and it wasn't our breakfast but this time a strong sturdy built gentleman stood outside our door and was speaking in Hindi to my auntie. It transpired he was offering to do a foot and leg massage, I jumped at the chance! However, this masseur was definitely more of a monsieur, with rather beefy arms. He took to the job with great relish and left no piece of flesh unpummelled. Whilst he was pulverising my muscles, I would wince out in pain and soon auntie was slapping this man on the wrist and shouting loud and clear in Hindi to stop as he was killing Baby. Suddenly he turned to me and asked me (in perfect English) whether this lady was my mother, and I replied "No, she's my auntie". He nodded his head and responded back with "No, I think she's definitely your mother"...!!

In fact, come to think of it, "Baby" was a word I often heard in auntie's presence for she had a gardener, a gate keeper, a sweeper, a man who came to do odd jobs which included delivering a newspaper, a lady who came in to wash the floors, a servant who made tea and coffee, another man to walk the dogs, and of course they all referred to me as Baby. I would catch sentences of Hindi spoken between Auntie and her help and invariably a glance would be made to me and the mention of Baby would turn up. It made me feel very cossetted and loved, I have to say!

A true story from my father...

One city gent, one girl and her hanky

It was 1944, I was 19 and a Naval Officer Cadet with the Royal Indian Navy, based in Bombay. It was the start of the rush hour evening traffic, when I boarded the already full bus.

Image source: Lou Morgan Photography

Every seat was taken, otherwise I would have given up my seat to the pretty young girl who followed me onto the bus.

I noticed when she went to pay the conductor that her white lace handkerchief flew out of her handbag and landed straight onto the lap of a city gent who was reading his large broadsheet paper.

A lot of sniggering followed, as passengers clearly saw the girl's predicament. Surely she wasn't going to pick her handkerchief up now?

The city gent could now hear the passengers laughing and slowly edged his newspaper down to take a peek at what was causing the amusement. To his horror he found all eyes were on him! He pretended to carry on reading and gave a quick look around his attire and saw what he thought was his shirt tail sticking out from his trouser flies. So, still holding the newspaper now with one hand, he used his other hand to push his "shirt tail" back into his trousers!

We finish with an event which happened only recently, on Sunday 19th July 2015 and it feels so right that I should add this here in my book as it captures the essence of an Indian community and my own experiences of that day...

This story is a fine example of social networking at its best, illustrating quite simply a network of folks from Bangalore, each with their own ancestral history going back over 170 years or more. Where Indians mingled with Anglo Indians, Tamils shared cups of tea with their Anglo Portuguese neighbours, where lively banter and daily conversations would take place. When a five minute walk down the road would take fifty minutes stopping to have a chat with their close knit community on the way to Russell Market or to the local bakery to get their fresh bread, cakes and biscuits. Neighbours would be happy finding the simple joy in being in each other's company, throwing open their doors to the community and in sharing their mutual love of food and cooking. Scents of the different aromas food wafting around in the air where grandma's would sit on their verandahs and discuss how their geraniums and chrysanthemums were doing that year. The closeness of a friendly tight knit neighbourhood where a coming together of different nationalities is evident.

Truly remarkable, after spending years researching all through my grandmothers' recipes I can totally understand and appreciate now why my grandmothers would be writing ingredients in their recipe book which calls for 40 eggs for their Christmas Cake recipe, with pounds of dried fruit, citrus peel and a good glass or two of their best brandy! This delightful community of Bangalore where doors would be thrown open at Christmas time or another perfect excuse to celebrate an event with their neighbours, family and friends, inviting everyone in for a glass or two of their favourite brew of homemade O.T., Ginger Wine and a slice of their Christmas Cake.

All my grandmas lived in Bangalore at some point in their lives, some were born in Madras and ended their years in Bangalore, but the family link has always been strongest in Bangalore.

However, let's get back to my story which happened just twelve days prior to this book going to press. My Sunday morning started off the way it always does, with a mug of coffee, my laptop and my thoughts. A sudden idea came to mind which prompted me to post on my Author Facebook page an urgent plea for help, to establish whether the two houses where both my great grandmother and my grandmother lived, were in fact still standing.

Months before, I had connected with several groups in Bangalore who had either food interests, historical photography or an interest in Anglo Indian heritage. Quite a few of the members were now living in different parts of the globe, but they all had one thing in common, they were unified by their love of their community, particularly a community that had seen some pretty dramatic changes over the past few years. India's third largest city, once known as the "Garden City" because of its many green spaces, had now earned the distinction of being India's Silicon Valley.

I threw out an urgent appeal to three groups I had recently barely connected with on Facebook – Photos from a Bygone Age, Richards Town Bangalore and also My Good Ol Bangalore. This was my exact Facebook message, sent at 5:52am on 19th July, which would have been just coming up to 10:30am their time in Bangalore and from a complete stranger (in their eyes) in England.

I NEED EVERYONE'S HELP TODAY, AS YOU MAY JUST KNOW THE ANSWER FOR ME, OR KNOW OF SOMEONE WHO HAS THE ANSWER...PLEASE READ THANKS!!

I have one last thing to sort out before my book goes to print this week and that's quite an enigma that I need solving... You see, I have a photograph of my grandmother Irene which was taken outside her home in Bangalore in the 1940s, her address at that time was known as 13, Jeremiah Road, Bangalore, her mother lived in Pettigrew Street op Xavier's Cathedral in St Johns so I'm hoping that Jeremiah Road might be around there too! I've looked up on Google Maps etc to find Jeremiah Road, but it must have been changed since 1948 to another name!! Can you help circulate or ask around in your family anyone who lived in Bangalore during the forties who might just know Jeremiah Road and pinpoint it out for me on a map so that I can locate it for my upcoming trip to India. I want to be able to see the road my grandmother lived on, maybe even that lovely old house is still there even! Here's that photograph for all you budding Sherlock Holmes!!!!! It will mean the world to me if I can find out the new name of her road and my publishing house can press the "go ahead" button for printing!!! Hoping you can help.

With kindest wishes,

Jenny Mallin

I sent out these two images of 13 Jeremiah Road, Bangalore. The first one of my grandmother, Irene with her dog, Laddie standing on the stone pathway to her house, and another close up of the front of her house, both of which were taken in the 1940s.

Within three minutes I got a response from Pradeep E Sinnas who sent me this message:

Now armed with my grandmother's house number, Pradeep jumped on his motorbike in the pouring monsoon rain and wrote back to me reporting on his findings.

Next to come on the scene was Vinay Bhatt. Vinay, with his son Sachin Bhatt waited for the rain to subside, as it was feet deep, drove around the neighbourhood taking some excellent photographs of both Jeremiah Road and Pettigrew Street. Vinay was breaking it to me gently:

Photos of No.13 will be with you soon. The house still exists! Though in a bad state. Here are the photos of 13 Jeremiah Street. Note that gate has been bricked up and sealed. So all pictures are from over the compound wall. I have compared this with the photo you have on your page and the building is identical! Regards, Vinay

Indeed grandma's house was sadly holding its own, this lovely old heritage house was still there in its rightful place amidst all the chaos and modernity of a busy sprawling metropolis with a modern apartment block "propping it up" and literally rubbing shoulders with grandma's house.

Vinay's son took some great shots which meant we could then easily identify the otherwise unknown identity of this crumbling aged house.

Sachin had managed to get in all the architrave detail, and the fact that the two pillars which marked the doorway entrance to her house was no longer there but sealed up with a wall with grass growing high on the other side. How grandma would have hated to see it now! When she lived there, the walls were all whitewashed and beautifully clean. However, I looked past all of this and only saw a house that still had its soul, it was like it was defiantly saying to the world, "look I'm still here..." and I felt so thrilled to imagine my grandparents and my mother living in this little house... Vinay also found a house a few doors down which had exactly the same front as my grandmother's did in the 1940s with the same pathway leading up to the front entrance.

 10/14 is a similar house two doors away but well maintained and a mirror image of 13

My thoughts turned to my great grandmother's house in Pettigrew Street and I wondered if anyone would find her house also! Within minutes, Vinay reported back with news that the house was no longer there, that all those lovely heritage houses were knocked down in the 1970s to make way for new development. Once back home, Vinay continued on with his quest...

Vinay Bhatt
July 19 at 2:07pm

Thanks for the opportunity to go on a treasure hunt on a Sunday! And in the process discover that my nursery teacher was related to you!

Hello Jenny, Many of my schoolmates lived in Jeremiah Road, Will see if any of their parents are still around. Most Anglo Indians in the locality sent their kids to either St. Germains High School (Boys) and St. Francis Xavier Girls High School. Both Schools have an active alumni association. My first teacher at school (1968) was a Miss Ball who lived on Jeremiah Road! Just wondering if Miss Ball stayed at No.13! Regards, Vinay Bhatt

My reply was: "Wait for this Miss Ball, is my relative."

So now we had some more relatives of mine who not only lived in Pettigrew Street (where my great grandma Maud lived) but had subsequently moved to Jeremiah Road (where my grandparents lived)! I do remember from a young age, hearing my mother say how the Balls were all great friends with the family, but of course we now know due to my research, that they were cousins by marriage.

Through numerous communications on my Facebook that morning I discovered so much of my other ancestors, the Balls. That Fred Ball (a cousin) owned quite a bit of property in that immediate area, and he rented out the property to both my grandparents and his two cousins, Miss Sybil Ball and Miss Rita Ball.   That the two sisters, Sybil and Rita were both teachers at St. John's School and St. Francis Xavier's High School, and I've since learnt that Rita Ball was also a teacher at St. Joseph's Convent, also in the same immediate vicinity as the other two schools. I was conversing with one of Miss Sybil Ball's pupils who remembers with fondness "sharing a cycle rickshaw in to school with Miss Ball". I further learnt how much respect and love their pupils had for them, one pupil admitting to being extremely distraught when realising that her excellent grades meant she was moving up a class, which meant that she was leaving Miss Ball's class. Here is Miss Rita Ball with her nursery class pupils of 1976.

Here is a photograph of a picnic which was taken in 1927, the only gentleman in the picture is my grandfather, Herbert Jeffries, the pregnant lady in the centre is his sister, great aunt Constance who you will remember from an earlier story, the girl in the white dress sitting on the blanket is my aunt Dolly, and the teenager girl holding her hat in her hands is my aunt Gwen, the rest I believe are all the Balls family. If I had to guess, I would say that Sybil Ball is the lady with the glasses, and Rita Ball was the lady on the far right. Sadly, despite all my enquiries asking if anyone can pinpoint the two sisters who were teachers – no-one is able to confidently identify them.

But we have not quite finished on my great grandmother Maud's search for her house! Here's a picture that Sachin Bhatt took of my grandma's road this week, which he successfully manages to capture the irony of new development with its meaningless "Keep City Green and Clean" signage holding a fine of 500 rupees to anyone who leaves garbage.

In actual fact, all one can see is actually garbage and debris, a new development has managed to wipe out and erase all signs of a once loved heritage road which might well have been tree-lined with stunning white washed walls, immaculately cut lawns and flower beds, all helping to create the image of Bangalore's "Garden City". One can only now grieve with a sense of loss and sadness of Garden City that used to be.   Great pity…

Melissa Arulappan was next on the case.

Jenny, I found out that my mum has a good friend who lives on Pettigrew Street. She and my mum used to sing together with the Bangalore Musical Association and know each other for many years. Tell me what you need and I can ask Lisa (her name) to check for you. Just FYI Pettigrew St is closer to St John's Church Road and Narayana Pillai Street. Jeremiah Road is closer to Coles Road/Mosque Road/St Stephen's Road. All in and around a 3-5 km radius. Regards Melissa

I thanked Melissa for her help and advised her that although I had no house number to offer her, I did have one image of the actual house. It's a particular favourite of mine since it captures so well an Anglo-Indian family during the reign of King George. It is a photograph you have already seen in my book, it's the wedding day of my great uncle Eugene and this photograph was taken at grandma Maud's home in Pettigrew Street, Bangalore in 1927.

Melissa armed with only this picture, came back to me very quickly with: Jenny, my mum's friend lives in an old house on 13 Pettigrew Street! Followed by, Mailing you as I think my mum's friend has honed in on a home close to Pettigrew Street where a Shandley family used to live... And, I think my mum's friend may have struck gold as far as recalling the house where your ancestors lived. Lisa says there used to be a Shandley family (she mentioned Maureen and my mum cannot recall the other name) who lived in a cottage right inside the compound of a house that belonged to Dr Goudinho. Lisa also mentioned this family later emigrating to England. I doubt there would have been too many of the same name and it must be your family. This cottage was however not on Pettigrew Street but on St John's Road which is very close to Pettigrew Street. It could be that there was a side gate that opened onto Pettigrew Street - I do not know as yet. I could go with Lisa and check it out if you like. Melissa

Thanking Melissa once more for her help, I replied saying how Maureen Shandley was a really close cousin of my mothers, that she was my closest "auntie" whom I had known all my life as she emigrated to London in the fifties. I finished off saying that this was most definitely my family. I waited with bated breath...for Melissa's next instalment!

Jenny, This is so much fun and I am glad we are getting so much closer. I just spoke with Lisa and she thinks her sister Charlotte Veeranna was a classmate of Daphne's (she is going to check with Charlotte) but the names she remembers are Daphne, Maureen and Maud. She also says her cousin Maurice Powell visited Daphne in Canada recently. So it's all the same then. Lisa is going to check more details with her sister but is quite sure that the Shandleys (at least Maureen and Daphne) lived in Dr Goudinho's house between St Francis Xaviers Church and St John's Church on St John's Church Road. She will however ask her sister if there were any Shandleys staying on Pettigrew Street although she does not think so. Maybe your aunt could not remember all the information but the name that struck was Pettigrew Street which is very close by. Lisa also remembered your story from the newspaper article so it all resonates. Am glad this is a happy Sunday for you!!! Melissa.

Melissa continued with her search and with her aunty Lisa and her mother's other friend they decided they would make the trek to that neighbourhood but Melissa came back to say that the monsoon weather was holding them back from walking to Pettigrew Street (Melissa explained that her two companions were her mother's two elderly friends who were now in their late seventies). Jenny, the rain put paid to my plans as these friends who were to show me around are elderly and I didn't want them walking around in the rains. Hopefully tomorrow. I prayed that night for good dry weather for them all, and the next day Melissa wrote back to me, with news that both Melissa and her aunty Lisa had managed to get there: Hi Jenny, Today was a better day - the rains had eased off by the time I went to Pettigrew Street and so I was able to walk down the street with my mum's friend as she recounted some of her childhood memories and how her family came to live on the street. Aunty Lisa must be in her late 70s. Troubled feet keep her from walking very well but she ambled along and spent about an hour with me. The street threw up a lot of surprises for her too. It is a very narrow street punctuated by a criss cross of roads and so Lisa too had not really walked down the entire street for a long, long time and was surprised at how much had been torn down. She showed me where her sister mentioned your great grandmother Maud Shandley lived but there is no house or cottage there anymore. It's on its way to becoming yet another concrete block of something. I have taken some pictures of the street - the nicer parts of it. Much of it is worn down, piled with garbage and run down recovered/accidents cars left by the neighbouring police station, rat infested, etc. We walked through it all and it was an experience. Regards, Melissa

Meanwhile, throughout that Sunday afternoon, I continued to receive messages from a community of people all linked with one theme: Bangalore. Miss Ball's pupils were all writing in fast and furious to me saying how much she played an important part in their lives, one person saying that before he went to school, he spoke no English whatsoever, but was clearly thankful to his nursery school teacher, Miss Ball for being the first person to teach him English. The messages continued all day, one after the other, even one enthusiastic lady quipping in with: "Oh how I <u>do</u> love a paper chase!" All heartfelt stories with immense fondness of this sweet and lovely lady who lived to well over 100 years of age! After 24 hours, the Paper Chase Trail had gone cold, all messages stopped. I had spent the entire day writing to each one of them thanking them for your contribution and decided to post on all three of their sites this special message: Dear Vinay, Pradeep, Dorothy, Phyllis, Smith, Blossom, Janet, Melissa and Peter....I am TRULY overwhelmed by your responses. In particular to Vinay and Pradeep for doing this amazing Paper Chase for me today, in spite of the rain. Wow, I look forward to meeting you all to say a personal "thank you" in December. All good wishes, Jenny It was now 7pm Sunday night in England, "India" had gone to bed but then suddenly out of the blue, Janet Hutchison sent me:

"In the 50s my grandmother used to visit an elderly "English" lady next to Dr Goudino's ...I was very young and cannot remember her name. Remembering seeing pics in an English magazine of Princess Margaret's wedding in her house. Could she be a relative of Jenny Mallin?"

Janet's post struck a chord in me, I have to say that I know my family were extremely proud of their English heritage (coming from Yorkshire via Benjamin Hardy who set foot in India in 1798 with the British Army) and it was obvious how proud my grandma Maud was about this as you can feel her pride in the way she noted down all her favourite English puddings and cakes throughout the grandmothers' legacy recipe book.

Janet's childhood memory of visiting an elderly English lady who lived next door to Dr Goudinho's and seeing pictures in an English magazine of Princess Margaret's wedding day (which was on May 6, 1960) convinced me that the person Janet met in 1960 was in fact my darling great grandma Maud. That would have placed my great grandma Maud in her eighties at the time Janet's grandmother visited her with Janet being tugged along behind her...!

Out of all my grandmothers, I do feel a close connection with Maud. I love her sense of pride, her precise neat handwriting, her orderliness, her obvious love of good old English puddings (Fair Rosamond Pudding) and the way she adored all of her family and her grandchildren, who lived with her in this tiny little cottage which sat within the compound of Dr Goudinho's property.

She was one of thousands of such ladies of that time, who shared the same amazing qualities: love, great inner strength, vigour and the capacity to override obstacles in their path! Those ladies were all fragile to look at and yet inside very strong women, they held the household together, they took time to get to know everyone in their neighbourhood, their tailor, the priest, the bakery man, even the milkman with his cow... These wonderful ladies held together a framework of contacts and friends, and as a result were the absolute bedrock and backbone to any community. You will still find them in Bangalore, Bombay, Calcutta and Madras – it's just a question of going out like Melissa did with aunty Lisa – and finding them!

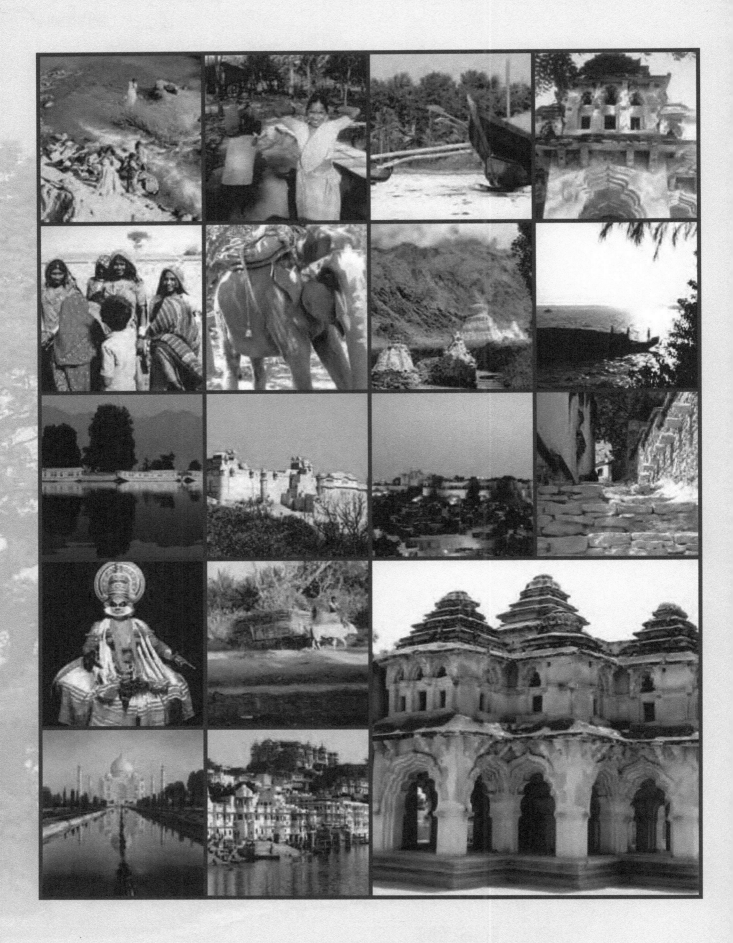

Grandmother's Pearls of Wisdom

Household Tips

⋆ For effective household cleaning, you need just four items: bicarbonate of soda, washing soda, white vinegar and lemon.

⋆ For burnt food on pans – leave a good handful of bicarbonate of soda overnight on the burnt food and by morning you will be able to remove it.

⋆ Mix a solution of equal parts of bicarbonate of soda and water and coat the inside of your oven, leave overnight then wipe with a damp cloth.

⋆ Just rub a little bicarbonate of soda with your fingers onto any stubborn teacup stains and they will instantly disappear.

⋆ To freshen a room just place a small bowl filled with a mixture of bicarbonate of soda and white vinegar or lemon juice and smells will be absorbed.

⋆ Sinks and baths can be made gleaming by diluting two tablespoons of washing soda with two litres of hot water.

⋆ Spray the toilet with white vinegar and then sprinkle with bicarbonate of soda, allow the two to fizz and react for a minute then scrub with a brush.

⋆ Brighten up your colours in your laundry by adding 1½ cups of white vinegar to your rinse water.

⋆ To whiten delicates in your laundry, soak items in a bucket of warm water with the juice of a lemon and allow to soak for 1-2 hours, wring out and then allow to dry in the sun.

⋆ To remove smells from the microwave add a slice of lemon to a small bowl of water, then microwave for 5 minutes and wipe clean.

⋆ For sparkling mirrors, mix 2 tbsp of lemon juice into water and spray.

⋆ Rub half a lemon over your chopping board and then scrub, it will remove all harsh smells and disinfect the board.

⋆ Draw a line of chalk across the floor of your pantry to prevent ants from entering.

⋆ Remove any furniture scratches with half a walnut, just rub it over the marks.

Beauty, Health & Nutritional Tips

* Splashing your face several times with cold water each morning will tone and tighten your skin.

* Two cups of vinegar into your warm bath will relieve aching muscles.

* For tired eyes, place a warm tea bag on each eye

* A teaspoon of honey is good for a sore throat and also bee stings.

* Cinnamon is one of the richest sources of antioxidants – one teaspoon of ground cinnamon has the equivalent level of antioxidants as half a cup of blueberries and one cup of pomegranate juice. Cinnamon is now recognised in keeping arteries healthy, managing blood sugar levels and is proven to lower cholesterol.

* Turmeric combined with ginger can reduce inflammation in arthritis. It is also a natural liver detoxifier. In India, turmeric paste is applied to wounds to speed the healing process, and people sip turmeric tea to relieve colds and respiratory problems.

* Ginger is excellent for stomach digestion and nausea. It is also thought to relax blood vessels, stimulate blood flow and relieve pain.

* Cloves are a natural toothache remedy – keep the clove close to the tooth and the oil from the clove will take the pain away. It is also regarded as an antihistamine. An effective expectorant, chewing on a clove with a crystal of common salt assists in the process of coughing up. And with its antiseptic properties, it can bring relief to the throat stopping a cough in the pharyngitis, when the pharynx is inflamed by boiling six cloves in 30ml of water which can be sweetened with honey and taking one teaspoon of this mixture, three times a day. It can also be a useful treatment for asthma.

* Nutmeg is known to be a powerful sedative and induces calm and sleep. Make sure you use no more than one nutmeg though as it's potently strong.

* Cardamom boosts energy. A tea made from cardamom is valuable for headache caused by indigestion. It is also used as a remedy in the treatment of depression. Known to stimulate appetite it can also aid indigestion, and is helpful in the elimination of toxins through your skin. It can also be useful for treating respiratory conditions like coughing, asthma and loss of voice. Daily gargling with an infusion of cardamom and cinnamon cures pharyngitis, a sore throat and can protect you from flu.

* Red chillies, chilli powder (cayenne pepper can assist in weight loss by speeding up the metabolism) – adding three chilli peppers to your daily diet can increase calorie burning after a meal by 40 to 100 calories and fat burning ability by up to 25 per cent.

* Saffron has traditionally been used to improve blood circulation and bruises. The active ingredient, Crocetin may also lower blood cholesterol and triglycerides in the body. Studies indicate that saffron can improve vision and is effective in the prevention of age-related macular degeneration, the commonest cause of blindness in the elderly.

* Garlic has been shown to protect against high blood pressure, infections, stomach ulcers and bowel disorders. In addition it has been known to slow down the growth of cancer cells and also strengthen the immune system.

* Possessing Vitamin E in abundance, Cumin excels in the maintenance of healthy skin and the prevention of premature aging. Being rich in iron makes this also beneficial for those who are anaemic.

* A great all-rounder for good health. Chia seeds is the only grain to be a complete protein, having the appropriate balance of all essential amino acids. Rich in calcium, it has twice as much potassium than in a banana and three times more antioxidants than blueberries.

* Hemp seeds are very helpful if you are at risk of diabetes, or are diabetic as they can control your sugar levels by allowing the quick absorption of glucose from the bloodstream and its conversion into energy. Just adding 4 tablespoons into your meals can help induce weight loss as it acts as a natural appetite suppressant and makes you feel fuller for longer. It can also reduce your food cravings significantly and give you more energy.

* High in zinc, Pumpkin seeds are a natural protector against osteoporosis. Known to improve bladder function and promote overall prostate health, this naturally effective compound is also effective in combating depression. Studies also indicate that pumpkin seeds can reduce inflammation without the side effects of anti-inflammatory drugs.

* Rich in magnesium, potassium, selenium, zinc and iron, Sunflower seeds can be beneficial in lowering blood pressure, and more importantly, in the repair of cellular damage while slowing the spread of cancerous cells, boosting the immune system and in the distribution of oxygen to the muscles.

* Due to the high content of phytoestrogens, Linseeds have been called nature's answer to HRT (hormone replacement therapy). Therefore it claims to have a positive impact on the unpleasant effects of the menopause, such as hot flushes and night sweats.

* High in niacin, folic acid, potassium, calcium, vitamin C, iron and fibre, Pomegranate juice and their seeds help to maintain a pregnant woman's health and encourages cell growth. Has been known to reduce cramps and sleep difficulties that often appear during pregnancy.

* Sesame seeds have been found to contain the highest amount of phytosterols, which are known to lower bad cholesterol and can improve the effectiveness of certain diabetes medication.

Kitchen Tips

* Spices like cinnamon sticks, cloves, peppercorns and seeds such as cumin and coriander will always benefit from toasting in a frying pan to bring out their essential oils prior to starting a recipe

* No more garlicky hands – just rub your fingers with a stainless steel spoon and like magic, it goes away. The metal neutralises the garlic fumes.

* Don't even think of peeling knobbly ginger with a potato peeler or a knife, use the edge of a teaspoon which goes into all the crevices and makes easy work of it.

* To check how fresh your eggs are, place them in a bowl of water, the freshest ones are at the bottom, if one side tips up then it's less fresh and you should use it soon, if it floats then it's past the fresh egg stage.

* For finely chopped ginger, just freeze the ginger first, then use it straight from the freezer onto a micro plane grater or cheese grater.

* Keep the pasta or potato water when boiled and use on your houseplants, they will love the nutrients.

* The best way to avoid tears when chopping onions is to always keep onions in the fridge. This will reduce the amount of enzymes released into the air, and has zero effect on taste.

* Chillies don't keep for long, but if you remove the stems and keep them in the fridge, they last much longer.

* When storing away and freezing curries, if you spray with non-stick cooking oil your tupperware containers beforehand you will get no discolouration or stains on the container.

* Odours from used tupperware containers can be sorted out with a pinch of salt in them before storing them away.

* Swap your sunflower oil for rapeseed oil – its low in saturated fat and contains omegas 3, 6 and 9 which all help reduce cholesterol and assist in the maintenance of healthy join, brain and functions. As it is high in mon-unsaturated fats, it is one of the only unblended oils that can be heated to a high frying temperature and not spoit its antioxidants, character, colour or flavour.

* To make a pan, non-stick – just add course sea salt to the surface of a hot pan until it is about 2cm thick and allow the salt to slowly burn until the salt turn to a dark brown colour. Discard the salt and with a kitchen paper towel dipped in oil, wipe the surface until it becomes shiny.

* The key to a successful omelette is in cooking it very, very slowly.

* An easy way of pitting cherries is to use a paper clip.

* When an annoying bit of egg shell has landed in the bowl by accident you can remove it easily by using the empty half of the egg shell, it scoops it up like a magnet.

* Adding a teaspoon of sugar to any dish requiring cooked tomatoes benefits from this addition.

* Skinning tomatoes are easy – just pop into a bowl of hot water and wait 5 minutes, score down one side and they slip off.   Same with sausages...

* A pinch of sugar added to the water when cooking any green vegetables help retain their brightness of colour.

* Just rub the inside of the pan rim with a little oil and your milk will not boil over. The same applies to noodles, spaghetti and potatoes.

* To keep cauliflower white when cooking, just add some milk to the water.

* Make easy work of slicing strawberries and kiwi fruit – use a boiled egg slicer.

* To ripen an avocado, simply place in a paper bag and leave overnight in an airing cupboard.

* To freshen up a crusty loaf, just run some water quickly over the bread and pop in a hot oven.

* You can keep potatoes longer before they start sprouting by placing them with an apple inside the bag.

* Make your own vanilla sugar by placing a whole vanilla bean in an airtight jar of sugar.

* Forgotten to bring butter to room temperature for that recipe? Just fill a glass with hot tap water and let it sit for a few seconds. Empty the water and place the glass upside down over the amount of butter required for the recipe. Wait one minute and the butter should be ready to use.

And, finally - I do hope you've enjoyed reading my book.

Would you consider writing a short review (just a line or two is fine) as to what you liked about it - positive reviews certainly help sway those customers who are considering making a purchase - your review would be most helpful to them in making that decision.

Please write to me at jennymallin@yahoo.com with your review.

Thank you.

Jenny Mallin

Recipe Index

Cakes, Sweets & Puddings

Milton Keynes UK
Ingram Content Group UK Ltd.
UKHW050318111223
433974UK00022B/97

A-Z
of
European
Coachbuilders
1919-2000

A-Z
of
European
Coachbuilders

1919-2000

James Taylor

Herridge & Sons

Published in 2017
by Herridge & Sons Ltd
Lower Forda, Shebbear
Beaworthy, Devon EX21 5SY

© Copyright James Taylor 2017

Design by Chris Fayers

ISBN 978-1-906133-78-8
Printed in China

Contents

Introduction
and
Acknowledgements

This book is the result of an interest in European coachwork that was triggered during the 1980s. It would be wrong to suggest that I have been working on it ever since, but in the years that followed I did collate whatever information came my way on the subject. It was only about five years ago that I began turning it into a more coherent form, and about three years ago that the exact shape of this book was agreed.

The *A-Z of European Coachbuilders* is deliberately intended as a first port of call for anybody with an interest in its subject, a handy and ready reference source. It certainly does not claim to be definitive on any of the coachbuilders included: most of those who have an entry here would make a book in themselves, and a small number already have. There is also plenty of information available on various internet sites, mostly painstakingly assembled by enthusiasts with an interest in one particular company or maybe a small group of companies. A lot of that material has inevitably fed into the present book.

So what exactly is covered? This book sets out to look at companies that provided special bodywork for cars, whether that was to individual commission or built in small volumes to create a special derivative of a manufacturer's mainstream range. It also looks at companies that have undertaken serial major bodywork modifications to production models, typically by creating open bodywork from closed types or by creating estate cars and the like from saloons. As for a time period, I have focussed on 1919-2000, the first date because it was the start of a new period in which the inventions of the Great War became of everyday importance, and the end date because it marks the end of the century in which coachbuilding (in the traditional sense at least) flowered and died.

The term "Europe" is very broad and, as the European Union has expanded since the 1990s, the goalposts have moved. My colleague Anders Clausager (who kindly read this book in draft form and made some useful suggestions) once jokingly suggested that Europe ends at Stalingrad! However, neither of us knows of any coachbuilders in that city, now called Volgograd. So I made a decision early on to limit the coverage to the eight continental European countries whose coachbuilders are probably of widest interest. They are Austria, Belgium, France, Germany, Italy, Netherlands, Spain and Switzerland. Some readers may find that is unjust, for which I apologise. To have included every eligible country would have resulted in a book many times the size and many times the cost.

Even so, I am conscious that this book's subject matter is very broad. So, borrowing some well-known words from that "harmless drudge" Samuel Johnson, I will beg the reader's forgiveness for what will surely be "a few wild blunders, and risible absurdities, from which no work of such multiplicity was ever free." They will be here somewhere, I am sure.

Information and photographs have come from a wide variety of sources over the years, and I could not list them all here if I tried. Photograph credits are listed where they are known, and here I would particularly like to thank the following to for filling gaps in the picture content: David Burgess-Wise, Giles Chapman, Erik Eckermann, Immo Mikloweit, Nikolaus Scheerbarth-Clasen and Rainer Simons.

I must acknowledge the importance of three highly informative books. These are:

- *Automobil-Specialkarosserien*, Halwart Schrader, BLV Verlagsgesellschaft, Munich 1985
- *Encyclopédie de la Carrosserie Française*, Serge Bellu, ETAI 2011
- *Schweizer Carrossiers*, Ferdinand Hediger, Swiss Classics Publishing 2013

Each one is highly recommended as a specialist work on its subject. I should also mention a small number of useful and entertaining web sites devoted to coachbuilding (although not exclusively to that from Europe). They are:

- www.coachbuild.com
- http://www.conam.info/carrosseriebouwers-beschrijvingen
- http://francois.vanaret.pagesperso-orange.fr

James Taylor
Oxfordshire, May 2017

Country by Country:
An Overview

The title of this book rather suggests that there was more in common among European coachbuilders than their geographical location. It is certainly true that the coachbuilders of one country were often influenced by those of another, but each of the countries covered here had a distinctive industry of its own.

Austria

Austria was a bit-part player in the European coachbuilding industry after 1919, not least because of the political and national border changes that accompanied the collapse of the Austro-Hungarian empire in 1918. Of its early coachbuilders, the most important was Armbruster which had begun as a carriage-builder many years earlier. Throughout the 1920s and the first part of the 1930s, Armbruster worked on high-quality chassis, but closed down in 1934.

Also well known in the 1930s was Keibl, which constructed some bodies on Mercedes-Benz chassis, including SS types. The company survived the Second World War but then struggled for business. Its salvation came in the contract to build the Volkswagen-based Denzel, which lasted from 1948 to 1959. Keibl also built a few early bodies for Porsche in 1948-1949, as did Kastenhofer, another company based in Vienna.

Belgium

Belgium did not develop a strong coachbuilding industry like that of neighbouring France or Germany, but it nonetheless became home to several high-quality coachbuilders during the 20th century. Like other countries, it of course had a number of carriage-building companies that dated from the 19th century, and of those D'Ieteren, Johnckheere and Vanden Plas all entered the motor vehicle business.

During the 1920s, Belgium had three important motor manufacturers, and it was FN, Imperia and Minerva who provided most of the chassis for domestic coachbuilders to work on. Pritchard & Demolin, Snutsel, Sprengers and Walch all provided bodies for FN; Matthys worked for Imperia until the car company took its body manufacture in-house from 1928. Minerva was well served by a number of coachbuilders, including Van den Plas in which firm they also invested. However, the dangers of such tight-knit

In Belgium, Vesters & Neirinck built this heavy-looking but well-proportioned four-door cabriolet in 1949 on an Austin A125 Sheerline chassis. *(Unknown copyright)*

arrangements were amply demonstrated when Minerva's demise in the mid-1930s took the coachbuilder with it. A few companies worked on foreign chassis, Emmel for example on the Ford Model T and De Wolf on Cadillac.

The worldwide economic troubles brought a downturn in demand during the early 1930s. FN stopped making cars, while Imperia and Minerva merged in mid-decade. So those coachbuilders still in business now worked more commonly with foreign chassis. Vesters & Neirinck did well, building bodies on Bentley and Rolls-Royce chassis and also on several American makes. D'Ieteren was still in business, but also opened car showrooms and took on assembly of Studebakers to keep the cash flowing.

The 1939-1945 war completely disrupted Belgian coachbuilding, and the industry that emerged when peace came was quite different and very fragmented. Vesters & Neirinck was one of the few companies to survive, but struggled to find business. D'Ieteren did not attempt to start up again, and turned wholly to its dealer activities. Much more in tune with the times were the small companies that arose to convert or modernise the Citroën Traction Avant, and these activities continued into the 1950s. Among the companies involved were Carrosserie Franco-Belge, Phlups, and TTT.

The 1950s saw the last of the great names go to the wall as Vesters & Neirinck turned to sunroof conversions of mainstream cars and then closed in 1956. Oblin started up with good intentions in 1951 but probably built no more than three bodies. Not until the 1960s were there significant changes. Jacques Coune, a car dealer, began to build special bodies with the aid of Italian craftsmen who had come to Belgium to seek work as Italy went through a tough economic period. IMA, too, began to convert Mercedes-Benz models to estate cars, and kept their business going until the late 1970s, latterly converting Saabs.

The 1980s saw a brief revival of coachbuilding in Belgium. Like their neighbours in Germany, some entrepreneurs saw the opportunity to create custom coachwork on prestige models from BMW and Mercedes-Benz to meet demand from the Middle East. Duchatelet (in business since 1968), EBS and L'Etoile all cashed in on the fashion, but it was short-lived and by the mid-1990s these companies had all closed down.

France

France was a pioneer in the motor industry and in the first three decades of the 20th century was the leading European car producer, losing that position to Britain in 1933. So it was no surprise that very many coachbuilders had sprung up to support the country's output of chassis. Many had in fact been founded before the arrival of the motor vehicle, as builders of horse-drawn vehicles, and some could trace their ancestry back as far as the 18th century. These companies had acquired a depth of skill that was denied to some of the newer start-ups.

France had also played a large part in the nascent aircraft industry at the start of the 20th century and, beginning around 1910 but especially after the Great War of 1914-1918, there was considerable influence on car construction from the aircraft industry. For the coachbuilders, the influence was mainly on construction methods, on ways of shedding weight, and on aerodynamics (although this was poorly understood for many years).

Very noticeable was the coachbuilding industry's focus on Paris, the social and fashion capital of the country as well as its seat of government. Large numbers of coachbuilders, both large and small, congregated in the suburban industrial areas of Neuilly-sur-Seine and Courbevoie to the west, and Levallois-Perret to the north-west. The many provincial coachbuilders tended to look to Paris for inspiration, and the very name of Carrosserie Parisienne de Bordeaux (Parisian Coachworks at Bordeaux) shows the all-pervading appeal of an association with the capital.

Elsewhere, coachbuilders tended to spring up close to chassis makers. So Lyons had its fair share. On the Mediterranean coast around Cannes, a high proportion of wealthy residents made it cost-effective for coachbuilders to operate in the area. In the later 1920s and 1930s it is said that such people often saw what they liked at a concours d'élégance event (a social and fashionable occasion at which coachbuilders showed their products in the hope of winning prizes and gaining business) and then asked a local coachbuilder to produce a replica. Yet the allure of Paris remained very strong. When the De Villars company was established specifically to build high-quality coachwork for wealthy southern residents, its workshops were located in Courbevoie.

As peace returned after the Great War, the leading coachbuilders who remained in business included Binder, Franay, Kellner, Labourdette and Letourneur et Marchand. But the new era seemed full of promise, and over the next decade many small coachbuilders came and went, while a handful of others established lasting reputations. Among those who seized the opportunity to begin business were Chapron (in 1919) and Hibbard & Darrin (in 1923).

However, the opportunities that many anticipated from the 1920s were tempered by the advent of mass production, which reduced the part played by traditional coachbuilding in car manufacture. Some coachbuilders turned to batch-building for the chassis makers, building runs of special bodies alongside their traditional individual commissions. Gauthier had already been building bodies for Peugeot before the war and in 1919 was bought out by the chassis manufacturer; Peugeot went on to establish a close relationship with Manessius, who later established close links with the French Fiat operation. Even the well-established coachbuilders played for safety in this new climate. Letourneur et Marchand set up a volume-

By 1938, the French firm of Letourneur et Marchand was building bodies with the sleek lines of this one, this time on a Delage D6 chassis. *(WikiMedia Commons/Buch-t)*

The elegant four-seater coupé body on this 1938 4¼-litre Bentley shows that the respected French coachbuilder De Villars could produce some strikingly individual designs. *(Simon Clay)*

production subsidiary called Autobineau, and Kellner established a similar business under the Janer name.

This was a period in which there were many experiments with body construction methods: flexible construction methods came from Dubos and Weymann, while several companies began to build all-metal bodies, sometimes adding aluminium panelwork to save weight. A very noticeable trend, begun in the 1920s but continued into the following decade, was for coachbuilders to develop new ideas and then sell licences for them. So the inter-war years saw such patents as the Baehr transformable design from 1919, Clairalpax (from Audineau), Plein Azur (from Dubos), Silentbloc (from Repusseau via Vanvooren), Toutalu (from Million-Guiet), Vutotal (from Labourdette in 1936) and of course the Weymann flexible system from 1922.

The after-effects of the 1929 Wall Street Crash accounted for a good number of the smaller coachbuilders who had been active in the 1920s, and some larger ones too. Yet the newly slimmed French coachbuilding industry lost none of its impetus or world-wide respect during the 1930s. A focus on aerodynamic designs, influenced of course by aircraft practice, had been growing at the close of the 1920s and continued into the new decade. Although the "pure" aerodynamic designs were usually not very attractive, elements of streamlining did become part of some designs produced in the Art Deco period, when they were often matched by imaginative use of colour.

By the middle of the decade, this led on to the sensuous and glamorous bodies pioneered by companies such as Fernandez & Darrin, Figoni & Falaschi, and Saoutchik. Yet while such designs certainly attracted attention, they did not take over entirely. Customers who wanted more conservative styles could still turn to coachbuilders like Binder, Chapron, Franay, Kellner or Vanvooren for a top-quality product. And even though mass production had taken over further down the market, the grand chassis of the time still typically attracted coachbuilt bodies. Delahaye, for example, never had its own body department.

Mass production had nevertheless not stamped out the taste for individuality further down the market, and the later 1930s saw the beginnings of an industry that focussed on transformations, modifying standard production models (notably the Citroën Traction Avant) to a greater or lesser extent. This was the start of a trend in coachbuilding that would become more widespread as the demand for traditional coachbuilt bodies declined. But not yet: first, the Second World War intervened to halt coachbuilding of all kinds in France between 1939 and 1945.

Not all the big names returned to the fray when peace came. Binder, for example, did not start up again. Chassis were in short supply and so was the money to build special bodies for them. The 1945 Pons Plan to rationalise the French motor industry allocated different market sectors to different motor manufacturers, and its effect on the coachbuilding trade was far-reaching. The surviving French makers of separate chassis – Delahaye, Delage, Hotchkiss and Talbot – fell into the "primarily for export" sector. As chassis were often bodied in the country of their destination, this robbed the French coachbuilding industry of work.

Still there was interest in transformations of less expensive mass-produced cars. The Traction Avant became a favourite, and many coachbuilders, both new and old, worked to produce individual derivatives. As the 1940s merged into the 1950s, so other French mass-produced cars increasingly became targets for the specialist coachbuilders and transformers, who simply worked with what they could get. So there were many transformations on the Citroën 2CV, Renault 4CV, and Panhard chassis throughout the decade. Meanwhile, many of the great coachbuilders closed down for lack of work. Only Chapron survived, notably building some fascinating low-volume conversions of the Citroën DS in the late 1950s and being rewarded with the contract to build the factory-approved cabriolet bodies for it in from early 1960s.

From the 1960s onwards, coachbuilding in France was almost all about transformations of one kind or another. Gété, for example, created special sporting versions of the Citroën DS. Small coachbuilders tended to specialise in conversions of one mass-produced model or another, and sometimes went out of business when the host car ended production. Few made any really lasting impression. The surviving long-established coachbuilders typically made ends meet by working as prototype houses for the major manufacturers. Chapron, for example, became a prototype house for Renault but closed when the car maker took that work in-house, and Chausson did similar work for several European makers but went under in 2007. New start-ups, meanwhile, reduced their business risks by operating as design houses or consultancies rather than actually building bodies.

Germany

As in France, many of the first German builders of car bodies had already been in business as makers of horse-drawn transport. During the first two decades of the 20th century,

Autenrieth, of Darmstadt in Germany, built a small number of bodies on BMW chassis as individual commissions. This cabriolet, on a 502, was built in 1955. *(BMW)*

a number became firmly established, and as Germany tried to settle back to normality after the end of the 1914-1918 war, the big names were Erdmann & Rossi, Hebmüller and Neuss. Papler already existed, but did not become a major player until the 1920s.

Germany's economic problems in this decade inhibited the growth of the coachbuilding industry, and the arrival of mass production also had a significant effect. After Ambi Budd was established as a volume builder of all-steel bodies in 1926, many companies sought stability in an alliance with one or more chassis makers. Kühn became the primary supplier of special bodywork for Opel; Baur focussed on batch production from 1927 (and went on to become a leader in its field); Zschau specialised in building small series of special tourer and cabriolet bodies for various German makers. Deutsch picked up a volume-production contract in 1927 when Citroën opened its German factory in Cologne, and then took on more contract work when Ford moved from Berlin to Cologne in 1930. Karmann had meanwhile had its big break as early as 1924 with a contract from AGA, and never looked back.

The disastrous economic period that followed the 1929 Wall Street Crash saw increasing unemployment and social disillusionment. Some coachbuilders went under (such as Kruck and Zander); some turned to commercial bodywork (such as Drögmüller and Kässbohrer); others sold out to bigger concerns (such as Neuss, which merged with Erdmann & Rossi in 1933). Papler survived by turning to batch-building for Ford, Adler and the German Citroën factory. Hebmüller began to batch-build cabriolet and open sports bodies for Ford and Opel, plus Pullman limousines for Ford. The early 1930s also brought a vogue for small, sporty and (most importantly) affordable roadster bodies by the likes of Musigk & Haas or Wendler.

Germany's new prosperity after 1933 was reflected in grander and more ambitious designs from German coachbuilders. Cabriolets on the larger chassis developed a distinctive style, which regularly featured a large and well-insulated hood that stood a long way proud of the rear bodywork even when folded down. Its weight required external landau irons for support. Hitler made life difficult for car importers, so German coachbuilders built almost exclusively on German chassis. The vogue for streamlining was reflected in a profusion of experimental cars, whose bodies were built to rigidly scientific aerodynamic designs by Dörr & Schreck, Voll & Ruhrbeck, and Wendler. Spohn incorporated aerodynamic features into some of its bodies for grand chassis such as Maybach.

German flamboyance in the 1930s was quite different from the French style. There were few designs like the pontoon-winged roadster that Erdmann & Rossi built for the King of Iraq. More generally, German bodies on the larger chassis had a confidence bordering on arrogance, with more than a trace of national pride. The largest companies were nevertheless those who had turned to volume or batch production for the chassis makers: Autenrieth, Baur and Deutsch were typical.

After 1939, German coachbuilders were obliged to contribute to the war effort. When peace returned in 1945, many were left with their premises destroyed or insufficient skilled staff, and closed down. Some, such as Ihle, turned to other business altogether; others, like Friederichs, moved into commercial body work. Yet others were marooned in the Soviet eastern sector of the country, where Hornig and Kathe were among those absorbed into the IFA state concern. Those who did survive had to get back into business slowly: Drauz was among those whose return to business was as a manufacturer of wooden hand-carts.

Car bodies were not needed. The shattered German economy needed small commercial vehicles, and companies like Hägele, Lueg and Miesen returned to work by building bodywork for them. From 1946, Hebmüller were building staff cars on Humber chassis for the British military and parcels vans for the post office. It took some time before any semblance of normality returned.

When it did, a major focus of coachbuilding was transformations of the Volkswagen Beetle. Drews began by building pick-up bodies on ex-military examples but was building special coupé bodies from 1949; Hebmüller built Volkswagen variants until its bankruptcy in 1952; Karmann did cabriolet bodies from 1949 (and right through until the 1970s); Rometsch and Dannenhauer & Stauss provided special bodywork for the ubiquitous Volkswagen. Reutter and Wendler probably would not have survived without contract work from Porsche after 1948, and even that company depended on the Volkswagen for its engines.

As the German Economic Miracle unfolded in the 1950s, the coachbuilders focussed on transformation work. Of the German cars in production, only the BMW 501 and its successors promised much hope for the traditional craft, as they still had a separate chassis. So Binz worked on light commercials for Mercedes-Benz, while Autenrieth and Deutsch made special bodies for Borgward and Opel. Baur got back into volume production through contracts with BMW, and for Karmann it was contracts for Volkswagen and (from 1965) BMW that helped ensure its survival. Vogt built estate conversions for Opel. Meanwhile, political events continued to have an impact. When the Berlin Wall was erected in 1961, Rometsch was left with so many skilled staff on the wrong side and unable to get to work that it had to abandon coach building and become a repair business. Others limped on a little longer: Deutsch closed down in 1972.

The late 1970s and the first half of the 1980s nevertheless brought a resurgence of activity, although not of the traditional coachbuilding kind. There was a boom in demand for bespoke and often extravagant conversions of the top-end BMW and Mercedes-Benz models, especially in the Middle East. So several companies sprang up to meet it: ABC-Exclusive, bbAuto, GCS Bennemann, Gemballa, SGS and Schulz-Tuning were among them. However, this market was short-lived and was dead by 1986. Only those companies which had also embraced performance enhancements remained in business. This change in taste provided an opening from the late 1980s for a company like Carlsson, for whom coachwork modifications were part of a much wider menu that centred on performance.

Closer to the everyday in the 1980s were more modest body transformations. Euler built some estate conversions on BMW 7 Series, Tropic built cabriolet conversions of several smaller cars, and Hammond & Thiede focussed on cabriolet conversions of the Opel Ascona.

Baur meanwhile had become firmly established as a mainstream maker of volume-produced bodies, with contracts from Audi and Porsche among others. However, the boom years of the 1980s did not last. A gradually diminishing volume of work from the major German manufacturers saw Baur in financial difficulties by the middle of the 1990s, and by the turn of the century the only survivor of the long-established German body makers was Karmann, which had wisely carved itself a niche as a specialist in folding-roof systems. Yet, a decade or so later, even Karmann was in trouble as manufacturers took more and more specialist work in-house.

Italy

The Italian coachbuilding industry had some individual characteristics from the beginning, most of them dependent on Italian social and cultural factors. Perhaps especially notable was that the successful companies generally remained within the ownership of their founding families. More so than elsewhere, local specialists survived by hand-building small numbers of bodies for a local "chassis" manufacturer and never showing much inclination to expand further: an example is Morelli, who built for Osca in the 1950s and 1960s.

As in other countries, many early coachbuilders grew out of companies originally formed to build horse-drawn vehicles. Varesina could trace its origins back to 1845, Castagna to 1849, Cesare Sala to 1887 – and Fissore was established as late as 1920 initially as a maker of horse-drawn vehicles. As the motor industry became more established, focussing on Turin in the northern steel-making area of the country, so coachbuilders tended to cluster in this area too. Not far away in Milan, Alfa Romeo also attracted local businesses to service its need for bodies.

Italian coachwork was largely but certainly not exclusively confined to Italian-built chassis before the Second World War. Only the grander coachbuilders such as Castagna built on foreign chassis. So although there was no doubting the excellence of the Italian creations, they were not as widely known as they later became. It was after 1945 that Italian companies pushed hard to gain business abroad, and during the 1950s there was a steady increase in awareness of Italian design that turned into a torrent of orders during the golden age of the 1960s.

By 1920, Castagna was Italy's largest coachbuilder, and its focus on attracting business from celebrities and royalty led it to build on many foreign chassis. Yet it was quite unlike most other Italian coachbuilders of the time, whose focus was on Italian-built chassis from Fiat, Lancia or Alfa Romeo. Gradually, some strong new companies entered the field, notably Touring (in business under a different name before 1926 when it was involved with airframe manufacture) and Zagato, whose founder had also been involved in the aircraft industry.

Among the established coachbuilders in the 1920s had been Stabilimenti Farina. The founder's younger brother broke away to set up on his own in 1930, supported by the promise of work from Lancia. Pinin Farina went on to become the most progressive of the Italian coachbuilders during the 1930s, mainly working on domestic chassis but

A rakish early creation by the great Italian firm of Bertone on a 1921 SPA 9000 Sport. *(David Burgess-Wise)*

also building on grand imported chassis from Germany or the USA. Yet, as in other countries, the turn of the decade was not a good time to be in coachbuilding. The global economic crisis saw some go under, such as Cesare Sala; Bertone survived by taking on repair work and moving into commercial bodywork as well; Savio moved into volume production for Fiat, and Viotti became a small-batch builder for Alfa Romeo, Fiat and Lancia.

This was the decade in which Ghia came to greater prominence, and the establishment of Italian factories by foreign makers helped to get Italian coachwork more widely appreciated. Yet Italian coachbuilders mostly remained faithful to domestic chassis and to their own inspiration, drawing relatively little from developments in countries such as France and Germany.

The 1939-1945 war disrupted coachbuilding and many makers became involved with military work. After 1945, many Italian coachbuilders – including Boneschi, Fissore and the newly-established Francis Lombardi – focussed on special bodies for the everyday models by Fiat, Lancia and other makers, who made their new integral-construction designs available as platforms for such work. Very noticeable was a new interest in business outside Italy, which would increase in the 1950s. Government policies, which focussed on providing work for Italians, supported these endeavours. Pinin Farina quickly made its mark with a 1946 design for Cisitalia, which would have a major influence on coachbuilding and design over the next few years.

The early 1950s saw Italian coachwork on several British chassis; indeed, it was a batch order for special bodies on MG chassis for the USA that saved Bertone in 1952. British manufacturers took notice and some came back with special commissions. Touring began with some cabriolet bodies on Aston Martin models in 1953 and ended up with a long-term licensing contract that covered Aston Martin production into the early 1970s. The Americans took an interest, too. Cadillac commissioned designs from Motto and Pinin Farina; Ford and Chrysler both worked with Ghia; Nash bought some Pinin Farina designs; and newcomer Vignale (founded in 1946) worked with racing driver Briggs Cunningham.

Pinin Farina was probably the most successful in

In Italy the characteristic Farina lines were in evidence on this 1950 Intermeccanica. *(David Hodges Collection)*

attracting foreign commissions, but few worked as hard after 1955 as Michelotti, who attracted work from Triumph in Britain and BMW in Germany. Stunning designs like Bertone's BAT cars for Alfa Romeo in 1953-1955 attracted worldwide attention, and as sports car makers Ferrari and Maserati gained an international reputation, so did the bodies Italian coachbuilders constructed for them. Meanwhile, many coachbuilders knuckled down to the less glamorous business of batch construction or conversions. Although new start-ups included Boano (whose founder had been with Ghia) and Frua (whose founder had been with Stabilimenti Farina), there were also closures. Castagna's market had vanished and the company went in 1954, and when Fiat set up its own bodywork department in 1957 there were repercussions around the industry.

The 1960s were a pinnacle when Italian coachbuilding and design dominated. The Italian GT became popular internationally from early in the decade, and Frua became particularly influential. New Italian makers of high-performance cars – De Tomaso and Lamborghini – brought the leading coachbuilders more work. Several European and American car makers began to turn to Italian companies for design and prototype production. Meanwhile, some more prudent companies anticipated the trough that would follow this peak. Pininfarina (now all one word) moved into mass production with government encouragement after a fire destroyed its factory, and produced several superb volume-production designs for Fiat and Lancia. Vignale moved into low-volume production of its own designs on Fiat platforms. Marazzi, formed from the ashes of Touring in 1967, quickly began to specialise in armour-plating, and Zagato embarked on small-volume production for Alfa Romeo and Lancia. New company Carrozzeria Eurostyle opened in 1968 but survived only a few years.

By the 1970s, the boom was over; Vignale (in 1969) and Ghia (in 1970) both disappeared, ultimately becoming part of the Ford empire. Italian coachbuilders moved increasingly into consultancy work for the major car manufacturers. Bertone, for example, did the 262C for Volvo. ItalDesign, established by Giorgetto Giugiaro in the late 1960s, soon became the most influential of the consultancies. There was intense competition: when Fiat wanted a convertible Ritmo, it evaluated designs from three different Italian houses before choosing one. Boniolo in 1975 and IDEA in 1978 were founded specifically as design consultancies, not as traditional coachbuilders.

There was a further thinning-out in the following decade. Michelotti closed on the death of its founder, and Pininfarina reinvented itself as a design and engineering consultancy for the motor industry at large. Bertone became firmly established as a volume manufacturer of cars, mostly taking on complete model-lines for major manufacturers. The trend continued during the 1990s, but there were signs of further retrenchment. Zagato turned away from production to focus on design and prototype build work. Stola focussed on building prototype and concept cars,

some for major makers. As the new century began, even Bertone found its contract manufacturing work drying up, and was eventually forced into bankruptcy. Pininfarina survived partly by developing an expertise in folding-roof designs to serve a new global fashion, and new start-ups (Spadaconcept and Torino Design, both in 2006) restricted themselves to consultancy work.

Netherlands

Few Dutch coachbuilders have been of any importance outside their own local area. A key reason is that the Netherlands has never had a domestic car industry of any size: Spyker built no more than 2000 cars before closing in 1926, and DAF cars did not come from the established truck maker until 1958. Nevertheless, a small number of coachbuilders did establish themselves by bulding on imported chassis during the inter-war years. By far the most important was Pennock, which remained in business until the early 1950s. Also notable were Veth and Van Rijswijk.

After 1945, the Dutch government attempted to help the country's economy by encouraging coachbuilding for export, and a number of prestige chassis were imported to further that aim. Notable was a batch of more than 100 Delahaye 135 chassis brought in during 1946 by the Lagerwij company in The Hague. However, Dutch coachbuilders suffered from the same problems with monocoque construction as did coachbuilders in other countries, and the industry did not survive the 1950s.

Spain

Much less information is available about Spanish coachbuilders than about those from other European countries, and that is a shame: there were some interesting Spanish companies in the inter-war years, such as Fiol and Capella. So regrettably there are fewer entries for Spain in this book than would have been ideal. Arguably the interruption of the Spanish Civil War in the mid-1930s and the subsequent Franco regime suppressed interest in products such as coachwork that had been designed for the wealthy. Even so, there was a brief revival in the early 1950s when Serra built bodywork for the Pegaso, which was intended as Spain's home-grown answer to Ferrari. It is certainly to be hoped that crucial information about Spanish coachbuilders has not been lost and that it will become available in the future.

Switzerland

In the early years of the 20th century, Switzerland had boasted a number of small car makers, and a coachbuilding industry arose to create hand-built bodies for the chassis they produced. Many of them had started off as builders of horse-drawn vehicles, and adapted gradually to the new motor vehicles in the first decade or so of the 20th century. Some continued to build horse-drawn vehicles alongside

Italsuisse of Geneva showed this well-resolved cabriolet based on the Opel Kadett at Geneva in 1964. Sadly, Opel were not interested. *(Author's Collection)*

bodies for motor vehicles into the 1920s. There were many of them, scattered through all the Swiss cantons and there was no particular congregation of them in any one area.

However, the picture changed after 1918. By the end of the First World War, all but two of the Swiss chassis makers had ceased activities. Of those, Pic-Pic went under in 1920 and Martini in 1934. Neither was able to provide enough work to keep all the coachbuilders afloat, and so the majority of Swiss bodies were built on chassis that had been imported into the country – from France, Italy, Germany, Britain and the USA.

At the start of the 1920s, the big names in Swiss coachbuilding were Geissberger in Zürich and Höhener in St Gallen. As demand for motor vehicles increased during the 1920s, so new names entered the picture, and by the middle of the 1930s both of those early leaders had gone under. A major factor for change was of course the global financial crisis that began in 1929.

Over the next few years, some Swiss coachbuilders changed their focus to commercial vehicles or to repair work, and others simply closed down. To support the industry, in 1931 the Swiss government reduced by 40% the import duty on foreign-built car chassis that were brought into the country to be bodied. This led to a boom for the Swiss carrossiers. The Swiss market was receptive to car makers from Britain, France, Germany and the USA, and as a result there were plenty of opportunities for custom

coachwork. Some of the importers also commissioned small batches of special bodywork for the models they brought in for sale in Switzerland.

In the early days, the majority of cars imported into Switzerland had come from France, and so it is not surprising that there was strong French influence on the early Swiss coachbuilders. However, German influence began to predominate in the 1930s, especially in the cabriolet designs with which Swiss coachbuilders were becoming increasingly associated.

Switzerland remained resolutely neutral during the Second World War, but coachbuilding nevertheless practically ceased in the country because there were no new chassis to be had. In the immediate aftermath of the war, supplies of new chassis remained problematical and once again some companies that had survived turned to other business, particularly commercial bodywork or repair work. Companies such as Baldenweg, Blaser and Eckert did not survive as coachbuilders.

Once again the Swiss government stepped in to help, this time altering taxation so that chassis bodied in Switzerland and then exported again were treated favourably. This new regime actually encouraged the Italian coachbuilder Carozzeria Ghia to set up a branch at Aigle in Switzerland in 1948 – and Ghia-Aigle would go on to become fully independent of the parent company in 1953. Meanwhile, there was a noticeable increase in the numbers of bodies built in Switzerland on chassis from Britain, where the government had also encouraged manufacturers to focus on export business.

However, the increasing prevalence of monocoque designs at the start of the 1950s made life hard for the traditional coachbuilder in Switzerland, as it did in other countries. A few tried hard to keep abreast of the times but many ended their involvement with car bodywork. Companies such as Langenthal, Reinboldt & Christé and Tüscher limped into the early 1950s; Worblaufen lasted a few years longer. Italsuisse was a new company formed in 1959, but did not last. Alongside Caruna, a newcomer formed in 1964 whose business was coachwork transformations, only Graber of the traditional coachbuilders survived, and that company ceased coachbuilding with the death of its founder in 1970.

A

ABC-Exclusive (D)
1983–1993, Bonn
ABC-Exclusive Tuning was founded in 1983 in Bonn, to capitalise on the booming market for bespoke custom bodywork. Most of its products were probably sold in the Middle East, and the majority of its bodywork conversions were done on the more expensive BMW or Mercedes-Benz models, although ABC-Exclusive also worked on Jaguar, Porsche and even Volkswagen models. The major transformations created convertibles (BMW 6 Series, Mercedes SEC) or stretched limousines and estate cars (Mercedes SE and SEL), but there were also wide-body kits and custom interior work. Like so many of its kind, however, this company went out of business when the market for such conversions declined, and closed its doors in 1993.

ABC-Exclusive: The company specialised in conversions of German-built cars, among them the BMW 6 Series coupé, which was turned into an attractive convertible.

ABC-Exclusive: The modifications to this W126 Mercedes-Benz S Class saloon were less radical, but the lowered suspension and bodykit were typical of their times.

ACB (F)
1934–c1991, Courbevoie, later Briare
Maurice Broual set up the Ateliers de Construction de Bécon (ACB) in 1934, with premises at 7 Rue Louis Ullach in Courbevoie, near Paris. In the 1930s, he specialised in conversions of popular cars such as the Citroen 11A, Georges Irat, Peugeot 202 and Simca Huit. His company's last appearance at the Paris Salon was in 1947.

Broual moved to Briare in the Loiret department in 1955, and opened a museum with his collection of classic cars. He subsequently specialised in 1930s-style replica bodywork under the name of the Ateliers de Construction, Carrosserie Broual. From 1983 there were also complete replicas of classic Talbot models, based on Peugeot running-gear.

Achard & Fontanel (F)
1907–late 1920s?, Lyons
Camille Fontanel was the coachbuilder, and Ernest Achard the businessman. They formed Achard, Fontanel et Cie at Lyons in 1907, with offices at 48-50 Rue Sainte-Geneviève and workshops at 8 Chemin des Platanes. For geographical reasons, many Achard & Fontanel bodies were on Rochet-Schneider chassis.

The company took out a patent for occasional seats in 1914 and another for a system of seats with folding backs in 1916. It claimed both the Russian and Greek royal families as customers. During the 1920s, Achard & Fontanel held licences for Audineau's Clairalpax system and for Baehr transformable coachwork. Its demise is not dated for certain but seems to have occurred by 1930.

AEAT (F)
See Ansart et Teisseire.

Aigner (F)
c1912–1927, Paris
Carrosserie Aigner was active in the period immediately before the First World War, from premises at 20 Rue de Villejuif in Paris. A known body is on a 1912 Delaunay-Belleville HB6, but no further details of this coachbuilder's work have come to light. Aigner merged with the coachbuilder Grümmer (*qv*) in 1927.

Akkermans (NL)
1811 to present, Oud Gastel
Founded in 1811, Carrosserie Akkermans was the oldest surviving Dutch coachbuilder at the time of writing. Its premises have always been at Oud Gastel in the Netherlands, and in the early part of the 20th century it played an important part in Dutch agricultural mechanisation.

The company subsequently moved into building car bodies, and worked on Delahaye chassis among others in the 1930s. In the 1950s, it constructed special bodywork for DKW and Volkswagen Beetle cars. The company now focuses on commercial bodywork, and includes ambulances, military and police vehicles, and bodies for TV companies among its work.

Akkermans: Coupé derivatives of the VW Beetle were fair game for coachbuilders before VW introduced its own Karmann Ghia model – and in some cases afterwards. This was the Akkermans contribution to the story.

Alin-Liautard (F)

c1910–c1930, Courbevoie

This French coachbuilder seems to have begun with the name of Alin et Liautard, with a trading address of 12-14 Passage Henri at Courbevoie in the Hauts-de-Seine department. Other names associated with them were Etablissements Alin-Liautard et Cie, and later Société Anonyme des Anciens Etablissements Alin-Liautard et Cie. Their address in the 1920s was 13 Rue de Bécon in Courbevoie.

In the years before the Great War they constructed aircraft fuselages as well as car bodywork, and this work seems to have inspired some quite daring designs. Many of these were on Grégoire chassis.

The earliest firm date for Alin-Liautard is 1910, when (they claimed) their work was the hit of the Paris Salon. The car was probably the extraordinary Grégoire "sous-marin" (submarine) coupé with a centre section that resembled the conning tower of a submarine. No less extraordinary was a "Triple Berline" (Triple Saloon) from the same period, built on a specially extended Grégoire chassis and elegantly recalling the days of the horse-drawn carriage.

The striking enclosed-drive Grégoire saloon (called a "torpille") on the company's stand at the 1912 Paris Salon was panelled in aluminium and incorporated a streamlined rear end. Its design was by the Romanian aerodynamicist Henri Coandă, who used an early wind tunnel to test a scale model.

Alin-Liautard's 1920s designs were generally more conventional, although to familiar shapes they sometimes added a dash of flair. Many bodies in this period were on Panhard et Levassor chassis, and others were on Talbot. Their best-known 1920s design was the Aérable, which (again according to the company's own claim) was the hit of the 1927 Paris Salon. This was essentially a saloon with a roll-top roof, which left the door windows and frames fixed in place when opened. The date of Alin-Liautard's demise is unclear, but the company did not survive the effects of the 1929 Wall Street Crash.

Alin-Liautard: Though falling outside the time span of this book, this "Triple Berline" body, dating from around 1910, is too spectacular to be left out.

Allemano (I)

1928–1965, Turin

Serafino Allemano set up his coachbuilding business in Turin in 1928. In the beginning, he concentrated on repair work, but by the mid-1930s he had realised that he had a talent for coachwork design. After the Second World War, Serafino's nephew joined the company, and Carrozzeria Allemano developed that side of the business to good effect.

Most Allemano bodies were open cars or coupés, and the company quickly gained a reputation for avant-garde styling. Early post-war bodies were mostly on domestic makes, including Ferrari 166S (1948), Alfa Romeo 2500 (1950), and Lancia Aurelia (1952). However, Allemano was not above contract work, and in 1951 built the stunning coupé body on a Cisitalia 202 to a design by Franco Scaglione of Carrozzeria Scaglietti.

Allemano: This beautifully neat little coupé dates from 1952 and was based on a Panhard Dyna. (*WikiMedia Commons/Luc106*)

From 1954, there was work on Maserati models, notably a series of 21 bodies on the A6G from 1954, prototype designs for the 3500 in 1957, and a further 22 bodies on the 5000 GT between 1959 and 1965. In the same period, Allemano was working on Fiats, beginning with three 1100 TV models in 1954 (to a Michelotti design). There was a four-door design for the Fiat 600 between 1955 and 1958, more bodies for 850s and 2200s, and a handful of aluminium-bodied Spyders on the Abarth 750 in 1958-1959. The year 1956 also brought a coupé on the Lancia Appia.

Allemano nevertheless did not confine its activities to Italian cars. On French chassis, there was a single Panhard

Allemano: Sharper edges became the fashion towards the end of the 1950s, and this design was for a 1957 Maserati 3500GT. (*David Hodges Collection*)

Allemano: Curvaceous and attractive, this was the firm's design for the Maserati A6G in the mid-1950s. (*WikiMedia Commons/ Rex Grey*)

Allemano: Another small-car success was this Fiat 750 Spyder dating from 1959. (*David Hodges Collection*)

Allemano produced this 1959 coupé on a Fiat-Abarth 2200. (*David Hodges Collection*)

Allemano: The sharper-edged designs continued into the 1960s; although similar to the earlier 3500GT design illustrated, this Maserati 5000 coupé has a wraparound rear window. (*WikiMedia Commons/Buch-t*)

Alpine: The first production Alpine was the A106, based on a Renault 4CV. (*David Hodges Collection*)

Alpine: The A110 of the 1960s was a distinctive and well-resolved design. (*Author photograph*)

Dyna 750 coupé in 1952, and in 1957-1958 the company made a number of Renault Dauphine coupés. Work on British makes included an Aston Martin DB2/4 coupé in 1953 and a Jaguar XK140 in 1956.

Among Allemano's last projects were a number of ATS 2500 GT models in 1963-1964. The company closed in 1965.

Allignol (F)
1918, Lyons
Carrosserie Allignol from Lyons is known for a single body, built on a locally-constructed Rochet-Schneider chassis for the Mayor of Lyons in 1918.

Alpine (F)
1954–1978, Dieppe
Alpine is generally known as a car maker in its own right, but its origins lie in special bodywork for Renault chassis.

Jean Rédélé was the son of the Renault agent in Dieppe, and in the early 1950s began racing modified Renault 4CVs in sports car events. In December 1952 he commissioned Giovanni Michelotti to design a coupé body which he then had built by Allemano and mounted on a Renault platform.

From this prototype, Rédélé developed the Alpine A106. He established the Société des Automobiles Alpine at the Avenue de Bréauté in Dieppe to build it, and the car – still based on a Renault 4CV chassis – entered small-series production in 1954. The bodies were made of fibreglass and were built by the Chappe brothers. The A108 of 1958 was again based on a Michelotti design, but modified by Alpine

as a 2+2 coupé; this was also built in Brazil as the Willys Interlagos, in berlinetta, coupé and convertible forms. The hugely successful A110 berlinetta followed in 1962.

During the 1960s, the Alpine company became very close to Renault, and by 1968 laid claim to the car maker's entire competitions budget. Renault took an increasing interest in Alpine products, and made its own revisions to the Trevor Fiore design for the 1971 A310. The 1973 petrol crisis led Alpine into financial problems, and Renault moved in and took over the business in 1978. The name remains today, but coachwork design is now by Renault.

Ambi Budd (D)
1926–1945, Berlin
The German Ambi Budd company became Germany's largest builder of car bodies during the inter-war years, developing a huge business on the basis of the steel-pressing methods developed by Edward Gowen Budd in the USA before the First World War.

Budd granted licences to some European car makers, notably to Citroën in France and to Austin in the UK, but

Ambi Budd: The Berlin body maker made the solid-looking two-door standard body for this BMW 321 dating from around 1939, which was actually assembled at Eisenach. *(BMW)*

Ambi Budd: This 1931 BMW 3/15 DA2 model carries an all-steel body. *(BMW)*

in Germany chose to establish a joint company with Ambi Maschinenbau; Ambi stood for Arthur Müller Bauten und Industriewerke. Ambi Budd, also known as ABP (Ambi Budd Presswerke), set up its steel pressing plant in 1926 in the old Rumpler factory in the Johannisthal district of Berlin. In 1928, the company moved to secure its position by taking a 26% stake in Adler, in collaboration with the Schroder bank in London.

The company was kept busy throughout the 1930s building complete bodies to fulfil large orders from chassis makers such as Adler, BMW, Ford, Hanomag and NSU. Unable to escape the German military build-up, by 1939 it was also building bodies for the Volkswagen Kübelwagen and Schwimmwagen, as well as mass-producing military jerrycans. During the war, it made parts for Focke Wulf fighter aircraft, and in 1943 was forced to move production underground after being targeted by allied bombers.

By the end of the war, the Ambi Budd plant was in ruins, and what remained of it fell into the Soviet sector of the newly divided country. The presses for the BMW 321

bodies were sent to Eisenau where they were used to create the post-war EMW cars, and the remaining production machinery was shipped to the Soviet Union. Ambi Budd was never revived.

Anders (D)
1920s, Leipzig

No substantial information is available about this coach-builder, which is known to have bodied a Ley T6 chassis in 1921.

Andreau (F)
1936–1941

Jean Andreau was strictly a designer rather than a coachbuilder, but his work on aerodynamic designs has earned him a place among the great French practitioners of the art.

He was in fact an engineer with very wide interests, which included subjects as diverse as wind power, jet aero engines and automatic gearboxes. However, his interest in aerodynamics seems to have been aroused when he was working on the design of shells for the French army during the First World War. His reputation as an aerodynamicist

Andreau: Aerodynamic principles governed the design of this body for the Peugeot 402 in 1936. It did not enter volume production. *(Peugeot)*

was made during a period with Chausson in the late 1920s, when the results of his experiments with wooden models and an Eiffel wind tunnel became widely known through a series of conferences and lectures.

Towards 1935, he worked with André Dubonnet on a futuristic streamlined car called the Dolphin, but its shape was too avant-garde for any car maker of the time to take it on. At about the same time, Peugeot asked him to design a streamlined body for their 402 chassis, and the resulting car with its teardrop-shaped body and huge rear fin was displayed at the Paris Salon in 1936. However, just six were built: public apathy and a worsening social and international situation led to the project being abandoned.

Andreau designed the streamlined body for Louis Delage's V12 circuit racer that was planned both to meet the new ACF rules and to challenge German domination of the international race tracks. Again, the car was constructed as a wooden model first and tested in a wind-tunnel. Severely damaged during testing for the 1937 French Grand Prix at Montlhéry, it did not compete but was rebuilt and displayed at the 1937 Paris Salon.

Andreau's reputation was such that George Eyston asked him to design the body for his 1937 Thunderbolt Land Speed Record car. Post-war, Andreau worked on the 1946 Mathis VL333 three-wheeler, which had an exceptionally low Cd of 0.20. However, although several prototypes were built, no production followed.

Anhaltische Karosserie-Werke (D)
1923–1925, Leopoldshall
This coachworks was named after the former Duchy of Anhalt in Saxony, which had become a free state under the Weimar Republic. It appears to have been active in the early 1920s, but no other substantial information is available.

Ansaloni (I)
1940s onwards, probably Bologna
The Ansaloni company seems to have been a small body shop, probably located in Bologna. In 1947, it constructed some simple two-seater racing bodies for the then-new Ferrari company on the 125S Competizione, and the year after also did a cycle-winged body on the 166 Corsa. There is some suggestion that early body design may have been done under contract by Franco Scaglione.

The Ansaloni name is also associated with some unidentified prototype work in 1952, and also with some open resort-type buggy conversions on the Fiat 126 of the 1970s.

Ansart-Audineau (F)
1920–1922, Neuilly-sur-Seine
Ansart-Audineau existed briefly at the start of the 1920s when established coachbuilder Audineau took on Jacques Ansart as a partner. The company operated from the existing Audineau premises at 41 Rue Ybry, in Neuilly-sur-Seine, and it was here that Ansart began to build the "transformable"

Ansart & Teisseire: A "demi-découvrable" (semi-folding roof) body on a late-1920s Renault. However ingenious this arrangement appears, it is clear that when it rains the rear passenger is going to get wet. (*David Burgess-Wise*)

bodies for which he later became well-known. He later bought the Audineau workshops, where he established Ansart & Teisseire, while Audineau moved elsewhere.

Ansart & Teisseire (F)
1922–late 1950s, Neuilly-sur-Seine
Les Anciens Etablissements Ansart et Teisseire was founded in 1922 at Neuilly-sur-Seine by Jacques Ansart and a Monsieur Teisseire, about whom nothing seems to be known. The company's initials gave rise to the name by which it is better known – AEAT – and it was based at the 41 Rue Ybry address where Ansart had formerly worked with Paul Audineau as Ansart-Audineau.

In the 1920s, Ansart et Teisseire made some skiff-type bodies with planked wood construction, but their focus was always on bodywork that could be transformed in some way. Early ones had side windows that could be removed and refitted at the rear to form a second windscreen for rear-seat passengers. The basic design of these had originated with Ansart-Audineau, from whom Ansart et Teisseire had acquired the patent. From 1926, there was also an opening fabric roof design, called the Toimobile. By the late 1920s, AEAT had become particularly associated with conversions of Citroën models, and in 1931 the company was bought by the local Citroën agent, Monsieur Luchard.

From 1935, AEAT became known for its "découvrable" or roll-top saloon, introduced that year for the new Traction Avant and patented in 1937. This used wooden beams to strengthen the body structure, and was adapted to suit other Citroëns as well, notably the more conventional B14 – although AEAT conversions on this model were far less common.

Having established its name as a modifier of the Traction Avant, AEAT offered a variety of other conversions of that model. These included a "Commerciale" conversion, which added a hatchback to a Traction Avant saloon to make a

Ansart & Teisseire: Rolltop conversions of the Citroën Traction Avant were popular in the late 1940s and early 1950s, and this one by AEAT dated from 1949.

vehicle similar to that available from the factory; there were certainly some custom-built one-offs, too.

AEAT also won a contract from the French Government to build a pair of scale-model Traction Avant roadsters which were presented to the two daughters of Britain's King George VI, Elizabeth and Margaret, in 1938. The models were designed to carry the princesses' dolls.

After the war, as the French car market slowly returned to normal in the late 1940s and early 1950s, AEAT revitalised a number of pre-war Traction Avant models with their roll-top conversion. A number of conversions were also done on Peugeot and Renault models. AEAT offered other modifications for the Traction Avant, including a larger boot and interior re-trims. From 1957, the company also had a roll-top conversion for the Citroën DS.

Antem (F)
1919–1997, Levallois, later Courbevoie
Antem was a leading French coachbuilder in the 1920s and 1930s. It was founded in 1919 by Juan Antem, the grandson of a family of wheelwrights from Majorca who had served an apprenticeship in France as a locksmith. Adopting the French version of his name, Jean Antem set up in business with a friend as Antem & Monroig Carrosserie in Levallois at the Rue Neuve-de-Villiers.

Although early work was mostly repairs, Antem & Monroig were also prepared to make body modifications, and they soon gained a reputation. In 1921 the company moved to larger premises at 15 Rue St Paul in Neuilly-sur-Seine, and by 1923 they were confident enough to show their work at the Paris Salon. By 1925, business was booming and the company took on a third partner, François Guyot, to become Antem, Monroig & Guyot. It moved to new premises at Rue des Ajoux in Courbevoie.

From the mid-1920s, the company was bodying not only popular French chassis by the likes of Chénard et Walcker and Renault, but also luxury chassis from Delage and Panhard et Levassor and expensive imported chassis from Mercedes and Rolls-Royce. Antem, Monroig & Guyot constructed fabric-panelled bodies using Weymann principles, and specialised in torpédo, skiff, coupé chauffeur and berline découvrable types. Characteristic was a low belt-line in a contrasting colour and this, together with concealed chassis frames, helped the cars to look lower and sleeker. The late 1920s also saw the company working on a number of utility-vehicle contracts, notably for the local police.

In 1929, Jean Antem was granted French nationality, and that same year he bought out his two partners and renamed his company Carrosserie Antem. During the 1930s, Antem established links with Ford, and obtained several contracts for van and ambulance bodies on Ford and Matford chassis. There was small-series production work for Ariès, but the company never ceased its bespoke coachbuilding activities. A highlight was the year 1935, when Antem showed a

Antem: Dating from around the time when Jean Antem became sole owner of the business is this formal coupé-chauffeur body on an eight-cylinder Mercedes-Benz Nürburg chassis. *(Daimler-Benz)*

Antem: This transformable saloon body was built on a Panhard & Levassor chassis around 1925, when the company was called Antem, Monroig & Guyot. *(David Hodges Collection)*

Delahaye 138S and a Hispano-Suiza K6 cabriolet at the Bois de Boulogne concours, along with some La Licorne cabriolets. La Licorne were sufficiently impressed to commission a small series of cabriolets on their 11/14CV chassis, and these became catalogued models with the name of Week-End.

During the Second World War, the Antem business focussed on repairs and on the construction of gas-producer

Antem: Elegant to a fault is this cabriolet body on a 1934 Bugatti Type 57 chassis. The long rear deck and rear spats gave the car an almost streamlined appearance without the excesses of the contemporary vogue for streamlining. *(David Hodges Collection)*

plants. In June 1941, they moved to a new workshop at 45 Rue Victor Hugo in Courbevoie, and when coachbuilding work resumed in 1946, Antem handed the business over to his two sons. Jean junior dealt with coachwork together with his father, while Jacques handled the mechanical side. The design talent of Jean junior attracted Delahaye, who commissioned the Antem company to design and build several small series of "coach" and cabriolet bodies on the 135 chassis, which was their main work in this period. A similar contract with Talbot followed.

Antem made sure of a regular flow of work by becoming involved with a variety of new projects as well. The company built bodies for Deutsch-Bonnet, constructed some minibuses with Renault engines, bodied some Mochet cycle-cars, and even modified a pre-war six-cylinder Citroën Traction Avant. From 1948, the company had its own showroom as well. In the early 1950s, Antem tackled the vogue for full-width bodywork with the coupé body on the Delahaye 235 chassis, and an attractive Bugatti Type 101 in 1953. Meanwhile, Jean junior and Jacques took an interest in racing as well and built the bodies for some competition cars in the early 1950s.

The early 1950s saw Antem construct some striking publicity vehicles, some from designs by former Delahaye designer Philippe Charbonneaux. But its time as a great carrossier was over., and it built its last car bodywork in 1955. In 1958, the company began building touring caravans and camper bodies, and from 1961 moved to new premises at Doudeville in the Seine-Maritime department and became Antem SA. Subsequent production included vans that doubled as market stalls.

Jean Antem died in 1972, and his two sons both died in 1986. Jean Claude Antem, son of Jean junior, took over for the next decade, but in 1997 the family decided to close the business while it was still profitable.

Antem: Styles were changing in the 1940s but Antem still created a distinctive cabriolet body for this 1946 Delahaye chassis. *(David Hodges Collection)*

Antem: A smooth 1949 coupé on a 2-litre DB (Deutsch-Bonnet) chassis.

Antem: Looking nothing at all like its parent saloon, this is a Citroën 2CV reclothed in 1955 with a two-door coupé body designed by Philippe Charbonneaux. It was among the last passenger car bodies from the company. *(David Hodges Collection)*

AR (F)

See Ateliers Réunis.

Armbruster (A)

1858–1934, Alsergrund

The Viennese firm of Armbruster built its first car bodies in or around 1910, but it was already a well-established and highly prestigious coachbuilder by this stage. Sebastian Armbruster had opened for business in 1858 as a carriage builder, and had built a reputation which had earned him commissions from the Austrian monarchy. However, Sebastian had died in 1889 and his two sons had taken over, Anton sharing the business with Carl.

In the beginning, Armbruster was at 4-6 Porzellangasse in the ninth district of Alsergrund. However, the Armbruster brothers opened a new and palatial workshop in 1897-1898 between Müllnergasse and Porzellangasse, and it was here that the car bodies were built. Carriage-building nevertheless continued into the end of the new century's second decade, probably ending when the Austrian monarchy collapsed in 1918.

Armbruster retained its reputation for high-quality coachwork throughout the 1920s, when it built on the leading prestige chassis of the day. Examples included the Mercedes S towards the end of the decade. Armbruster coachwork is known on Austro Daimler 635 and on Stutz DV32 chassis in the early 1930s, and the company favoured helmet-shaped front wings with no running-boards on its roadster and cabriolet designs. However, Armbruster was in financial difficulties in the early 1930s and closed in 1934. There is no direct connection between the company and the US company Armbruster Stageway, which builds limousine bodies and funeral cars.

Assmann: Dating from 1925, these are delivery vans for the Eisenach post service with bodywork by Assmann on Dixi 6/24PS chassis. (BMW)

Assmann (D)
1920-1939, Eisenach

The brothers Ernst and Karl Assmann founded their business at Eisenach in 1920, initially focussing on the construction and repair of horse-drawn wagons. An early advertisement shows that the company was also prepared to rebuild and modernise older cars.

Nevertheless, the Dixi plant was nearby, and by 1925 the company had unsurprisingly begun to build car bodies for its neighbour. Assmann built a number of special bodies on Dixi chassis, including distinctive vans for the ADAC (German automobile club) roadside assistance crews, and delivery vans after 1928. By the mid-1930s, the company was also ready with some prototype sports bodies. The company fell into the eastern sector of Germany after the 1939-1945 war and in fact still exists, although only as a car repair business.

Ateliers Réunis (F)
c1990, Ecquevilly

Les Ateliers Réunis, also known as AR, was established in 1989 or 1990 by Philippe Aubry and Jean-Pierre Fruleux on the Petit Parc industrial estate at Ecquevilly in the Île-de-France region. Aubry had earlier founded the French classic-car magazine *Auto-Rétro*.

The company's main product was a shooting-brake conversion of the Jaguar XJ-S, based very heavily on the Lynx Eventer conversion that originated in the UK. There were plans to build a numbered limited edition of 40, but production ended after somewhere between five and 20 had been built.

Aubertin (F)
Early 1900- c1925, Levallois-Perret

Georges Aubertin probably established his coachworks in the early 1900s, and had addresses at 19 Rue Greffühle and 4-6 Rue Albert de Vatimesnil, both in Levallois-Perret. There is little information about his early work, although a 1917 body for a De Dion Bouton is known.

From the early 1920s, Aubertin began using the Weymann Flexible Body Patent, but he also continued to build metal-panelled bodies. Aubertin bodies are known on Georges Irat chassis (1923) and on a 1921 De Dion, the latter being a panelled skiff type.

In 1923, Marcel Pourtout became workshop foreman, and two years later he bought the Aubertin business. When Pourtout set up his works in Bougival, the Aubertin premises in Levallois passed into Citroën ownership.

Audineau (F)
1924-1928, Neuilly-sur-Seine

Paul Audineau set up his coachworks in 1907 at 41-43 Rue Ybry in Neuilly-sur-Seine, and immediately claimed to be a specialist in lightweight bodywork. To this end, Audineau et Cie used slim ash frames and small windows, the latter because glass is much heavier than wood.

From 1920, he took on Jacques Ansart as a partner, but the partnership lasted only until 1922, when Ansart formed another company with a Monsieur Teisseire. Ansart & Teisseire took over the old Audineau premises, and the renamed Carrosserie Française Paul Audineau moved to 57-79 Route de la Révolte in Levallois.

Audineau: The lightweight aluminium pillars of the Clairalpax design made for a more airy interior, as this 1920s advertisement boasts. Oddly, the Clairalpax name is not used here; there is just a mention that the pillars are made of light Alpax aluminium alloy.

Still working on lightweight designs, Audineau patented his Clairalpax design in 1924, which used aluminium pillars. The company became closely involved with the advanced cars planned by the Bucciali brothers in the middle 1920s, and in 1926 announced a rolltop design called Clairalpax Cielouvert, which was licensed to a number of other French coachbuilders. However, the works closed down in 1928.

Auer (D)
1895-1949, Cannstatt

Surprisingly little information is available about the Auer coachworks, even though it was well respected in the first half of the 20th century. Christian Auer founded his wagon works in Cannstatt near Stuttgart in 1895, initially to construct luxury horse-drawn vehicles. As the Daimler works was in Cannstatt itself and the Benz works not far away at Mannheim, it was inevitable that the company should become involved in car body construction, and its first example was built in 1899. Most of Daimler's bodies up to 1903 came from the Auer works, although once the car maker had its own body works the quantities decreased. Nevertheless, by the end of 1906 Auer claimed to have built around 1500 bodies for Daimler vehicles – a large number by the standards of the time.

Auer went on to specialise in high-quality bodies to individual commissions, and as a result became associated with the more expensive chassis. The majority seem to have been on German chassis, such as Benz, Maybach, Mercedes and of course Mercedes-Benz. At least one Auer body was nevertheless built on a Czechoslovakian Tatra chassis in the early 1930s.

Auer: A 7-litre 1927 Maybach W5 cabriolet. (*Erik Eckermann Archive*)

Auer: The low roofline, shallow screen continuing into the roof and "aerodynamic" tail mark out Auer's body on this 1931/32 Mercedes-Benz 460 Nurburg. (*Erik Eckermann Archive*)

It appears from the records of Stuttgart Chamber of Commerce that Auer was absorbed into the Boku-Maschinenfabrik of Stuttgart in 1949.

Austro-Tatra (A)
1948-1951, Simmering

Karosserie Austro-Tatra was formed out of the Austro-Tatra car company that had been building Czech-designed Tatra cars under licence at Simmering near Vienna. Production of these ended in 1948, and the company kept itself going by taking on a contract to build a small number of bodies for the new Porsche 356 that was at the time being built at Gmünd in Austria. This work lasted from 1948 to 1949, and was followed by the construction of 203 special four-door Volkswagen cabriolets for police and fire services in 1950-1951.

Autenrieth (D)
1922-1964, Darmstadt

Karosseriebau Autenrieth was one of the best-known German coachbuilders between 1922 and 1964.

Georg Autenrieth and Fritz Eisenlohr founded the Weinsberg coachworks in the town of the same name near Heilbronn in 1912. Ten years later, Autenrieth chose to go it alone and set up his own coachworks in Darmstadt, with an address at 72 Feldbergstrasse. His was the first such business in the town, and he was soon building bodies for the eight-cylinder Röhr that was constructed in nearby Ober-Ramstadt.

The 1920s and 1930s saw Autenrieth building individual cabriolets, coupés and saloons on a variety of other chassis, including Adler, Audi, Horch, Maybach, Mercedes-Benz, NSU and Opel. However, the most significant relationship was with BMW, for whom Autenrieth began work in the mid-1930s. The coachbuilder made over 1000 two-door and four-door cabriolets for the 326 chassis, and these were sold through BMW showrooms as part of the chassis-maker's standard range. There were some one-offs, too, including a 326 with sliding doors. Autenrieth also built some bodies on other BMW chassis – the 320, 321, 328 and 335.

During the 1930s, Autenrieth employed over 400 people and was among the largest German coachbuilders. Many of its creations had been successful in concours d'élégance competitions, and unsurprisingly it was given the task of building some of the first cabriolet bodies on the Volkswagen (then still known as the KdF-Wagen). However, during the Second World War its premises were diverted to making military matériel, and it also managed the Illgische paper works at Nieder-Ramstadt, where it made aircraft sections.

After the war, the company resumed its link with BMW. Georg Autenrieth died in 1950 and the business was subsequently run by his two daughters and by Franz Trüby, his son-in-law who had become technical and development chief. From 1952, there were cabriolet and coupé bodies for the BMW "Baroque Angel" 501 and 502 models, which were stylish and pricey alternatives to the standard two-

Autenrieth: There was a deliberate similarity of line about many bought-in bodies on BMW chassis in the 1930s. This 1937 Autenrieth design on the 320 chassis bears comparison with the Ambi Budd body for the 321 on page 21. *(BMW)*

Autenrieth: The 335 was BMW's largest model from 1939, and the firm was responsible for its elegant cabriolet bodywork. (David Hodges Collection)

Autenrieth: The coupé body for the BMW 502 echoed the sweeping lines of the parent Baroque Angel saloons, and yet was utterly distinctive. These models were built in small numbers during the second half of the 1950s. (BMW)

door cars. Some were radically different from the factory offering, without even the traditional BMW twin-kidney grille. Individual commissions included a hugely expensive four-door cabriolet for a Hamburg lawyer on a 1959 V8-engined 502 V8 3200 Super, and a four-door limousine on the 502 from the same period.

The 1950s also brought cabriolets on the Borgward Isabella and a little-known one on the early Citroën DS. There was a Jaguar XK120, too. Much better known, however, are the cabriolets and coupés built in small numbers on Opel Rekord and Kapitän models from 1957 to 1962. These were often distinguished by additional chrome and by tail fins in the style of the time.

However, the increasing use of monocoque construction in the motor industry reduced Autenrieth's ability to create individual designs. Unwilling to continue in business as a simple body repair shop, the company closed its doors in 1964. Its last car was a cabriolet-limousine based on an Opel Rekord A.

Autobineau: The company built the body on this 1948 Delage 3-litre to a design by Letourneur et Marchand.

Autobineau (F)
1924-1973, Neuilly-sur-Seine

Autobineau was an offshoot of Letourneur & Marchand, established in the 1920s to produce batches of special bodies for the major chassis makers. The name of Autobineau was in fact the telegraphic address of the parent company: Letourneur et Marchand were at the Boulevard Bineau on the Ile de la Jatte at Neuilly-sur-Seine.

The first contract was with Delage and was a run of 2000 bodies for the D1 chassis; this was later extended to 4000. Autobineau had a workforce of over 200, and was capable of building three or four bodies a day. All its first work was for Delage, but when that company ran into difficulties in 1933, and Delahaye took control, Autobineau bodies began to appear on Delahaye chassis as well.

From 1936, there were special bodies for other companies as well, notably Amilcar, Georges Irat, La Licorne and Unic. After the Second World War, Autobineau retained its links with Delage and Delahaye, building some of the more ordinary bodies for these two marques until they disappeared in 1954. Autobineau then turned to commercial bodywork and was producing cabs for Unic heavy trucks when it finally closed in 1973.

Ava-Flynn (F)
1989-1994, Ajaccio

Automobiles Ava-Flynn International was a company in Ajaccio, Corsica, which converted around ten Saab 900 saloons into stepped-roof estate cars at the start of the 1990s. The company also built a six-wheel low-loader version of the Ford Sierra P100 pick-up.

Ava-Flynn: This stepped-roof estate-car design for the Saab 900 was perhaps not the most elegant of conversions.

B

Baehr (F)

1920s, Paris

Gustave Baehr was the proprietor of Saint-Didier Automobile in Paris, which he claimed was the largest sales outlet for motor cars in Europe. Though not himself a coachbuilder, Baehr developed a design for "transformable" bodywork that was widely used by coachbuilders in France and abroad during the 1920s. It was first seen at the Paris Salon in 1919, when the coachbuilder Belvalette showed a body that used the patented Baehr system.

The Baehr system allowed the side windows and their frames to retract into a housing behind the front seat, so simplifying the transformation from closed to open car. A second version in 1922 simplified the system further, and the two types were available together for some years to suit different types of coachwork.

Balbo (I)

1914–1954, Turin

Alfonso Balbo established Carrozzeria Balbo in 1914, at 78 Corso Parigi in Turin. His first bodies were on locally-built Fiat chassis, and included saloons, coupés, spiders and light commercial types as well. However, he also worked on Lancia chassis and a particular success was his two-door saloon design for the Trikappa in 1922.

Balbo died suddenly in 1926, but his close associate Carlo Follis picked up the reins and carried on with the business under the name of Carrozzeria Successori Balbo (Balbo Coachworks, successors). By the 1930s, the company was turning out one car a day, notably saloons, cabriolets and roadsters on the Fiat 6C 1500 chassis. However, the Second World War brought an end to Balbo's success, the company's premises in the Corso Parigi being completely destroyed by bombing.

Balbo: The company worked closely with Fiat for much of its existence. This cabriolet design on the Fiat 1100B chassis would certainly have turned heads at the start of the 1950s. (*David Hodges Collection*)

When the war ended, Balbo moved to new premises in the Via Gorizia, and again drew up a series of body designs for Fiat chassis; there were coupé designs and, unusually for the period, four-door saloons as well for the 1100, 1400 and 1500 models. Balbo also created special bodies for the Alfa Romeo 6C 2500 and the Lancia Aurelia and Aprilia, a notable one-off being an Aurelia coupé in 1951.

Supplementing its coachbuilding activities, Balbo also developed a two-seat microcar that was announced at the

Balbo: A tidy coupé on a Fiat 8V of the early 1950s. (*David Burgess-Wise*)

1953 Turin Motor Show as a roll-top coupé. Despite a nod to American styling with a chromed "jet engine" air intake on the nose, the Balbo B400 offered nothing really new, and no series production followed. A year later, in 1954, the company closed its doors.

Baldenweg (CH)
1920–1938, Geneva

François Baldenweg was of Alsatian origin and was a foreman with car maker Pic-Pic (Piccard et Pictet) in Geneva. When that company failed in 1920, Baldenweg decided to set up in business on his own, initially as a coach trimmer. However, on 15 August 1922 he changed the nature of his business to that of coachbuilder. By 1924, he had a workshop at the Rue du Léman.

Over the next few years, the Baldenweg company constructed bodies on many of the more expensive chassis, including Delage, Hispano-Suiza and Isotta-Fraschini. They regularly had a stand at the Geneva Show to display their latest creations, and Baldenweg is credited with constructing the first-ever Swiss four-door cabriolet. Most of their output consisted of touring and luxury bodies on French chassis, but there were also sporty two-seaters on smaller chassis from Delage and Hispano-Suiza.

By 1929, Baldenweg had moved to the Rue Jean-Jaquet, and in 1932 the business was taken over by the next generation. Edouard Baldenweg began a re-orientation of the business from coachbuilding towards repairs and maintenance, and this was continued from 1946 when his brother François junior took over.

The Baldenweg company still exists today in the repair and maintenance business, focussing on marques such as Lancia, Mercedes-Benz and Rolls-Royce. Its current premises are in the Rue Saint-Julien, at Carouge near Geneva.

Balzer (D)
1925–1957, Ludwigsburg

The Balzer coachworks became best known for commercial bodywork, but in the 1920s constructed passenger car bodies on a variety of chassis.

Karl Balzer had worked for the coachbuilders Utermöhle and Auer as well as for Daimler in Bad Cannstatt before he established his own coachworks at Ludwigsburg in 1925. Over the next few years, he became best known for bodywork on Mercedes-Benz chassis, and some of his creations won awards at concours d'élégance events. Balzer's speciality was removable roofs that allowed saloons and coupés to be converted into open cars, and the company's bodywork is known on Adler, Horch, NAG, Opel and Wanderer chassis. There was even a saloon body for a Bentley 3-litre in 1927.

However, Balzer soon began to focus on commercial bodywork, and during the 1930s became well known for its ambulances, advertising vehicles and other special-purpose types. From 1937 it was known as Balzer & Kienle, Paul Kienle having been with the business since its early days.

During the war and early post-war years, Balzer focussed on repair work. Its premises were destroyed by an incendiary bomb in 1944, but the company survived and in the late 1940s was known for making removable hardtops to suit Mercedes-Benz 170 models. Before long, it switched entirely to commercial bodywork for trucks and buses. The founder died in 1957, but his descendants carried on the family business, which still existed in 2015 as an automotive repair specialist.

Bangille (F)
1920s

Jules Bangille is known to have built bodies on several Delahaye chassis in the 1920s, but little else is known about his company.

Barailhé (F)
To 1920s, Neuilly-sur-Seine and Courbevoie

Carrosserie Automobile L Barailhé had its head office at 6 Rue d'Armenonville in Neuilly-sur-Seine, and additional premises at 43 Rue de la Garenne in Courbevoie. The company offered a variety of car bodies before the Great War, and promised a rapid turnaround of 15 days if the customer ordered a standard design. Bodies could be had in the white or fully finished. Barailhé closed in the early 1920s and its premises passed into the hands of Guettault.

Barbier (F)
1935, Cannes

Carrosserie Barbier was from Cannes, and is known for the bodywork on a La Licorne 8CV that was seen at a concours d'élégance at Cannes in 1935.

Barbier, Tulié et Cie (F)
1920s, Paris

Operating from premises in Paris at 5 Place de la Porte-Champerret and 5 Avenue des Chasseurs (Place Wagram), Barbier, Tulié et Cie built bodywork for chassis by makers like Citroën and La Licorne. They developed a system of insulation for bodywork which they called Isothermie, and which they claimed was able to keep car bodies cool in summer and warm in winter.

Bargin & Beckerich (F)
c1901–1920s, Neuilly-sur-Seine

The Anciens Établissements Bargin & Beckerich were at 85 Rue Borghèse in Neuilly-sur-Seine, and there are traces of their activity between the start of the 20th century and the 1920s. The company later became the Société Parisienne de Carrosseries (SCPA).

Barou (F)
1940–1972, Tournon-sur Rhône

Jean Barou set up his business at Tournon-sur Rhône in the Ardèche in 1940, but for the first few years he was obliged to build lorry cabs and trailers for bicycles under the German Occupation. In the late 1940s, he created a handful of roadsters based on Simca Six or Huit chassis, and then moved on to touring cabriolet bodies on Simca

and Delahaye chassis. Other Barou bodies were on Talbot Lago and Jaguar XK120 chassis, but in the early 1950s the company turned to the creation of publicity vehicles, eventually closing in 1972.

Baumann (CH)
1937–1950, Burgdorf

Baumann Carrosserie remains in business today as a coachwork and boat repair business at Burgdorf in Switzerland. Between 1937 and 1950, the company built a number of rolltop saloon conversions on the basis of the Citroën Traction Avant.

Baur (D)
1910–1998, Stuttgart

The Baur company was founded in 1910 with headquarters in the Berg suburb of Stuttgart, and remained a family-owned business until its insolvency in 1998. By the 1930s it had become one of Germany's leading coachbuilders, and for 40 years from the early 1950s until the early 1990s it had very close links with BMW. Primarily known for its cabriolet bodies, Baur developed the ability to produce full production runs of bodyshells of all types, and became hugely respected in the German motor industry for this. The company still existed at the time of writing, but under new ownership and with a focus on prototype work rather than batch production.

In its early days, Baur Karosserie- und Fahrzeugbau GmbH carried out individual body commissions and dealt with repair work, but by 1912 it was already showing signs

Baur: Unusual features of this cabriolet on a BMW 3/20 chassis from about 1934 are the curved top to the windscreen and the scallop in the rear body that would have allowed the hood to sit low down. *(BMW)*

Baur: Although Mercedes-Benz built most of its own coachwork at Sindelfingen, this sporty-looking 380 saloon of the early 1930s was by Baur. *(Daimler-Benz)*

of individuality and in that year took out its first patent. The business took an important step forward in 1927 with its first batch-production order. This was for Wanderer, and Baur went on to build 200 bodies of various types over the years to 1935. Prominent among these were cabriolets, and it was also a cabriolet design that associated Baur with luxury brand Maybach for the first time in 1927. From 1929 and throughout the 1930s, there were cabriolet and Pullman limousine bodies on several Horch chassis too. The early

1930s brought some work for Mercedes-Benz, including a four-door saloon on the short-lived 380 chassis.

The second half of the 1930s saw Baur continuing its work for Wanderer while adding body production for BMW (the 320 and 326 models, and the 320 Sport Cabriolet from 1938). Between 1936 and 1941, the company also took on the development and production of cabriolet bodies for three DKW models (the F5, F7 and F8). There was a single

Baur: Bodies on the eight-cylinder Horch chassis were something of a speciality in the mid-1930s. This 1935 Pullman Cabriolet on the 850 chassis was very much aimed at the wealthy and at political VIPs. *(VW-Audi)*

Baur: BMW turned to Baur for its "house" coupé bodies on the 502 chassis in the early 1950s. The design can be compared with the Autenrieth offering pictured on page 28. (BMW)

convertible saloon for the Ford V8 chassis in 1936, a Sport Cabriolet on the Lancia Aprilia from 1938 and a convertible Opel Admiral in 1939.

During the 1939-1945 war, the Baur workshops were turned over to the production of a variety of automotive items, including truck chassis, cable trucks, and power generators. Allied bombing of Stuttgart reduced the Baur factory to rubble and it was some years before Baur was once again a force within the German motor industry.

Nevertheless, from 1949 Baur was back in the game building bodies for the DKW F10 models, and also secured a contract from IFA in Soviet-controlled East Germany, who were constructing copies of pre-war DKWs in the old Horch factory at Zwickau. Baur's role was to provide a more modern design of body for limited numbers of these cars on the revived pre-war F8 chassis. This business lasted until 1952,

and between 1950 and 1953 Baur was also involved with the development and production of the Dyna Panhard Veritas.

However, Baur's return to the forefront of German coachbuilding began in 1953 with a contract to supply the bodies for the new BMW 501 saloon. This was followed in 1954 by the contract to design and build the "house" two-door coupés and both two-door and four-door cabriolets on the 501 and 502 chassis. Contracts with Maico (for the short-lived 500) and Auto Union (for the 1000 SP) followed in 1956 and 1957 respectively.

The early 1960s brought body production for the BMW 700 convertible (2597 built) and subsequently the 700 LS coupé, and in 1963-1964 Baur also built the hood assemblies for the DKW F12 convertible. The close relationship with BMW was strengthened further from 1967, with the arrival of the convertible 1600 (1682 built, 1967-1971), and later 2002 as well (200 built, 1971).

Even though the relationship with BMW remained fundamental to Baur's business in the 1970s, the company also worked for other German car makers. From 1973 to 1979 it built the bodyshells for the Bitter CD coupés, and from 1976 it handled the Opel Kadett Aero convertible bodies. Baur also gained the contract for the little-known Bitter Aero that was based on the Kadett. The Baur BMWs of the 1970s began with the safety-conscious "Top Cabriolet" on the 2002 with its fixed rollover bar. (The basic design was similar to Porsche's Targa style, but that name could not be used because it was protected as a trademark.) It was no doubt on BMW's recommendation that Baur built the dozen BMW Diana conversions of the 2002ti

Baur: The Top Cabriolet on the BMW E21 3 Series became a catalogued model. (David Hodges Collection)

bb Auto: The
Porsche 928 Targa
caused a stir at
the 1979 Frankfurt
Motor Show.
(Author's Collection)

for BMW dealer and former racing driver Hubert Hahne in 1971. Then came the 1978 Top Cabriolet on the E21 3 Series. Initially an aftermarket conversion, the model was quickly taken on as a catalogued BMW variant although Baur continued to build it and constructed 4595 examples before production ended in 1982.

The 1980s also saw Baur working for Audi and for Porsche. For the former, they built suspension assemblies for the Quattro between 1980 and 1991, and the carbon Kevlar bodies for the lightweight Sport Quattro from 1984. Between 1985 and 1988 they constructed the bodyshells for the Porsche 959 and assembled the complete cars on their own assembly line. Most of Porsche's special-order interior leatherwork was also done at Baur, and it was Baur who built the prototype 944 cabriolets in the late 1980s.

For BMW, Baur's work in the 1980s began with the bodies for the BMW 7 Series saloons, a task which ran from 1978 to 1987. Between 1983 and 1991, it was a Baur-designed cabriolet body on the second-generation E30 3 Series, although this time the bodies – more than 14,000 of them – were actually constructed by BMW themselves in both Germany and South Africa. Though Baur also built a prototype Top Cabriolet for the E36 3 Series in 1987, BMW chose instead to build its own full cabriolet design, awarding Baur the contract for final assembly of the Z1 sports car and the construction of its space-frame. This work lasted from 1989 to 1991. Returning to the charge, Baur made its Top Cabriolet available as a limited-volume conversion between 1992 and 1996. The car retained the four doors and window frames of the standard saloon.

However, a gradually diminishing volume of work from the major German manufacturers saw Baur in financial difficulties by the middle of the 1990s, and in 1998 the larger part of the company was sold to IVM Automotive, which in turn was sold to the Swedish Semcon company in 2007. Baur's work since 1998 has largely been out of the limelight, as the company has focused on prototype work for companies such as Audi, Ford and Porsche. Nevertheless, at the Geneva Show in February 2002 it emerged briefly from the shadows with a convertible based on the Mercedes-Benz G-Class; this G-Cabrio XL also featured a lengthened body.

Baxter-Gallé (F)
Late 1920s, Paris

The Baxter-Gallé company had premises on the Champs-Élysées in Paris and was an offshoot of the coachbuilder Gallé *(qv)* in the late 1920s. It is known to have bodied a Packard chassis and displayed this at the 1930 Paris Salon.

bb Auto (D)
1973–1986, Frankfurt-am-Main

The brothers Rainer and Dieter Buchmann established their business in 1973 as bb Auto Exclusive Service KG and initially specialised in special paintwork and interiors for Porsche models. However, from 1976 they also began modifying the bodywork, and a notable example was the so-called Flatnose version of the 911 Turbo which borrowed its pop-up headlights from the contemporary 928. There were also major modifications for the Volkswagen Polo and Golf models.

From 1978, the Buchmann brothers became more ambitious and worked with Eberhard Schulz to produce a complete car – CW311 "dream car" that was then the fastest road car in the world. From the start of the 1980s, bb also began working with Mercedes-Benz. A striking early work was the "1930s look" 600 model built for King Khalid of Saudi Arabia, and from 1985 there was the Magic Top Mercedes-Benz; this was a C126 S Class coupé with a retractable roof section, of which ten were built. Work

bb Auto: This retro-styled limousine was created from one of the final Mercedes-Benz 600 limousines, and featured a lengthened wheelbase as well as the obvious body modifications.
(Author's Collection)

bb Auto: The Magic Top Mercedes was essentially an SEC coupé with a retractable roof section. (*WikiMedia Commons/ NearEMPTiness*)

on Porsches continued, too, and a sensation at the 1979 Frankfurt Show was a targa-top 928 model, with completely restyled rear end and high-quality audio units installed in the targa bar. Five were made.

However, bb – officially bb GmbH & Co KG Autos since the early 1980s – was hit hard as the demand for exotic one-offs collapsed in mid-decade and the company filed for bankruptcy in spring 1986. More recently, Rainer Buchmann launched a comeback for the company when he presented the "bb Moonracer" based on a 1980 Porsche 911 Targa at the Frankfurt Motor Show in September 2014.

Beer (D)
1920s, Zwickau

Very little information is available about the Karosseriewerk Beer, which is known to have built a saloon body on an Audi chassis in 1923 and a delivery van body on an Ego chassis the following year.

Belvallette: A "coupé limousine" on a Hispano-Suiza chassis. (*David Burgess-Wise*)

Belvallette (F)
1892–1933

Jean Baptiste Belvallette built horse-drawn vehicles in Boulogne from 1804. His two sons followed him, one remaining with the Boulogne business and the other moving to Paris in 1850. The former's son married a daughter of Charles Binder and then established his own business at Neuilly, with an address at 21 Rue Duret. Alfred Belvallette's first bodywork was for a Panhard et Levassor chassis in 1892, which made him one of the very first French builders of car bodywork. Early Belvallette bodies were distinguished by innovations, among them a system of rubber mounting blocks designed to reduce the transmission of noise and vibration into the body. From 1910, aluminium panels were used to reduce weight, and by 1914 Belvallette was building close to 400 bodies a year.

Belvallette & Cie resumed coachbuilding after the Great War, and pioneered the use of the Baehr transformable body patents with an exhibit at the 1919 Paris Salon. In 1925 the company bought out the Mühlbacher coachworks, and then took over the clientele of the Rothschild coachworks. From 1927 Jean Belvallette took over the business from his

Belvallette: A Voisin wearing a "torpedo transformable" body built according to Baehr patents. (David Burgess-Wise)

father, continuing the policy of bodying top-quality chassis by the likes of Delage, Hispano-Suiza, Renault, Rolls-Royce and Voisin. Sadly, it was this close alliance with the luxury end of the market that ultimately ruined Belvalette; the business was unable to survive the Depression and closed down in 1933.

Bérard (F)
1991 on
Bérard Automobile Design was established in 1991 and worked on transformations of volume-produced cars, including the Mercedes-Benz SLK, from premises at 18 Rue Bourgneuf in Saint-Étienne. In more recent years, Bruno Bérard has moved into other areas of design.

Bernath (CH)
1938–1946, La Chaux de Fonds
Willy Bernath built a total of 24 cabriolet bodies in eight years as a carrossier. All were on pre-1940 chassis, and the

Bernath: Seen here in unrestored condition is this striking drophead coupé on a 1933 Alfa Romeo 6C 1750 chassis, with the firm's characteristic wide horizontal grille and concealed headlamps. (Nikolaus Scheerbarth-Clasen)

majority were rebodies. Just three are known to exist today, a 1933 Alfa Romeo, a 1938 Citroën and a 1938 SS Jaguar.

Bernath was born at La Chaux de Fonds in the Swiss canton of Neuenberg, and went to Germany in the early 1930s where he learned the craft of panel-making as an apprentice in Hamburg. He finished his apprenticeship in Zurich and took up his chosen trade, but for a time his first love was skiing, at which he was a champion performer. He spent some months in the USA, where the latest trends in car body design made a big impression on him. Returning to La Chaux de Fonds, he joined the body shop that his father had founded in 1924. From 1938 he began building complete bodies to customer order as Auto Carrosserie Willy Bernath.

Characteristic of the Bernath bodies were full-width grilles, sometimes with the headlights concealed behind them and sometimes with the lights integrated into the chromed grille bars. These were some of the earliest horizontal grille designs. Both front and rear wings flowed into the main body, and there were wheel spats on some bodies; sometimes these were on the front as well as the rear wings. Bernath liked pointed bonnets, with a chrome strip to mark them off from the lower body; sometimes, the chrome strip ran the full length of the body as well. Body frames were made of steel tube, over which Bernath added aluminium panels, and the construction method has sometimes been likened to the Superleggera design from Touring. Other influences on the designs were Pinin Farina and Hermann Graber, and the Bernath cabriolets often included a touch of Art Deco as well.

Almost all the chassis bodied by Bernath were European: Alfa Romeo, Citroën, Fiat, Jaguar, Lancia, Mercedes-Benz and Talbot-Lago. Though the company continued working during the Second World War, it built very few bodies after 1945. The last was in 1946, probably on an Auburn 851 chassis dating from 1936. That year, the Bernath company became insolvent and closed. Willy Bernath himself became a car dealer in the Jura canton, and died in 1991.

Bertin-Cholet (F)
1980s, Rugles

Bertin-Cholet Carrossiers Constructeurs were at Rugles in the Eure region of France, and specialised in specialist conversions of Citroën and related Peugeot products in the 1980s. They worked on GS and C35 models, but were best known for a cabriolet-cum-pick-up conversion of the related Citroën LNA Entreprise and Peugeot 104 ZS models that was available in 1983-1984. These conversions had factory approval, and came as either Marina or Targa types, the latter being the luxury model. No more than about 10 of the Citroën version are thought to have been built, further production being inhibited when Talbot announced a volume-produced cabriolet aimed at the same market.

Bertone (I)
1912–2014, Turin

Carrozzeria Bertone became one of Italy's most important coachbuilders during the 20th century, and the company's prolific output was matched by its influence internationally. Several major designers started their careers with Bertone, which began as a small coachbuilder and designer and went on to become a major player in the Italian motor industry, with its own large construction capacity as well.

Founder Giovanni Bertone came from a farming family. He had worked as a carriage wheelmaker, and from 1907 was employed at car-maker Diatto in Turin. In 1912, he set up his own carriage building and repair shop in the Corsa Pesciera. Though forced to close his business during the Great War, Bertone started up again when peace returned and expanded his activities to include car bodywork. He moved to new and larger premises at Monginevro in 1920, with 20 staff.

In 1921, Carrozzeria Bertone signed its first major contract, for a torpedo-type body on the SPA 23S chassis. Next came work for Fiat, with the Fiat 501 Sport Siluro Corsa competition car. Well-located at the centre of the emerging Italian car industry in Turin, Bertone began

Bertone: A Ceirano awaits panelling in the workshops, 1921.
(Giles Chapman)

Bertone: Dating from the early 1930s, a typically neat cabriolet design for the Fiat 508 Balilla chassis. *(Fiat)*

Bertone: The young Nuccio Bertone showed a sure hand in his cabriolet design for the Lancia Aprilia of the later 1930s. *(Lancia)*

building bodies for Aurea, Chiribiri, Diatto, Fast and SCAT. He was soon working with the city's two largest car makers, Fiat and Lancia.

Lancia work in particular furthered Bertone's career. Vincenzo Lancia commissioned him to carry out small-batch production of special bodies on standard chassis. However, when Lancia asked for a metal monocoque body in large volumes, Bertone felt that it would go against his skills as a coachbuilder. Lancia built their own body plant to do the job, and not surprisingly were putting fewer commissions out to Bertone by the end of the decade. Although the Lancia work did not dry up altogether – Bertone bodied 1928's Lambda VIII Series – and there were individual commissions for private customers, the business was in a precarious state by the end of the decade.

Bertone survived by taking on repair work and moving into commercial bodywork as well. In 1932 Giovanni's son Giuseppe (known as Nuccio) joined the business, and their determination to return it to health was helped when Fiat introduced the little Balilla in 1933, so giving Bertone the chance of creating a variety of new bodies on this popular chassis. Nuccio Bertone toured the length and breadth of Italy promoting the company's business, and his efforts were successful. As the coachbuilding work increased, so the business took on more staff and moved into larger premises at 225 Corso Peschiera.

For Bertone, the 1930s were characterised by several innovative and bold designs, such as the 1934 Fiat 527S Ardita 2500 with its striking headlamps faired into the bonnet sides, and the Fiat 1500 Aerodinamica of 1937. The latter also showcased Nuccio Bertone's talent as a designer, and later designs such as the Lancia Aprilia Cabriolet and the Fiat 1500 Torpedo made clear that the younger Bertone would have a great deal to offer.

Bertone: Not quite every design was a winner. This 1948 cabriolet on the Fiat 1100 chassis shows American influences and is surprisingly dumpy, if nonetheless neat. *(Fiat)*

The 1939-1945 war saw Bertone obliged to build for the military, an example being an ambulance on the Lancia Artena chassis. But coachbuilding did not stop altogether, and Bertone constructed a few bodies on Lancia Aprilia chassis and a notable special cabriolet on a Fiat 2800, commissioned for the racing driver Giovanni Lurani Cernuschi.

Recovery was slow after the war ended; there were few chassis to be had from Italian car makers. So Nuccio Bertone spent his time as an amateur racing driver, an activity that also brought him some valuable motor industry contacts. Although Carrozzeria Bertone built a few bodies on Fiat chassis, the company was effectively moribund. As a last ditch attempt to keep the business alive, Giovanni and Nuccio bought a pair of MG TDs and clothed them with new bodywork in time for the 1952 Turin motor show. The gamble paid off: US importer Stanley Arnolt placed an order for around 100 bodies on the later MG TF chassis, and followed this a year later with orders for a design on the Bristol 404 chassis.

Bertone: This Stanguellini Berlinetta from 1953 used a front end design also deployed for a Fiat 1100 TV roadster. *(David Hodges Collection)*

By this time, two important things had happened. Nuccio Bertone had taken over the reins of the company from his father in 1950, and in 1952 he had engaged the talented Franco Scaglione as head of design. The designs for Arnolt attracted attention, and 1953 marked the beginning of a fruitful relationship with Alfa Romeo, beginning with the Giulietta Sprint that was intended on its introduction in 1954 for a limited run of 1000 cars. In fact the car would become Bertone's staple product for more than a decade, and nearly 40,000 were built before production ended in 1965.

Encouraged by Nuccio Bertone's willingness to push the boundaries of design, Scaglione also designed the stunning series of aerodynamic show cars for Alfa Romeo, the three Berlinetta Aerodinamica Tecnica (BAT) models that gained Bertone international acclaim between 1953 and 1955. Further aerodynamic research led to the Abarth 750 Record, which set ten world records at Monza in 1956.

For NSU in Germany, Bertone designed the Sport Prinz, and the production of this car from 1957 demanded further expansion. A new factory was opened at Grugliasco on the outskirts of Turin in 1959; by now, Bertone had 550 employees. The end of the 1950s also saw a series of milestone sports berlinetta models, notably the Alfa Romeo Giulietta Sprint Special, the Aston Martin DB2/4 and the Maserati 3500GT.

Scaglione's successor at Bertone was Giorgetto Giugiaro, who was in charge of design from 1959 to 1965 and later became a leading designer and coachbuilder in his own right. Giugiaro helped Bertone to define the Italianate GT that became popular internationally in the early 1960s. Notable designs from the company were the Alfa Romeo 2600GT (and the later Gordon Keeble which looks just like it), a pair of Ferrari 250GTs, the Maserati 5000GT and a special body on the Aston Martin DB4 GT that was known as the Jet and became Nuccio Bertone's personal transport.

Bertone: The three BAT cars (the letters stood for Berlina Aerodynamica Tecnica) were part of an experiment conducted for Alfa Romeo. This is the 1953 BAT5, the first one turned into a full-size car. (*WikiMedia Commons/Gregory Moine*)

Meanwhile, for Simca in France there was the 1000 Coupé, and for BMW in Germany the elegant but low-volume 3200CS. Bertone also designed the promising ASA 1000, also known as the "Ferrarina", which sadly never reached the market. A link with Iso led to the Iso-Rivolta GT 300 and 340 models, and to the Grifo, and there was interest from the USA as well when Chevrolet commissioned the Corvair Testudo, which nevertheless remained a show car.

For Alfa Romeo, Bertone did the Canguro show car, and followed this in 1965 by the production Giulia GT. There was a slightly unhappy coupé design for the Jaguar S-type, too.

Marcello Gandini took Giugiaro's place as chief designer in 1965, and led the Bertone design studios until 1980. Meanwhile, major commercial success came with the Fiat 850 Spider, of which Bertone built nearly 140,000 between 1965 and 1972. Production was ramped up yet again to cope with the demand, and between 1966 and 1968 Bertone's

Bertone: Designed by Franco Scaglione, the 1954 Arnolt-Bristol coupé announced Bertone's return as a major force in the automotive design world. (*David Hodges Collection*)

Bertone: Scaglione's sure touch delivered this prototype Alfa Romeo Giulietta Spider in 1956, but the car maker chose a Pinin Farina design for production. *(David Hodges Collection)*

Bertone: Very much Bertone and not very Jaguar, this 1957 body on an XK150 chassis has similarities to other Bertone creations on chassis such as the Maserati 3500GT. *(David Hodges Collection)*

body output increased by around 40%. This allowed the company to continue attracting international attention with exotic designs, such as the Lamborghini Miura in 1966, and the 1967 Marzal and 1968 Espada for the same maker. Regular customers included Alfa Romeo and Fiat, for whom Bertone designed the Montreal and Dino Coupé respectively in 1967. Another ground-breaking concept was the futuristic 1968 Carabo, built on the chassis of an Alfa 33.

By the start of the 1970s, the Grugliasco factory had a 1500-strong workforce. There was more work early in the decade for Lamborghini, as the Espada was followed by the Jarama and the Urraco. At the 1970 Turin Show, Bertone presented the stunning Lancia Stratos Zero concept, which went on to inspire aspects of the Lancia Stratos Stradale rally coupé.

Founder Giovanni Bertone died in 1972, aged 88. That year, the Fiat 850 Spider gave way to the Bertone-designed X1/9, which became another major commercial success with 160,000 examples built over 16 years. However, the oil crisis of 1973-1974 persuaded the company to switch focus from supercars to practical everyday models, and although there were more concepts and supercar designs, Bertone increasingly began to look at city cars as well. So after 1972's Maserati Khamsin and 1973's Ferrari 308 GT4 and breathtaking Lamborghini Countach came the Audi 50 and Innocenti Mini 90 in 1974. The Fiat Abarth 131 Rally followed in 1975, and the prototype Alfa Romeo Navajo in 1976. A link with Volvo led to the 262C model of 1977, which is sometimes seen as one of Bertone's less aesthetically successful designs but which was important commercially for the company, which took on the entire manufacture of

Bertone: Still utterly distinctive more than five decades after it was new, this is the Alfa Romeo Giulietta Sprint Speciale. The design was the culmination of some late 1950s ideas; a 1960 model is shown. *(Author's Collection)*

Bertone: The 1962 Iso Rivolta GT coupé was another striking design. *(David Hodges Collection)*

Bertone: From the drawing board of chief stylist Giugiaro came the 1965 Iso Grifo coupé. *(David Hodges Collection)*

Bertone: The 1966 Spyder version of the ASA GT showed Bertone's effortless ability to achieve long and lean proportions. *(David Hodges Collection)*

Bertone: The public first became aware of new head stylist Marcello Gandini when his sleek coupé design for the Lamborghini Miura was announced in 1966. This is a later 1971 example. *(David Hodges Collection)*

Bertone: Combining elements of earlier show cars, the 1968 Lamborghini Espada was another Gandini design triumph. *(David Hodges Collection)*

the car in Turin. Many of these designs by Gandini had a distinctive angularity, reflected also in the Citroën BX that was released in 1982, and continuing to influence Bertone design as late as the 1987 Skoda Favorit.

The 1980s saw Bertone firmly established as a volume manufacturer of cars. From the start of the decade, the company took over responsibility for sales of the Fiat X1/9 and Ritmo Cabrio, as well as their manufacture. A joint venture with Volvo in 1985 led to the 780, a two-door saloon designed and built by Bertone, and from 1987 Bertone also handled production of the Opel Kadett Cabrio for GM Europe. Coupé and cabriolet versions of the Astra followed. A further interesting venture was the assembly of the Freeclimber off-road vehicle, in which Bertone combined a Daihatsu design with BMW engines under its own brand; there was a later Freeclimber II, as well. Other important design work was done for Citroën, who engaged

Bertone: The Lamborghini Jarama, seen here as a 1973 model in S guise, had some similarities in appearance to the 1969 Iso Lele. Both were designed by Marcello Gandini. *(David Hodges Collection)*

Bertone: Gandini's 1968 Carabo was a concept car built on an Alfa Romeo 33 Stradale platform. The car was an early pioneer of the wedge shapes popular in the 1970s and was less than a metre tall. Its pioneering scissor doors anticipated the Lamborghini Countach. *(David Hodges Collection)*

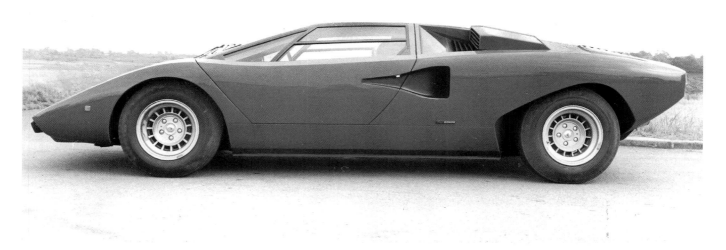

Bertone for the distinctive design of the BX saloon of 1982 and the XM saloon at the end of the decade.

Volume production at Bertone in the 1990s centred on cabriolet versions of the Opel Astra and Fiat Punto from 1993, and again Bertone carried out the full manufacturing process. Meanwhile, the company began to focus on the technological innovation needed for low environmental impact vehicles. The ZER (Zero Emission Record) of 1994 set records for electric cars after the Blitz barchetta concept of 1992 had pointed the way forward. 1994 also saw Gruppo Bertone become the first manufacturer in Italy to be awarded the ISO 9001 quality certification. Meanwhile, concept cars continued to promote the company's design skills: the Karisma, a four-seater berlinetta on a Porsche base, the Kayak in 1995, a coupé on a Lancia K base, the Slalom 'coupé de chasse' on an Opel Calibra base, and the Enduro 4x4, an SUV based on the Fiat Brava.

Bertone: Gandini pulled it off again with his design for the Lamborghini Countach, first seen in prototype form (as here) in 1971 and available in production from 1973. *(David Hodges Collection)*

Sadly, Nuccio Bertone died on 26 February 1997, and his widow Lilli took over the running of what was by now known as Gruppo Bertone (the Bertone Group). The first decade of the new century was a less happy one for Bertone. It built the slow-selling C1 motorcycle for BMW between 2000 and 2002 but, like other "contract" manufacturers such as Karmann and Baur in Germany, the company found its work drying up, and was eventually forced into bankruptcy. Only the Stile Bertone design centre survived, and the Grugliasco factory was sold to Fiat in 2009. The workforce was reduced to around 300. In 2008 designer Jason Castriota moved from Pininfarina to become Bertone's design chief, but he left after less than a year and was replaced by Mike Robinson.

Bertone: The firm's first design for Maserati was the Khamsin of 1974, again by Marcello Gandini. This is a later car, with the louvred nose added in 1977. (David Hodges Collection)

Bertone: The Lamborghini Jalpa represented Bertone supercar styling from 1981. (David Hodges Collection)

Bertone: The other side of the Bertone business was the production of low-volume derivatives of mainstream cars. This is the company's cabriolet conversion of the Fiat Ritmo (Strada in the UK) dating from 1983.

In May 2011, Stile Bertone was obliged by the Italian bankruptcy court to sell off six concept cars from its museum in order to raise money for its survival. By summer 2014, it was all over, although the licensing rights of the Bertone brand had been sold in 2013 to a Milanese company called Bertone Design which intended to revive the brand in various fields outside the automobile industry.

Besset (F)
1920–1940, Annonay

Carrosserie Besset was established as a wagon-maker at Annonay in the Ardèche by Joseph Besset in 1913. From 1920, Besset turned to car bodies, his first being on a Roland Pillain chassis. Like many other small coachbuilders, he took out a licence for Baehr transformable bodies, and during the 1920s built coachwork on a variety of chassis. These included Berliet, De Dion Bouton, Delage, Delahaye, Diatto, Farman, Hispano-Suiza, Peugeot, Renault, Rochet-Schneider and Voisin. One of its last car bodies was for a Bugatti Type 57, which featured the Vutotal windscreen design patented by Labourdette.

However, from 1927 Besset turned increasingly to bus bodies, suspecting that mass-produced cars would damage the traditional coachbuilding trade. During the 1930s, he developed new methods of construction and from 1938 turned definitively to bus bodywork. A downturn in business persuaded Jospeh Besset to retire in 1951, but the business continued and, after several changes of name, survives today at the heart of the Iveco empire.

Beutler (CH)
1946–1987, Thun

The Swiss coachbuilder Gebrüder Beutler (which translates as Beutler Brothers) was active mainly in the late 1940s and 1950s. Both Fritz Beutler, who specialised in panelwork, and younger brother Ernst, whose speciality was design, had learned their trade at the Ramseier coachworks in Worblaufen and, when the Second World War came to an end, they set up their own business at Thun, in the canton of Berne.

Like so many other Swiss coachbuilders of the period, Beutler was best known for coupé and cabriolet bodies.

Beutler: The firm bodied this Porsche 356 as a cabriolet in 1949.

Beutler: The Swiss coachbuilder's take on a Jaguar XK120 dates from 1952, and presents a very different picture from the factory original. (Author's Collection)

Its earliest bodies were cabriolets on Salmson and Healey chassis, and then in 1948-1949, the company was commissioned to build six of the eight Porsche cabriolet prototypes. The volume contract, however, went to Gäser (qv) in Stuttgart. Beutler's first coupé was on a Bristol 401 in 1949, and in 1950 there followed a Bristol cabriolet to a very different design. There were also some re-bodies in this period, on pre-war BMW 328 chassis.

In the 1940s and 1950s, the brothers constructed bodywork on Austin Atlantic, Bentley, Bristol, Jaguar, Jowett, Lancia, Packard and Simca models, among others. Most were one-off designs, such as a Citroën 15-Six Traction Avant coupé in 1953 and a DS cabriolet in 1959.

Beutler: This coupé design on the six-cylinder Citroën Traction Avant remained unique. (Citroën)

Beutler: The firm's characteristic lines are again in evidence on this 1957 Volkswagen coupé, which also has a Porsche 356 engine. (WikiMedia Commons/ Detectandpreserve)

More numerous were conversions of the VW Beetle, which Beutler would convert into a pick-up, and there were even estate conversions, although these were overtaken by the appearance of VW's own Type 2.

Beutler also built a number of 2+2 coupés on the VW Beetle from 1954. However, these never received factory recognition, and in consequence the supply of chassis was restricted, which in turn limited the numbers Beutler could build. Nevertheless, the design was refined over the years, and Beutler even produced different versions for the European and American markets, the latter having a wider grille, sharper tail fins and over-riders on the bumpers. By the end of the decade, this design had achieved quite wide renown. There were a few similar bodies on Porsche 356, too.

Between 1957 and the early 1960s, Beutler also built six coupé bodies on BMWs, perhaps not least because that company's big saloons still had a separate chassis on which the traditional work of a coachbuilder could be performed. However, the 1960s were hard times for coachbuilders in Switzerland, and Beutler changed the focus of its business

Beutler: This late 1950s coupé design for the V8-engined BMWs always looked a little old-fashioned. There were minor variations from one example to the next. (*BMW*)

to bodywork repairs. In the 1970s, the company worked with the Worblaufen coachworks to create a body from original drawings for a 1930s Bugatti chassis, but that was a highlight. Fritz Beutler died in 1986, and his brother closed the business for good in 1987.

Bierhake (D)
Late 1950s, Babenhausen
The Bierhake company, based in Babenhausen near Bielefeld, is known for a pair of identical ambulance bodies on BMW V8 chassis that it constructed in 1958. One of these, a 501 V8 which left the BMW works in January 1956, was apparently fitted with a six-cylinder engine as part of its transformation. The bodywork was lengthened by around 20cm, but the chassis was not altered. Other known details suggest that this vehicle, at least, was created on a very tight budget.

Billeter et Cartier (F)
1919–c1940, Lyons
Billeter & Cartier set up their business in 1901 close to the Rochet-Schneider factory at Lyons, and forged links with

that company which remained close until the end. Briefly renamed Quantin & Billeter in 1917, the company returned to its old name in 1919. It was one of many coachbuilders to take out a licence for the Baehr patents.

Although Rochet-Schneider chassis formed the bulk of the Billeter & Cartier business before the car maker turned to commercial and bus chassis in 1932, there were many prestigious bodies on other chassis. The company built some bodies on Bugatti, and in 1933 there was a striking high-roof limousine on a Renault Vivastella for pioneer cinematographers, the Lumière brothers. The link with Rochet-Schneider remained strong, and Billeter & Cartier constructed a number of commercial and bus bodies for that company, but did not survive the Second World War.

Binder (F)
1902–1939, Paris
The Parisian coachbuilder Henry Binder was one of France's leading exponents of the art for nearly 40 years. Never avant-garde in his designs but always elegant, Binder bodied only top-quality chassis from the beginning.

The Binder coachbuilding story goes right back to 1806, when the saddle-maker Johann Jakob Binder left his native Wurttemburg for Paris. The carriage works he opened there employed 400 workers by the middle of the century and enjoyed the patronage of royalty and nobility as well as the upper middle classes in all the major countries of Europe. Henry Binder was the youngest son of the family, and around 1860 he founded his own coachworks in the Rue Colisée near the Champs-Elysées. On his death in 1901, the company passed to Maurice Cottenet, an Arts et Métiers engineer who had joined the business in 1880 and now retained the established trading name of Carrosserie Henry Binder.

There were still horse-drawn carriages before the Great War, but from 1920 the Binder business plunged into

Binder: Formal and imposing in the Binder tradition, this saloon on a Panhard et Levassor X31 chassis dates from 1921. *(David Hodges Collection)*

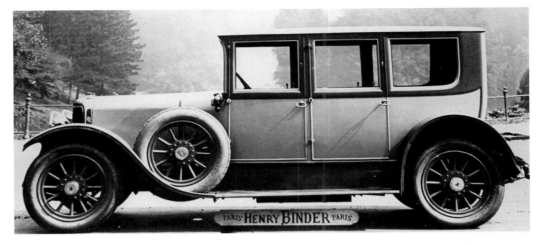

Binder: Built on a Peugeot 184 chassis from 1928-1929, this was a "transformable" body. *(David Hodges Collection)*

Binder: This coupé de ville with folding hood was one of the types for which the firm was well known. The chassis is a Renault Reinastella from 1930. *(Author's Collection)*

Binder: This coupé de ville body with more conventional fixed roof was built on a 1930 Hispano-Suiza chassis. *(Author's Collection)*

building coachwork for the leading car chassis of the day. Although they held a Baehr licence, most Binder bodies were saloons, limousines and coupés de ville – there were few torpedos – and Binder's reputation put the company at the very top level of French coachbuilding. From 1928, Léon Aboucaya took charge of the business.

Despite the contraction of the coachbuilding market in the 1930s, Binder continued to do well. The company bodied some 200 Hispano-Suiza chassis, and its grand and formal bodies were found on chassis by Bentley, Delage, Mercedes-Benz, Minerva, Panhard & Levassor, Peugeot,

Binder: Another formal body, this time on a Panhard 8DS dating from 1932. (*Author's Collection*)

Binder: In the coachbuilder's own photograph, this is a coupé de ville on a 1936 Hispano-Suiza K6 chassis. (*Author's Collection*)

Binder: Mounted on a later Renault Reinastella chassis, this elegant coupé de ville again shows the coachbuilder's sure touch. (*David Hodges Collection*)

Renault, Rolls-Royce and Voisin. Famously, Binder also built bodies for two of the six Bugatti Type 41 Royales, one being the 1931 Coupé de Ville and the other a conversion of the Esders roadster to a coupé de ville in 1939.

When war broke out in September 1939, Binder immediately closed its workshops. After the war was over, it did not resume its coachwork activities but instead joined forces with coachbuilder Janssen in 1946 to become Binder-Janssen and sell GM cars, especially Cadillacs. This business continued into the 1960s, but the coachworks business was formally closed down for good in 1951.

Binz (D)

1936–present, Lorch

The Binz company is known primarily for its specialist commercial bodywork, which embraces ambulances, hearses and military vehicles, but it also has a long-standing relationship with Mercedes-Benz, for whom it builds extended-wheelbase limousines.

Michael Binz had worked for Daimler and for the coachbuilder Baur before he founded his own company in 1936 as the Lorcher Karosseriefabrik Binz & Co in Lorch. The company grew quickly, and between 1936 and 1945,

Binz: This was the Binz ambulance body for the Mercedes-Benz "Ponton" models of the 1950s. The same design was adaptable to estate car use. *(Daimler-Benz)*

the Binz works built mainly taxis, trucks and cabriolet conversions of standard production cars, along with a few ambulances. Between 1945 and 1955 its primary work was building lorry cabs for a number of German manufacturers.

The 1950s saw the company working closely with Mercedes-Benz on a variety of special bodywork for that company's cars. There were ambulances, taxis, long-wheelbase conversions, estate conversions of the W186 "Adenauer" limousine, and pick-up conversions (for export) of the medium-sized Ponton saloons. A few BMW saloons were also turned into ambulances, and between 1954 and 1958 Binz even built its own motor scooters.

Collaboration with Mercedes-Benz intensified during the 1960s, and Binz continued to construct ambulance and long-wheelbase derivatives of the company's cars. A new factory was constructed at Ilmenau in 1991, although development remained at Lorch. Binz is today known as Binz GmbH & Co. KG. It builds all the catalogued Mercedes-Benz long-wheelbase limousines derived from standard production saloons, and continues to make hearses and other special bodies for Mercedes-Benz cars.

Blaser (CH)
1927–1939, Burgdorf

Walter Blaser did his apprenticeship as a wagon maker, and worked briefly in that business before setting up his own workshop in Burgdorf to build bodies for motor vehicles in 1927. The company turned its hand to whatever was required, and early products included a tractor cab and a body modification for a Model T Ford. However, there were also individual car bodies on a number of chassis, including Delage, Ford and Martini.

In 1933, Blaser was joined by Johannes Burkhardt, who took over the administrative side of the business. Within a few years, Burkhardt had become an equal partner with Blaser, and the company was renamed Blaser & Burkhardt. It continued to build commercial bodies, and in the later 1930s specialised in tippers and trailers, but there were also several cabriolet bodies built as individual commissions.

Binz: Broadly similar in concept was the van body for the Mercedes "Ponton". *(Daimler-Benz)*

Notable was an elegant cabriolet on Ford V8 chassis that was exhibited at Geneva in 1935. Its key characteristic was a fully-disappearing hood, which folded into the boot to leave the rear of the body uncluttered. Similar designs were also built on Chevrolet and Delage chassis. The Ford V8 remained a favourite for Blaser & Burkhardt's work, and the company built a variety of bodies for it, ranging from cabriolets to limousines and even vans. Grander chassis also passed through the Burgdorf workshops: there were some bodies on Mercedes-Benz and even two on Rolls-Royce. Of the latter, one was a 20/25 chassis that was bodied as a hotel taxi, and the other a Phantom that was bodied as a limousine.

The outbreak of war in 1939 disrupted the business. Blaser & Burkhardt employed a number of Austrians, who were summoned back to their home country to join the military. The two principals of the company also fell out with one another, to such an extent that Walter Blaser decided to leave the company he had founded. For a time during the war years, he worked for the coachbuilder Gangloff. Many years later, he returned to Burgdorf and made a business from building such things as bus seats.

Johannes Burkhardt meanwhile renamed the company Burkhardt & Cie, and remained in business at Burgdorf until 1956. Under him, the company built no more car bodies, but focussed exclusively on the commercial vehicle market.

Blaser & Burkhardt (CH)

See Blaser.

Bloch & Fernandez (F)

c1928–1932, Paris

This short-lived Parisian coachbuilder united Marcel Bloch (who became Marcel Dassault of aircraft fame) with the banker J Fernandez. When Bloch chose to move into the aircraft industry, Fernandez briefly carried on alone, then joined forces with Howard Darrin in 1932 to form Fernandez & Darrin. Known coachwork from Carrosserie Bloch & Fernandez includes a coupé transformable on Panhard et Levassor 35 CV chassis.

Boano (I)

1954–1957, Grugliasco

Felice Mario Boano, usually known as Mario, learned the coachbuilding trade with Carrozzeria Ghia. When Giacinto Ghia died in 1944, Boano was one of the two employees designated as his successors, and together with Giorgio Alberti he took over at the helm.

At Ghia, Boano worked on several pioneering low-roofline designs with Luigi Segre. Among these were the 1950 Lancia Aurelia, the 1953 Karmann Ghia (for Volkswagen), a number of berlinetta bodies on the Ferrari

Boano: This early (1955) design was for the Abarth 1100 model. *(David Hodges Collection)*

Boano: American designer Raymond Loewy commissioned the company to build one of his designs on a Jaguar XK140 chassis in 1956. *(Author's Collection)*

166 Inter and some Alfa Romeos. However, in 1953 Boano decided to leave Ghia and set up on his own.

He established Carrozzeria Boano at Grugliasco in 1954, together with his son Gian Paolo and Luciano Pollo. Initial work was for Alfa Romeo, but Boano soon moved on to other brands, such as Abarth and Ferrari. The Ferrari relationship began early: in 1954, Boano was commissioned to construct a coupé body for the 250 Europa to a design by Raymond Loewy, but after objections by Pinin Farina (Ferrari's favoured coachbuilder) the project was cancelled and the strikingly unusual body was modified to fit a Jaguar XK140 chassis. The car was then displayed at the 1955 Paris Salon. So the first Boano-bodied Ferrari was a one-off 250 GT cabriolet in 1956, and in that year the company took over some of the 250 GT body production from Pinin Farina, using a design close to that of Pinin Farina's 250 GT Europa prototypes. There were 63 of these in all. An interesting exercise was a one-off body designed by Raymond Loewy for his own use, and built by Boano on the chassis of a Jaguar XK140 in 1956.

However, in 1957, Boano was offered the chance to establish a new styling studio at Fiat in Turin. The opportunity was too good to miss, so he brought production at his own company to an end and closed it. The work was passed on to his partner Luciano Pollo and his son-in-law,

Boano: Alfa Romeo 1900 Super coupé, 1955.

Boano: The firm created this body on a 1955 Alfa Romeo 1900 Super Sprint.

Boano: Volume work came from Ferrari, for whom Boano built 250GT coupés to a Pinin Farina design. This is a 1957 car. *(Author's Collection)*

Ezio Ellena, who had been employed at the Boano works. These two established a new company, Carrozzeria Ellena.

Böbel (D)
1950s, Laupheim
Very little is known about this coachbuilder, which built the pillarless saloon bodies for the Wendax 750 car in 1950-1951 and also built prototype bodies for the Champion 250 and Trippel SK10 of the same period.

Boldt & Lieske (D)
1919–1928, Berlin
Karosserie-Werke Boldt & Lieske specialised in conversion work, especially turning saloon cars into dual-purpose vehicles. Sometimes a simple box was added at the rear, and sometimes a platform for carrying items. In its later years, the company also undertook some cabriolet conversions. Some sources give the company's dates as 1923 to 1927.

Boneschi (I)
1919–present, Milan
Carrozzeria Boneschi was always primarily associated with Italian car makers, although it also built a limited number of bodies on other chassis. The company was active as a builder of car bodies between 1919 and the 1960s, and subsequently became a builder of commercial vehicle bodies. It has since built just one prototype car body for Lancia, the marque with which it was always most closely associated.

The Boneschi company was founded in Milan by Giovanni Boneschi in 1919. Its initial focus was on coachwork for luxury cars, but success proved elusive. Then in 1922, the Milanese Lancia dealer Enrico Minetti suggested to Boneschi that special bodywork on the new Lancia Lambda chassis might find a ready audience. He was right, and Boneschi built a limited number of bodies for the new model. Between 1924 and 1926, Boneschi also worked with the Italian branch of Citroen, but then returned to Lancia chassis. The later 1920s and the 1930s saw some of Boneschi's best-known creations, on the Dilambda, Astura and Aprilia chassis, and from 1933 the company moved to new premises at Cambiago.

Allied bombing destroyed the Boneschi factory during the Second World War and, although it was rebuilt in 1946, Boneschi himself died that same year. Direction of the business passed to Bruno Pezzaglia, who had been the works manager and chief designer. He steered the business in a new direction, establishing a link with Alfa Romeo and focusing on that company's 6C 2500 chassis from 1952. Among the Boneschi creations were some saloons for political figures of the time, and then from 1953 the company built a small series of special bodies on the 1900 chassis. There was work for Fiat, too, with the wooden-framed Giardinetta station wagon on the 1100 chassis from

Boneschi: The company was lined up to build the convertible bodies on the post-war Isotta-Fraschini 8C chassis with rear-mounted engine. Sadly, only prototypes were built.

Boneschi: A cabriolet body on the Fiat 1400 in 1950. (David Burgess-Wise)

Boneschi: The firm's interpretation of the Maserati 3500GT.

Boneschi: Alfa Romeo 6C 2500S with cabriolet body, 1950. The side grilles seem a little overblown and there are tinted perspex panels above the windscreen.

1949, and Boneschi was not too proud to turn down a commission for a special Fiat 1100-based publicity vehicle in 1951. This was for toothpaste manufacturer Binaca, and the vehicle's body was shaped like a toothpaste tube.

The link with Lancia had not been broken, however, and in 1953 Boneschi began building special bodies for the Aurelia B53 series. From 1957, there was then a small series of "Weekendina" station wagons on the Alfa Romeo Giulietta. The early 1960s brought work for Alfa Romeo (some convertibles and coupés on the 2600 chassis) and

Lancia (a Flaminia Spyder Amalfi in 1962, with a design by Rodolfo Bonetto). But coachwork commissions were drying up, and Boneschi was taken over by the Milan-based Savio arm of the Fiat Group, to be turned into a maker of commercial vehicle bodies. Since then, the Boneschi name has made a single appearance on a car body, which was that of the 1987 Lancia Thema Gazzella coupé prototype. Its Cambiago factory was sold in 2006, and Boneschi now exists only as a name within Fiat's Savio Group.

Boniolo Design (I)
1975–present, Padua

Boniolo Design was founded as an industrial design agency by Francesco Boniolo, and works in a number of fields in addition to that of automotive design. It has worked with a number of major Italian car makers as well as with Ford and Volvo, and has produced a number of concept designs. These include the Coupé Goal, Ferrari Mamba, the Soleado

Cross-country vehicle, the SUV Invader and (in 1981) the Michelotto Ferrari 308 GT/M IMSA competition car, of which three were built. In 2007, the company also designed a shooting brake conversion of the Aston Martin Vanquish (called the EG after its owner's initials) which was constructed by restoration specialist Quality Cars of Barbariga di Vigonza.

Boulogne (Arthur Boulogne) (F)
1920s, Levallois-Perret

La Carrosserie Arthur Boulogne was based at 5 Boulevard Bineau in Levallois-Perret and mainly bodied medium-sized cars from the likes of Delage and Panhard et Levassor. The company was active throughout the 1920s but appears not to have survived the Depression.

Boulogne (Eugène Boulogne) (F)
1900s–late 1920s, Levallois-Perret

Carrosserie Eugène Boulogne et Fils had workshops at 54 Rue du Bois in Levallois-Perret but its offices were at 148 Rue de Courcelles in Paris' 17th Arrondissement. The company opened at the start of the 20th century and remained in business until the late 1920s.

Bouracq & De Costier (F)
1920s, Boulogne sur Seine

Little is known about this company, which seems to have created some quite showy bodies. In 1925, Bouracq & De Costier built a pair of mahogany-bodied Isotta Fraschini torpedos, and at the 1927 Paris Salon, the company showed a Hispano-Suiza torpedo and a Delahaye saloon upholstered with snakeskin. Other bodies from the company were for Bugatti chassis. The De Costier brothers parted company with Monsieur Bouracq in 1927 and kept the business going as De Costier Frères until 1931.

Bourgeois-Luchard (F)
1920s, Paris

This company was set up in 1919 by Paul Luchard as a car showroom in Paris, and was among the first Citroen dealers. During the 1920s, the company also built some luxury bodies, notably showing a limousine with division on Voisin 18CV chassis at the 1924 Paris Salon, along with a closed coupé on Citroën 5CV chassis that was specifically intended as a lady's car. Both bodies had a basketwork finish. It is unclear whether there were any more; Luchard focussed on his showroom business and the company closed in 1945.

Bourgois (F)
1920s, Levallois-Perret

Carrosserie Bourgois was another one of the myriad small coachbuilders who clustered around the Levallois-Perret district in the 1920s. The company was at 33 Rue Fazillau, where it specialised in fabric-panelled saloon bodies on chassis such as Delahaye and Hotchkiss.

Bouveret (F)
1930–1956, Andelot

The Bouveret involvement with coachbuilding goes right back to 1777 when Jean-Simon Bouveret began building horse-drawn vehicles at Andelot in the Jura region. His grandson Louis Bouveret joined the business around 1920, and the focus switched to car bodywork. During the 1930s, the garage at Rue du Maréchal-de-Lattre-de-Tassigny changed to become a body repair shop, changing again to a mechanical repair shop in 1956.

Brandone (F)
1923–1963, Cannes

Etienne Brandone learned his trade as a saddle-maker in Nice, moving to Lyons and the workshops of the coachbuilder Billeter & Cartier around 1911. In 1923 he set up in business with his brothers Pierre, a coachbuilder, and Dominique, a mechanic, creating Carrosserie Brandone at 69 Rue d'Antibes in Cannes.

The choice of Cannes was a shrewd one; the area was full of wealthy clients who saw the styles they wanted at concours d'élégance events and wanted a replica or near-replica made locally. So the Brandone business came to specialise in exactly that, which has sometimes confused the attribution of its products in later years. Not that Brandone lacked creativity as well, as a few individual bodies bear witness; it was simply that the overwhelming demand was for copies of the great Parisian coachbuilders' work. There was no change in the approach when Etienne Brandone's son Pierre joined the business in 1930, gradually assuming a more and more important rôle in its running.

Brandone's first car body was on a Peugeot chassis. In the inter-war years, the company clothed chassis by Alfa Romeo, Ballot, Bugatti, Citroën, Delahaye, Hispano-Suiza, Minerva, Rolls-Royce and Voisin – the grandeur of this list coming naturally from the preferences of the company's wealthy clients. Some of these cars won prizes at concours events on the Riviera.

During the war, Brandone built about 40 electric cars under the Electraph name, advertising these both from its address in Cannes and from addresses in Paris (79 Avenue des Champs-Elysées and 24 Rue Quentin-Bauchart). After 1945, Brandone returned to the charge, building bodies on Alfa Romeo 1500, Delahaye 148L, Ford Vedette, Peugeot 402 and Talbot T23 models. As the demand for coachbuilt bodies declined, so Brandone's business ended, although Pierre Brandone spent a period with the British coachbuilder James Young in 1952, where he was responsible for a striking Bentley sports saloon. The Brandone business was formally closed after Etienne died in 1963.

Brianza (I)
1932–c1939, Milan

Carrozzeria Brianza appears to have been founded by some former Zagato employees at a time when Zagato was going through a bad patch. Even Ugo Zagato himself acted as a

Brandone: An opulent yet relatively restrained drophead coupé on a 1930s Hispano-Suiza. (*David Burgess-Wise*)

consultant to the company while his own coachworks was briefly in liquidation, and Brianza was actually located in the old Zagato works at Viale Brianza – from which it clearly took its name.

Brianza exhibited some of its earliest bodies at the Milan show in April 1932, three on Alfa Romeo chassis and one on Maserati. These two companies would provide most of the work for Brianza over the next few years, and there were racing bodies on the small Maserati 4CS chassis as well as on larger Alfas, such as the 6C 1750 GS and the 8C 2300 Lungo. Brianza created just one roadster body for a road-going 4CS, and was responsible for the bodies on the special Alfa Romeo 8C 2600 Monza racers campaigned by Scuderia Ferrari.

As business became harder to get in the later 1930s, Brianza diversified its activities. Among other things, the company became an agent for Dux producer-gas systems, but it was unable to survive and had gone under by 1940.

Brichet (CH)
1920–1933, Geneva
Francois Brichet had worked with a number of Parisian coachbuilders before returning to his native Switzerland

and establishing his own coachworks in 1920. Although his early bodies were mainly open torpedo and tourer types, Brichet soon developed a broad range of offerings. He also moved on from everyday marques such as Amilcar and Citroën to clothe some of the grander chassis from about 1924, and these included Delage, Hotchkiss and even Rolls-Royce. Notable was a special faux-cabriolet body on a Mercedes-Benz S in around 1928, and there were bodies on American chassis as well after these became more readily available in Switzerland in the early 1930s. The reasons for the company's demise in 1933 are not clear.

Brissonneau & Lotz (F)
1950s, Creil
Brissonneau & Lotz is best known for its railway rolling stock, but after a new factory was built at La Rochelle in the 1950s, the original plant at Creil was turned over to car production. The car was designed by racing driver Louis Rosier and was a cabriolet, designed in conjunction with Italian coachbuilder Rocco Motto and used Renault 4 CV running gear. It was introduced at the 1956 Paris Salon and 220 examples were made before it became clear that the project lacked financial viability. The Creil factory was then sub-contracted to build bodies for the Renault Floride, and Brissonneau & Lotz ended its brief flirtation with the body building business.

Brissonneau & Lotz: The Louis Rosier cabriolet based on Renault 4CV running gear was the company's first attempt to get into car manufacture. *(David Hodges Collection)*

Broual (F)

See ACB.

Bruegge (D)

1920s?, Frankfurt-am-Main

The Bruegge name seems to have been used by the Gemeinschaft Deutscher Bruegge-Werkstätten for car bodywork in the 1920s, but no other information is available.

Buchmann (D)

See bb.

Buhne (D)

1919–1939, Berlin

Heinrich Buhne set up his coachworks in Berlin in 1919, and quickly moved from sub-contracting work to employing his own team of skilled men. The business specialised in bodies for taxicabs at first, and a large proportion of the taxis operating in Berlin during the 1920s were of Buhne origin. One basic body design suited multiple chassis, and there were examples on Adler, Ford, Opel, Pluto, Presto and Steyr chassis among others.

Buhne also built tourers on chassis such as Dixi, and for Hansa chassis offered a "Kombinationswagen" – a four-seat tourer whose rear compartment could be turned into a load bay when required. In the 1930s, Buhne built numerous bodies on the Berlin-assembled Ford V8 chassis. There were special coupés and limousines to individual order, too, on

chassis including Adler, Austro Daimler, Brennabor, Buick, Cadillac, Mercedes and Rolls-Royce.

The company survived the Second World War but the focus of its body building activities changed. In the 1940s Buhne built bodies for post office and police vehicles, probably mostly on Ford chassis. The company later became known for special advertising vehicles, with bodies shaped to resemble toothpaste tubes or cigarette packets. Buhne also became involved with hotel and department store interiors, and finally closed its doors in 2005.

Bunau-Varilla (F)

1925, Paris

Etienne Bunau-Varilla was the son of a civil engineer who had been involved with building the Panama Canal. A pioneer aviator and sportsman, he founded the Société de Vente des Automobiles Bugatti with a few friends in 1920 with a showroom at 116 Champs-Elysées, where Pierre de Vizcaya sold sports Bugattis. Convinced of the importance of aerodynamic coachwork, with which he had experimented on pedal cycles in 1910, in 1925 he showed a Panhard "transformable" at the Parc des Princes concours.

Busson (F)

1928–1933, Nanterre

Guillaume Busson was an early aviator and became a pioneer of semi-aerodynamic coachwork in the late 1920s, operating from premises at 6 Rue des Basses-Fontenelles in Nanterre. A particular Busson trait was rear wings that were blended as far as possible into the sides of the body. A remarkable faux cabriolet on Citroën C6 chassis in 1929 was probably as close to the post-1945 concept of envelope bodywork as anyone had come at the time, although it could hardly be described as elegant.

Busson's ideas appeared on several chassis, ranging from the small Rosengart 5CV up to a Rolls-Royce Twenty, for which he built a striking sports coupé body in 1928. A streamlined body for a Delahaye 138 record car in 1933 was also his but, discouraged by a generally cool public reception to his ideas, Busson decided to throw his lot in with Gaston Grümmer *(qv)*, and closed his own business.

Bunau-Varilla: This 1925 Panhard wears a pleasing tourer body with aerodynamic tail. *(David Burgess-Wise)*

Busson: This Citroën B14F cabriolet dating from around 1928 shows advanced design ideas for its time: note how the rear wings are minimised to allow maximum width in the body. *(Author's Collection)*

C

Candelaresi (F)

c1921–1935, Lyons

Candelaresi was one of the leading coachbuilders in Lyons during the 1920s, operating from premises at 76 Rue Neuve-de-la-Villardière. The company was noted for its American-style coachwork and built on chassis by local constructor Barron-Vialle as well as better-known marques. Some sources suggest the company did not survive beyond 1928, by which time it was building convertible saloon bodies to the Aérable style patented by Alin-Liautard. Others suggest that Candelaresi became less active in the early 1930s and closed in 1935.

Capella (E)

1852–1959, Barcelona

Carrocerias Capella was founded by Francisco Capella Riera in 1852, and was subsequently run by three more generations of the same family. Always based in Barcelona, the company became one of Spain's most important coachbuilders and was well known in continental Europe before the time of the Spanish Civil War.

Capella's son took over the business after his father's death in 1899, and guided its transition from horse-drawn to motor vehicles. By 1907, the company was working on Hispano-Suiza chassis and was also building bodies for public transport vehicles. By the 1920s, the founder's three grandsons were involved as well, and one, Fermin Capella, had gained a close knowledge of modern coachbuilding in France, where he had spent some time working at Kellner.

The 1920s and early 1930s were Capella's golden age, with coachwork of many different types on a wide variety of chassis. The company even scored some successes at concours d'élégance events held in France. Most of its work was on Spanish-made chassis, notably on Hispano-Suiza and Elizalde, plus a few for Ricart. However, there were examples on several French makes – Bugatti, Delage, Delahaye and Renault – and on British Austin and Rolls-Royce too. Capella became the Spanish importers of Chryslers at the start of the 1930s, and this gave them access to other American chassis. There would be examples of their work on Cadillac, Graham-Paige and Packard chassis in the next few years.

However, during the Spanish Civil War the company was nationalised and was obliged to construct armoured vehicles and the mobile-classroom bodies for the trucks of Franco's Catédras Ambulantes rural educational initiative. Spain became closed to imports, and Capella focussed on commercial bodywork but also rebodied some older car chassis with more modern styles to give them a new lease of life.

In the 1950s, the company became involved with a number of micro-car initiatives, building bodywork for such cars as the three-wheel Jurka. However, most of its

Capella: The car nearest the camera in this shot of a Capella showstand in the 1930s is a Phantom II Rolls-Royce.

work was now on commercial vehicles; the market for grand coachwork had disappeared. By 1957 Capella was building hearses and in 1959 the company closed down for good.

Carde (F)

1900–1920s, Bordeaux

The Carde company was founded in 1860 and by 1900 – when it began making both cars (a short-lived venture) and motor bodies – had a staff of 1250, making it one of Bordeaux's biggest employers. It even had a branch at Saragossa in Spain. In

the 1920s Gustave Carde made "Frégoli" bodies for locally-assembled Model T Fords. Named after a vaudeville quick-change artist, the "Frégoli" was an ingenious "transformable" body which could be converted from a car into a truck, but was unusual in that its sides were planked in mahogany. Carde also built ambulances for the Russian front at his Bordeaux-Bastide factory during the Great War.

Carlsson (D)

1989–present, Gut Wiesenhof

Carlsson Autotechnik GmbH is not only a modifier of bodywork but has also created a popular range of alloy wheels and a number of performance enhancements. The company has always specialised in Mercedes-Benz models, but has also produced performance conversions for Citroën, Honda and Toyota.

The company was founded in 1989 by brothers Rolf and Andreas Hartge, with premises at Gut Wiesenhof, a manor house near Merzig in south-west Germany. It took its name from Swedish rally driver Ingvar Carlsson, who was a successful driver for the Mercedes-Benz rally team.

Carlsson initially offered only mild body modifications and interior changes. In 2006, it began a new push into the US market, and from 2007, the company embarked on a coachbuilding programme with fashion designer Etienne Aigner. Their first joint work was a coachbuilt Mercedes-Benz CL 65 coupé, called the Carlsson Aigner CK65 RS Eau Rouge and finished in two-tone paint. (Eau Rouge is the famous corner at the Spa Francorchamps race track in Belgium.) Then at the 2010 Geneva Show Carlsson presented a rebodied (and, of course, performance-tuned) Mercedes-Benz SL600 called the C25. Less ambitious Carlsson modifications remain available for every model in the current Mercedes-Benz range.

Carrosserie de Boulogne (F)
1920s, Boulogne-sur-Seine
The Carrosserie de Boulogne had premises at 55 Rue de Sèvres in Boulogne-sur-Seine. It is known to have built bodies on Unic chassis and on a 1924 Lorraine-Dietrich.

Carrosserie Française (F)
1920s
There is almost no information about this French coachbuilder, except that it constructed an elegant "torpédo ponté" body on a 1924 Delage chassis.

Carrosserie Générale Automobile (F)
c1920–c1934, Courbevoie
The Carrosserie Générale Automobile had premises at 10 Rue de l'Abreuvoir at Courbevoie. It is known to have built several bodies for Delage, and as late as June 1934 constructed the body on a Bugatti 57 chassis. The company is generally thought to have closed not long afterwards.

Carrosserie Industrielle (F)
c1903–1920s, Paris and Courbevoie
The Etablissements de la Carrosserie Industrielle had two addresses in Paris. These were 10-12 Rue Tourneux, and 17-19 Rue de Seine in Courbevoie. The company is known for bodywork on a 1903 Darracq 8hp and on a 1920 Grégoire 132B torpédo.

Carrosserie Moderne (F)
1920s
This company is known to have collaborated with Georges Messier, building a fabric-bodied saloon with aluminium bonnet for one of the Messier cars with their technically advanced air suspension systems in the later 1920s.

Carrosserie Parisienne de Bordeaux (F)
1920s, Bordeaux
Based in Bordeaux but clearly feeling the need for a link with the more prestigious city of Paris, this coachbuilder used the Baehr patents during the 1920s.

Carrosserie Profilée (F)
1920s, Courbevoie
La Carrosserie Profilée was another one of the myriad establishments in the Courbevoie area of the Parisian suburbs. Its address was 16 Rue Armand Sylvestre. As the company name suggests, its focus was on modern coachwork styles. Notable was a drophead body on a Bugatti Type 30, designed by Jean de Vizcaya and built in 1926.

Carrosserie Universelle (F)
Late 1920s, Neuilly-sur-Seine
Based at Neuilly-sur-Seine, La Carrosserie Universelle took over the business of the Valéry company (qv) in the late 1920s.

Car Système Style (F)
1981-1989, Redon
Car Système Style was a trading name of Concept Auto SA, based at 12 Quai Jean-Bart in Redon (Ile-et-Vilaine). The company was founded by stylist Gérald Maillard and engineer Patrick Faucher and was known for its modified Renault 4 and Renault 6 models, which were turned into open buggies, lightened and given greater ground clearance. From 1984, Yves Rousteau joined the business and work began on the Belle-Ile pick-up, which was based on a Renault 5 and was ready by 1988. About 90 were built (all painted blue) before the company closed in 1989; the design was subsequently taken on by Gruau, who built a further 500 with slight modifications.

Caruna (CH)
1964–2006, Dietikon
The name of Caruna came from the German description of what this Swiss company did: CARrosserie Und NeuAnfertigung (Coachwork and New Build). More formally Carrosserie Caruna AG, it was based at 10A Bergstrasse in Dietikon, near Zurich.

Established in 1964, Caruna first attracted attention in 1969 with the Caruna Spider, a somewhat odd-looking roadster with a VW chassis and a Porsche 914 engine. This was built in small numbers until 1974. A variety of open models followed, such as the Caruna Staccato, which was another rather odd-looking two-seater. However, the company then switched from creating complete cars to modifying existing designs, and 1977 brought an attractive

Caruna: Convertible derivatives of the Mercedes W126 were a speciality. (*Author's Collection*)

cabriolet on the Datsun 180B SSS which was built in small numbers. Caruna tried working on US cars, too, and produced an open version of the Pontiac Firebird.

Between 1980 and 1987, Caruna was particularly noted for convertible derivatives of the Mercedes-Benz W126 S-Class models. However, by the 1990s the focus of its work had changed, and Caruna was working on such things as sliding doors for minibuses. The company finally closed on 30 June 2006.

Castagna (I)
1849–1954 & 1994–present, Milan

Carrozzeria Castagna was a highly regarded Milanese coachbuilder in the 1920s and 1930s, who constructed high-quality bodies on most of the prestige chassis of the period.

The company can trace its origins back to 1849, when Carlo Castagna took over the horse-drawn vehicle business of his employer, a Signor Ferrari. By the turn of the century, the company had begun to build car bodies, its first being

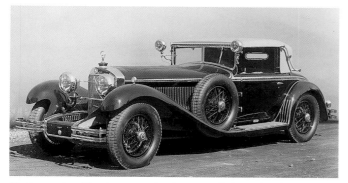

Castagna: Looking heavy and rather grand, this cabriolet was built on a Mercedes SS chassis. *(Daimler-Benz)*

Castagna: The upright look of this transformable saloon hints at both American and Germanic influence. The chassis is a supercharged Mercedes-Benz from the late 1920s. *(Daimler-Benz)*

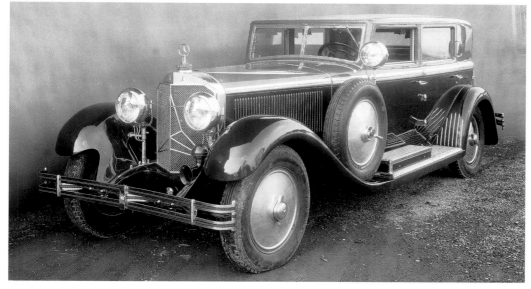

Castagna: Another late-1920s supercharged Mercedes, in this case a 630K: again the look is both upright and heavy, and suggestive of American and German influences. *(Daimler-Benz)*

Castagna: 1935 Four-seat cabriolet on the Alfa Romeo 6C 2300 GT series B.

on a Benz quadricycle, and had soon built some notable examples. By 1915, Carlo Catagna had passed the business over to his son, Ercole, who intensified the focus on top-of-the-range chassis. By 1920, Castagna had become Italy's largest carrozzeria, with around 400 employees.

Ercole Castagna rode the glamorous celebrity culture of the time, and made a point of selling his cars to film stars, royalty and even the pope. Castagna bodies were found on chassis such as Alfa Romeo, Daimler, Duesenberg, Hispano-Suiza, Isotta Fraschini, Lancia and Mercedes-Benz. A Castagna characteristic was ornate grille decorations.

However, the 1930s were less happy. The collapse of the US economy at the start of the decade took away one of Castagna's largest markets, and the wider effects of the Depression saw the company enter a difficult period. After the Second World War, Castagna was unable to regain its old markets as demand for special coachbuilding diminished, and the demise of Isotta Fraschini in 1949 removed the company's major client. The company closed in 1954.

The Carrozzeria Castagna name was revived in 1994 by Italian businessman Umberto Pietra, although there was no connection to the old company beyond the name. Pietra commissioned Gioacchino Acampora to design a striking concept car based on the Alfa Romeo SZ, and displayed it at the Geneva Motor Show in March 1995. The car was called the Vittoria, after Pietra's daughter. Between 2004 and 2011, Carrozzeria Castagna also built a small series of special versions of the BMW Mini, and from 2008 there were special conversions of the Fiat 500 as well.

Cesare Sala (I)
1887–1933, Milan

Carrozzeria Cesare Sala was established in Milan in 1887 as a carriage-maker. It built carriages for members of the Austrian aristocracy, but began building car bodies at the start of the 20th century as the popularity of the new motorized transport began to grow.

The company was already recognized as a creator of the very finest coachwork, so it was no surprise to find that Cesare Sala was soon building bodies on the most prestigious Italian car chassis. There were elegant and opulent examples on Alfa Romeo, Fiat, Lancia and Isotta Fraschini. However, operating at the top end of the business, Cesare Sala was unable to survive the effects of the Great Depression, and the company closed its doors in 1933.

Chapelle & Jabouille (F)
c1930, Paris

Chapelle & Jabouille Carrossiers were located in the Levallois district of Paris and are known to have built bodywork on Citroën C6 chassis.

Chappe & Gessalin (F)
1950–1974, Saint-Maur-des-Fossés

Carrosserie Chappe was founded around 1930 but its car coachwork activities belong to the period after World War II. It was a pioneer of lightweight coachwork, particularly using GRP, and was associated with French sporting marques such as Alpine and Deutsch-Bonnet, and with the Panhard CD.

In 1946, Amédée Gessalin joined his three brothers-in-law, Abel, Albert and Louis Chappe, in the business at Saint-Maur-des-Fossés; some years later, his son Jean Gessalin would take over from his father on the latter's death. Chappe Frères et Gessalin built lorry cabs for Delahaye and ran a car repair business, but in the early 1950s began to create lightweight bodywork for competition specials. From 1954, the company became closely involved with the nascent

Cesare Sala: Fairly typical of grand Italian coachwork of the late 1920s is the body on this Isotta-Fraschini 8ASS, the performance version of the manufacturer's powerful eight-cylinder model. (WikiMedia Commons/Luc106)

Alpine marque, and over the next decade built bodywork for the A106 and A108 models. It also worked with less well-known makers, such as UMAP and Arista, as well as René Bonnet and Panhard. From 1960, the company moved to new premises at Brie-Comte-Robert.

The growth of Alpine saw Chappe & Gessalin edged out of the business, and so they decided to create a rival marque using Simca running-gear. From 1966, they began to build the CG 1000, which later evolved with larger engines. Production ended in April 1974 after 517 CG cars had been built, and the company closed.

Chapron (F)
1919–1985, Neuilly-sur-Seine; later Levallois

Chapron was one of the great French coachbuilders of the 20th century, noted for his restrained good taste and supreme elegance. The coachbuilder produced both unique bodies to order and small-run conversions, and it was to Chapron that successive French Presidents turned for their official limousines and parade cars in the period from 1950.

Henri Chapron established his company at Neuilly-sur-Seine in August 1919, and initially specialised in bodywork for Ford Model T chassis, although he built bodies for many

Chapron: This well-resolved cabriolet is on a 1932 Delage D8S chassis. *(David Hodges Collection)*

Chapron: This time on the Delahaye 135 chassis, Chapron again demonstrates his mastery of proportion with a cabriolet body. *(David Hodges Collection)*

Chapron: Delahaye again, and this time the body is an attractive "coach", or two-door saloon. (*David Hodges Collection*)

Chapron: This cabriolet body is on a post-war Delahaye chassis from 1951-1952. Chapron had clearly adapted well to post-war styling trends. (*David Hodges Collection*)

Chapron: The chassis is a Delahaye 235MS from 1953, and the coupé body is, as always, beautifully proportioned. (*Salon Privé*)

Chapron: 1954 Hotchkiss Manceau saloon, relatively up to date but hardly inspiring.

Chapron: A rare failure: the lines of this cabriolet body on a 1956 Grégoire chassis seem unhappy. Nevertheless, Chapron supposedly built ten like it. (*David Hodges Collection*)

other marques as well. In December 1923, he decided to move to nearby Levallois, and by the end of that decade was working on the grand French chassis of the day, from the likes of Delage, Hotchkiss, and Talbot. However, it was from 1935 that Chapron's real reputation was established, after he produced a pillarless saloon on the new Delahaye 135 chassis for that year's Paris Motor Show.

Always tasteful and restrained despite the contemporary taste for flamboyance, Chapron focussed on Delahaye chassis while working on almost all the other grandes marques of the day; Cadillac, La Salle and Rolls-Royce were among the marques he worked on, and his designs were particulary appreciated in Britain, where he regularly exhibited at the London Motor Show.

Chapron: The mid-1950s were not Chapron's best period. Here, he was asked to modify a Bentley Continental into a cabriolet with a more modern rear wing line. *(David Hodges Collection)*

Chapron: A series of conversions based on the Citroën DS put the firm back in the limelight from the late 1950s. This is a La Croisette cabriolet from 1958; Chapron would later be responsible for the "factory" DS convertibles. *(Author's Collection)*

Chapron: This sleek coupé was the Le Paris model, again dating from 1958. *(Author's Collection)*

Chapron: The coachbuilder's name was prominently applied to these Citroën conversions. (Author's Collection)

Chapron: A one-off cabriolet built from a Rover 3-litre in 1962. (Chapron)

Chapron: If France had had a royal coachbuilder, it would have been Chapron. This is one of two special parade cabriolets built for presidential use on the basis of the Citroën SM in the 1970s. (Citroën)

After World War II, Chapron's close association with the Delahaye marque continued. The coachbuilder did not rush to embrace new design trends, but assimilated elements of them gradually, blending modernity and conservatism in some exceptionally pleasing designs. From 1952, it was a Chapron design that became the standard body on the Delahaye 253 chassis, and there was work on Delage, Hotchkiss and Salmson models too. But the market for traditional French "grands routiers" was declining rapidly, and Chapron recognised that to stay in business he would have to work on mass-produced models. So from 1955 his choice fell on the new Citroën DS – mass-produced but technologically advanced and therefore respectable in a way that few other mass-produced cars of the time were.

Over the next six years, Chapron constructed no fewer than 389 special DS convertibles and coupés, all built by hand and with multiple variations to suit the taste of individual customers. Then from 1961, he began

producing a standardised two-door "décapotable" that was sold through Citroën dealerships as a catalogued model, building 1365 examples before production was halted in 1971. When the Citroën SM was introduced in 1970, Chapron created two special variants of his own, but these were produced only to order, and there were just seven Mylord convertibles (which revived a Chapron name from the 1930s) and eight four-door Opera saloons. This close association with Citroën earned Chapron a formidable reputation as a creator of elegant convertibles, and it was to him that Rover turned in 1962 for a convertible design exercise on their 3-litre saloon.

Notable Presidential conversions in this period were a convertible limousine in 1956 based on a 15-Six for René Coty, and a 1968 extended DS Présidentielle for the De Gaulle government. In 1972, Chapron constructed two SM Presidential models for Georges Pompidou, and these cars remained in use right through until the mid-1990s.

As late as 1976, Chapron was still coming up with new ideas, and that year exhibited special versions of the small Peugeot 104 ZS and larger 604 saloon. Henri Chapron himself died in 1978, but his widow continued to run the company for a few more years. In this latter period, it retained close links with Citroën, building some luxury derivatives of the CX model. The Chapron business finally closed in 1985; it had become heavily dependent on prototype work for Renault, and had no option but to close its doors when that company took the work back in-house.

Charles (F)
1920s, Villeurbanne
The coachbuilder E Charles is known to have built a transformable body on a Voisin C3 chassis in 1925. The company's address was 25 Cours Tolstoï in Villeurbanne (Rhône).

Chatellard (F)
1930s, Toulouse

Carrosserie Chatellard is known from a single example of coachwork dating from the inter-war period. The company was based in Toulouse.

Chaussende (F)
1899–1920 Lyon

Monsieur Chaussende set up a coachworks at Villeurbanne, near Lyon, in 1899 and formed links with Lyon area chassis makers Pilain and Cottin-Desgouttes. The company survived only briefly into the post-war era, forming an alliance with Faurax (qv) in late 1919.

Chausson (F)
1907–2007, Asnières; later Courbevoie

Chausson Frères was established in 1907 by brothers Gaston and Jules Chausson at 28 Rue Malakoff in Asnières (Hauts-de-Seine). The company's original business was the production of cooling radiators, and this continued to expand until the early 1930s. Meanwhile, Chausson had moved to 11 Avenue Dubonnet in the heart of the Courbevoie motor industry near Paris.

Following the Depression, Chausson decided it was prudent to look for additional lines of business, and began by taking out a licence to build Coquille trunks for cars. It capitalised on Ford's move into Europe, and in 1934 obtained the contract to build all-steel bodies for the new Matford marque. Between 1936 and 1940, the company built around 24,000 bodies for these cars, and in the same period took over the Chenard & Walcker factory at Gennevilliers where it built a further 5700 similar bodies for that marque. There were bodies for Citroën in this period, too.

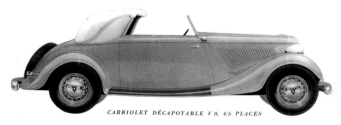

CABRIOLET DÉCAPOTABLE V 8, 4/5 PLACES

Chausson: In the second half of the 1930s Chausson built thousands of bodies on Ford chassis. This is a 4/5-seat V8 cabriolet, which would wear the French Matford badge.

During the Second World War, Chausson began building buses, and this activity continued after the war, accompanied by the construction of lorry cabs. To its earlier association with Ford, Chausson added a new one with Simca, turning out many thousands of standard bodies for that marque before 1963. Chausson built the GRP bodies for the Deutsch-Bonnet HBR5 between 1953 and 1957, opening a special department for the purpose. A further new factory was opened at Reims in 1957. There was more volume-building work for Panhard and Renault (the Floride coupé and cabriolet) in this period, and it was to Chausson that Citroën turned for the shells of its SM range from 1970. In 1972, Chausson acquired the old Brissonneau & Lotz factory at Creil, where it took over assembly of the Opel GT. That same year, it opened a new factory at Gennevilliers.

Chausson then became involved in prototype construction for a number of European makers, and during the 1980s forged several links with design studios. However, these attempts did not prosper and by 1990 Chausson was reducing its size, first closing factories at Asnières and Meudon, then the Gennevilliers plant in 1993 and the Creil plant in 1995. The business lasted until 2007, when the remaining factories were closed – exactly a century after the firm had been established.

Chavet (F)
1920s, Neuilly

Carrosserie Marcel Chavet was a small French coachbuilder of the 1920s, with premises at Neuilly. The company held a Weymann licence and used that system for some of its closed bodies, which were generally unadventurous in design.

Chesnot (F)
To early 1920s, Courbevoie

The coachworks of G Chesnot were at 93-101 Boulevard Saint-Denis and at the Rue Hudri in Courbevoie. It is not clear when the company opened for business or when it ceased operations, but Chesnot appears to have bodied a 1910 Delage TR as well as a 1912 Lorraine-Dietrich SLF and a 1920 Piccard-Pictet R2.

Chevalier (F)
1920s, Lille

Chevalier was the Voisin concessionaire in Lille, and is known for an imposing-looking torpedo body on a 1926 Voisin C3L chassis.

Chiattone (CH)
c1914–c1930, Lugano

A Chiattone was a Swiss constructor of bodywork based in Lugano. The company is known to have been building both touring car and ambulance bodywork on Benz chassis around 1914, but is best known for its bodywork on Bugatti chassis, notably a cabriolet on a 1930 Type 49 chassis.

Clabot (F)
c1946–1950s, Alfortville

Robert De Clabot set up his coachworks at 15 bis, Rue du Pont d'Ivry at Alfortville (Val-de-Marne). His primary business was in conversions based on the Citroën Traction Avant cabriolet, most notably with variations on a heavily chromed "shark-nose" style that was clearly inspired by the 1938 Graham. This same design was available for other models, and at least one is known to have been built on a Delage D8.

Clabot: This extraordinary post-war Traction Avant cabriolet shows clear influence of the 1938 Graham. (Author's Collection)

Clairalpax (F)

Clairalpax was not a coachbuilder but a patented coachwork design using aluminium pillars. It was invented by the coachbuilder Audineau (qv).

Clauzet (F)

c1959–1960s, Bretagne-de-Marsan

This French provincial coachbuilder attempted to make his mark with angular and ungainly bodywork for the Citroën 2CV that he displayed at the Paris Motor Show in 1959. Atelier de Carrosserie Métallique Albert Clauzet was at Bretagne-de-Marsan (Landes), on the Route de Grenade, and in 1960 he followed up with his own interpretations of the Panhard Dyna and Borgward Isabella. All three designs probably remained unique.

Clauzet: The Clauzet 2CV was certainly different, but not pretty. (Author's Collection)

Cloché (F)

1920s, Neuilly

Almost nothing is known about the coachbuilder Cloché from Neuilly. The company is known to have created a torpedo body on Delahaye 102M chassis, but that is all.

Coenen (NL)

1940s–1970s?, The Hague and Utrecht

The WF Coenen company of The Hague was always best known for the sunroofs in which it specialised from the late 1940s, and for such accessories as radiator blinds. However, in the late 1940s and early 1950s it also carried out some rolltop saloon conversions, notably on the Citroën Traction Avant although one was also done on a 1952 Austin A40. The Coenen sunroof patents later passed to Hollandia at Vermeulen, and today Coenen continues in business as a bodyshop.

Coggiola (I)

1966–present, Turin

Sergio Coggiola spent 14 years with Ghia, initially as a designer and latterly as chief of the prototype build department. In 1966, he left to set up his own business near Turin and specialise in the production of prototype vehicles. Among other things, his work has focused on fatigue behaviour and torsional rigidity in body design.

Early contract work was for Saab in Sweden, and Coggiola worked on the Sonett III that was in production from 1970 to 1974. He also built the prototypes for the Saab 98 Combi-Coupé in 1974-1976, but this did not go forward to production. From 1978 the company had some involvement with the Saab 9000, which became a production model in 1985 and lasted until 1998. Coggiola also worked on the Lancia Thema Coupé, which shared its Type Four platform with the Saab 9000 (as well as the Alfa Romeo 164 and Fiat Croma).

Coggiola has constructed a number of concept cars for major manufacturers, including the Dunja Lancia Fulvia HF (done with Glasurit and designer Sessano) and the 1971 Volvo Coupé ESC. Work for Fiat has included the Punto Surf and Brava Sentiero, while the company also had an involvement with the Volvo 262C (which was ultimately attributed to Bertone) and, with Paul Farago, on the Pontiac CF 428.

Cognat & Piot (F)
1912–1921, Lyons

JS Cognat and A Piot set up their coachworks in April 1912, taking over from the Roesch company which claimed to be Lyons' oldest coachbuilder. Cognat & Piot had two addresses, at 30 Rue Duguesclin and 40 Rue Montbernard, the latter being the workshops. The Peugeot museum has a 1911 Type 127 bodied as a torpedo by this company, which became Piot & Barbary in 1921 when the principals changed.

Colli (I)
1931–1973, Milan

Giuseppe Colli set up Carrozzeria Colli in Milan in 1931, together with his four sons, Mario, Candido, Beniamino and Tarcisio. The company built both racing and touring bodies, specialising in the use of aluminium.

Its first cars were racers that used Fiat 1100 mechanical elements, and these were followed by others based on the engines and running-gear of Fiat 500s and Lancia Astura and Aprilia cars. During the Second World War, Colli's workshops were turned over to aircraft work.

Returning to the coachwork business after 1945, the company built a prototype "flying car", the Aerauto PL 5C in 1946. There were a couple of bodies on Alfa Romeo 6C 2500SS chassis, others on the Lancia Aprilia, a Fiat 6C 1500, and a Fiat 500 barchetta for the 1947 Villa d'Este event. In the 1950s, Carrozzeria Colli worked with Alfa Romeo on cars like the 6C 3000, and a one-off body on the Disco Volante, while retaining its racing links through the 1955 Arzani-

Volpini that used a twin-supercharged Maserati engine. The 1960s were mainly occupied with more work for Alfa Romeo, constructing estate cars on the Giulietta and Giulia.

Contamin (F)
Late 1940s

Contamin was a manufacturer of crane cabs, but in the late 1940s bodied a single Talbot Lago T26 GS chassis as a sports coupé. The car was driven at Le Mans in 1949 and 1950 by André Chambas and André Morel.

Coune (B)
1962–1970, Brussels

Although the Brussels coachbuilder Jacques Coune made his name with some strikingly handsome special bodies in the 1960s, he had actually been in business since the middle of the previous decade, maintaining mostly quality and sports cars from a workshop in the Kroonlaan (Avenue de la Couronne). In the beginning, he had worked for his father's business, Central Pièces Auto, which had specialised in imported parts after the Second World War and also assembled Panhards for the Belgian market.

Jacques Coune's own business embraced agencies for the Abarth and Iso makes, and his showroom was in the same building as the famous Garage Francorchamps, which later became one of his most important sales outlets. In the early 1960s he became a co-founder of the Ecurie Nationale Belge, which campaigned Abarths and Ferraris. It was for this team that Coune bodied an unsuccessful Formula 1 car

Colli: One of a couple of coupés on the Alfa Romeo 6C 2500SS bodied by Colli. This one is from 1951.

Coune: There were probably only ever four of these Volvo cabriolets, all built in 1963. (Author's Collection)

Colli: Estate, "Giardinetta", version of the Alfa Romeo Giulietta 1300, 1957.

Coune: The Belgian coachbuilder built a few estate conversions of the BMW 1800 in the 1960s. (Author's Collection)

Coune: The MGB Berlinette, of which 56 were made.

that combined an Emeryson chassis with a Maserati engine and was driven by Lucien Bianchi in 1963.

Many of Coune's employees were specialist coachbuilders from northern Italy, and with such skills readily available it was a natural step for him to move into the construction of special bodies. Among his first creations were some open versions of the Volvo 122S, a two-seater roadster and four four-seater cabriolets. He made some estate cars, too, notably from BMW 700 and BMW 1800 models, and then a very well-resolved design in 1964 on a Mercedes 300SE. Other estates included a Peugeot 404, and Coune produced a series of hardtops to suit open DKW, Fiat 1500 and MGB models. From 1963 to 1965, Coune displayed his latest creations at the annual Brussels Autosalon.

However, his best known creation was undoubtedly the MGB Berlinette, of which 56 were made before BMC put their own MGB GT coupé into production. The car was a major attraction at the Brussels Autosalon in 1964, but its pronounced Italian styling influences persuaded MG management not to take it as a catalogued model. The car remained in production at the Coune workshops until 1968. In the mean time, Coune had designed a targa-roofed MGB variant called the Gemini Spider in 1966 (which remained unique), and in 1967 had moved to new premises at Vanderkindere in Brussels.

Meanwhile, as the Italian economy gradually improved, so Coune lost many of his skilled Italian staff, who returned to their homeland. Among his final projects was a Peugeot 204 Coupé de Ville, and in 1970 he closed the coachbuilding business.

Crouzier (F)
c1925–1936, Moulins

Carrosserie Crouzier Frères was established at Moulins (Allier), initially at 163 bis Rue de Bourgogne and later

on the Route Paris-Nice. The company held licences for Weymann fabric bodywork, for the Baehr "transformable" patents and for the Clairalpax patents of Paul Audineau. In the mid-1920s, Crouzier was successful in Concours d'Elégance events at Vichy and Deauville, but was never widely known. Known bodies were a Weymann-type Brougham on Panhard 10 CV chassis, a so-called cubist Bugatti, and a roadster on Peugeot 401 chassis for the actress Mistinguett, the latter in 1935.

Currus (F)
1902–1975, Paris

Carrosserie Currus was established in 1902 when the old-established Perrotin & Bollinger coachbuilding company passed into new ownership and began to add motor car bodies to its traditional horse-drawn fare. The company was initially based in Paris's 13th Arrondissement, at the Rue Poliveau but with showrooms in the Boulevard de l'Hôpital.

From 1906, Currus formed an alliance with Carrosserie Rolland (formerly Chastel & David) and moved to new premises at 16-18 Rue Watteau. Early bodies included a small series of torpedos on Citroën B2 chassis, designed by Labourdette; later examples of this body were mounted on B14 chassis. However, Currus also worked on more prestigious chassis in the 1920s, such as Delahaye, Hispano-Suiza and Panhard & Levassor.

Touring coach bodywork had been part of the Currus business since the early days, and from the early 1930s the company focussed increasingly on this and on commercial bodies. A single body on Delahaye 175 chassis in 1950 did not lead to a revival of the car bodying business, and Currus was better known in the following decades for special bodywork on police vehicles, as well as its buses, coaches and lorries. The two Currus factories, by then at Mâcon and Ivry, finally closed in 1975.

D

D3 (F)
1986–present, Paris
D3 was founded by Bernard Pène in 1986 and has mainly been involved in the creation of prototypes and concept cars for the likes of Citroën, Renault and Hyundai. The company was absorbed into the Matra group in 2002 and subsequently into the Pininfarina group in 2003.

Dannenhauer & Stauss (D)
1950–1957, Stuttgart
In the 1930s, Gottfried Dannenhauer was with Reutter in Stuttgart, where he worked on some of the early Volkswagen prototypes. After the war, he set up a body shop with his son-in-law, Kurt Stauss. They specialised in repair work initially, but they had wider ambitions.

These were realised with the body for a Volkswagen-based sports cabriolet. The design came from two designers called Wagner and Oswald, who had studied under streamlining pioneer Wunibald Kamm and had already built a prototype streamlined Volkswagen. This was the inspiration for the hand-built cabriolet body that Dannenhauer & Stauss offered between 1950 and 1957, building it on the Volkswagen floorpan and running-gear that. Around 100 are thought to have been made, and the design evolved over the years; there are said to have been three hardtop coupés as well. The company also built special cabriolet bodies for DKW, and from 1956 there were also 10 examples of a fibreglass-and-

Dannenhauer & Stauss: Two shots of the firm's very sucessful transformation of the Volkswagen Type 1. (Erik Eckermann Archive)

polyester coupé designed by Günther Ahrens of Karlsruhe on that company's F-93 chassis.

The arrival of the Volkswagen Karmann Ghia killed the market for the expensive Dannenhauer & Stauss cabriolets, and the company ceased coachbuilding. The DKW Monza coupé remained available through DKW dealer Fritz Wenk in Heidelberg, body production being done by the local firm of Massholder. Between 115 and 155 were built in total. Dannenhauer & Stauss still survives today in Stuttgart's Augustenstrasse, but as an automotive repair business.

David (F)
c1900–1930s, Paris
Carrosserie F David was formed at the start of the 20th century with premises at 54-56 Boulevard de l'Hôpital in the 13th Arrondissement of Paris. The company is known to have built some bodywork on Panhard & Levassor chassis, but during the 1930s turned to building commercial vehicle bodywork. The coachbuilder Clément Kelsch spent part of his apprenticeship in the David workshops.

Davy (F)
c1930–c1931, Puteaux
Carrosserie Davy had premises at 3 Rue Collin in Puteaux (Hauts-de-Seine) and is known to have specialised in coachwork on Citroën C6 chassis around 1930. The company had a stand at the 1931 Paris Motor Show, but probably did not survive much longer.

De Costier Frères (F)
Late 1920s, Boulogne sur Seine
This was a later continuation of the company that had begun as Bouracq & De Costier (qv).

Deissner (D)
1920–1929, Köthen
Carosseriefabrik August Deissner & Sohn was active in the 1920s at Köthen in the Anhalt district of Saxony and had a staff of around 80 people. It worked primarily with chassis by Audi, Dux and Presto.

Delcourt (F)
1930, Vertus
Pierre Delcourt from Vertus (Marne) was an inventor in the automobile field rather than a coachbuilder, but his study

Delcourt: The saloon body on this 1930 Citroën C4 remains Delcourt's only known work. (Author's Collection)

of aerodynamics led him to create an extraordinary special body on a Citroën C4 chassis in 1930. The closed body was constructed from paper-mâché on a metal framework.

Dens (B)
1920s–1930s?
L & A Dens Frères were active in the late 1920s and around 1930, when they are known to have built some bodies on Minerva chassis. Among these were a 12hp Type AN in 1928, a convertible on the MB chassis in 1930, and another on an M-4 the same year.

Denzel (A)
1948–1959, Vienna
Wolfgang Denzel was a Viennese who built himself a sports car around modified Volkswagen running-gear, and used it to win the 1948 Austrian Alpine Rally. Its all-aluminium body had a broad similarity to that of the Porsche 356, and that no doubt added to its appeal. Denzel put it into small-volume production, and built around 300 examples before closing his business in 1959.

Derouault et Jongen (F)
c.1920–1930s, Neuilly-sur-Seine
Almost nothing is known about Carrosserie Derouault et Jongen, which was based at Neuilly-sur-Seine. Its office was at 7 Rue du Lieutenant-Boncour and its workshop was on the Boulevard de Courbevoie. The company had a licence to build transformable bodies using the Baehr patents. A torpedo on Delahaye Type 108 chassis is known from 1930.

Design Performance (F)
1987 and later, Yvelines
This design studio was founded in 1987 in Yvelines by Erick de Pauw and produced a number of show concepts. It amalgamated with two other small design companies in 1999 – Outilmole and M3D – to become Groupe Design Performance and has continued to work on concept designs.

Deslandes (F)
1980s, Villeneuve-sur-Allier
Guy Deslandes founded Deslandes Design at 21 Rue Pasteur, Trévol, Villeneuve-sur-Allier. His aim was to create a cabriolet version of the Citroën CX and by 1983 he had designed such a conversion which he called the Orphée. A coupé derivative called the Avrilly followed, and the cars appeared at some French shows in 1983-1984, but only a handful were built.

Deslandes: The Orphée cabriolet conversion of the Citroën CX remained a rarity. *(WikiMedia Commons/Andrew Bone)*

Deutsch (D)
1916–1971, Cologne
Deutsch was a highly respected conversion specialist, known particularly for its work on German-built Fords between the 1930s and the 1950s.

The firm could trace its origins to 1913, when Karl Deutsch took over the established coachbuilder J W Utermöhle GmbH, which had headquarters in Cologne and a branch in Berlin. This pioneer German coachbuilder had been working with Horch chassis since 1901, and initially Deutsch renamed the business as the Westdeutsches Karosseriewerk (West German Coachworks), concentrating activities at the existing works in the Braunsfeld district of Cologne. The start of the Great War in 1914 made this a somewhat inauspicious time to be starting out in business,

Deutsch: A neat cabriolet on the Ford Model B.

Deutsch: Later in the 1930s came this style of drophead coupé body on the Ford V8.

Deutsch made some Isabella Coupés for Borgward. *(Giles Chapman)*

Deutsch: Cabriolet bodies for the Ford Taunus represented good business for Deutsch. This is a 1951 example. *(Author's Collection)*

Deutsch: This cabriolet conversion of the Ford Capri was built under licence from the British coachbuilder Crayford. *(Author's Collection)*

but Deutsch secured a contract to build trailers for the German army. In 1916, he renamed the business again, this time as Karl Deutsch GmbH.

After the Great War, Deutsch began to build individual bodies to customer order, and soon developed a name for open bodywork. Many of these were designed by O Kuhler, and several were successful in concours d'élégance events. However, the company's big break came in 1927 with a contract from the German Citroën plant in Cologne, and over the next few years Deutsch bodied around 1000 B14 chassis as taxis, cabriolets and delivery vans. The business continued to expand with a small series of cabriolets for Horch from 1930, and further opportunities came along when Ford moved its

German headquarters from Berlin to Cologne in 1930. The first Deutsch-bodied Fords appeared in 1932 on the Model B chassis, and these cabriolets took on the name Rheinland from August 1933. Commissions for series of bodies followed from the Ford branch in the Netherlands, too.

During the 1930s, the Deutsch business became one of Germany's major builders of car bodywork. By 1934, it was turning out between eight and ten bodies a day, and by 1938 the figure was 30 a day. Some of these cars were shipped to Ford in the Netherlands as well.

After the Second World War ended in 1945, Werner Deutsch took over the company from his father. Ford once again became the company's biggest customer, taking cabriolet bodies for its Taunus models, although costs and complication rose thanks to the Ford reliance on monocoques rather than separate chassis after 1952. Demand for cabriolets also began to fall, and although Deutsch aimed high by taking on the legendary Johannes Beeskow, who spent two periods with the company in 1949-50 and then 1953-56, it was market conditions which would dictate the future of the business.

Between 1955 and 1957, a contract with Borgward – for around 1000 cabriolet conversions of the Isabella and Isabella coupé – kept the company busy. Then from 1964, Deutsch picked up the cabriolet work for Opel when Autenrieth closed down. The Ford business disappeared in the mid-1960s, however, when the company dropped cabriolets from its range. Undeterred, Deutsch developed its own conversions of some models, such as the P7, and built them in small numbers to customer order.

From 1969, Deutsch took on a licence to build a convertible Ford Capri to a design by the UK firm of Crayford, but the safety debate was already limiting demand for open cars and the model did not sell as well as expected. Plans for a closer association with Crayford came to nothing and the final blow came when General Franco vetoed a big Spanish contract. Deutsch built its last car body in 1971 and closed down the following year.

Deutsche Industrie-Werke (D)
1920–1928, Berlin

This company, in the Spandau district of Berlin, was the holder of a Weymann licence by 1927.

De Villars (F)
1925–1945, Courbevoie

Carrosserie De Villars was founded and funded by the American millionaire Frank Jay Gould, who owned a string of hotels and casinos on the French Riviera and was himself a resident of Nice. He established the company in 1925 at 53-55 Boulevard de la Mission-Marchand in Courbevoie, at first largely to maintain the high-quality cars of his friends. Before long, the focus changed and De Villars began to provide top-class coachwork on top-class chassis for fellow wealthy Americans living in France. The plan was to limit production to 25 bodies a year, but in practice the company never attracted anywhere near that many orders.

The De Villars name came from Gould's son-in-law, Roland De Graffenried De Villars, whom he put in charge of the business. However, De Villars left the company before long, apparently after some sort of disagreement, although he allowed his name to remain in the interests of the family business. In his place, Gould hired Charles Guignedoux, who inspired the small workforce to create bodywork of the highest quality. The elegant lines, flowing curves and subtle shapes of De Villars bodies were highly regarded, and they were invariably individual commissions for the prestigious chassis of the day. Known examples include Bentley (in 1935 and 1938), Bugatti (1930), Cadillac V16 (1934), Chrysler Imperial (1932), Delage (1933 and 1938), Delahaye (1938),

De Villars: The company built high-quality coachwork on high-quality chassis, such as this 1929 Hispano-Suiza H6B. *(Author's Collection)*

De Villars: This formal saloon de ville on a 1935 Renault chassis has some interesting design elements; few other coachbuilders of the time would have risked those long rear wings, for example. (David Hodges Collection)

Hispano-Suiza (1936), Lancia (1929), Minerva (1931), Renault and Rolls-Royce (1938). There may also have been a Mercedes-Benz 500K in 1936.

The business did not survive beyond the Second World War, and in 1945 its premises were bought by Jean Daninos, who then owned an aircraft panel company but would later create the Facel Vega.

DeWolf (B)
1920s, Brussels
The Belgian coachbuilder Frans DeWolf is known for bodywork on some grand chassis of the 1920s, including a closed body on a 1922 Minerva and a Cadillac coupé-cabriolet in 1929 or 1930.

D'Ieteren (B)
1897–c1935, Brussels
The D'Ieteren company is best known for its coachwork in the first four decades of the 20th century, but in fact its origins go right back to the start of the previous century. Today, the company is the Belgian importer for the Volkswagen Audi Group and several other leading brands.

Jean Joseph D'Ieteren moved from the Netherlands to open his small workshop near the centre of Brussels in 1805, when Belgium was still a part of France. He began as a wheelwright, but soon moved on to build complete wagons. On his death in 1831, he was succeeded by his two sons Adophe and Alexandre. After a period in Paris to learn more about the design and construction of wooden bodies for carriages, Alexandre opened a new and larger workshop in Brussels' Nieuwstraat in 1857. When his sons Alfred and Emile succeeded him in 1873, they moved the company again, this time to Steenweg in Charleroi. It was Alfred and Emile who changed the name of the company to the one familiar from the car bodying era, calling it D'Ieteren Frères (D'Ieteren Brothers). From 1884, they became official carriage suppliers to the Dutch Royal Household, and subsequently received a number of awards for their work. They then began to supply carriages to the Belgian Royal Court as well.

D'Ieteren: This neat cabriolet with its side step replacing conventional running-boards was built on a Mercedes-Benz SS around 1929. (Daimler-Benz)

The first D'Ieteren car body was made in 1897, and over the next decade the company grew bigger, moving in 1906 to new premises at 50 Maliestraat in Elsene (Ixelles). Alfred's sons, Lucien and Albert, now took over and the business switched entirely to car body building. In 1919, the D'Ieteren business became a limited company with the name of Anciens Etablissements D'Ietereren Frères. After 1926, most D'Ieteren bodies were built for export, and the company's main markets were in Argentina, Egypt, the Netherlands, Spain, Portugal and the USA. From 1931, D'Ieteren took out a licence to build the patented Toutalu (all-aluminium) body designs held by Million-Guiet (qv) in France. When built by D'Ieteren, these carried the name of Supra-légère.

Over the first four decades of the 20th century, the D'Ieteren business built bodies for more than 100 different chassis, of which the most notable were Delahaye, Duesenberg, Hispano Suiza, Impéria, Isotta-Fraschini, Mercedes, Minerva, Panhard, Peugeot and Renault. Around 6000 bodies are thought to have been built in all. However, from the start of the 1930s, the coachbuilding business was in Albert's hands; Lucien created a separate company as a hedge against the effects of the Great Depression, selling American cars and trucks from brands such as Auburn, Pierce-Arrow, Rockne and Studebaker. Then to avoid heavy taxation, D'Ieteren started assembling Studebaker chassis and bodies for the Belgian market at the Maliestraat premises in 1935.

There was no more coachbuilding after the Second World War, and the company was renamed SA D'Ieteren NV in 1947. In 1948, Lucien's son, Pierre D'Ieteren, obtained the Belgian sales franchise for Volkswagen in 1948, and his company retains it to this day. The premises in Vorst that had been built for Studebaker assembly also began to turn out Volkswagens, and from 1950 he added the Porsche franchise to his business, followed by Packard in 1955. The early 1960s also saw D'Ieteren building around 700 roadster bodies for the Porsche 356.

On Pierre's death in 1975, his son Roland took control of the D'Ieteren empire, and further extended the list of its Belgian import franchises. The service and maintenance side of the business was also built up. Coachbuilding was still in the family genes, however, and in more recent years Roland D'Ieteren took a share in the revitalized Touring Superleggera company.

Dietrich (CH)
1914–c1930, Basle

Very little is known about the Swiss coachbuilder Otto Dietrich, who established his business in Basle in 1914. He is generally thought to have specialised in building bodywork on the grander chassis, and those known include a Landaulet Coupé on a Rolls-Royce 40/50 and a Berlina body with sun roof on a Lancia chassis. This last was built in 1929, but nothing more is known of the coachbuilder, which probably disappeared during the economic crisis of the next few years.

Dietzsch (D)
1930s, Glauchau

Ernst Dietzsch's coachbuilding business, the Karosseriefabrik Dietzsch, was active at Glauchau in Saxony during the 1930s. Among its bodies was a grand cabriolet on a 1932 Horch V12 chassis. After the 1939-1945 war, Glauchau fell into the eastern sector and the Dietzsch business was amalgamated with other coachbuilders to work on IFA products.

Ditting (CH)
1928–1979, Zürich

Despite the spread of dates associated with this company, the Zürich firm of Adolf Ditting actually seems to have built very few bodies. It was founded in 1928 as Adolf Ditting Carrosserie – a general body shop, specialising in the construction, conversion and repair of vehicle bodies. However, in 1944 the company diversified into the design and manufacture of food slicing machines.

In 1949, Adolf Ditting modified a Riley 2½-litre saloon for his wife's use, producing an attractive modernisation of the standard style. However, the food preparation machinery business was expanding, and from 1954, the Ditting range was extended to include coffee grinders.

Adolf Ditting died in 1972. His business became a limited company under the name Ditting AG, and continued to grow. By this stage, coachwork construction seems to have ceased, although the original body shop remained open. In 1976, a new factory in Bachenbülach was opened to accommodate the food machine business and, although the body shop remained in Zürich, it had become a sideline and was sold in 1979. Ditting remains a leading manufacturer of machines for the food industry.

Dörr & Schreck (D)
1919–1939, Frankfurt am Main

Jakob Dörr had established himself in business as a wheelwright as early as 1890, but after the First World War he joined forces with Matthias Schreck in a new coachwork business at Frankfurt am Main. In the 1920s and early 1930s, they specialised in individual bodies for luxury chassis, such as Maybach, but also bodied Adler, Bugatti, Horch and Opel chassis.

Dörr & Schreck also built a number of streamlined bodies to designs by Freiherr Reinhard von Koenig-Fachsenfeld, and several of these were on Maybach chassis. An Opel Super Six chassis with light-alloy coupé bodywork by Dörr & Schreck achieved a maximum speed of 164km/h (102mph) in 1936.

From the mid-1930s, Dörr & Schreck also built small batches of cabriolets and sports bodies for Adler. However,

Dörr & Schreck: This well-proportioned cabriolet was built for the Prinz von Waldeck und Piermont on a Maybach Zeppelin chassis in 1939. (Author's Collection)

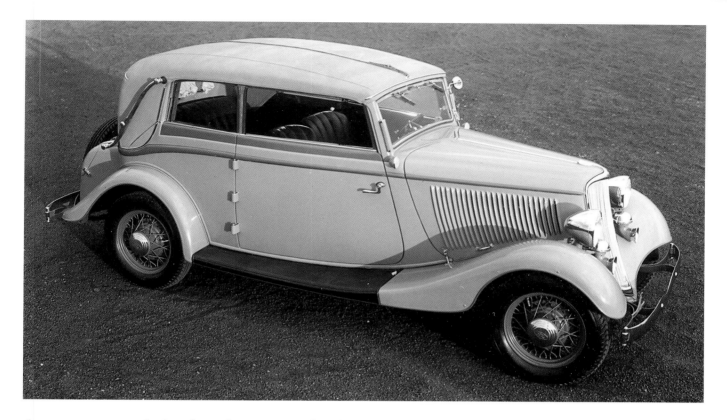

there were no more bodies from the company after the Second World War. Dörr had died, and Matthias Schreck rebuilt the company as a body repair shop, which lasted into the 1960s.

Drauz (D)

1900–1965, Heilbronn

Gustav Drauz founded his carriage works at Heilbronn in 1900, but before long was fielding orders for car bodies from NSU. Other makers followed, and by 1911 the company had grown to employ a staff of 200. It had also gained a reputation both at home and abroad for the excellence of its work. During the war years, Drauz built ambulances and field kitchens, but returned to the coachwork business when peace came and began to specialise in cabriolet bodies.

The company continued to grow, and from 1925 Gustav Drauz junior joined. NSU remained a customer, and was joined in this period by Adler and Fiat. In this period, Drauz was best known for its cabriolet bodies, often quite unusual in design. There were individual commissions as well as the batch production of cabriolets, and from 1931 the major customer for Drauz coachwork was the German Ford branch in Cologne.

Meanwhile, after 1930 the business was effectively divided into two. That year, Drauz bought the old Schebera coachwork company, and transferred the custom body building to that. It also bought out Karosserie Alexis Kellner GmbH, which became a subsidiary from 1932. In 1933, this company began line assembly of all-steel cabriolet bodies and of lorry cabs. Among the chassis with all-steel Drauz

Drauz: This Ford Rheinland four-seat cabriolet model dates from about 1935. *(Author's Collection)*

cabriolet bodies were the BMW 319/1 Sport Cabriolet of 1935, and the broadly similar 329 model of 1937. Drauz was the supplier of the Cabrio-Limousine bodies for Ford Eifel chassis in the late 1930s. Meanwhile, the company had also begun to build trailers and bus bodies for companies such as Magirus-Deutz.

The Drauz works in Heilbronn were completely destroyed in an air raid in 1944 and, like many other German companies, Drauz returned to business after the Second World War as a manufacturer of wooden hand-carts. However, from 1947 there were orders for bus bodies once again, and from this point onwards Drauz began to specialise in such work. Nevertheless, the old customers for car bodies such as Ford and NSU also gradually returned, and Drauz found itself building bodies for new customers DKW and Porsche as well. Among its early products were the DKW delivery vans, and Drauz also built bodies for the Ford FK 1000, the Champion 400 and the Porsche 356 Convertible D, of which 3514 examples were built between 1958 and 1961. The D in its name actually stood for Drauz.

By 1965, Drauz had a staff of 700. However, in July that year the company's coachbuilding interests were bought by NSU, and Drauz re-focused on tooling and equipment. Major customers were mostly from the region around Heilbronn, and included Audi, Porsche and Daimler-Benz. Through a series of subsequent mergers and take-overs, Drauz became Krupp Drauz, then ThyssenKrupp Drauz, and finally ThyssenKrupp System Engineering, a member of the ThyssenKrupp industrial group. The company made the aluminium bodies for the Lamborghini Gallardo (which was assembled by Audi) and today supplies body panels and assemblies for Audi, Porsche and Mercedes-Benz cars.

Drews (D)
1945–2001, Wuppertal

In 1945, brothers Gerhard, Erwin and Werner Drews set themselves up as Karosseriebau Drews with an address at Rauental 36, in Wuppertal-Oberbarmen, to the east of Düsseldorf. They began by creating pick-up trucks from ex-military Volkswagens to meet demand for light commercial vehicles in West Germany.

In 1947, the Drews brothers also created the streamlined body of a monoposto AFM racer, which Emil Vorster campaigned successfully in German events. Their next move was a modern two-seater cabriolet design for the Volkswagen platform chassis, using aluminium panels over a steel tube framework. Shown at the first West German Motor Show in Rheydt in 1949, this was expensive but attracted an estimated 150 orders between 1949 and 1951. Drews willingly catered to individual requirements, with the result that no two cars were exactly alike.

Drews: This 1949 cabriolet on the Volkswagen was an important model in getting the firm established. (Author's Collection)

Drews: The basic cabriolet body design from the Volkswagen was adapted to suit the 1950 Ford Taunus De Luxe. It looked rather dumpy, but was in keeping with contemporary taste. (Author's Collection)

Drews: Built in 1951, the Dyna-Veritas prototype was not followed by volume production. (David Hodges Collection)

Drews: Putting the hood up on the Drews cabriolet did not really help the car's looks. This one was pictured at the Berlin Motor Show in 1951. (Author's Collection)

From 1950, the same basic design was adapted to suit the Ford Taunus, but now as a four-seater and with rear "fins" like those of a 1948 Cadillac. Over the next few years, Drews also built a number of one-off cabriolet bodies on other chassis, notably one on an Alfa Romeo and a handful on the Mercedes 220. The first half of the 1950s also saw a very American-looking convertible body for the VW Beetle that was built at the VW plant in Curitiba, Brazil.

Meanwhile, Drews continued to build bodies for sports and racing cars. There were examples on AFM and Veritas chassis and, in the later 1950s, on the DKW Formula Junior. The company also built the body for a prototype Dyna-Veritas, but the project to build these cars in Belgium did not get off the ground. Notable bodies in the later 1950s included a 1958 DKW 3=6 Spyder, a metal-panelled open car not unlike the DKW Monza coupé. Drews also built the bodies for AFM-engined Opel and Fiat cars.

The 1960s saw Drews still in business as a specialist coachbuilder, but its focus was now on restoration and maintenance. There was one throwback to the old days in 1984, when the company created the monoposto body for a BMW-engined Scampolo racer. The company remained in the specialist bodywork business until 2001, under the leadership of Joachim Drews, a descendant of the founders.

Driesen & Oblin (B)
1920s
Almost nothing is known about this company, which built a coupé-chauffeur on a Minerva chassis in 1927. It is presumed to have been Belgian, and may possibly have had a connection with the later Brussels coachbuilding firm of Oblin *(qv)*.

Driguet (F)
Early 1900s–1936, Paris
The Driguet business could trace its origins back to 1836, when it was founded as a wagon-maker at l'Yonne in Saint-Florentin. Louis Driguet, son of the founder, added funeral carriages to the company's repertoire and then, at the start of the 20th century, moved to Paris and set up in business as a builder of motor vehicle bodies with two of his sons.

Based in the Boulevard de l'Hôpital in the 13th Arrondissement, the company became Driguet Frères and in the early 1920s enjoyed strong links with Panhard & Levassor. It then turned to creating the popular transformable bodies, mainly on more popular chassis from Citroën, Panhard and Renault, but with the occasional Delage or Hispano-Suiza as well. Then from 1936, it moved to new premises and ceased car body production, focussing instead on emergency vehicle bodywork.

Drögmuller (D)
1920–1931, Heilbronn
Karosserie Drögmüller built both car bodies and commercial bodies during the 1920s, but appears to have concentrated on commercial business after 1931. The company had certainly become a bus body specialist by the late 1940s, and in 1992 became the German branch of the Volvo bus division.

Drouet & Gaucher (F)
1920s, Courbevoie
Drouet & Gaucher Carrossiers had premises at 12 Avenue de Saint-Denis in Courbevoie throughout the 1920s, but probably did not survive much beyond 1930, when they had a stand at the Paris Salon. They offered both open and closed bodywork, with either fabric or metal panelling.

Dubos (F)
c1925–c1950, Neuilly-sur-Seine; later Puteaux
The Dubos company originally traded as Louis Dubos Carrossier from premises in the Rue de Sablonville at Neuilly-sur-Seine and built horse-drawn vehicles. Its conversion to building bodies for motor vehicles in the mid-1920s is said to have been reluctant.

Its early designs used flexible mountings between body and chassis to reduce noise transmission, although the actual shapes were fairly conventional. By 1928 it was focussing on its own design of folding-roof coachwork, designed by Louis Dubos and known as the Plein Azur. It built this on chassis such as Delage and Hotchkiss, and also licensed the design to Ottin *(qv)* in Lyons. The company

Dubos: The "Gascogne" coupé body for the Delahaye 135 chassis was introduced in 1949 and was a design by Philippe Charbonneaux. *(David Hodges Collection)*

Dubos: The lines of the Gascogne coupé are clear in this contemporary advertisement. *(WikiMedia Commons/Ctellal)*

also held a licence for Weymann fabric bodies. Notable bodies were an aerodynamic saloon for Panhard at the 1933 Paris Salon and the original Renault Vivastella two-door saloon in 1934. Dubos bodied some Delahaye chassis in the 1930s, and built the final cabriolet bodies for Voisin, as well as coupés on that company's C30 chassis.

After the Second World War, the company passed into the hands of Louis Dubos' two sons. Now known as Dubos Frères, Carrossiers, it moved to 11 bis Rue Jean-Jaurès in Puteaux. Notable were a small series of coupé bodies for Delahaye and some Talbot Lago Record cabriolets to a design by Talbot's designer Carlo Delaisse. However, the company closed down in the early 1950s, perhaps reflecting the early stages of a decline in French coachbuilding.

Dubost & Perret (F)
Later 1920s, Lyons

Dubost & Perret was established in September 1926 with premises at 11 Boulevard des Brotteaux in Lyons. Its speciality was saloon bodies that could be turned into open cars simply by removing the roof and supporting pillars; the company seems also to have offered demountable roof conversions for existing torpedo-type bodies.

Duchatelet (B)
1968 to present, Liège

The Duchatelet name is primarily associated with opulent conversions of Mercedes-Benz models for the Middle East, but the company has also done similar work on other prestige models (such as Ferrari, Jaguar, Porsche and Rolls-Royce) since the start of the 1980s. Its work has often been marketed under the name of Carat by Duchatelet.

Frederic Duchatelet set up Carat Duchatelet International SA as a coachwork conversions business in Liège during 1968. The address was 413 Rue Winston Churchill. However, real recognition did not come before 1981, when Duchatelet displayed a modified Mercedes-Benz 450SEL at the Geneva Show, and then took it to the Cannes Film Festival and on a marketing tour of the United Arab Emirates.

Duchatelet's willingness to meet the Arab taste for ostentation was a major factor in the company's success. The main bodywork of the car might be altered in relatively subtle ways, such as with an SEC-style sports grille on an S-Class saloon, or it might be given a convertible roof or a major limousine extension. Duchatelet also produced at least one gullwing-door C126 SEC in the 1980s, although this was based on a conversion by Sbarro. Duchatelet was prepared to refinish the bodies to customer choice, even using multiple coats of Chinese lacquer or even gold leaf. Interiors would be transformed with four individual seats with full electrical adjustment and top-quality leather in a variety of styles and to the customer's choice of colour. Some cars had electrically operated folding tables, special centre consoles, and accessories from the top designers such as Cartier, or crystal from Val Saint Lambert.

From 1983, Duchatelet also set up an armouring division, and this subsequently accounted for a large proportion of its work. In the same year, the company introduced a range of affordable accessories such as bodykits and interior modifications, and these broadened its market and its reputation in Europe, Japan and the USA. Mercedes-Benz

transformations of various types continue to account for around 95% of the Duchatelet work today.

Duchemin (F)
1920s and 1930s

Very little is known about this coachbuilder, except that the company bodied a Delage in 1928 and that it modified the body of a Citroën 11CV that was entered in some concours d'élégance in 1939.

Dumas (F)
1920s and 1930s, Bordeaux

Very little is known about the work of this Bordeaux coachbuilder, which was founded in 1922 by Maurice Dumas. There were bodies on various chassis, including Citroën, Georges Roy and Bugatti. When demand for bodywork dried up, the company became a bodywork repair business, and still existed in the ownership of the original family as Carrosserie Dumas in 2012.

Dupont (F)
1920s

This coachbuilder is known only from a torpedo body built on a Renault MC chassis in 1924.

Duquesne (F)
1920s, Tourcoing

Carrosserie Automobile Charles Duquesne was active in the 1920s and appears to have built both luxury bodies for cars and commercial bodies. The company picked up on the skiff style pioneered by Labourdette and is known for a torpedo body on Hispano-Suiza chassis. It operated from 84 Rue d'Hondschoote in Tourcoing.

Duriez (F)
1945-1951, Paris

Before World War II, the Parisian firm of Automobiles Duriez was best known for its industrial vehicles, although it also dabbled in cars with such things as a four-speed gearbox conversion for the Citroën Traction Avant. As the war ended, Duriez converted a number of C4 and C6 Citroën cars to small forward-control trucks with electric power (known as Transition Duriez types), and in the later 1940s created a

Duriez: As much conversion as coachwork, this was the Duriez Jeep from the late 1940s. (*Author's Collection*)

wooden body for war-surplus Jeeps. Its sole venture into car bodywork was a Renault 4CV cabriolet in 1950. More than one was built, and the model was shown at the Paris Salon in 1951. However, a high price dissuaded buyers.

Durisotti (F)
1956–present, Sallaumines

Durisotti was founded in 1956 and has always been best known for its commercial coachwork. Among others, it has also created special pick-up type vehicles from Peugeot estate cars. The company is based at Sallaumines in the Pas-de-Calais.

Duval: The roadster body on this 1929 Amilcar was an early Duval creation. (Bonhams)

Duval (F)
1920s–1949, Boulogne-sur-Seine

Carrosserie Charles Duval opened for business at Boulogne-sur-Seine in the mid-1920s, some of its earliest bodies being on Amilcar and De Dion Bouton chassis. and a BNC that was shown at the 1927 Paris Salon. Duval built mostly on smaller and less expensive chassis, and over the next few years built bodies on Amilcar, BNC, Chenard & Walcker, Derby, La Licorne, Lombard and Matford chassis. By the end of the 1930s it was looking to American chassis, and in 1937 built a cabriolet on a Chevrolet Master chassis. However, the company was in financial difficulties by this time, and although the Duval name appeared on a Chevrolet cabriolet in 1949, the company closed down.

Duvivier (F)
Active 1920s-1930s, Levallois-Perret

The Duvivier business was founded in 1890 in Levallois-Perret as a maker of horse-drawn vehicles. After the Great War, R Duvivier took out a Baehr licence to build transformable bodywork for motor vehicles but, unlike many other companies that took the same licence, it was able to develop its own ideas as well. Notable was a torpedo body on a Hispano-Suiza chassis built in 1921 for the King of Spain, and Duvivier soon began to specialise in luxury bodywork. There were bodies on Ballot, Delage, Cadillac and Voisin chassis among others, and the company had a particularly strong relationship with Peugeot. Duvivier forged links with the Gallé (qv) coachworks, but it was too late. The company's reliance on the luxury end of the market caused its collapse in the early 1930s as that market imploded.

E

EBS (B)
1981–1994, Tervuren

Ernst Berg was a Dutch architect and racing driver who set up a coachwork and conversion business at Tervuren in Belgium, clearly aiming to capitalise on the nascent 1980s demand for custom bodywork. Ernst Berg Styling took on two bodywork specialists from bb, Figueras and Moreira, and before 1985 focussed mainly on conversions of BMW 6 Series and Mercedes-Benz SEC coupés. EBS built an estimated 30 BMWs and 50 Mercedes, predominantly cabriolets.

From 1985, the company abandoned individual custom bodywork in favour of producing cabriolet conversions for major motor manufacturers. At the 1986 Geneva Motor Show it showed a cabriolet version of the Renault 5, and this was ready to go into production in 1986 when a change of top management at Renault led to a change of heart. EBS decided to press on alone, buying complete cars from Renault. However, the original business plan had depended on Renault supplying bare shells to EBS, and the extra work involved made the conversion no longer viable financially.

A Type II version was drawn up under Michael Kaag, with a much simpler and more cost-effective design that lacked the attractive features of the first version but did allow EBS to make a profit. Encouraged, EBS went on to design and build more convertibles, modifying Lada Samara and Rover 100 models. There were some other custom conversions, too, including an estate car on the Renault 25.

However, EBS was in financial trouble by 1994. Michael Kaag bought the company from the receivers and renamed it ACT. ACT Research NV now works in the commercial bodywork conversion business from premises at Kortenberg.

Eckert (CH)
1918–1947, Zürich

Heinrich Eckert's coachworks in Zürich could trace its origins right back to 1806 when it was founded as a wagon-maker. Before the Great War, the company held German patents for touring limousine bodywork, and during the 1920s it often constructed these bodies on chassis of American origin, such as Buick, Dodge and Essex. In all, Eckert is reported to have sold more than 200 such bodies in eastern Switzerland. Eckert himself became the first president of the Swiss coachbuilders' association (Verband Schweizer Carrosserie-Industrie). In later years, the company's focus was on repair work.

Eggli Frères (CH)
1918–1947, Lausanne; later Vevey

The original Eggli Frères company was involved in building vans on the Fiat 501 chassis and "Cars Alpins" for the Swiss Post Office. A later company of the same name, based in Vevey, built touring coaches and buses, and in 1967 constructed a hearse on Cadillac chassis.

Egli (CH)
1902–1932, Basle

Adolf Egli was one of the earliest Swiss coachbuilders to work on motor cars, and built a number of bodies, especially on local chassis such as Martini. In 1918, the company was a founder member of the VSCI (Verband Schweizer Carrosserie-Industrie or Guild of the Swiss Coachbuilding Industry).

Egli became known for sporty touring and luxury cabriolet bodies on the larger imported chassis, including Peugeot, several American makes and also Rolls-Royce. A characteristic of some of these bodies were special front seats that slid forwards automatically when being folded down, to give easier access to the rear. Egli was a well-respected coachbuilder, but did not survive the Depression and closed down in 1932.

Eichelbaum (D)
c1922–1925, Berlin

Karosserie Eichelbaum GmbH was established in Berlin's Brandenburgstrasse some time around 1922, but very little information is available about its activities. An early offering was a Sport Phaeton body, possibly on Benz chassis.

Elgé (F)
1920s, Bordeaux

The Elgé coachworks was established by Roger-Louis Maleyre in Bordeaux. Little is known about the company except that it bodied around 15 Bugatti chassis in the 1920s. At least one of these, possibly on a Type 35 chassis, had quite extraordinary lines. Elgé was a pioneer of aerodynamic bodywork, and in 1924 Maleyre made his own chassis, using a locally-built CIM engine, and created a fabric-covered saloon body with a low overall height of just 50 inches.

Ellena (I)
1957–1966, Turin

Carrozzeria Ellena was formed in 1957 when Mario Boano accepted a job with Fiat to establish and run its new styling department, and was unable to continue running his own coachbuilding company. At the time, he was building a Pininfarina-designed coupé body for the Ferrari 250GT because Pininfarina lacked capacity, and he passed this contract on to Ezio Ellena, his son-in-law. Ellena set up the new company in tandem with Boano's former partner, Luciano Pollo.

The first eight Ellena bodies were identical to the Boano versions, but 41 more were built with a raised roofline. From 1958, Pininfarina took over production at its new Grugliasco factory, and Ellena moved on to other work. The company's biggest commercial success was a delivery van based on the Fiat 600 Multipla, but it also constructed about 100 luxury coupés based on the Fiat 1500 and some spyders on the Fiat 850. The 1960s also brought work with Abarth,

and there were Ellena bodies on the Abarth 1000 and the Fiat-Abarth 2200 coupé. However, business was slow and Ellena closed down in 1966.

Emmel (B)
1924–1926, Brussels

The Emmel coachbuilding company was led by a Monsieur Ven de Waele, and is known for the special versions of the Ford Model T which it marketed under the Emmel name. Emmel offered two body styles, a two-seater sports torpedo capable of over 100km/h and a four-door saloon. Both had a Ricardo cylinder head and Delco coil ignition, and the chassis was also lowered. The first example was probably built in 1924, but production did not begin until December 1925 and seems not to have lasted for long.

Engelhard (D)
See Vereinigte Werkstätten für Karosserie- und Wagenbau.

Enzmann (CH)
1957–1968, Schüpfheim

The Swiss Enzmann company made its public debut at the 1957 Frankfurt Motor Show, with a glass-fibre cabriolet body for the Volkswagen Beetle chassis. This was marketed as the Enzmann 506, the number coming from the number of the company's stand at the show. Enzmann senior owned a garage and hotel in Schüpfheim, and the sports bodywork was the creation of his sons. It was manufactured at a boatyard in Grandson, and the Enzmann could be bought as a complete car or as a body for DIY fitment. Around 100 were built before Volkswagen declined to supply further chassis, seeing the car as a rival for its own Karmann Ghia model. However, supplies of the original body remained available until 1968.

Some cars were fitted with uprated engines, including Porsche 356 types, and were used in competition. At the start of the 21st century, the descendants of the Enzmann family started production of a New Enzmann at Bischofszell, again designed for Beetle chassis.

Elgé: A very idiosyncratic "aerodynamic" body on a 1925 Bugatti. (David Burgess-Wise)

Ellena: The Fiat-based 850 Spyder was a strikingly attractive sports two-seater, distinguished by its pointed nose. (David Hodges Collection)

Enzmann: This GRP-bodied cabriolet was one of many attempts to exploit the basic Volkswagen chassis in the 1950s. (David Hodges Collection)

Erdmann & Rossi (D)
1906–1949, Berlin

Willy Erdmann set up in business as a carriage maker in Berlin in 1898. In 1906, car salesman Eduard Rossi joined him and the company began to focus on car bodywork, changing its name to Karosserie Erdmann & Rossi.

After Rossi died in an accident in 1909, Erdmann decided to sell the company to his chief accountant, Friedrich Peters. The name was already well established, however, and so Peters retained it. During the First World War, the company constructed post vans and ambulances, and dealt with repairs.

However, once the war was over, Erdmann & Rossi turned for business to the luxury market. They bodied German chassis such as Horch and Mercedes, other Europeans such as Bugatti and Minerva, and after becoming the German distributor for Rolls-Royce and Bentley also bodied examples of both marques. The company was capable of building two or three bodies a week, and employed around 200 craftsmen. In the inter-war years, its name became synonymous with glamour and style.

Business was booming in the 1930s, and in 1933 the company took over the Neuss carrosserie that was located nearby in the Halensee district of Berlin. Customers included Prince Bernhard of The Netherlands and King Ghazi of Iraq, for whom Erdmann & Rossi created an outrageous Mercedes-Benz 500K roadster with its wheels

Erdmann & Rossi: With its folding hood tucked neatly away at the back, this body was built on a Mercedes-Benz S chassis in 1929. *(Author's Collection)*

Erdmann & Rossi: The coupé body on this Horch 853 chassis was the very embodiment of motoring prestige when the car was new in the late 1930s. *(WikiMedia Commons/MPW57)*

Erdmann & Rossi: Almost half of all Mercedes-Benz 500K models sold in bare chassis form went to Erdmann & Rossi for bodies. This two-door saloon dates from 1936 and is a unique design with glass panels in the roof above the windscreen. *(Daimler-Benz)*

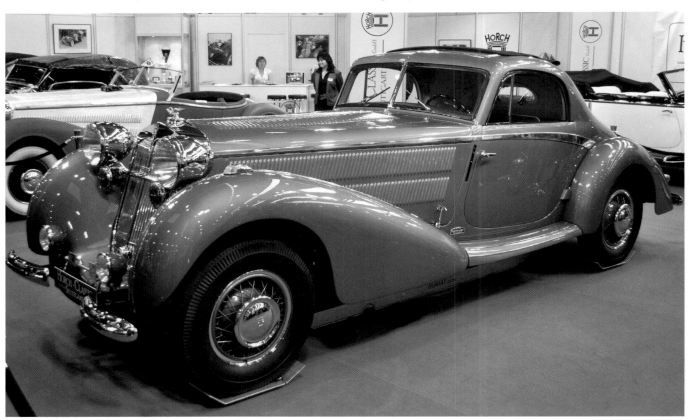

Erdmann & Rossi: This astonishing roadster body was built for the King of Iraq on a Mercedes-Benz 500K chassis in 1935. Although unique, it was inspired by an earlier design on a Mercedes 290 chassis. (Daimler-Benz)

Erdmann & Rossi: Mixing upright British front end design with a solid-looking German passenger cabin, this is a 1939 two-door sports saloon body on a Rolls-Royce Wraith chassis. (David Hodges Collection)

concealed in fully-enclosed pontoon wings. There were bodies for most of the grand chassis of the period, including American makes such as Packard. Erdmann & Rossi also developed a healthy business in making the interiors of passenger aircraft.

In 1937, Friedrich Peters died and ownership of the company passed to his brother, Richard Peters. However, the golden age of luxury coachbuilding was already coming to an end. Erdmann & Rossi limped through the late 1940s but built their last body on a Maybach SW 42 chassis in 1949. The company still exists, but as a body repair shop.

Esclassan (F)
Late 1920s to early 1950s, Boulogne-sur-Seine
Henri Esclassan was primarily a maker of panels, and from the late 1920s he supplied wings, boot lids, roofs, trunks and other items to several of the major French car makers, of which the nearest to him geographically was Renault at

Billancourt. After the Second World War, Esclassan became an official of the TAI (Tôlerie Industrielle Automobile, or Society of Industrial Automotive Panel-makers).

From around 1947, he also responded to market demand in France for new designs by producing kits of panels that would transform the appearance of existing mass-production models. Among these were panels for the Renault 4CV and the Citroën Traction Avant, and both were marketed under the Splendilux name. For the latter, the appearance of the car was thoroughly changed with a new grille, new front wings, new rear wings and an enclosed boot that incorporated the spare wheel; all these panels were simple bolt-on substitutions for the originals. Similar panels were used on cabriolet models, but these retained their original rear panels. Splendilux only converted a small number of cars, although they sold several kits for others to fit.

In the early 1950s, Esclassan gained a contract to build panels for a first series of 38 Salmson 2300 Sport models, but

Esclassan: This early Salmson 2300 Sport has panels from the Esclassan coachworks. (*Author's Collection*)

Esclassan: Inspired by General Motors' 1951 Le Sabre concept car, this is one of a pair built on Salmson chassis in 1952. It could not be called attractive. (*Author's Collection*)

eventually lost the job to Chapron. Shortly after the 1952 Paris Salon, Esclassan also built a pair of cabriolets on Salmson chassis that incorporated a number of elements inspired by the 1951 Le Sabre concept car from General Motors.

Etablissements Lyonnais (F)
1906–c1920, Lyons
The Société Lyonnaise des Carrosseries pour Automobiles was founded in February 1905, apparently in order to build car bodies designed by the Parisian carrossier Védrine. In May 1906, the company moved premises and was renamed the Etablissements Lyonnais de Carrosseries pour Automobiles. Some sources argue that the company did not survive beyond 1918, but a limousine body is known on a 1920 Renault Type EU chassis.

Euler (D)
c1980–c1983, Frankfurt
The Euler Group is a BMW franchised dealer in Frankfurt. Not normally associated with custom coachwork, the company created a well-proportioned estate car from a BMW 7-Series saloon in the early 1980s. Several examples were built, mainly or possibly only on 745i models. Some were shipped to the USA and at least one is said to have been made from a right-hand-drive 7-Series for the UK.

Eurostyle (I)
1968–1970, Turin
Carrozzeria Eurostyle was a short-lived coachbuilder based in Turin. It made its debut at the 1968 Turin Motor Show with a pair of coupés based on Fiat running-gear, called the City 125 and the Hidalgo 1000. The same two cars, slightly restyled, were shown again at Turin in 1969. Turin 1968 also saw the introduction of the LMX Sirex 2300HCS, a Ford-powered fastback designed by Franco Scaglione for which Carrozzeria Eurostyle built the fibreglass bodies. Production began in late 1968 and only 43 cars were made. Just one was a convertible with removable fibreglass hardtop, which was shown at Geneva in 1969.

Carrozzeria Eurostyle's last known product was a quite extraordinary estate-type body based on a Porsche 914, shown at Turin in 1970. This was said to have been designed by Albrecht Goertz, and just two examples were made. The company seems to have closed down in 1970, although some sources claim that production of the LMX Sirex continued as late as 1972.

F

Facel Metallon: The first Bentley Cresta cars were built by Facel Metallon to a Pinin Farina design, but the second batch (of which this is a 1951 example) were both designed and built by Facel. *(David Hodges Collection)*

Facel Metallon (F)

1945–1964, Paris

The name of Facel comes from the initials of the Forges et Ateliers de Construction d'Eure et Loir (Forges and assembly workshops of the Eure and Loir region) which was set up by Jean Daninos in 1939. Daninos joined forces with Metallon in 1945 with the intention of making all-aluminium coachwork. The new company had premises at three different sites: prototype work was done in Courbevoie, in the old De Villars works; cars were built at Dreux and Colombe; and the Amboise works was the home of the stamping presses for panels and for aviation material, as well as for manufacture in stainless steel.

The company perfected the basic technique of all-aluminium construction for the body of the Dyna Panhard, of which it built 45,565 examples between 1946 and 1953. Facel Metallon went on to build many bodies to outside designs. These included those for the Simca Huit Sport (a

design by Michelotti for Pinin Farina, of which 23,500 were made) and the Bentley Cresta (another Pinin Farina design, of which 17 were made). Later, the company also constructed 9632 examples of the Delahaye VLR all-terrain vehicle.

From 1948, the company established a luxury coachwork department where many later designs were created by Daninos in collaboration with the chief engineer of Facel Metallon, Jacques Brasseur. These two were responsible for the bodies on several Simca models, including the 1951 Aronde Week-End and Coupé de Ville and the 1956

Facel Metallon: Another Pinin Farina-Facel collaboration, this Simca Huit Sport model dates from 1951. *(Bonhams)*

Facel Metallon: Even though the Bentleys were built to a common design, there were minor differences from one car to the next. *(WikiMedia Commons/Rex Grey)*

Facel Metallon: There are distinct similarities to the Simca Huit design in the body of this 1954 Ford Comète Monte Carlo. *(David Hodges Collection)*

Facel Metallon: The company eventually constructed their own cars. This is a Facel II model dating from 1962-64. (*David Hodges Collection*)

Océane and Plein Ciel. They also did the Ford Comète, of which 2200 were made, and the second version of the Bentley Cresta that was at the 1951 Salon.

From 1954, the company manufactured the Facel Vega luxury sports models for which it is best known, but eventually ran into financial trouble and closed down in 1964.

Faget-Varnet (F)
1945–1953, Levallois-Perret
The industrial body company established by Jean Faget and Henri Varnet set up a car bodywork division in 1945. That year, the company became involved in the construction of a

one-box taxi design on the Renault Juvaquatre chassis, but this went no further than a prototype.

In 1948, Faget-Varnet perfected an all-metal body construction which reduced weight as compared to traditional wood-framed types, and was also used under

Faget-Varnet: Superb use of curves characterises this cabriolet body on Delahaye 135M chassis dating from 1949. (*Author's Collection*)

Faget-Varnet: The body for the 1948 Wimille certainly broke new ground, but it was not fertile ground. (*David Hodges Collection*)

Fantuzzi: This car started life as a 1963 Ferrari 250GT Lusso with coupé body by Pininfarina, but received modifications by Fantuzzi a few years later. (*Author's Collection*)

licence by Gramond *(qv)*. A number of strikingly attractive bodies on the Delahaye 135 chassis earned plaudits at concours events although they incorporated no major stylistic advances. Notable were a coach at the 1948 Paris Salon and a cabriolet the following year. This latter incorporated three complementary curves in side view – one for the front wing, one for the body side and one for the rear wing.

Stylist Philippe Charbonneaux worked with the coachbuilder to create the 1948 Wimille with its rear-mounted Ford V8, but the company was not to last. Its last notable creation was a two-door saloon body on a Delahaye 235 chassis that was shown at the Paris Salon in 1952.

Falco (I)
To 1926, Milan
Carrozzeria Falco was a coachbuilder in Milan founded by Vittorio Ascari, and is best known as the predecessor of Carrozzeria Touring. Among its specialities were lightweight airframes. The company was ailing by 1926, when it was bought by Felice Bianchi Anderloni and Gaetano Ponzoni in 1926, who changed its name to Touring *(qv)*.

Fantuzzi (I)
1957–present, Modena
Medardo Fantuzzi was born in 1906 and took on work for Maserati from 1929 until their withdrawal from racing in

1957, building the bodywork on almost all of the factory's single-seaters and on sports-racers such as the 350S and 200S from the early 1950s. He was also responsible for a beautiful barchetta on a 1953 OSCA 1500 chassis.

He then set up in business with his brother Gino as Carrozzeria Fantuzzi in Modena, and quickly took on the construction of sports and single-seater bodywork for Ferrari when their regular carrozzeria, Scaglietti, was overwhelmed with demand for Ferrari road car bodies.

Fantuzzi's first Ferraris were the 250TR Spyder and the initial works team of three 250TR59s. From 1959 to 1966, Fantuzzi built most of the bodies for Ferrari Formula 1 cars, as well as a number of one-off roadgoing Ferraris. However, in the second half of the 1960s he fell out with Enzo Ferrari and broke his ties with the company.

Fantuzzi subsequently worked with Tecno, the racing team of the Pederzani brothers in Bologna. He did body work for De Tomaso, and for Scuderia Serenissima and its parent, Automobili Serenissima. Meanwhile, his son Fiorenzo had set up a repair shop in Modena, specialising in body work on classic Italian sports and sports-racing cars. Medardo Fantuzzi died in 1986, and Fiorenzo continued to use the Carrozzeria Fantuzzi name until he retired in 1990.

Farina (I)
1919–1953, Turin

The work of Stabilimenti Farina – more strictly Stabilimenti Industriali Giovanni Farina SA – is sometimes confused with that of the better-known Pinin Farina, later known as Pininfarina. In fact, the two companies were related: Giovanni Farina was the older brother of Battista "Pinin" Farina, who learned his trade at the older company. A third member of the family became important in the motor industry, too: this was Giuseppe "Nino" Farina, the first Formula 1 world champion, who was a son of Giovanni Farina.

The Stabilimenti Farina workshop was established in Turin shortly after 1900, but its significant coachbuilding history is generally considered to have begun in 1919. During the 1914-1918 war, Stabilimenti Farina focussed on production of war matériel, and among other things was involved with aircraft production. After the war, it wholeheartedly embraced car bodywork production, and during the inter-war years built bodies for all the major Italian chassis makers, including Alfa Romeo, Fiat, Isotta Fraschini, Itala and Lancia. From 1935, styling was overseen by Pietro Frua, who would eventually set up his own coachbuilding company in 1944.

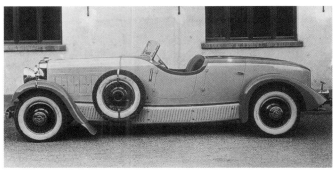

Farina: 1931 Cadillac V16 2+2 Spyder, perhaps a surprising incarnation for a Cadillac.

After the hiatus of the 1939-1945 war, Farina returned to car bodywork production, building a number of bodies for the new sports car brands such as Ferrari and Maserati. Among its employees was Alfredo Vignale, who learned the coachbuilder's trade here before leaving to set up his own coachworks in 1948. However, Farina never seemed wholly at ease with the all-enveloping style that was popular in the late 1940s, and some of its creations seemed heavy and unadventurous. The company finally closed down in 1953.

Farina: The older company was still at the height of its powers in the mid-1930s, and this coupé body on a Lancia Astura dates from 1935. *(Coys Auctioneers)*

Farina: 1934 Alfa Romeo 6C 2300 Turismo with rather neat saloon body, in which the central door pillars are angled to match the windscreen.

Farina: Though attractive, this berlinetta body on an early Ferrari 166 Inter did not break any new ground. In search of new ideas, Ferrari would switch to the younger and more adventurous Pinin Farina company a few years later. (WikiMedia Commons)

Farina: There was a heaviness about the berlinetta bodywork for this 1951 Siata Daina. (David Hodges Collection)

Faurax/ Faurax & Chaussende (F)
1903–1963, Lyons (Monplaisir from 1920)

The Faurax business was originally established in Paris by PF Faurax in 1808 to build horse-drawn vehicles. Nearly a century later, in 1903, it relocated to Lyons and became part of the burgeoning car industry there. There is an unconfirmed suggestion that Faurax & Cie was associated with the coachbuilder of the same name that operated in Geneva in the pre-1914 period.

After the 1914-1918 war came some rapid changes. The first was in November 1919, when Faurax & Cie took on a new partner and became the Société Nouvelle des Etablissements Faurax, G Jarsaillon & Cie. Just a year later, the company joined forces with the coachbuilder Chaussende, becoming Faurax & Chaussende and moving to Monplaisir.

The new company held a licence to build Baehr transformable bodies and built a number of touring car bodies during the 1920s. However, it soon refocussed on commercial bodywork and entered a partnership with Berliet. In 1963, Berliet took over the Faurax & Chaussende works, turning it into its Lyons branch.

Farina: On the Siata 208CS in 1953 Farina created a purposeful, aggressive, style.

Farina: The so-called "Flying Jaguar" was built on a Jaguar XK120 chassis in 1952. It was very much a Farina design, and quite a shock to Jaguar enthusiasts. (Author's Collection)

Faust-Design (D)
1986, Cologne

Faust-Design was based in Cologne and built just one special body, which was a gullwing-door conversion of a Mercedes-Benz 500 SEC. The company was presumably hoping to ride the wave of enthusiasm in the Middle East and elsewhere for extreme conversions of the S-Class models in the 1980s, but disappeared without trace after displaying its work at the Essen Motor Show in 1986.

Most converters who put their name to gullwing-door Mercedes SECs in the 1980s started with a basic conversion by Styling-Garage or one of the other big names. However, Faust-Design built its own car from a crash-damaged SEC, adding wide-body styling that was probably inspired by the Koenig Specials design.

Fehler (CH)
c1925–1928, Berne

Very little is known about the Fehler coachworks in Berne. However, the company is known to have worked with the Santschi coachworks on the construction of at least three bodies in the mid-1920s. These were sporting bodies on Alfa Romeo and Salmson chassis, and a saloon on a Bugatti chassis.

Felber & Fils/Felber Frères (F)
1835–c1931, Paris; later Puteaux

The Felber company was founded in Paris in 1835 by Charles Felber, and entered the automotive industry in 1898, its earliest known work being displayed at that year's Paris Salon. By the turn of the century, Felber had produced around 120 car bodies, some of which had gone to foreign royalty which included the Russian court. During the Great War, the Felber works manufactured ambulance bodies.

From 1919, the workshops moved to Puteaux and the company became Felber Frères under the direction of its founder's two sons, Victor and Charles junior. It rapidly became busy, employing some 300 staff and building 300 bodies a year while also undertaking repairs on 900 more. There were Felber bodies on a wide variety of chassis, including Ballot, BNC, Hispano-Suiza, Hotchkiss, Lorraine-Dietrich, Renault and Voisin. Yet despite its success, the Felber company never really developed a distinctive style of its own. From the early 1920s the company held a licence for Baehr transformable coachwork, and in the early 1930s it took out a licence for the Hibbard & Darrin design with its triangular B-pillar and trapezoid side windows. However, the company closed its doors in the early part of the1930s.

Fernandez/Fernandez & Darrin (F)
1932–1937, Paris and Boulogne-sur-Seine
Initially but briefly in business with aviation pioneer Marcel Bloch-Dassault, the French-domiciled South American banker J Fernandez gave his name to a new coachwork company in Paris. Inspired by the Barker coachwork he had seen in the Alain Resnais film *Stavisky* on a Rolls-Royce Phantom II (in fact the prototype 24EX), he worked only on top-quality chassis. The Fernandez company lasted in this form until 1932, when it was joined by Howard Darrin, the American stylist fresh from the break-up of Parisian coachbuilder Hibbard & Darrin.

This was not an auspicious time to establish a new coachbuilding company because the effects of the 1929 Wall Street Crash were still being felt, but Fernandez & Darrin found new outlets in Europe, and especially in Britain, where the company set up a separate production facility at Kilburn in north-west London. Darrin's work made imaginative use of colour and aerodynamic shapes, and continued in the original Fernandez tradition of being built only on prestigious chassis. By 1934, he was designing sleek coupé-chauffeur models, one notable design being seen first on a Renault Nervastella at the 1934 Paris Salon and then repeated on a Rolls-Royce 20/25 and on a pair of Hispano-Suiza chassis for the Rothschild family in Britain.

For more conservative clients, Darrin had a cabriolet coupé de ville design with a fixed rear roof, typically for such chassis as the Hispano-Suiza K6. The company built three cabriolets on Bugatti 57 chassis in 1935-1936, but the glory years were over. In autumn 1937, Howard Darrin went back to his native USA, where he was able to call himself "Darrin of Paris" in his new business on Hollywood's Sunset Boulevard. The Fernandez & Darrin business closed down.

Figoni/ Figoni & Falaschi (F)
1923–1955, Boulogne sur-Seine
Although the Figoni & Falaschi partnership was not formed until May 1935, Giuseppe Figoni had already built his reputation as a coachbuilder in France. A native of Piacenza in Italy, Figoni had moved to Paris with his family at the age of three in 1894. From the age of 14, he was apprenticed to a wagon-maker called Vachet. After military service in the Great War, he returned to Paris, and in 1923 founded his own business under the name of

Figoni: Creative use of paint was a characteristic, as seen on this 1929 Bugatti Type 43/44 roadster. (Author's Collection)

Figoni: The front wing braces are unmistakably Voisin, but the body on this 1934 C27 chassis is unmistakably Figoni. *(Author's Collection)*

Figoni: This 1927 Figoni torpedo body on a Ballot RH chassis only briefly hints at what was to come later. *(David Hodges Collection)*

Carrosserie Automobile in Boulogne-sur-Seine at the heart of the French motor industry.

By this stage calling himself Joseph, Figoni set up initially as a body repair shop, but was soon modifying existing bodies and by 1925 was building complete bodies himself. He worked on several types of chassis, including Alfa Romeo, Ballot, Bugatti, Delage, Delahaye, Duesenberg, Panhard and Renault. Ballot become a major customer, and Figoni built 65 bodies on the company's chassis between 1925 and 1931, including a lovely torpedo which he showed at the 1927 Paris Salon.

Figoni: Neat and stylish is the body on this 1932 supercharged Alfa Romeo 8C 2300 chassis. This was the only short-chassis example of the model bodied by the firm. *(Eventageous PR)*

Figoni: Striking use of colour makes this elegant coupé body on an Alfa Romeo 1750 GS chassis an outstanding success. *(Concours of Eelegance)*

Figoni & Falaschi: Even the plate bearing the company's details had a style of its own. *(Author's Collection)*

Figoni & Falaschi: Unmistakable again, but this time from the combined talents of Figoni & Falaschi. The chassis is a 1937 Delahaye 135M. *(Author's Collection)*

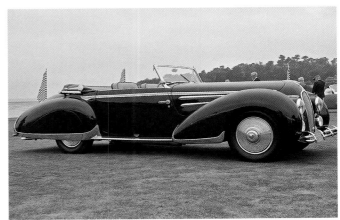

Figoni & Falaschi: The company's ability to create eye-catching bodywork remained intact in the 1940s, even though the designs were less flamboyant than before the war. This is a 1949 El Glaoui cabriolet on the Delahaye 135M chassis. *(WikiMedia Commons)*

Figoni was also fascinated by aircraft design, and created the aerodynamic racing bodywork for the Alfa Romeo 8C 2300 that won Le Mans in 1932. At the 1933 Paris Salon, he showed a sporting body on the new Delahaye Type 138 18CV chassis. This was an immediate success, and made Figoni a top choice for Delahaye buyers.

This growing success led Figoni to form a partnership with Ovidio Falaschi, who was in a position to finance the expansion that was Figoni's logical next business step. Falaschi was also experienced in the automotive business and had his own firm ideas about styling, although in practice he confined himself largely to looking after the financial side of the business.

The typical Figoni body was a stylish coupé or cabriolet with curvaceous, flowing wings that conveyed an air of sensuality. Figoni enjoyed working with the fashion designers of the day, whose ideas and textures he often matched in his coachbuilt bodies. His usual method was to begin with a simple sketch, transferring the design to the intended chassis by making up iron bands to represent the shapes, and then making an ash wood frame to which the hand-formed metal would be attached. Nevertheless, bodies might be tried with several different configurations until their creator was satisfied with the lines. Figoni particularly enjoyed experimenting with colour, and used the latest metallic paints to give his cars dramatic combinations of two and even three colours.

Not surprisingly, the Delahaye 135 chassis was an early candidate for the attentions of the new Figoni & Falaschi company, and an example with all-enveloping teardrop-shaped wings, incorporating the sensuous curves that Figoni favoured, became the sensation of the 1936 Paris Salon. The style, augmented by strips of chrome, would be built onto 11 Delahaye chassis in all, and onto several other chassis from the grand French makers of the 1930s.

It was followed in 1937 by another defining icon of the

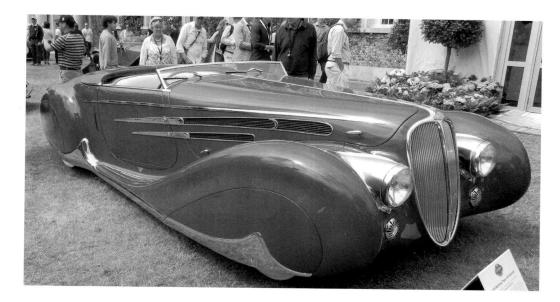

Figoni & Falaschi: … and the elegance continued: this later body with the teardrop wings and enclosed wheels dates from 1939 and is on a Delahaye 165 chassis. *(Author's Collection)*

era – the streamlined Teardrop Coupé body on a Talbot Lago T150C SS chassis that was destined for an Indian Maharani. Ten cars were eventually built, all with the same flowing and voluptuous lines, egg-shaped side windows and a streamlined tail. Some had a tail fin; most had plenty of chrome decoration.

However, these were not the only designs from Figoni & Falaschi. There were less extravagant cabriolets built in small series on the Chrysler Eight and Lancia Belna chassis, and the 1936 Paris Salon had a particularly attractive design on the Delage D6-70. The company also worked on the Talbot T150 chassis, and bodied a Voisin C27 for the Shah of Persia – although the design was quite conventional and Gabriel Voisin himself did not like it.

When France was occupied during the 1939-1945 war, the Figoni & Falaschi premises were requisitioned for the manufacture of aircraft components; some sources say it made primarily heaters and electric radiators. The company was able to begin coachbuilding again after the war, and unsurprisingly worked predominantly with the Delahaye 135 chassis. However, some of the magic had already gone: these late 1940s creations were influenced by a desire to match or outdo American styling trends, and the peaked bonnets of the seven "Narwhal" bodies built on Delahaye 135 chassis in 1946-1947 were simply ugly. There were more sober designs in this period, too, notably the series of 18 El Glaoui cabriolets on Delahaye chassis (named after the buyer of the first one, who was Thami El Glaoui, the Pasha of Marrakesh,).

The company's last great designs dated from 1948 and 1949, and were produced for Delahaye and Talbot Lago Type 26 chassis. By this time, the market for the grand and elegant designs for which Figoni & Falaschi were famous had shrunk drastically, and in 1950 Ovidio Falaschi decided to retire. Joseph Figoni kept the business going for a few more years in partnership with his son. There were a few bodies on the new Delahaye 235 chassis, some Delage

D6 3-litres and a pair of Bentleys. Figoni also worked with Citroën and on the Autobleu project that Ghia had abandoned. It was inevitable that volume manufacture should enter the picture as the traditional custom-building market fell away, and Figoni did a run of 500 bodies on the Simca Sport chassis for the Algerian and Tunisian markets. However, in 1955 Simca terminated its supply of chassis, and this loss of business brought about the demise of the Figoni company.

Figoni ended his career as a concessionaire for the Lancia marque in France. A grand total of around 1150 bodies had come from the companies owned jointly or separately by Joseph Figoni and Ovidio Falaschi in just over three decades of coachbuilding, and many of them are still considered to be among the most beautiful ever built. Nevertheless, there have always been dissenters. For some tastes, the archetypal Figoni & Falaschi designs were excessively ornamental; one British wag referred to them as "phony and flashy" while Jaguar founder William Lyons somewhat waspishly described them as "positively indecent".

Fiol (E)
Barcelona, 1910s to 1930s
Baltasar Fiol was one of the most highly regarded Spanish coachbuilders of his time, and worked on a number of the

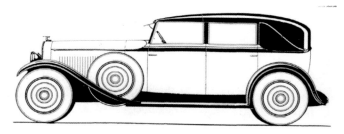

Fiol: Described as a "double cabriolet transformable" is this body by the Barcelona coachbuilder Fiol on a Hispano-Suiza J12 chassis, designated in Spain as a 56 BIS.

grander chassis. There were bodies for Rolls-Royce 40/50 and Phantom models in the 1920s, and Fiol had his own stand at the 1925 Paris Salon.

In the 1930s, Fiol became an agent for Dodge and Adler, and constructed bodies on several American chassis, including Cadillac, Dodge and Packard. However, the company was probably best known for its coachwork on Hispano-Suiza chassis from the Spanish arm of the company in Barcelona, and there were examples of this from at least 1916 until the later 1930s.

Fioravanti (I)
1987–present, Moncalieri, near Turin

The Fioravanti name has been inextricably linked with Ferrari since 1964, although Leonardo Fioravanti did not set up in business himself until 1987. In that year, he left his job at Pininfarina, where he had been a designer for nearly 24 years and established his own design studio. This started life as a provider of architectural design services for the Japanese market, although Fioravanti himself never lost contact with the automotive world. He spent the years from 1988 to 1991 working for the Fiat Group, initially as the deputy General Manager at Ferrari and then as head of the Fiat design studio. From 1991, Fioravanti returned full-time to his own company, and turned it into a concept studio, working especially closely with Ferrari.

Fioravanti's own links with Ferrari dated right back to 1964, when he joined Pininfarina as a designer after graduating in aerodynamics and car body design from the Milan polytechnic. Here, he was responsible for several Ferrari designs, the greatest of which was the 1968 365 GTB/4 Daytona. His other designs included the P5 and P6 concept cars, the 365 GT4 2+2, the 512 Berlinetta Boxer, the 308 GTB, and the 288 GTO. By the end of his time with the company, Fioravanti had risen to become Managing Director and General Manager of the research department.

Since 1991, the Fioravanti company has produced several concept cars, mostly exhibited under the Fioravanti name although the 2001 Fioravanti LF became the Alfa Romeo Vola. The company also designed the retractable glass roof that was used on the 2005 Ferrari 575 Superamerica. In 2008, the company joined Ferrari's new Portfolio custom-building programme and became responsible for special coachwork. Its first special coachbuilt Ferrari was the one-off SP1 of 2008, based on the F430 and constructed for a Japanese collector.

Fissore (I)
1920–1984, Savigliano

The Fissore company was best known for its work after the Second World War, although by that stage it had been established for more than a quarter of a century. It worked with a variety of manufacturers, of whom the most notable were Fiat, Auto Union-DKW, and Monteverdi. A relative of one of the company's founders also established a separate company, Rayton Fissore.

Carrozzeria Fissore was founded in 1920 at Savigliano (Cuneo) by four brothers, Antonio, Bernardo, Costanzo and Giovanni Fissore, to build carriages and horse-drawn agricultural vehicles. However, it soon became clear that the future lay in car bodywork, and by the end of the 1920s the Fissore company was taking its first steps in that direction.

During the 1930s, Fissore mainly modified production cars. From 1936, Bernardo took control of the company and the work expanded to include hearses, mail vans and small buses as well as special bodies for cars. When the Second World War came, the Fissore company was drawn into military work, building a variety of truck-based bodies such as mobile surgeries and mobile offices.

Once the war ended, private cars once again became the primary focus, although there were still some commercial-vehicle bodies, some ambulances and some hearses. Fissore's future direction was most clearly indicated by the Giardinetta estate car for Fiat, based on their 1100 saloon model. However, the company attracted more attention with a 1953 coupé design on the same chassis, called the 1100 TV Fissore Coupé. Fiat followed through with a string of commissions for variants of the Multipla and 600, but Fissore's big success was with the series-built 1500 and 1600S coupés and spiders from 1959.

From 1958, Fissore had a major contract with Auto Union-DKW in Germany, and designed several models for manufacture and sale in South America. First came a restyled DKW F93 called the Belcar in saloon form and

Fissore: The 1964 De Tomaso Vallelunga was one product of the relationship between the supercar maker and Fissore in the 1960s. *(David Hodges Collection)*

Fissore: The Elva 2-litre 160 was built to a design by Trevor Fiore. (*David Hodges Collection*)

Fissore: Again drawn up by Trevor Fiore, this wedge-shaped coupé was shown on a TVR chassis in 1965. (*David Hodges Collection*)

the Vemaguet as an estate car, which was built in Brazil. This was rebodied in 1964 as a two-door saloon sold as the Vemag Fissore, which was much less successful. There were also coupé and spider derivatives of the German-built Auto Union 1000 models, manufactured in Argentina and Spain as well as in Brazil.

In 1962, Fissore developed and built a small series of bodies for the Osca 1600 GT, consisting of 22 coupés and two convertibles. Then, as the Osca business wound down, Fissore sought work elsewhere. An interesting Elva-BMW GT 160 S with rear-mounted 2-litre engine shown at Turin in 1964 led nowhere, but the same show also marked the start of a collaboration with De Tomaso. Fissore designed the body for the mid-engined Vallelunga, and built several prototypes, including a unique spider. However, Alejandro de Tomaso had a stake in Ghia at the time and had the production bodies built there.

The 1965 show brought a modified Volvo P1800 and a small city car called the Aruanda, but neither led anywhere. By contrast, the wedge-shaped TVR Trident coupé at that show, drawn up by Fissore designer Trevor Fiore (né Frost), did enter production – albeit through one of TVR's dealers who bought the rights to it – and remained available until 1976. It was also Trevor Fiore who proposed a wedge-shaped

successor to Alpine's A110, and this eventually became the production A310 after some modification.

By the mid-1960s, Fissore was employing around 200 people. Still seeking a lucrative long-term contract, in 1969 it concluded a deal with Monteverdi in Switzerland that would shape its whole future. The deal began with the body manufacture of the High Speed 375S, which had been designed by Frua.

Small numbers of other designs were still coming from Fissore. The 1969 Turin Show had the Mongho 650, a little coupé designed by local stylist Aldo Sessano around uprated Fiat 500 mechanical elements that remained a one-off. Also based on Fiats were the Sabrina, a special-bodied Multipla, and the related Marinella beach-car version. Anxious to retain a close relationship with Fiat, Fissore took on the 127-based Maina Gipsy open fun car that its designers had been unable to produce themselves, and in 1971 introduced it in modified form as the Fissore 127 Scout. Many were built, and several were exported. Early versions had a fibreglass body over a tubular metal frame, but from 1974 pressed metal bodywork was used. Fissore designed a smaller follow-up called the Poker and based on the Fiat 126, but a plan for production in Greece was never realised. Still hoping to secure more work for Fiat, Fissore developed a convertible body for the company's Ritmo (badged as a Strada in the UK), but lost the contract to Bertone's rival design.

Other attempts to secure lucrative contracts saw Fissore build a four-door convertible prototype of the Opel Diplomat B, but Opel did not bite. There was also a small sporting coupé based on the Autobianchi A112 and called the Otas, but this too failed to bring Fissore the business it needed. Probably as a precaution, Bernardo made his firm a limited company in 1971, appointing his daughter Fernanda as President and his son Sergio as Vice President. Increasingly, however, it was the Monteverdi deal that provided a steady flow of work and ensured Fissore's survival in the 1970s.

The original High Speed design ceased production after a copyright suit, and Monteverdi came up with a new shape

Fissore: The 1977 Monteverdi Sierra was based on a Plymouth Volare with some extensive body modifications. (David Hodges Collection)

which some believe was by him while others attribute to Fissore. However, Fissore never claimed as their own any of the Monteverdi High Speed designs with which they were involved, although there was no doubting the resemblance between the Monteverdi Hai of 1970 and Trevor Fiore's A310 design for Alpine. The company nevertheless did acknowledge the Monteverdi 2.8 Turbo, a three-door coupé based on a Ford Granada that did not enter production, as their work.

Monteverdi's prediction of 100 cars a year was never realised until the 1976 introduction of the Safari off-roader, which was based on an International Scout. But the volumes were still higher than Monteverdi could handle with their traditional production methods. Ironically, Fissore had gained the contract to build the first Monteverdis because of limited production capacity at the Frua works; now their own capacity limitations meant that some of the High Speed cars were actually constructed by two smaller coachbuilders, Poccardi and Embo. Monteverdi pumped money into the company to facilitate a switch to more industrial production methods, and in return took a stake in Fissore.

Sensing perhaps that the dependency on a relatively small company like Monteverdi might ultimately prove risky, Fernanda Fissore established a separate company in 1976 with her husband, Giulio Malvino. This became Rayton Fissore. Their action was not misguided, for at the

end of the decade Monteverdi took full ownership of the original Fissore company. From around 1980, Monteverdi had its four-door Range Rover conversions built at the Fissore works, but by 1984 the Swiss company was in trouble. When it closed that year, it took Fissore with it, and the coachbuilding business was liquidated shortly afterwards.

Fleury (F)
1920s, Thonon-les Bains
Little is known about Carrosserie E Fleury, which operated from Thonon-les Bains in Haute-Savoie, on the shores of Lake Geneva. Among its creations was a formal landaulet, built on a Delage chassis in about 1928.

Fontana (I)
1950s, Padua
There have been several different coachbuilders with the Fontana name, but the best known is Carrozzeria Fontana from Padua, which bodied a number of racing Ferraris for the Marzotto brothers in the 1950s.

Franay (F)
1903–1956, Levallois-Perret
Carrosserie Franay was a leading French coachbuilder in the first half of the 20th century. Jean-Baptiste Franay was apprenticed as a saddle-maker with Henri Binder in Paris,

Franay: This superb coupé de ville body was built in 1934 on a Hispano-Suiza 54CV chassis. (David Hodges Collection)

Franay: Also dating from 1934, this two-door saloon on a Hispano-Suiza J12 chassis demonstrates Franay's versatility. *(Author's Collection)*

Franay: The company returned to coachbuilding in 1946 with this body on a Delahaye 145 chassis; its crouching stance made it look fast even when standing still. *(David Hodges Collection)*

Franay: Although there is a hint of uncertainty about the rear quarters of this 1949 two-seater on a Talbot-Lago T26 chassis, it is much more assured than many contemporary efforts by lesser coachbuilders. *(WikiMedia)*

and left to set up his own business in 1903. His coachworks at the Rue du Caporal-Peugeot were responsible for solid but unexciting bodies in the period up to his death in 1922.

The business then passed to his son Marius Franay, an engineer who was a product of the Arts et Métiers technical college in Paris. He refocussed the business on building luxury bodies for the top makers of the day, and the company rapidly rose to fame. In the 1930s, Franay was especially known for its coupé-chauffeur bodies, and was often successful in the popular concours d'élégance events of the

period. The company was one of the last coachbuilders to specialise in coupé de ville bodies, a style which had become anachronistic in the economic circumstances of the period, but produced a variety of supremely elegant and discreetly stylish types. There were Franay bodies on many leading

Franay: Underneath this grand and imposing limousine body hides the running-gear of a six-cylinder Citroën Traction Avant. This French presidential limousine was completed in 1956, with design input from Philippe Charbonneaux. (Citroën)

chassis of the time, including Bentley, Cadillac, Delage D8-100, Duesenberg J and SJ, Packard and Rolls-Royce. Those on Hispano-Suiza chassis included an aerodynamic "coach" for the King of Romania on a 12-cylinder model, and a K6 coupé de ville for the actor Harry Baur. Also notable was a 1938 coupé de ville parade car for the French President, Albert Lebrun, on a Renault Suprastella chassis.

In the meantime, Marius Franay had diversified his activities, as insurance against the long-term effects of the Depression in the early 1930s. In 1935, he established a second business called LTC (Laboratoires de Travaux Cinématographiques) at Saint-Cloud, which went on to have a long and successful career in post-production work for the cinema.

After the disruption of the Second World War, Franay started in the luxury coachbuilding business again, and was ready for the 1946 Paris Salon with a cabriolet body on a pre-war Delahaye 145 12-cylinder racing chassis. The company went on to build a number of bodies on newer Delahaye chassis, some sensuously flamboyant Bentleys and Talbot-Lagos, and there were a dozen on Rolls-Royce as well.

However, this was an era of diminishing opportunities for the traditional coachbuilder. Marius Franay died in February 1954, and the company's stand at the 1955 Paris Salon was its last. Its last two bodies were a Bentley Continental and the special French Presidential limousine on a Citroen 15/6 chassis, to a design by Philippe Charbonneaux. The company closed down in 1956.

Franco Belge (B)
1940s–1950s, Ghent
Carrosserie Franco-Belge is best known for its conversions of Citroën Traction Avant models. It constructed convertibles on the basis of the 11 and BL models, of which there were three types, and on the 15-Six, of which there were two different designs.

Frech-Hoch (CH)
c1919–c1935, Sissach
The Swiss Frech-Hoch company is still operating today and is well known for its commercial and coach bodies. However, in the 1920s and 1930s it was also active as a builder of car bodywork.

Emil Frech-Hoch founded his wagon works at Sissach in 1899, working on horse-drawn vehicles for his first two decades in business but turning the company into a builder of bodies for motorised vehicles after 1919. Frech-Hoch built touring bodies on Fiat chassis, closed bodies on Pic-Pic and American chassis, and bodies for light commercial vehicles. There were also a few luxury bodies on chassis such as Cadillac, Chrysler and Cord, and a roadster is also known on a Bugatti Brescia chassis from about 1927. However, the car bodying business ceased some time in the mid-1930s.

Freidenberg & Vernède (F)
Late 1940s, Montélimar
The Freidenberg & Vernède company is remembered for a single body on Delahaye 135M chassis. The style showed great promise, and has been described as worthy of the great Parisian coachbuilders. Unfortunately, the client failed to pay. The car was sold to the Charrière bus company, and nothing more is known of its constructor.

Frey (CH)
1920s, Zürich
Almost nothing is known about the Zürich coachworks owned by a certain P Frey. The company advertised a touring body and a landaulet-taxi (the latter probably on a Martini chassis) in 1922 but there is no further information except that the company also became involved with bus bodywork.

Friederichs (D)
c1905–1939, Frankfurt
Heinrich Ludwig Friederichs founded his carriage-building business on 1 July 1840 in Frankfurt, and the company had a distinguished history as a maker of carriages for royalty before it began making bodies for cars. The company passed from father to son Carl in 1876 and then down to grandsons Heinrich and Rudolf in 1900, and it was this generation that began building car bodies, some of the earliest being on Benz chassis from about 1905.

Heinrich Friederichs took out a patent for cabriolet bodywork early on. In the 1920s, there were bodies for Adler, Benz and Daimler chassis, and Friederichs worked for Austro Daimler, Horch and Steyr as well as meeting private orders for bodies on LaSalle and Peugeot chassis. The company's coachbuilding activities came to an end in 1939, when the Second World War broke out. However, the company remains in business as a commercial body builder, now known as Carl Friederichs GmbH. Very few Friederichs car bodies are known to survive, the earliest being on a 1926 Maybach W5 chassis.

Frua (I)
1944–1983, Turin

The Frua name was at its peak in the 1960s, when Pietro Frua's designs were at the leading edge of Italian design and were very influential on the direction of car styling. He was a prolific designer and is credited with more than 210 designs. Although much of his work was for Italian car makers, he also designed a number of bodies for British and German companies.

Pietro Frua was born in 1913. His father Carlo worked for the Fiat body department, and Pietro was trained as a draughtsman at the Scuola Fiat in Turin. From there, he joined Stabilimenti Farina at the age of 17, and worked his way up to become the company's Director of Styling at the age of 22. It was here that he met his pupil and lifelong friend, Giovanni Michelotti, who took over from him as Farina's styling chief when he left after a disagreement with Attilo Farina to set up his own design studio in 1937.

However, styling work was in very limited demand during the war years of 1939 to 1945, and Frua eked out a living by designing children's cars, electric ovens and kitchen units, and even a monocoque motor scooter. Then in 1944 he was able to buy a bomb-damaged factory in Turin. He hired 15 staff (among whom was Sergio Coggiola, who would found his own carrozzeria in 1966) and set himself up as a car design studio that he called Carrozzeria Pietro Frua.

Business was not brisk in the beginning. Frua's earliest known design is a Fiat 1100 Sport Barchetta, dating from 1946. Then came a commission from Maserati, who asked Frua to style some bodies for their new A6G sports chassis. Between 1950 and 1957, Frua built 19 spyders and seven coupés in three different design series, including some on the A6GCS racing chassis. However, an offer from Ghia was too good to resist: in 1957, Frua sold his business to that company and was appointed as its Head of Design, taking over from Michelotti as head of design at Ghia-Aigle as well.

Frua: Despite the fussy grille design, there is a light sportiness about the body on this 1951 Maserati A6G 2000. *(David Hodges Collection)*

Frua: Again a fussy grille design rather spoils the essentially right lines of this berlinetta body on a 1953 Panhard Nardi NarDyna. *(David Hodges Collection)*

The late 1950s saw Frua contributing to the design of the Volvo P1800, which was primarily Pelle Petterson's work but is sometimes credited wholly to Frua. For Borgward, he designed a coupé on the small Lloyd Alexander, which was then built in small numbers by Ghia-Aigle. He was probably responsible for the Renault Floride coupé (called the Caravelle in English-speaking countries), but fell out

Frua: This body dates from 1954 and is on a 1.3-litre Ermini. *(David Hodges Collection)*

with Ghia director Luigi Segre over who deserved the credit for the car's design. As a result, Frua left Ghia to set up his own design studio again. This time, he called it Studio Technico Pietro Frua.

There was no shortage of business. After Ghia-Aigle ceased coachbuilding in 1959, former employee Adriano Guglielmetti set himself up as Carrosserie Italsuisse, and called upon Frua to do most of his design work. It was probably Frua's company who built all the Italsuisse prototypes, too. His designs for Italsuisse included a pontoon-bodied Volkswagen Beetle in 1960, a Maserati 3500 GTI coupé in 1961, and a pair of bodies for Studebaker, who were trying to revitalise their range. In 1964, there was an attractive spyder based on Opel Kadett running-gear.

Frua also established a lasting relationship with Maserati in 1963, beginning with that year's Quattroporte saloon and going on to the acclaimed Mistral of 1965. The Borgward connection came good, too: Frua had been engaged to

Frua: The body for the AC428 of 1965 was quite distinctive even though it pandered to the contemporary vogue for Italian GT designs. (*David Hodges Collection*)

Frua: The Maserati Mistrale of 1969 saw Frua still using design cues that had worked on the AC428. (*David Hodges Collection*)

Frua: Many of the mid-1960s designs shared the ideas Frua had set out on the AC 428. This is a Glas 2.6-litre coupé. (*David Hodges Collection*)

Frua: The origin of the Monteverdi Hai design is still disputed: was it by Frua or by Trevor Fiore – or perhaps even both? *(David Hodges Collection)*

Frua: Both Frua and Trevor Fiore had input to the design of the 1971 Monteverdi 375C. *(David Hodges Collection)*

Frua: Launched in 1976, the Maserati Kyalami had a body that Frua restyled from that of the De Tomaso Longchamp at the request of Maserati's then owner, Alejandro de Tomaso. This is a 1980 example. *(David Hodges Collection)*

By the 1970s, Frua was no longer in such demand. Few makers called on his legendary ability to design and construct a fully functional prototype in ten weeks, and a fastback coupé body in glass-fibre commissioned for the Ford Escort Mexico in 1971 came to nothing. The fashion for Italian styling was on the wane, and the excitement of Frua's regular appearances at the annual Turin Motor Show was no longer there. In 1982, Frua was diagnosed with cancer. He died a few weeks after his 70th birthday in June 1983, and the company that bore his name closed down.

FTI Design (F)
1950 on, Enghien-les-Bains

French-born designer Louis Lepoix took up residence in Germany after working on aircraft for the French military occupation forces during 1945. Two years later, he founded FTI Design, whose initials stood for Form Technik International. This was and remains primarily a design house, and its most famous piece of design is probably the Bic biro. The company has also been involved with a number of vehicle designs, including for cars.

Lepoix was invited by Pierre Marco, then in charge at Bugatti, to put forward ideas for the shape of the new Bugatti 101 in 1952, although the prototypes were built by several different coachbuilders. Most of FTI Design's vehicle work in the 1950s then centred on lorry cabs, for makers such as Berliet, Hanomag, Magirus-Deutz, Pegaso and Steyr. It was responsible for the design of 1958 Farmobil light agricultural truck and acted as a consultant on some all-terrain vehicles for Lohr in 1977-1978.

In the 1960s and 1970s, FTI Design worked on car designs with several German manufacturers. Among these were Volkswagen, for whom work was done on a new saloon from 1969 and on a compact car from 1977. There was work on a BMW coupé in 1978, too. The company later became involved with urban-car projects, and worked on the 1972 Universal one-box compact car for Steyr and the 1973 Urbanix, neither of which entered production.

design the body for the planned Hansa 1300, which was to replace the Goliath 1100, but the design remained unused when Borgward went bankrupt in 1961. In 1963, that design was adapted to become a new saloon for the German car maker Glas, and Frua went on to design other bodies for them: a small GT coupé and related cabriolet, and a large 2600 V8 coupé. All these later gained BMW badges when Glas sold out in 1966, but despite submitting some interesting proposals that included a special 2002ti saloon in 1972, Frua was never able to interest BMW in further designs.

In 1965, there was the 428 convertible for the British car maker AC, and this was followed in 1967 by a coupé version. There was a one-off Jaguar coupé in 1966. Another customer was the Swiss Monteverdi company, for whom Frua designed its first car in 1967 – the High Speed 375S – and a later model called the 2000 GTI that did not see production. Actual production of the 375S went to Fissore because the Frua works had limited capacity, but the Monteverdi connection remained as Frua designed the Hai 450 that did not progress beyond the prototype stage – although some sources credit the design to Trevor Fiore.

G

Gaborit (F)
1923–c1925, Paris and Levallois-Perret
Jean Gaborit was an ambitious young man who set up his coachwork business in 1923 in the heart of the French motor industry at Levallois. He was aged just 19 at the time. He employed contract workers to build his first car body, a saloon on Sizaire-Berwick chassis that was noted for the quality of its construction. Encouraged by this initial success, Gaborit took on his own staff at the workshop in Levallois.

Gaborit: An impressive limousine body by Jean Gaborit on a 1922 Farman.

Over the next couple of years, Gaborit's reputation spread and his work was rewarded with several prizes at concours d'élégance events. The company had its own premises in Paris. At the 1923 Paris Salon, the company showed a cabriolet on a Hispano-Suiza 32CV chassis, a saloon on a Renault 40CV and a coupé-limousine on a Farman chassis for no less a figure than the Shah of Persia. The business expanded, and employed 150 staff at its height, but it looks as if Gaborit had over-reached himself and his coachbuilding company folded during 1925.

Gaertner (D)
1912–1927, Bremen
The Gaertner company (always spelled that way, and not with an umlaut) was founded as a wagon-building business in 1880 by Carl Heinrich Louis Gaertner. There was little demand for car bodies in the early days, but in 1906 the first chassis maker set up business locally. This was NAMAG (the Norddeutsche Automobil- und Motorenwerke AG, or North German Automobile and Engine Works Ltd), which had links with Norddeutsche Lloyd. As NAMAG had no bodyshop of its own, it passed most of its Hansa-Lloyd chassis to Gaertner to be bodied, and the company was renamed Bremer Wagen- und Carrosserie-Werke GmbH (Bremen Wagon and Carriage Works Ltd) to suit.

From 1912, NAMAG effectively took over the coachworks, which was now renamed Louis Gaertner AG. The business was turned over to the production of ambulances and military trucks during the Great War, but when peace came Wilhelm Kunz quickly rose to the top. He had joined the company in 1914 as head of the construction department, and from 1921 he also became head of the Rembrandt coachworks in Delmenhorst; later he worked with Borgward as well. However, NAMAG collapsed in 1927 and took the Gaertner business with it. The factory was bought by Carl Borgward and Wilhelm Tecklenborg and became the Goliath plant.

Gallé (F)
1909–c1930, Boulogne-sur-Seine
The heyday of this French coachbuilder was in the 1920s, but Louis Gallé had begun building car bodies as early as 1909 and the company could trace its origins right back to 1840. The Gallé characteristics were conservative lines allied to a high quality of execution, although the company also built some unusual barrel-sided bodies which featured rounded door bottoms. There were examples on many of the grand chassis of the period – Hispano-Suiza, La Salle, Peugeot, Rolls-Royce and Voisin among them. A torpedo body on Bentley chassis also won a concours prize in Paris in 1928.

Gallé: A Hispano-Suiza H6B with two-seater drophead body.

In the late 1920s, Gallé was commissioned to design a complete range of bodies for the Belgian marque Minerva, but by the time of the 1930 Paris Salon there was clearly trouble within the company. That year, a breakaway company called Baxter-Gallé had a Packard on display at the show. The parent company subsequently forged links with Duvivier (qv) in Levallois-Perret and absorbed the small Parisian coachbuilders Currus and Girard (qqv). However, these links were short-lived as Gallé succumbed to the downturn in demand that affected all specialist coachbuilders at the start of the 1930s.

Gangloff (CH)
1903–1936, Geneva, then Berne (from 1928)
Founded in 1903 by Georges Gangloff, the company which bore his name went on to become one of Switzerland's most important coachbuilders after the Great War. It expanded greatly, establishing new branches in Colmar (1919, over the border in France and a major coachworks in its own right; see below), Zurich (where it took over the Geissberger business in 1926 or 1927), and Berne (1928). From 1928, the Berne premises became the company's headquarters.

The Swiss branch of Gangloff was the main supplier of bodies for Pic-Pic until that company's demise in 1924 but

Gangloff: A Bugatti Type 57 Atalante. (*David Burgess-Wise*)

also bodied a number of other chassis. Among these were Ansaldo, Delage, Hispano-Suiza, Isotta-Fraschini, Martini, Mercedes-Benz and Minerva; there were some bodies on American chassis, too, such as Hudson. The Colmar branch became independent in 1930 and became very well known and respected for its work on Bugatti chassis.

However, the parent company struggled in the economic downturn of the 1930s, and became insolvent in 1936. The business was broken up, the car body side becoming Carrosserie Séchéron and the rest of the business becoming three separate divisions that focussed on commercial and bus bodywork, on commercial trailers and on funicular railway vehicles. The renaissance of funicular railways in the 1970s made Gangloff an international operation.

Gangloff (F)

1930–present, Colmar

The French branch of Gangloff is closely associated with chassis-maker Bugatti. From the earliest times, Bugatti gave work to the Widerkehr coachworks in nearby Colmar, a long-established business founded in 1818 which had supplied horse-drawn vehicles to several of the European royal households during the 19th century. However, owner Louis Widerkehr retired after the Great War, and rented his premises to Georges Gangloff, whose coachbuilding business already had several branches in Switzerland. Gangloff continued very much where Widerkehr had left off, giving the Colmar business his own name and developing the close links with Bugatti. In 1930, Gangloff took full ownership of the business, which took on the name of Société Française de Carrosserie Gangloff.

In the mean time, Gangloff had appointed Gottlieb Moore and Paul Horlacher as directors of the Colmar business during 1927. These two men strengthened the relationship with the Bugatti works in Molsheim, and before long Gangloff was building the bodies for nearly

Gangloff: A 1934 Bugatti Type 57.

half of all new Bugattis – about five cars a month. Some of the body designs originated with Bugatti, but others were pure Gangloff creations. The relationship between the two companies became so close that it is sometimes difficult to be certain which one was responsible for a given design.

In 1935, the Colmar branch of Gangloff took over the coachbuilding and saddle-making business of a Monsieur Durr, which they renamed the Société Française de Carrosserie Gangloff. Particularly notable in this period were five bodies to Gangloff designs – three coupés and two cabriolets – on the Bugatti 57S chassis.

The links between Bugatti and the Gangloff coachworks were so close that the demise of the car maker in the early 1950s also brought about major changes for the coachbuilder. With its major market gone and the alternatives in the car business diminishing, Gangloff turned to the manufacture of bus bodies and abandoned car coachwork.

Gangloff: 1935 saw the production of this pleasing cabriolet body on a Type 57 Bugatti. *(Giles Chapman)*

Gangloff: A drophead coupé by Gangloff on a Type 57S, 1937. *(Giles Chapman)*

Gangloff was responsible for this body on a Type 101 Bugatti in 1953.

Garnier (F)
c1900–c1929, Paris

There is no substantial information about this Parisian coachbuilder, which seems to have been active from the turn of the century and to have disappeared at the end of the 1920s.

Gastell (D)
1920s, Mainz

The Gastell brothers established Waggonfabrik Gebrüder Gastell in the Mombach district of Mainz. They are known to have been active in the 1920s, when they bodied Maybach and Rabag-Bugatti chassis.

Gauthier (F)
1911–1919, Lyon-Villeurbanne and Beaulieu-Audincourt

Most of Henri Gauthier's activity as an independent coachbuilder took place before 1919. He had established a company at Lyons as early as 1885, and won a local award in 1894 before moving into the bicycle and motor-cycle business some time around 1905 as a maker of saddles and saddle-bags. By 1910 he was also looking at opportunities in the aircraft business.

Recognising the potential of the new car industry, Gauthier opened a second factory, this time further north at Beaulieu-Audincourt. The Peugeot factories were close by, and Peugeot became a major customer. By the start of the Great War, Gauthier claimed to be building as many as 5000 bodies a year and had become one of France's largest coachbuilders. One of its proud boasts in 1914 was that it held the only French franchise for using "tissus biasés" in hoods, which the company guaranteed were both waterproof and tear-proof. Although the Gauthier company survived the Great War, its importance to Peugeot persuaded the car maker to take it over during 1919.

Gazelle (D)
Dresden

The Karosseriefrabrik Gazelle name was used by Rudolf Stange & Co of Dresden. However, the dates of this company and details of its activity are not available.

GCS Bennemann (D)
1980s, Herzogenrath

Günther Benneman specialised in coachwork modifications on German cars during the boom years of the 1980s. His workshop at Herzogenrath, near Aachen, constructed a number of convertibles and otherwise modified derivatives of the Mercedes W126 S-Class models, many of which were destined for Middle Eastern customers. Some of the Benneman cars were converted under contract to other firms, including Koenig-Specials and Gemballa, who then completed them and sold them under their own names.

GCS Bennemann are believed to have built 41 convertibles on the C126 SEC (including three with hardtops), and 9 four-door convertibles on the W126 saloon. There was one ultra-long wheelbase landaulet, which is sometimes wrongly attributed to Schulz-Tuning. In the mid-1980s, the company also did a number of body conversions on Porsche 911 and 944 models.

As the market for extravagant conversions of this type dried up in the early 1990s, Bennemann closed his coachbuilding business and went on to run a fitness centre.

Geissberger (CH)
1903–c1927, Zürich

The C & R Geissberger Carrosserie could trace its origins back to 1850, when Johann Caspar Geissberger took ownership of a blacksmith's business at Seefeld near Zurich. The business expanded to take on wagon manufacture, and in 1880 Johann was joined by his two sons, Caspar and Robert. It was these two who would take the company into the automotive business in the early years of the 20th century, but not before a railway rolling-stock subsidiary (formed in 1895) had been split off from the main company as the Schweizerische Wagons- und Aufzügefabrik AG. Known as SWS, this company would also build some car bodies in the 1920s.

Meanwhile, Geissberger had become Switzerland's most important coachbuilder by 1914, building bodies for most of the early Martini, Saurer and Turicum chassis. The 1914-1918 war brought a hiatus in the business but Geissberger was active again from 1920. The company worked on American chassis for a time, but soon returned to European makes such as Delage, Hispano-Suiza and Peugeot. There was at least one body on a Mercedes-Benz 630.

By the middle of the decade, however, the business was struggling, and in late 1926 or early 1927 it was taken over by the Swiss branch of Gangloff. In 1937, ownership of the former Geissberger business passed to Langenthal.

Gemballa (D)
1981 to present, Leonberg

The Gemballa company is primarily associated with performance tuning of cars such as Porsche, McLaren and Mercedes-Benz, but it has also done some body modifications and major transformations on these vehicles.

It was founded in 1981 by Uwe Gemballa at Leonberg near Stuttgart in Germany. The company's main focus in the early days was on aftermarket parts for Porsche models, but inevitably owners of other high-performance exotics began to come to Gemballa for performance and associated body changes. Some of the Mercedes-Benz SL and SEL models that carried the Gemballa name in the 1980s had coachwork modifications by other specialists, such as Styling-Garage and Sbarro, while Gemballa's contribution was new interiors, special equipment (such as cameras instead of mirrors), bodykits and special paint. There was at least one conversion of a Ferrari Testarossa in this period.

During the 1980s, Gemballa creations on Porsche cars acquired names such as Avalanche, Cyrrus and Mirage. Characteristics were ostentatious wide-body styling and a swathe of high-tech equipment. Audio company Pioneer used Gemballa vehicles in their advertisements and brochures for several years. The cars were always extremely expensive and were built in low numbers.

The Gemballa body conversions of the 1990s became more subtle to reflect changing customer tastes. The company meanwhile continued to provide performance upgrades, and expanded by opening a new branch in California, where many US sales were being made. In the first decade of the new century, the company's main focus was still on Porsche models, but there were also some individual commissions on other makes such as Ferrari. Many customers were in the Middle East.

In early 2010, Uwe Gemballa went missing, and was found shot dead in South Africa later that year. Some believe that he was murdered in the course of a money laundering operation that went wrong. The German authorities seized the Gemballa factory in May that year and closed it down. However, CEO Andreas Schwarz and investor Steffen Korbach were able to buy the brand rights and name rights later that year and re-established the company as Gemballa GmbH.

In 2011, the revitalised company established a racing division to promote its performance work. By 2013, the listed Gemballa models were predominantly based on Porsche and McLaren cars, although individual commissions were always welcomed.

Germain & Chapiron (F)
1920s, Lyons

Germain & Chapiron was a small French coachbuilder, active at Lyons during the 1920s. Among others, it is known for a late-1920s body on a Bugatti Type 44 chassis.

Gété (F)
1960s, Méteren

Carrosserie Gété SA is known only for its conversions of the Citroën DS. Owner Henri Bossaert commissioned the Italian coachbuilder Frua to draw up a two-door body based on a wheelbase shortened by 470mm, and the first car was a coupé that was shown at the Paris Salon in 1960 under the name of the GT19 (note that the name of Gété is a pun on the French pronunciation of the letters GT). Tail fins were a notable feature, adding length and balance to the design.

Gété: As the "signature" on this picture makes clear, the Gété was designed by Italian coachbuilder Frua. (*David Hodges Collection*)

Ghia: An Alfa Romeo 6C 2500 bodied in 1946.

Ghia: US manufacturers began to take an interest in the Italian styling houses in the early 1950s, and Ghia was asked to design a coupé body for the 1953 Cadillac 62 chassis.

Gété built just 18 of these cars (although the number is disputed), including some cabriolet derivatives, and then moved on to build DS conversions of their own design. These were considerably less distinguished than the Frua body and the company seems to have gone out of business within a few years.

GFG
1980s
GFG was another German coachbuilder of the 1980s that made a brief living from converting Mercedes-Benz S Class models. Extended wheelbases were their speciality, but the company also put its name to at least one "gullwing" SEC coupé. Some features of this car, badged as a 5000 GFG, suggest that the base conversion may have been the work of Styling-Garage or one of its sub-contractors. GFG also made a number of Mercedes-Benz SSK replicas, naming them 500SK models and basing them on modern Mercedes-Benz mechanical components. Most of GFG's output was probably exported to the Middle East.

Ghia (I)
1915–1970, Turin
Carrozzeria Ghia SpA was one of the most famous Italian design and coachbuilding companies for a period of around half a century. The name still exists, but since 1970 has been owned by Ford, who used it until 2010 as a type designation for its best-equipped models in several markets.

The company was established in 1916 with premises at 4 Corso Valentino in Turin. Initially it was known as Carrozzeria Ghia & Gariglio, the two partners being Giacinto Ghia and a colleague called Gariglio. Early bodies were made of lightweight aluminium, and the company came to international notice in 1929 when an Alfa Romeo 6C 1500 it had bodied won that year's Mille Miglia.

The 1930s saw Ghia creating some extravagant special coachwork for Italian chassis, and the company's products were found on Alfa Romeo, Fiat and Lancia models. Particularly notable was the Sport Coupé it designed for the Fiat 508 Balilla.

Like many other companies in the automotive business, Ghia was reduced to building necessities during the Second World War. The company survived for the first few years by building carts for the Italian army and by making bicycles. However, in 1943 its Turin factory was destroyed by Allied bombing, and Giacinto Ghia died of a heart attack in February 1944 while supervising rebuilding work.

His widow was determined that the family business should carry on, and offered what remained of it to Felice Mario Boano, whom Ghia had chosen as his eventual successor, and to Giorgio Alberti, another of his close associates. These two now began to look beyond the Italian borders for new customers.

In 1948, Ghia established a subsidiary company at Aigle in Switzerland, where government policies favoured coachbuilding on imported chassis as long as they were subsequently exported. (Ghia-Aigle has a separate entry in these lists.) Approaches to various US makers bore fruit, too, and Ghia established links with Ford, for whom it built the 1955 Lincoln Futura design study. Even more productive was a link with Chrysler, whose chief designer Virgil Exner became a close partner for 15 years. At the start of this relationship, no fewer than eighteen Chrysler Ghia Specials were constructed between 1951 and 1953 as Chrysler tried to steal leadership of post-war design in the USA. In 1956, Chrysler returned to Ghia for the construction of their Norseman concept coupé, which was lost when the liner

Ghia: Between 1951 and 1953, the company built several bodies for the Ferrari 212 Inter. There were just four of these coupés in 1952. *(David Hodges Collection)*

Ghia: This striking body was built in 1953 on a Fiat 8V chassis, and was known as the Supersonic. Eight examples were built, and Ghia re-used the basic shape on both Aston Martin and Jaguar chassis later. *(WikiMedia/Braniff747SP)*

Ghia: The wide grille mouth appeared again on this 1954 Alfa Romeo 1900SS. *(WikiMedia/Simon Davison)*

Ghia: The Turin coachbuilder essayed more than one body for Jaguar chassis in the 1950s, including this example on an XK140. *(David Hodges Collection)*

Andrea Doria sank en route to the USA and was never seen in public.

Closer to home, the big success came with a coupé design for Volkswagen that went into production at the Karmann works in Germany as the VW Karmann Ghia coupé in 1955. Ghia's coupé on Armstrong-Siddeley chassis that was shown at Turin in 1952 nevertheless failed to prompt any orders.

There were major changes in 1953. The factory relocated from Turin to Agostino da Montefeltro, and designer Boano left to set up his own coachworks. In his place came Luigi Segre. The latter's 1953 cabriolet design for Renault on the Frégate was rejected in favour of a rival proposal from French coachbuilder Letourneur et Marchand, but the Ghia name continued to ride high with several bodies for Ferrari in the mid-1950s. All these carried an air of exclusivity thanks to their low-volume production at the Ghia factory.

In 1957, Ghia bought out the Frua coachworks, and took on Pietro Frua as its new head of design. However,

he soon fell out with Luigi Segre over which of them had designed the Floride coupé for Renault, and left Ghia to set up on his own again. Segre died in 1963, and from 1965 Giorgetto Giugiaro came to Ghia as head of design after a stint at Bertone. Over the next two years, designs such as his De Tomaso Pampero and Mangusta, Fiat Vanessa, and Maserati Ghibli created waves in automotive design. In 1966, Ghia also became involved in small-volume

Ghia: Based on Renault 4CV running gear, the Autobleu coupé was introduced in 1953 with a body designed and built by Ghia. The engine was at the rear, so the coachbuilder avoided using its trademark wide grille at the front! *(David Hodges Collection)*

Ghia: When Volkswagen wanted a coupé derivative, it approached Karmann in Germany to build it, and Karmann in turn asked Ghia to design it. This was the original (pre-1958) Karmann Ghia coupé. *(David Hodges Collection)*

Ghia: The Karmann Ghia was developed into a cabriolet as well. This is a 1959 example. *(David Hodges Collection)*

manufacture of the Giugiaro-designed Ghia 450 SS; a total of 52 were made over the next year or so, using Chrysler running gear and a Plymouth Barracuda chassis.

However, in 1966 the Ghia company was sold to Ramfis Trujillo; and Trujillo in turn sold it to Alejandro De Tomaso in 1967. Ghia had some involvement in the development of the De Tomaso Pantera, but before this became available in 1971, De Tomaso had decided that he could not run the coachbuilding company at a profit and began to look for a buyer. In 1970, he sold his shares in Ghia to the Ford Motor Company, whose main interest was in the legendary name. The Ghia design studios became an Italian outpost of the Ford empire, and from 1973 the Ghia name and its famous red and blue shield badge began to appear on the best-equipped versions of several Ford ranges in Europe. From 2010, the name disappeared from the cars, having outlived its usefulness as a marketing tool.

Ghia: From 1961 there was a new Karmann Ghia coupé, again styled by the Turin company. This is a 1966 model with the larger 1600 engine. (David Hodges Collection)

Ghia: There was a pleasing lightness of touch about this coupé body for the six-cylinder Fiat 2300 and 2300S models of the 1960s. (David Hodges Collection)

Ghia: The body of the Maserati Ghibli was designed by Giorgetto Giugiaro during his time at Ghia, and was announced in 1966. It was an early indication of Giugiaro's skill as a designer. (David Hodges Collection)

Ghia: Even Ghia could make mistakes, and this ponderous body for a planned revival of the Duesenberg marque in 1966 was one of them. In fact, the design was by Virgil Exner; the chassis was a Chrysler. (David Hodges Collection)

Ghia: The 1968 Serenissima Ghia coupé was an individual commission on a De Tomaso Mangusta chassis that did not enter production. The design was by Tom Tjaarda. (David Hodges Collection)

Ghia-Aigle (CH)
1948–1988, Aigle, and Lugano (1954-1958)

Changes in Swiss government policy in the late 1940s, favouring coachbuilding for export on imported chassis, opened an opportunity for the Italian Carozzeria Ghia to expand its activities. Premises were found at Aigle, and in late 1948 under the leadership of Dr Pierre-Paul Filippi from Turin, a new branch was established. There was no financial involvement by Ghia, but the company granted its Swiss offshoot a licence to use its designs, and sent experienced craftsmen to Switzerland to train the new company's staff. The Swiss company became known as Ghia-Aigle, and specialised in cabriolet and coupé designs, typically building around ten or a dozen bodies a year.

The first bodies in 1949 were probably built largely in Turin and were simply finished at Aigle, and those for Alfa-Romeo 6C-2500SS and Delahaye 135 chassis in this period were unmistakably designed by Ghia's Mario Felice Boano. Among the earliest cars actually built at Aigle was a Fiat 1500 coupé in 1949, although again the design was clearly by Boano.

However, from 1951, Boano engaged a young Giovanni Michelotti to design for Ghia-Aigle. That year, the company also took on the Swiss agency for Ferrari, and one result was that it became the only coachbuilder outside Italy to body examples of the 212 chassis. There were three bodies on Jowett Jupiter chassis in 1951, and a pair of 1930s Bugattis were rebodied the following year. Coupé and cabriolet bodywork followed on Fiat, Jaguar, Lancia, MG and Singer chassis, and the Ghia-Aigle designs for the Panhard Dyna eventually clothed around 30 chassis.

Ghia-Aigle: A quite distinctive Panhard Coupé Grand Sport, 1954.

Ghia-Aigle: This unique sports coupé was built on a Studebaker Champion chassis in 1955. Ghia's skill in dealing with the proportions of this large car is unquestionable. *(Unknown copyright)*

Meanwhile, the Swiss company became wholly independent from its Italian parent in 1953, and in late 1954 established new headquarters in Lugano. Over the next few years, Michelotti designs appeared on Alfa-Romeo, Daimler Regency, Fiat 103TV, Lancia, Lotus and even Studebaker chassis. There was also an ambulance conversion of a Cadillac and, as further proof that Ghia-Aigle could think beyond coupé and cabriolet designs, the company built the limousine body on a prototype BMW 505 in 1955, but this rather unhappy design did not make production.

Michelotti left Ghia-Aigle to set up on his own in 1957, and in 1958 the Swiss company returned to its earlier home at Aigle. Meanwhile, Pietro Frua had sold his carrozzeria to Ghia, and became that company's head of design. He now took over responsibility for design at Ghia-Aigle as well, and among the characteristically Frua shapes that emerged were bodies on Alfa-Romeo 1900SS and Jaguar XK150 chassis.

Ghia-Aigle: Built in 1954 on a Chevrolet Corvette chassis, this unique coupé was designed by Michelotti. *(David Hodges Collection)*

Ghia-Aigle: This 1956 Jaguar XK140 carried the wide grille characteristic of Ghia-Aigle's Italian parent company. *(David Hodges Collection)*

Ghia-Aigle: Another large-car challenge in 1955 was the prototype BMW 505 limousine. Michelotti was responsible for the design, which was not an unqualified success. The car did not enter production. *(Author's Collection)*

Ghia-Aigle: A most unusual choice of chassis for this creation: it was built on a Lotus 1100 Le Mans in 1957. There was also a roadster version of the design. *(David Hodges Collection)*

The Swiss company also attracted an order from Lloyd in Germany to build a series of 49 coupés to a Frua design on the Alexander chassis.

However, the company built no more special bodies for passenger cars after 1959. Instead, it turned to commercial bodies and to repair work, remaining active until late 1981, when a liquidator was called in. The business finally closed its doors in 1988.

Gienapp (D)
Hamburg
No information is available about the activities of the Karosseriewerke Gienapp, which was located in Hamburg.

Gillotte (F)
1896–1929, Levallois (Courbevoie from 1920)
In the years before the Great War, Gaston Gillotte's company was primarily responsible for coupé and torpedo bodywork. It subsequently specialised in two-door and four-door saloon bodies, but did not survive the 1929 economic crisis.

Gindine (F)
1928
The Gindine company is known for a faux-cabriolet on a Talbot chassis and an undistinguished Voisin 14CV cabriolet, both new in 1928.

Girard (F)
Early 1900s–c1931, Paris
2 Rue des Éclusses Saint-Martin, Paris 10
Very little is known about the Parisian coachbuilder Carrosserie Eugène Girard Fils, which was established at the start of the 20th century. It is known to have held a licence for the Baehr transformable bodywork in the 1920s. Absorbed by Gallé after the 1930 Paris Salon, it collapsed early in the new decade, probably at the same time as Gallé itself went under.

Giron (F)
1935
This French coachbuilder is known only for a spectacular cabriolet body, built in 1935 on a 1930 Voisin C15 chassis.

Gläser (D)
1864–1952, Dresden
Gläser-Karosserie GmbH was a major German coachbuilder which was particularly noted for its cabriolet designs in the 1930s. Based in Dresden, it fell into the eastern sector of Germany after the Second World War, and was absorbed into the state-owned motor industry. A vestigial Gläser company also survived in the west until the early 1950s.

The company was founded in Dresden in 1864 by Carl Heinrich Gläser to build horse-drawn vehicles. Based at 6 Rampische Strasse, it soon acquired a reputation for quality and was building for the Dresden royal family by 1865.

Gläser: Dating from 1923 and built on a Dixi chassis, this streamlined body was built to a Paul Jaray design. *(Author's Collection)*

Gläser: Cabriolets were a speciality, and Pullman cabriolets even more so. This one is on a 1931 Mercedes-Benz Nürburg 460 chassis. *(Daimler-Benz)*

Gläser: Another cabriolet body on a Mercedes-Benz Nürburg 460 chassis, this time dating from 1933. *(Daimler-Benz)*

Gläser: The two-seat sport-cabriolet body on BMW's 1.2-litre 303 model of 1933-1934 was a Gläser confection. *(Unknown copyright)*

Gläser: This attractive cabriolet body on Steyr 220 chassis was an exhibit at the 1939 Berlin Motor Show. *(WikiMedia Commons/ Public Domain)*

Gläser's firm actually bought in the basic carriages from a wagon works owned by Friedrich August Emil Heuer and then "dressed" them to suit its customers. In 1885, Heuer married Gläser's daughter; in 1898 he became a partner in the Gläser firm; and when Carl Gläser died, he took control.

The move into car bodywork in the early years of the 20th century was a natural progression. The company built its first car body in 1902 on a Mercedes chassis, and before the First World War had developed special hardtops for touring cars. During the 1920s, Gläser took on a Weymann patent, and was soon building bodies on a variety of prestigious chassis. The company forged strong links with the German arm of General Motors and there were several Gläser bodies on Buick, Cadillac and later Opel chassis. However, the company began to struggle as the world economic crisis deepened, and ran into financial difficulties when General Motors cancelled a major contract; in 1932, Georg Heuer committed suicide. His brother Emil, already an old man, took control of the business but the financial problems persisted, and Emil Heuer himself died in 1934.

Meanwhile, the Gläser business was being restructured at the behest of the Dresdner Bank, and Gläserkarosserie GmbH – effectively a new company – was founded in summer 1933. At its head was Willy Bachmann, who had married into the Heuer family in 1929, but Georg Heuer's

Gläser: The cost of building bodies for the Porsche 356 America Roadster led Gläser to ruin. The design was in fact by Erwin Komenda at Porsche. *(WikiMedia Commons/Detectandpreserve)*

two sons, Georg and Erich, were responsible for much of the success that followed. So too was the Dresdner Bank, which was also involved with the restructuring of the Auto Union group and ensured that Gläser would provide plenty of bodies for its Audi, Horch and Wanderer brands.

Yet not all Gläser bodies in this period were on prestigious chassis; there were individual commissions for Hanomag, Opel and Steyr, too. In addition, Gläser built series-production types, such as the Sport-Cabriolet on the 1933 BMW 303 and designs for German Fords, including some of the low-volume special bodies for the Ford Eifel in the later 1930s. The company's cabriolet designs, which were the work of Georg Heuer junior, became particularly noted.

Nevertheless, the company also built a variety of more traditional styles, including coupés, landaulets, limousines, phaetons, and Pullman saloons. A Gläser characteristic was folding top mechanisms that were easy to use, and for which the company took out several patents. There were bodies on American chassis such as Buick, Cadillac, Chevrolet, Chrysler and Hudson until the Nazi government of the 1930s obstructed such imports.

After 1935 the company also built special bodies for military staff cars on Steyr chassis, and specialist military conversions of Ford and Opel trucks as well. The late 1930s saw involvement with components and sub-assemblies for fighter aircraft, and when war came in 1939 the Gläser factory was turned over entirely to production of military vehicles and aircraft components for the Luftwaffe. In February 1945 it was destroyed by Allied bombing, but Erich Heuer was able to retrieve some of the machinery and equipment and put it into storage. Once the war was over, he started up in business again, this time in Ullersricht bei Weiden in the Oberpfalz region, which fell into the western sector of Germany.

The site of the original Gläser factory was now in the Soviet-controlled eastern sector of Germany, and when rebuilt it became the Karosseriewerk Dresden (KWD), as part of the state-owned VB automotive industry. It built bodies for IFA, Wartburg and AWZ cars, and was involved in developing the plastic bodywork for the latter. After Germany was reunified in the 1990s, KWD was privatized, and since 1994 has been a supplier of automotive components.

Meanwhile, Erich Heuer was able to attract some contracts

from the newly established Porsche company. He built between 100 and 250 Cabriolet bodies for the Porsche 356, and a further 16 bodies for the legendary aluminium Porsche 540 "America Roadster". However, the America Roadster cost far more to build than planned, and Gläser lost money on every one. This contributed to the company's bankruptcy, and in November 1952 the Gläser coachworks closed for good. The unfinished Porsche contract went to Reutter.

Glüer (D)
1920s
Very little indeed is known about Glüer, who advertised car bodywork in around 1923. It appears that the bodies, both closed and open types, may have been of modular construction, and that customers were required to supply only the running-gear of their choice. The system seems not to have caught on.

Goosens & Mercken (F)
1920s, Puteaux
The Carrosserie Parisienne Ch Goosens & M Mercken built both luxury car bodies and commercial bodies during the 1920s.

Graber (CH)
1925–1970, Wichtrach
Carrosserie Hermann Graber is probably the best-known of the great Swiss coachbuilders. Graber himself had learned the coachbuilding trade from his father, and in 1925 took over the business at Wichtrach, near Berne. He initially continued building horse-drawn vehicles, but in 1927 constructed his first car body – a two-seater cabriolet on a Fiat 509 chassis. Two years later, his body on a Panhard-Levassor 20CV chassis won the Concours d'Elegance in St Moritz and immediately brought Graber international attention.

Graber was primarily a builder of cabriolet bodies, and in the 1930s he became renowned for both the excellence of his designs and the high quality of his craftsmanship. Commissions came in for special bodies on chassis as diverse as Alfa Romeo, Bentley, Bugatti and SS Jaguar, and there were small series of bodies on American Duesenberg and Packard chassis, too.

Graber: This 1935 torpedo body on a Hispano-Suiza 54CV chassis is thought to be the work of the Graber concern. *(David Hodges Collection)*

Graber: The size of the Cadillac V12 chassis must have made it hard to get the proportions of a two-door cabriolet right, but Graber succeeded only too well on this 1931 order for the King of Egypt. *(Author's Collection)*

Graber: Built in 1950, this coupé was on a short-chassis Talbot Lago Grand Sport. *(David Hodges Collection)*

Graber: There were 17 Graber bodies on the Bentley Mk VI chassis, most of them cabriolets. *(John Divall)*

Graber: The lines on this elegant Talbot Lago Grand Sport T25 drophead from 1953 could only have been penned at Wichtrach. *(David Hodges Collection)*

Graber: As the Swiss Alvis importer, Graber unsurprisingly created a number of one-off bodies on the cars in the 1950s. This is an early cabriolet. *(Author's Collection)*

Graber: This is another early 1950s Alvis; the "special" bodies on Alvis were usually accompanied by "Super" badges. *(Author's Collection)*

Graber: Alvis were sufficiently impressed to commission a volume-production body from Graber, although they had it built in the UK. This was the 1955 prototype, on TC21/100 chassis. (*David Hodges Collection*)

Graber: The TD21 Series II coupé was an update of the firm's earlier Alvis designs. (*John Divall*)

Graber: The company continued to build special bodies on Alvis chassis long after the car maker had adopted his design for production. This superb cabriolet was the 1963 Geneva Show car. (*Author's Collection*)

After the Second World War, Graber focussed his attention largely on British-built chassis. He acquired distribution rights for Alvis and Rover, building special bodywork on these chassis whenever he could, and he also bodied a number of Aston Martin, Bentley, Jaguar, Lagonda and Rolls-Royce types. There were bodies on French and Italian chassis,

too, notably from Alfa Romeo and Delahaye, and from about 1948 Graber moved from a modernised pre-war style with clearly-defined wings to smooth pontoon shapes.

However, it was with Alvis chassis that Graber would be primarily associated in the post-war years. He built his first Alvis body to customer order in 1950, and later proposed an elegant, modern-looking two-door coupé body for the 3-litre TC21/100 chassis. Alvis adopted the design for their new TC108G model, and the early examples were actually built by Graber. Alvis then decided to buy the rights to the design and have it made in Britain for the revised TD21 model by Willowbrook, and later by Park Ward. The design lasted in production until the demise of the Alvis car business in 1967.

Graber meanwhile continued to build special-order bodies for Alvis chassis at the rate of around ten a year; typically, these were more rakish than the upright-looking original. As the Swiss concessionaire, Graber was also willing and able to modify both running-gear and engines to customer order.

By the time of his death in 1970, Hermann Graber had built more than 800 bodies, but the coachbuilding activity now stopped. The business continued, now under the control of his widow and specialising in the repair and maintenance of car bodywork. Between 1980 and 1996, the company also had a Ferrari franchise, and was well known for its major restoration work on both German and Italian sports cars.

By then known as Graber Sportgarage, the business was sold to the well-known Swiss classic car restorer Markus Scharnhorst, and its activities were relocated to larger premises in Toffen. The company remains active in the classic car field, selling, maintaining and race-preparing classic and historic sports cars.

Gramond (F)
1900-c1950, Bordeaux

Ateliers Gramond claimed to have been established in 1900, but is known for its work in the years after the Second World War. In the late 1940s, it held a licence for the Faget-Varnet (qv) all-steel body patents, which it used in a number of bodies for Delahaye chassis. Gramond was responsible for both coupé and cabriolet bodies on the Delahaye 135, but did not survive the downturn in demand for coachbuilt bodies in France in the early 1950s.

Grange & Martel/ Grange Frères (F)
1920s, Valence-sur Rhône

Brothers Emile and Leon Grange set up their first business 1920 with Charles Martel as Grange & Martel, but Martel soon left to set up in business with his brother-in-law as Ravistre & Martel (qv). The Grange brothers continued in business alone as Carrosserie Grange Frères, and are thought to have been early pioneers of metal body framing. An example of their work is a fabric-bodied saloon built on a 1927 Turcat-Méry chassis.

Groulard (F)
1920s

Monsieur Groulard was a French engineer who in 1928 constructed an extraordinary four-door saloon body made of reinforced concrete. The chassis appears to have been a Citroën, and the rationale behind the exercise appears to have been to make the body fire-proof. Needless to say, the result was very angular and, equally needless to say, there seem to have been no follow-ups even though Groulard patented his invention.

Gruau (F)
1980s–1990s, Laval

Société M Gruau et Fils is primarily associated with commercial bodywork, of which it is one of the major French builders. However, the company has also dabbled in the car body business. It built the 205 Utilitaire for Peugeot in the 1980s, and at the 1982 Paris Salon showed its own leisure-vehicle concept, called L'Escapade 2000. In 1990, it took on the manufacture of the Renault 5 Belle Ile pick-up conversion that had been designed two years earlier by Car Système Style at Redon (qv). The company built 500 of these in all, to a slightly modified design.

Grümmer (Etablissements Grümmer) (F)
c1914–1930s, Paris

The Grümmer family originated in the German city of Aachen, where they had been master coachbuilders since the 17th century. One branch of the family had moved to Brussels and subsequently to Paris, and here one of the sons, Antoine Joseph Grümmer, worked for the old-established Morel company, which built horse-drawn vehicles. Just before the start of the Great War, he and his brother Gaston took over the Morel business and re-named it Etablissements J Grümmer. Still building horse-drawn vehicles, they specialised in the luxury end of the market.

The Great War brought new influences to bear on the Grümmer business. Gaston's time as an aviator had given him a keen interest in aerodynamics, and it had become clear that the market for car bodies was increasing as that for horse-drawn vehicles diminished. So the family business changed its focus, becoming a builder of car bodies and changing its name to SA des Etablissements Grümmer. It built several bodies for Lorraine-Dietrich, but Gaston was keen to explore new ideas, and in 1924 left the business to set up on his own. Antoine kept the business alive, and in 1927 absorbed the Parisian coachbuilder Aigner. Nevertheless, the Grümmer coachworks went out of business in the early 1930s, at about the same time as Lorraine-Dietrich.

Grümmer (Gaston Grümmer) (F)
1924–1935, Clichy

The coachwork business that Gaston Grümmer founded at Clichy in 1924 after leaving Etablissements Grümmer (qv) went on to enjoy a much wider reputation than the family firm. Gaston's real interest was in incorporating aircraft techniques into car construction, but while he developed his ideas, his company kept abreast of the latest coachwork developments elsewhere by taking on licences to build other patented modern designs. It held licences for Baehr transformable bodies (although Grümmer seems to have

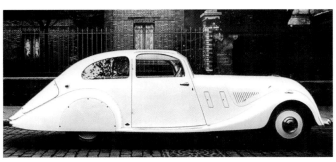

Grümmer: The Aéroprofil body was the result of Grümmer's work on aerodynamics with Guillaume Buisson. This example dates from 1934 and is on a Renault Nervasport chassis. *(Unknown copyright)*

used the Aldi name on those he built), and took on a licence for Weymann fabric-panelled bodies as well.

From 1926, the company also had a licence from Forotowsky to build "surbaissé" (ultra-low) bodies, where lightweight bodywork was combined with panels that ended below the centre-line of the axles. Among the earliest of these was one built on a 1926 Voisin C5 chassis, and there were later examples on Panhard chassis. Nevertheless, Grümmer coachwork was soon distinguished by a unique style as well as by the use of these modern techniques.

The surbaissé bodies were built in collaboration with Etienne Bunau-Varilla who, like Grümmer himself, had been an aviator. By the end of the 1920s, Grümmer was working with another former aviator, Guillaume Buisson, in an attempt to develop aerodynamic body designs. Clearly still keen to keep ahead of the game, Grümmer patented a design called the Extensible TS in 1930; this used a body module to turn a two-seater body into a four-seater when required.

At the 1933 Paris Salon, Grümmer finally showed the fruit of his work with Buisson – a design called the Aéroprofil. The show car was on an Alfa Romeo chassis, and Grümmer subsequently built similar bodies on Citroën Rosalie, Delage D8, Hotchkiss, Peugeot 601 and Renault Nervasport chassis. The integrated headlamps, streamlined wings and grille, and sloping tail were all features that would later typify the streamlined era in the mid-1930s. The 1933 Paris Salon also saw the debut of a Grümmer design called the Hirondelle (swallow) on a Hispano-Suiza chassis; the same design was also used on the Delage D8.

Gaston Grümmer continued working under his own name until 1935, but closed his coachworks down that year.

Guérin (F)
1920s, Limoges
Carrosserie Guérin is known for a torpedo body which it constructed in 1926 on a Panhard et Levassor 16CV Six Type 57 chassis. Little more is known about the company.

Guettault (F)
1920s, Neuilly-sur-Seine
The Guettault brothers moved into the premises formerly occupied by the Barailhé coachbuilding business in the

1920s. They specialised in bodywork for luxury chassis, and examples are known on Bugatti, Delahaye, Hispano-Suiza and Rolls-Royce. The last known trace of the company is at the Paris Salon in 1930.

Guilloré (F)
1937–1954, Courbevoie
Alphonse Guilloré opened his coachworks at Courbevoie-sur-Seine in the late 1930s, and focussed his efforts on chassis by French makers, notably Delahaye, Delage and Talbot. From 1937, he built a series of two-door closed bodies to a Delahaye house style, sharing the work with Chapron.

Resuming work after the Second World War, Guilloré again focussed on the great French marques, and created some extremely attractive open and closed bodies on the Delahaye 135 chassis. There were small numbers on Delage chassis, too. Most of these bodies retained the separate wings of 1930s cars, and all of them typified the elegance of the best French coachbuilders of the period. By 1949, Guilloré was using pontoon-type wings in the contemporary idiom. The company bodied the second Bugatti T101 chassis in 1952, although one school of thought is that the body was actually one for a Delahaye that had been modified to suit the new chassis.

Like so many others, Guilloré found his business restricted by the demise of the great French chassis-makers. From 1952, he began building truck cabs for Citroën, but closed down in 1954. Guilloré bodies often have much in common with Chapron designs, and are sometimes mistaken for the work of the better-known carrossier.

Gygax (CH)
1896–1936, Biel
Jean Gygax founded his coach works in 1896 at the Freiestrasse in Biel. His first car bodies were built on Swiss-made chassis, but by the 1920s he was building all-weather types on a variety of makes. The company had around 30 employees at this stage.

Gygax moved on to luxury car chassis, creating some cabriolets on Cadillac, Isotta-Fraschini and Minerva chassis, but he continued to work with other makes. One example was a Vauxhall ASX which he bodied as a cabriolet for the 1933 Geneva Show. From 1932, Alexis Kellner came to work for Gygax, after his own carrosserie in Berlin had failed. The company was briefly renamed as Kellner & Gygax, but in 1936 the company was sold to Paul Leichti, who renamed it Carrosseriewerke AG.

In 1948, Carrosseriewerke AG moved to Nidau, and the company still exists as a body repair shop.

Gyselinck (B)
1930s, Anderlecht
Belgian coachbuilder Fernand Gyselinck specialised in convertible coachwork with a fabric hood that could be opened and closed rapidly by just one person at a time when such operations usually needed at least two people.

H

Hägele (D)
1940s–1950s?, Mössingen

Karosseriebau Hägele is known to have built estate cars and commercial bodies (vans and pick-ups) on Mercedes-Benz 170V chassis in the late 1940s. In the mid-1950s, it is also believed to have built hearse bodywork for at least two Mercedes 180 models.

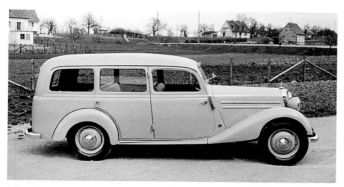

Hägele: Several small coachbuilders constructed estate bodies on the Mercedes-Benz 170V chassis in the late 1940s, and this was the Hägele version. *(Daimler-Benz)*

Hägele: From the same company came a pick-up truck on the Mercedes 170V, one of many types available in immediate post-war Germany. *(Daimler-Benz)*

Haizer & Herrmann (CH)
1926–1929, Zurich

This small Swiss company was responsible for constructing a streamlined body on a Chrysler Type 72 chassis to a design by aerodynamicist Paul Jaray.

Hamet (F)
1920s

The Hamet company was one of many small coachbuilders to have a licence for the Baehr designs in the 1920s, but it is also known to have constructed conventional bodies. Among the recipients of these was at least one Panhard et Levassor.

Hammond & Thiede (D)
1980s, Würzburg

Several companies considered creating a cabriolet out of Opel's two-door Ascona in the early 1980s, including Michelotti, Tropic and Hy-Tech in Crailsheim. However, the company which actually brought the idea to market was born out of an idea by Michael Thiede, a BMW dealer in Germany. Securing financial support from the George Hammond Group, an old-established British business with headquarters in Dover, he had the car designed by IAD in Britain. Testing was carried out by Porche at Weissach (although the company was unwilling to publicise its association with Opel at the time). The contract for construction of the cars went to Voll (qv) in Germany, at Würzburg-Heidingsfeld; body reinforcement and the convertible top added about 30kg to the weight of the original saloon.

The Ascona cabriolet was introduced in 1983 and was initially available only through the Munich Opel dealer Häusler, although it later went out through the whole Opel network. In Britain, RHD versions were sold as the Vauxhall Cavalier Convertible. However, when Voll went bankrupt in 1984, it was bought by those behind the Ascona cabriolet project, becoming Hammond & Thiede. This company also had offices in Sulzbach am Main and Dover.

Between 1984 and 1988, a total of 2873 cabriolets to this design were built, around half of them with right-hand drive. Early models carried a Voll maker's plate; later ones had Hammond & Thiede identification.

Hänni (CH)
1920s–1930s, Zürich

Alfred Hänni specialised in creating roll-back roofs for saloon bodies, and examples are known on Bugatti and Rolls-Royce chassis, as well as on an unidentified American chassis. The company also created an attractive MG PA roadster body in 1935.

Habsburg (D)
1930s, Berlin

When Drauz of Heilbronn (qv) bought the premises and patents of the Berlin-based Kellner company (qv), it turned over the company's old workshops to the production of bodies for Fords built in Berlin. These were built under the name of Karosserie Habsburg, and were mostly cabriolets on the Model A chassis, apparently using former Kellner patents.

Hartmann (CH)
1929–1939, Lausanne

Willy Hartmann learned the coachbuilding trade in Paris, initially with Labourdette and then at the Renault works. He returned to his native Switzerland in 1927 and set up

Hartmann: Often considered Willy Hartmann's masterpiece was this Cadillac V16 from 1937, clearly inspired by some of the more extravagant French coachbuilders. *(David Hodges Collection)*

Heber: This attractive faux-cabriolet body was mounted on a Delage GL some time around 1925. *(David Hodges Collection)*

his own coachworks in Lausanne, focussing primarily on cabriolet bodies for new chassis but also building some new bodies for older chassis. There were cabriolets on Chevrolet, Dodge, Hotchkiss, Mathis and Voisin chassis, and sketches survive showing proposals for a Minerva chassis too. A Graham chassis received a roadster body in 1930.

Several Hartmann bodies won awards in the concours d'élégance events of the early 1930s, but the company is particularly noted for a glamorous torpedo on a 1937 Cadillac V16 chassis that commentators have suggested resembles the work of French coachbuilders such as Figoni & Falaschi or Saoutchik. The car survives, but has been rebuilt with non-original features.

During the 1939-1945 war, Hartmann turned to building trucks for the Swiss Army and farm vehicles. When the war ended, the company confined its activities to repair work and commercial bodies. It built just one more car body, a cabriolet on a Fiat 1100 chassis in 1960. Willy Hartmann retired in 1977 and closed his business down.

Hauser (CH)
1955, Zofingen
Jakob Hauser AG built just one coupé body in 1955 on a Fiat 1100c chassis. The company still exists as a repair workshop.

Heber (CH)
1890–c1930, Geneva
Very little is known about the Charles Heber coachworks, which is thought to have been founded in 1890. It is known to have constructed a cabriolet body on Alfa Romeo RLSS chassis in 1925, a faux-cabriolet on a Delage GL in about 1925, and a sports saloon on a Rolls-Royce Phantom in 1927. No more recent bodies are known.

Hebmüller (D)
1889–1952, Wülfrath
Karosserie Hebmüller was an important builder of car bodies in Germany between the end of the First World War and the early 1950s.

Joseph Hebmüller, born in 1865, was a wheelwright with the wagon-maker Sauer in Barmen, near Wuppertal. After Sauer went bankrupt, he took the business over in October 1889. His four sons, Joseph, Paul, Emil and Erich all joined him, and Karosseriewerke Joseph Hebmüller Söhne continued in the wagon-building trade.

In the early years of the 20th century, the company began building car bodies as well, and after Joseph Hebmüller died in 1919, his four sons continued to take the business in that direction. Early work included a limousine body on

Fiat chassis and a delivery van on the Ford Model T. The business expanded, and in 1924 an additional works was established in Wülfrath, followed by a third in the same town in 1936. The 1924 works was taken over from car maker Wilhelm Körting, a customer business which had run into financial difficulties. Low rents in Wülfrath soon made this the main works, while the Barmen works was turned over to repair work.

Customers in the 1920s included Austro-Daimler, FN in Belgium and Dürkopp in Bielefeld; Hebmüller built high-class bodies for them, either as individual commissions or in small batches. There were also bodies for the Austro-Daimler ADR Sport, Mercedes-Benz SS and the Bugatti Type 40.

In the 1930s, Hebmüller also worked for mass producers like Ford and Opel, building cabriolet and open sports bodies on their chassis. From 1936 the three works were building cabriolets and Pullman Limousines for Ford, Hanomag and Opel, the Fords being on lengthened V8-engined chassis. The war years 1939-1945 saw them building military vehicles and decoy aircraft designed to lead Allied bombers astray.

At the end of the war they were quick off the mark and from 1946 were building staff cars on Humber chassis for the British military and parcels vans for the post office. However, it was Volkswagen who now became Hebmüller's major customer. Hebmüller built three prototypes of a two-seater cabriolet in 1948 with an elegantly curved long rear deck, and that summer VW ordered 2000 examples. Production began in 1949, and was soon swelled by an order for a four-seat Police cabriolet with fabric doors. All the two-door cars had two-tone paintwork, in black and red or black and ivory. However, only 696 examples were built: a major fire destroyed the Hebmüller works on 23 July 1949. Production of the police version was also disrupted, and the final examples of that are thought to have been constructed by Papler.

Hebmüller rebuilt its works and got production under way again in 1951, but the insurance pay-out on the fire did not cover the cost of the modernisation it undertook at the same time. Hebmüller had a staff of some 700 and plenty of work, for Borgward, DKW and others, but the financial situation deteriorated. So in May 1952 the company was obliged to close its doors. A further dozen or so VW cabriolets were built from parts by Karmann, and the works was bought by Vidal & Sohn from Hamburg-Harburg, who later sold it on to Ford.

Heidemann (D)
1950s, Munich
Heidemann built a unique ambulance from a six-cylinder BMW 501 in 1956 for the Bavarian Red Cross.

Heimburger (CH)
1904–c1930, Basle
The Heimburger business was founded as a saddlery in Basle in 1814, and was still family-owned when it built its first car bodywork in the early years of the 20th century.

Hebmüller: The early cabriolet has become something of a legend among Volkswagen enthusiasts. (*David Hodges Collection/ David Burgess-Wise*)

Hebmüller: The fabric-door police cabriolet was in production when the works was destroyed by fire. (*Author's Collection*)

Hermès: Special trim and other features created the Bugatti Veyron Fbg par Hermès in 2008. (WikiMedia Commons/ Xavigivax)

The owner's son, Otto, spent four years learning the trade at the Rothschild coachworks in Paris, returning in 1912 and putting his experience to good use in the family business. By 1914, the Heimburger reputation had attracted business from the Russian tsar, for whom a body was constructed on Martini chassis.

Later work included an attractive coupé body on an Adler chassis in 1919 and an elegant coupé de ville on a Cadillac chassis in 1924. The company's last known car design was a rebody for a Rolls-Royce Silver Ghost. Heimburger turned to commercial bodywork and repair work, probably at the end of the 1920s or start of the 1930s and remained in business until 1995. The workforce and some of the company's assets were taken over by Carrosserie Wenger (qv).

Hermès (F)
Since 1929, Paris
The Hermès company is well known as a leather specialist, but has had occasional involvement with the automotive world as well. In 1929, it constructed the external trunk for the Weymann-bodied Bugatti Royale, and in May 1953 did the special trim on a Ferrari 250MM for Princess Saddrudin Aga Khan.

In the 1980s and 1990s, Hermès trimmed a Volvo 240 saloon and a 960 limousine, as well as a Renault Super 5. March 2008 saw the introduction of a Bugatti Veyron Fbg par Hermès at the Villa d'Este concours (the "Fbg" was short for Faubourg; the Hermès company is located in the Rue du Faubourg Saint-Honoré). The same year Hermès prepared a special show version of the Citroen 2CV for the model's 60th anniversary. Most recently, in 2009 the Como dealer group in Paris commissioned a limited edition of 10 Smart cars to celebrate 10 years of the marque; known as the Smart Toile H, these were individually trimmed by Hermès.

Hess (CH)
1882–present, Bellach
The Swiss body builder Hess is primarily known today for its bus, trolleybus and commercial vehicle work, but it also constructed many car bodies in the first half of the 20th century. The company dates from 1882, when Heinrich Hess set up business in Bellach, near Solothurn. It began building buses, especially charabancs ("cars Alpins") when his sons Arnold and Emil took over the business in 1919.

Hess car bodies included some early all-weather types, as well as open touring types, luxury limousines and cabriolets, and from the mid-1920s the company held a Weymann licence. There were bodies on a wide variety of chassis, from small Amilcars to grand Minervas, with examples on Alfa Romeo, Buick, Farman, Fiat, Martini, Pic-Pic, Peugeot, Stoewer and others. However, the world-wide recession led Hess to concentrate on bus and commercial bodies from 1933.

After 1947, Hess moved to new premises in Bellach. The company briefly returned to car building in 1956 when it constructed the bodywork for the unique Soletta 750 prototype, a small car intended purely to demonstrate Willy Salzmann's patented flexible drive shaft.

Hess: Possibly the only surviving example of Hess's work is this two-door Sports Saloon on a 1932 Alfa Romeo 6C 1750 chassis. *(Nikolaus Scheerbarth-Clasen)*

Heuliez (F)
1920–2009, Cerizay

Heuliez was at its peak as a maker of car bodywork between the late 1970s and the first decade of the 21st century, when it undertook design and construction of small-run niche models for several major manufacturers. Between 1985 and its demise in 2009 it constructed more than 450,000 cars. It was also once a major force in the French bus and coach building industry.

The company was established in 1920 by Adolphe Heuliez, who started by making horse-drawn carts. From 1922, Louis Heuliez took over the business, and in 1925 made his first move into the car market with the bodywork for a Peugeot 177B. In 1937, the company set up a subsidiary company for the production of buses, and this went on to become very successful. It was eventually sold off in 1991 to the Renault and Volvo combine.

Car body activity at Heuliez was nevertheless a sideline for many years. In 1962, the company built a four-door cabriolet version of the Citroën DS, which it went on to build in small quantities without factory approval. But by the end of that decade, Heuliez had begun to make a determined effort to break into the car bodywork market. The plan seems always to have been to make small-volume niche models or conversions that the major manufacturers could not make economically themselves.

At the 1968 Paris Salon, Heuliez showed two conversions based on Simca production models – an 1100 pick-up and a 1501 coupé. Soon afterwards, the company was awarded the contract to build the platforms for the new Simca 1301 and 1501 range. Citroen also gave it the job of building the special bodyshells for the limited-production rotary-engined Citroen M35, and Renault turned to Heuliez to build the doors of the Renault 8.

Heuliez' attempt to gain the attention of the major French car makers had succeeded thus far, and its next step was to create its own designs. At the 1970 Paris Salon, Heuliez showed a VW-Porsche styled by Jacques Cooper, and the

Heuliez: Conversions on standard car models included this ambulance on the Citroën BX. *(Author's Collection)*

Heuliez: Never common, this conversion was based on the Renault 5. The "van" name was intended to suggest its use as an MPV. (*Author's Collection*)

following year established a dedicated styling studio under Yves Dubernard, who was recruited for the job. Among his earliest creations was a Peugeot H4 taxi, shown at the 1972 Paris Salon. In January 1978, Heuliez established its new research centre under the name of DEA.

During the 1980s, Heuliez attracted plenty of business from the major French manufacturers, building small-run or specialist models. Peugeot was the earliest customer, having its extended-wheelbase 604 limousine built by Heuliez, a total of 180 being constructed between 1978 and 1984. Peugeot followed up with the low-volume 205 Turbo 16, which was assembled by Heuliez from 1985, and there would be other contracts later.

Renault came next, and it was Heuliez who converted the quirky 5 Le Car Van models, of which some 450 were built (with the spare wheel mounted on the tail and opera windows in the rear sides) between 1979 and 1984. After this came the Renault 5 Turbo from 1980 and the long-wheelbase Renault 25, of which 132 were built in 1985-1986.

For Citroën, who were of course by this stage part of the PSA Group with Peugeot, Heuliez built a number of estate models in the 1980s and 1990s. These were the BX estate (from 1983) and BX Break (1985-1993), the CX Break (1989-1991) and XM Break (1992-1999), and the Xantia Break (1995-2000). It built the high-performance BX 4TC in 1986, and three versions of the Visa in 1984: the Visa Chrono, Visa Mille Pistes and Visa Convertible. It was the association with Citroën that probably steered Heuliez towards its later interest in electric cars, when the coachbuilder was entrusted with the production of the Saxo électrique (1996-2003) and AX électrique (1995-2000).

Meanwhile, Yves Dubernard had left the original Heuliez design studio in 1984, and the company opened a new studio in Turin under Marc Deschamps. Here, it produced a number of prototype and concept designs in the 1990s, and also an ambitious model based on the Lamborghini Diablo. Among these concepts was the Heuliez Intruder, a 1997 design for a SUV roadster-coupé.

The Heuliez strategy at the start of the 21st century was to make itself indispensable in an expanding specialist area of car bodywork. Retractable roofs were the coming thing, and Heuliez established links with the Webasto sunroof company. A first statement of intent was shown at Geneva in 2000, where Heuliez revealed an extended-wheelbase Peugeot 607 for the French President. Known as the Paladine model, this had a six-window body with a retractable rear roof.

Heuliez subsequently assisted in the development of the roofs for the Nissan Micra C+C, the Opel Tigra Twin Top and the Peugeot 206 CC, which latter entered production in 2001. From 2004, the company took on the entire assembly of the Opel, so combining its roles of small-volume builder and specialist designer. Heuliez made more than 350,000

Heuliez: A one-off conversion was this Peugeot 604 limousine for French President Valéry Giscard d'Estaing. (*WikiMedia Commons/Thomas Doerfer*)

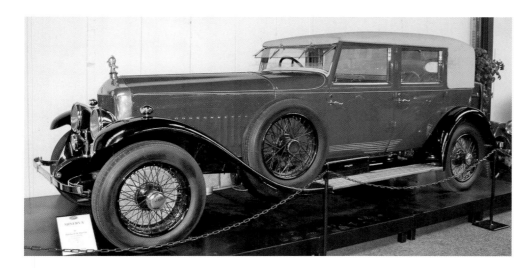

Hibbard & Darrin: Among their early bodies on the Minerva chassis, to which they owned the sole French distribution rights, was this majestic faux convertible on a 1928 AC type 30CV chassis. (*WikiMedia Commons/André Ritzinger*)

units of the Peugeot before production ceased in 2007 and, probably hoping to gain more business from Peugeot, developed an interesting four-door coupé-cabriolet concept based on the Peugeot 407. The Macarena project had a folding glass roof and was shown at Frankfurt in 2007, although no production followed.

Meanwhile, Heuliez had also embarked on another new venture, probably anticipating the eventual loss of their small-volume work for the major manufacturers. The new venture was the development of a hybrid electric car called the Cleanova, and was carried out in conjunction with the Dassault Group.

However, Heuliez was badly affected in 2006 when Opel asked for a 75% cut in Tigra production as a consequence of poor sales. The body company laid off around a quarter of its staff and by October 2007 was in trouble, requesting state protection from its creditors. In August 2008, the Indian car firm Argentum took a 60% share of the company, while the French state investment firm CDC took a minority interest. Argentum's aims were to create a global design company and to tackle the market for electric cars, and at one stage Heuliez was scheduled to start production of the German-developed Mia electric car in 2011.

Sadly, by 2009 the whole business had collapsed. It was due to be taken on by Krief Consulting, but that company also went under. The remains of Heuliez were sold in June 2010 to a conglomerate of BG Industries (from France) and the German Con-Energy AG, with assistance from the Poitou-Charentes region.

Hibbard & Darrin (F)
1923–1931, Paris
At the start of the 1920s, Thomas Hibbard came to France with the intention of establishing a branch of the Le Baron coachbuilding company he had founded in his native USA with Raymond Dietrich. In practice, he set up a new business in Paris in the spring of 1923 with a fellow American, the stylist Howard Darrin. Workshops were established at nearby Puteaux.

Hibbard & Darrin: This Renault 40CV wears a "double cabriolet" body, impressive for its sheer length.

Hibbard & Darrin: The choice of royalty: King Alfonso XIII of Spain is seen here with his convertible town car on a Duesenberg J chassis from 1930. (*Author's Collection*)

Their first efforts as Hibbard & Darrin were conventional, but the pair aimed high and obtained the sole distribution rights in France for the Belgian Minerva chassis. It was on a Minerva 30CV that they mounted a striking transformable torpedo body, showing the result at the 1926 Paris Salon. Characterised by trapezoid windows and a triangular B-pillar, the style was soon imitated by others, and the Hibbard & Darrin reputation was made.

Hibbard & Darrin: Representing the finest that money could buy in 1930 is this Duesenberg J model with convertible Victoria body. (*WikiMedia Commons/Craig Howell*)

The company concentrated on bodies for the prestigious chassis of the time, working on makes such as Duesenberg, Hispano-Suiza and Rolls-Royce as well as the Minerva that they imported. Renault commissioned them to design the 1929 range of bodies for their flagship model, the Reinastella, but part of the arrangement seems to have been that these should not carry Hibbard & Darrin identification plates.

The 1929 Wall Street Crash and the subsequent Depression led to the end of the partnership. Thomas Hibbard sought security in the arms of General Motors, returning to the USA in 1931. Howard Darrin took the risk of staying in business, and linked with the banker Fernandez in 1932 to form Fernandez & Darrin (qv).

Hofkens (B)
1926–1927, Antwerp
The coachbuilder Hofkens is known for its bodies on Belgian-made Minerva chassis, including a type AG 16hp in 1926 and a type AF 30hp in 1927.

Höhener/Höhener's Erben (CH)
1920–1935, St Gallen
Ulrich Höhener established his workshop at St Gallen 1896, and became one of the best-known builders of horse-drawn vehicles in Switzerland. Drawn inevitably towards the nascent automobile business, he was building car bodies by 1912 and possibly earlier on chassis such as the locally-made Martini.

Höhener became a founder member of the Swiss Coachbuilders' Federation (VSCI) in 1918, but died in 1923, leaving the company to his children. They picked up where he had left off, renaming the business Höhener's Erben (Höhener's successors). The 1920s brought sporting bodies on Amilcar, Bugatti, Ctiroën, Fiat and Renault 6CV chassis, large open tourers on Martini and Pic-Pic types, and closed bodies on the likes of Fiat, Martini, Peugeot and Presto. American chassis were not ignored, and there was a cabriolet on a La Salle in 1930. The early 1930s also saw Höhener building a Lancia Lambda "balloon" car (a tourer with demountable roof) and a number of bodies on Martini chassis as the bankrupt concern sold these off to coachbuilders in 1934. The company also took out a licence for the roll-roof "Sun Saloon" conversion designed by Arbenz in Zurich.

However, Höhener had also been active in the commercial vehicle business, constructing buses and fire engines for local use. By 1935, it seems to have gone over entirely to commercial bodywork, and eventually moved on to devote all its resources to repair work.

Holvoët (F)
1930s, Lille and Roubaix
The Holvoët company, of which there seem to have been two related branches in France, was one of many that held a Clairalpax licence in the 1930s. The Lille branch was run by Alphonse et Pierre Holvoët, while the Roubaix branch was known as Louis Holvoët et Fils.

Hornig (D)
1906–1945, Meerane
The Hornig coachworks built car bodies for the first half of the 20th century, but was absorbed into the East German state automobile industry after the Second World War.

The company's origins were in 1869, when wheelwright Gustav Reinhold Hornig set up business as a wheelwright in Meerane. It was 1906 before the transition was made to car bodywork, and Hornig's first creation was a saloon body on a Presto chassis. From that point on, his reputation spread locally.

Hornig was able to establish business relationships with major automotive companies, including Audi, DKW, Horch and Wanderer, and also some of the smaller ones such as Elite, Presto, Rex and Simplex. The company took on an internationally renowned designer, Erich Lüsebrink, to cater for the demand. Among other chassis bodied in the 1930s were Mercedes-Benz (the 380) and Ford (the Eifel convertible).

However, Hornig did not survive the Second World War. Meerane fell into the eastern sector of Germany, and the Hornig works was initially obliged to produce such

Hornig: A 1935 Audi UW 8/40 drophead with dickey. This model had front wheel drive. *(Erik Eckermann Archive)*

necessities as horse-drawn carts, boxes for vegetables, and hand carts. When car body construction did resume, Hornig had ceased to exist as a separate company, and its works had been integrated into the state-owned IFA organisation.

The Meerane factory was one of those involved with production of the IFA F8 and later the F9 convertible saloon. From 1955 there were trucks and truck cabs; in 1956 Wartburg coupés were added; and then there were Trabants from 1958, with their Duraplast bodies being made in Meerane. Production of these, and of their military and utility derivatives, continued until 1991, when the factory was finally closed.

Huber & Brühwiler (CH)
1930–1941, Lucerne
Huber & Brühwiler are known only for building a pair of streamlined bodies to Paul Jaray designs that were used for research and demonstration purposes. Both were constructed in 1934, one on Audi 2-litre chassis and the other on a Mercedes-Benz Type 200.

Hornig: An attractive, though not terribly distinctive, drophead on a 1939 Audi 920, this time with rear wheel drive. The front end could be mistaken for that of a contemporary Fiat. *(Erik Eckermann Archive)*

IDEA (I)
Since 1978, Turin

IDEA is an acronym of the name Institute of Development in Automotive Engineering. It was established in 1978 as an automobile design and engineering company and since 2002 has been wholly owned by Rieter Holding Ltd.

The company has had input to a number of volume production models, and for its first few years mainly acted as a consultancy to the Fiat Group. For Fiat itself, IDEA worked on the Tipo (1988), Tempra (1990) and Palio (1966). For Lancia, it worked on the Dedra (1989), Delta (1993) and Kappa (1994), and for Alfa Romeo it had input to the 155 (1992).

Foreign car makers have used IDEA increasingly since the early 1990s, welcoming its European orientation for models destined for that market. Japanese makers have included Nissan (the Terrano II that was a twin of the Ford Maverick in 1993) and Daihatsu (the Move, 1995). From Korea has come work for Daewoo (the Nubira, 1997) and Kia (the Rio, 2000), and from India has come work for Tata (the Indica, 1998; the Indigo, 2002; and the Nano, 2008).

Ihle (D)
1930–1941, Bruchsal

Brothers Rudolf and Fritz Ihle set themselves up in the coachwork business at Bruchsal in 1930, using the business name of Gebrüder Ihle. From 1933, they began to focus specifically on creating more stylish and sporting bodywork

Ihle: The Sport Type 600 was a special-bodied version of BMW's 3/15 built from 1933 to 1937. *(Rainer Simons)*

Ihle: A strong resemblance to the contemporary BMW is evident in the styling of this 900 roadster, which could be based on BMW, Fiat or Opel chassis. *(Rainer Simons)*

for mundane small cars, and their first success came with a more modern style for the Dixi 3/15 (later BMW 3/15), which still used the basic shape of the 1920s Austin Seven on which it was based. This all-steel body was called the Ihle Sport Type 600, was always painted bright red and boasted a sporty, pointed tail. Customers could buy a kit to convert their own vehicles or could have their cars rebodied in Bruchsal. The Ihle brothers also sold complete cars, created from second-hand vehicles which they had overhauled mechanically and rebodied. The Bruchsal factory set up a special production line for these bodies in 1934.

Ihle became more ambitious, and the company's conversion work often went beyond a straightforward rebody to include new fittings and sometimes even a lengthened chassis or an uprated engine. In 1936, the company introduced its Sport Type 800 body, which could be adapted to suit DKW (F1, F2, F4 and F5), Hansa or Ford Eifel chassis. As before, the favoured style was based on archetypal racing and sports designs, often recalling those of the 1920s. The earliest Ihle conversions had a rectangular grille, although later ones on all makes of chassis had a style similar to that of 1930s BMWs. It is not true, however, that BMW took its famous twin-kidney grille from an Ihle design.

At its peak in the 1930s, the company employed 50 staff. Later in that decade, Ihle also worked on larger models from the likes of Opel, but by this stage they faced much increased competition from other coachbuilders who were offering stylish alternatives to the standard mass-produced bodywork. So although the Dixi/BMW conversions and others remained available until 1941, the company supplemented its income from the start of the 1940s by producing miniature cars for fairgrounds and amusement parks.

During the Second World War, the Ihle workshop was given over to building precision weapons and DKW-engined portable water pumps, and the staff increased to 150. When peace returned, the company saw no future in a return to coachbuilding and sold its Dixi body line to BMW. Instead, it now focussed completely on the fairground miniature cars.

Many of these were made from fibreglass, and one especially notable example was a miniature Mercedes 300SL, which was powered by an 8hp Hirth petrol engine. However, the company closed down in 1985 after bankruptcy followed the death of both Ihle brothers.

IMA (B)
Malines, 1965–1973

IMA was established in 1951 in Brussels as an importer of various foreign car makes, including Mercedes-Benz. The initials of its name stood for Importeur de Moteurs et d'Automobiles (Importer of Engines and Cars). In 1954 it moved to new premises at Malines (called Mechelen in Flemish).

IMA: The Universal estate car was a neat conversion of the Mercedes-Benz "Fintail" saloons. This is a 1966 230S model. *(Daimler-Benz)*

IMA: The trick was repeated with equal success on the later W115 or "Stroke 8" models, of which this is a 220D. *(WikiMedia Commons/Mercedesgek)*

Between 1965 and 1973, IMA was responsible for a factory-approved estate car conversion of Mercedes' saloons, which was known as the Universal. There were 2754 examples on the "Fintail" saloons between 1965 and 1968, and a further quantity on the later W115 range.

IMA then began building Saab 99 models for the local market, an arrangement that continued until 1978 when IMA closed down.

Italdesign (I)
1968 to present, Moncalieri
Italdesign was founded in 1968 as the Studi Italiani Realizzazione Prototipi SpA (Italian Prototype Construction Studio Ltd) by Giorgetto Giugiaro and Aldo Mantovani. Giugiaro already had an impressive list of automotive design achievements behind him, and became responsible for the research and style departments, while Mantovani took charge of planning and development.

Deliberately based in the Turin region, near the heart of the Italian motor industry, the company went on to offer car

Italdesign: Among the earliest manufacturers to use Italdesign was Alfa Romeo, who commissioned a Giugiaro design for their 1971 Alfasud. *(Alfa Romeo)*

Italdesign: The Bizzarini Manta show car was a powerful statement of intent by the newly independent Giugiaro in 1968. *(WikiMedia Commons/Brian Snelson)*

Italdesign: Keen to demonstrate that his company did not plan to be tied to volume-production designs, Giugiaro constructed the Caimano show car on the basis of an Alfasud in 1971. (*David Hodges Collection*)

Italdesign: Also dating from 1971 was the Maserati Bora supercar. (*David Hodges Collection*)

Italdesign: Work for the VW Group began with the Audi 80 of 1972. (*VW-Audi*)

makers all over the world a one-stop shop for the design, prototyping, testing, project management and production implementation of a new model. Italdesign's primary focus has always been on design for mass production, and it has not built special bodywork for individual customers.

During the 1970s, Italdesign widened its scope beyond the automotive industry to embrace other areas of product design. Projects have included sewing machines for Necchi in Italy, cameras for Nikon in Japan, and watches

for Seiko in Japan. At the start of the 1990s, Italdesign became a business group with the new name of Italdesign Giugiaro, and in 1992 it established a Spanish subsidiary, Diseño Industrial Italdesign Srl, in Barcelona, to work with manufacturers in that country. This subsidiary was later renamed as Italdesign Giugiaro Barcelona SL.

In May 2010, some 40 years after the two companies had first worked together, the Volkswagen Group bought a 90.1% stake in Italdesign through its Italian subsidiary

Italdesign: The 1972 Alfa Romeo Alfetta showed Italdesign's mastery of the everyday saloon. *(Alfa Romeo)*

Italdesign: A hugely important milestone in the company's history was the contract to design the first-generation Volkswagen Golf that went on sale in 1974. *(Volkswagen)*

Italdesign: BMW turned to Italdesign when they needed an eye-catching but practical body for their 1978 M1 supercar. *(BMW)*

Italdesign: Also shown in 1978 was the Megagamma MPV concept for Lancia. Unfortunately Lancia's owners at Fiat got cold feet and this pioneering design was shelved. *(Fiat)*

Lamborghini Holding SpA. The Giugiaro family retained the rest, and both Giorgetto Giugiaro and his son Fabrizio continued to play leading roles in the activities of the company, which by this time employed some 800 staff.

From the beginning, the company's reputation depended on Giorgetto Giugiaro himself. He is regarded as one of the greatest car designers of all time, and has certainly been one of the most prolific. His designs have included several volume-selling models as well as extraordinarily attractive prototypes and concept cars, and much of the genius of his work lies in its simplicity and essential rightness of line.

Giugiaro's talent was first recognised by Dante Giacosa, technical director of Fiat, who recruited him to the company straight from school in September 1955. However, Giugiaro found the Fiat environment stifling, and in 1959 left to join Bertone. Here, he matured as a designer under the guidance of Nuccio Bertone, showing his talent on some exceptional coachbuilt cars like the Aston Martin DB4 Jet

Italdesign: The Aztec was a concept car from 1988 with an Audi engine and Lancia Integrale four-wheel-drive system. Driver and passenger spoke to each other by intercom. (*David Hodges Collection*)

Italdesign: Japanese car maker Subaru turned to Italdesign for its 1991 SVX (also sold as the Alcyone) coupé. The wide windows with their fixed upper sections were a notable feature. (*Subaru*)

(1961), the Maserati 5000GT (1961) and the Ferrari 250 GT SWB (1962), and then on volume-production cars such as the Alfa Romeo Giulia GT (1963) and the Fiat 850 Spider (1965). Bertone's Chevrolet Testudo (1963) and Alfa Romeo Canguro (1964) prototypes were also his work.

In 1965, Giugiaro moved to Ghia as head of design, and immediately produced a number of designs that played a major part in reviving Ghia's flagging fortunes. These included the Maserati Ghibli and De Tomaso Pampero, both revealed in 1966.

Giugiaro's desire for independence soon asserted itself, however, and in February 1967 he established Ital Styling as his own company, while continuing to freelance for Bertone. From this era comes his design for the Fiat Dino coupé, built by Bertone and released in 1967. Wholly independent from 1968 with Italdesign, Giugiaro immediately made an impact with the Bizzarini Manta concept car at that year's Turin Motor Show. This was very much a statement of intent, and before long Italdesign was working on a number of projects for major car manufacturers. Since then, the company has been responsible for large numbers

of production models, among them such best-sellers as the first Volkswagen Golf in 1974, the Fiat Uno in 1980 and the Fiat Punto in 1993. All three embodied the Giugiaro principle of linear simplicity.

A complete list of cars drawn up by Italdesign is beyond the scope of this book, but it is worth noting that the list of makers who have used Italdesign's services includes Alfa Romeo, Audi, BMW, Bugatti, Chevrolet, Chrysler, Daewoo, Daihatsu, DeLorean, Fiat, FSO, Hyundai, Isuzu, Lamborghini, Lancia, Lexus, Lotus, Maserati, Morris, Renault, Saab, SEAT, Ssang Yong, Subaru, Suzuki and Volkswagen.

Italsuisse (CH)
1959–1967, Geneva
In the late 1950s, Adriano Guglielmetti was employed by Ghia-Aigle in Switzerland, and there he met the Italian designer Pietro Frua, who was working for the company on a freelance basis. At the end of 1959, Guglielmetti left Ghia to set up his own company, which he called Carrosserie Italsuisse, and he called upon Frua for every one of its designs. The company's name reflected its use of Italian

styling from a Swiss base, and its logo incorporated the Swiss and Italian national flags.

The first Italsuisse premises were a small workshop in the Carouge district of Geneva, in the Rue de la Pyrotechnie, and the company's first design was ready in time for the Geneva Show in March 1960. This was an attractive four-seat coupé called the Sun Valley and based on the Volkswagen 1200, with more than a hint of the Chevrolet Corvair in its design. One story has it that there was interest from the USA and that an order came from Israel for 5000 examples. However, Volkswagen refused to supply the necessary platforms, perhaps because it was already working on the broadly similar 1500 Karmann-Ghia coupé for 1961 introduction.

Also from 1960 were two designs on the Studebaker Lark. Italsuisse followed up in 1961 with a Maserati 3500 GT coupé and a Fiat Giannini Spyder, and in 1964 there was an Opel Kadett A Spyder.

In 1965 or 1966, the company moved to new premises in the Route du Pont-Butin, in the nearby Geneva suburb of Petit-Lancy. Still hoping to attract major orders from regular stands at the Geneva Show, it created variations on the Jaguar E-type, a convertible in 1965 and a coupé in 1966. However, the big orders were not forthcoming and Italsuisse made its last appearance at Geneva in 1967, with a fastback coupé for Autobleu that was based on a Peugeot 204 and was its tenth design from Pietro Frua.

J

Jackey (F)
1920s
The French coachbuilder Jackey is known for bodies on Bugatti chassis, including a racing body on a Type 30 in 1927 and one at the 1928 Paris Salon.

Jacobi (D)
1920s, Hanover
There is no detailed information available about Carosseriewerk Gebrüder Jacobi, although its name clearly indicates that more than one Jacobi brother was involved in the business.

Jacobsen & Steinberg (D)
1956, Berlin
Jacobsen & Steinberg was a Berlin manufacturer of boats that is known for a single two-door cabriolet on BMW 503 chassis, built as a private venture in 1955. The car had a somewhat Italian appearance and was notable for having a body built from GRP and polyester.

Jacobsen & Steinberg: This interesting cabriolet based on a BMW 503 had GRP bodywork. *(Copyright unknown)*

Jähnig (D)
1891–1945, Lommatzsch
Walter Jähnig Automobile was founded in 1891 in Lommatzsch, Saxony, as a builder of agricultural vehicles and later carriages. Although it advertised its willingness to produce bodywork to individual commissions or in series, little is known about its activities. It is likely that most of the company's output was commercial bodywork. During the 1939-1945 war it was involved with the production of war materiel and was closed down in 1945.

Janer (F)
1930s, Paris
Janer was a subsidiary of the Kellner (qv) coachbuilding company, established in the early 1930s to handle low-volume body production for the major car makers. Kellner wanted to keep this business separate from its established high-class custom-building business, although in practice the small runs of saloons and cabriolets that Janer built were designed by the Kellner stylists. The products of the Janer (JAcques KellNER) company were particularly associated with Ford V8 chassis.

Janet (F)
1930s, Paris
Carrosserie René Janet is known to have built a coupé body on a late 1930s Voisin C30, characterised by a curious layered grille.

Janoir (F)
1925–late 1930s, Saint-Ouen
Louis Janoir was a pioneer of all-metal bodywork in France during the 1920s, but car bodies were only a part of his business. He had been educated as an engineer, and was wealthy enough to indulge in the sport of flying before the Great War. One of his chosen mounts was a Deperdussin seaplane that had a metal monocoque structure at a time when most aircraft still had wooden frames and a canvas outer skin, and this almost certainly influenced his later coachwork construction methods.

In 1916, he founded Janoir Aviation at Saint-Ouen, building a small number of his own aircraft but mainly repairing and later building Spad XIII fighter planes. In 1920, he joined the Chantiers de Provence and became a principal shareholder before leaving to establish his own motorcycle and sidecar business in Saint-Ouen. Here, he also built a number of cyclecars between 1921 and 1922.

Car bodies followed from about 1925. Janoir took out a licence to build bodies using the Baehr patents, but he improved on this by creating an all-aluminium frame and by developing interchangeable body elements. The results were lightweight bodies that were also practical to build and to repair.

Although Janoir bodies were built on a number of quality chassis, including those by Delahaye and Delage, their main interest lay in their construction rather than their shapes, which broke no new ground. The company survived until the end of the 1930s.

Janoir: This advertisement from the 1920s promoted Janoir's use of high-strength aluminium framework and interchangeable body elements. *(Author's Collection)*

Janssen (F)
Early 1900s–c1937, Paris; later Levallois-Perret

The Parisian coachbuilder Janssen & Cie was established at the start of the 20th century at 158 Boulevard de la Gare, Paris 13, later moving to 93 Rue Gide in Levallois-Perret. It was always associated with luxury coachwork before the Great Depression.

Increasingly close links with Panhard & Levassor enabled the company to survive the Depression, and it was Janoir who built the last cabriolets and limousines on the Panhard drop-frame CS and DS chassis in 1937. The company ceased coachbuilding at the end of the 1930s, and in 1946 joined forces with the coachbuilder Binder to sell Cadillacs and other General Motors products in France as Binder-Janssen.

Joly (F)
1905–1930s, Paris; later Clichy

Founded in 1905 by two brothers as Joly Frères, this Parisian company was mainly known in the 1920s and 1930s for its work with Fords. Its original address was 194-196 Rue Marcadet, Paris 18, but it later moved to 162 Boulevard Victor-Hugo in Clichy and changed its name to Louis Joly.

Among the products offered by the later company was a Ford Model A with wheelbase extended by 300mm and configured as either a saloon, a "familiale" or a taxi.

Jonckheere (B)
1902–c1932, Roeselare

Jonckheere has been best known since the early 1930s as a Belgian manufacturer of bus and coach bodies. However, between 1902 and the early 1930s it was also a builder of car bodies.

The company was founded in 1881 by Henri Jonckheere in Beveren, near Roeselare in western Flanders, and began by building horse-drawn vehicles. In 1902, the company built its first car bodywork, and over time came to specialise in luxury bodywork for the more expensive chassis, including Bovy, FN, Métallurgique, Minerva, Pipe and Rolls-Royce.

The Jonckheere premises were completely destroyed during the Great War, and when the company started up again afterwards, Henri Jonckheere's son Joseph began to think internationally because he believed that diversification was the best safeguard for the company's future. In particular, he suspected that domestic manufacturers would suffer when the Belgian market was opened to US manufacturers in the early 1920s.

So from 1922, Jonckheere began building bus and coach bodies. Car body construction continued, and a notable example was on Minerva chassis in 1927. However, the bus and coach work rapidly became the company's major activity, and in the early 1930s it abandoned car body production altogether.

Jousse & Parsy (F)
1900s–1920s, Montargis

Founded at the start of the 20th century, Jousse & Parsy were best known for their torpedo bodies. Although they were still active in the 1920s, the company appears to have gone out of business before the end of the decade.

K

Karmann (D)
Since 1901, Osnabrück

Karmann today is a major body design, production and assembly plant that serves car manufacturers not only in Germany but also in the USA and in other European countries. It began life as a small coachbuilder, and began to take on volume-build contracts for German chassis manufacturers in the 1920s. However, its real success was largely due to its early grasp of how to alter a monocoque structure, which enabled it to make cabriolets and coupés from existing saloon designs when other coachbuilders were still struggling with the new body technology. One result was that Karmann was always best known for its cabriolets, and the company had become an acknowledged world leader in the field by the 1980s.

The company can trace its origins back to 1901, when Wilhelm Karmann took over the Klage carriage works that had been established in Osnabrück in 1874. To this day, many vehicles built by Karmann carry a small wagon wheel emblem, which reflects the coat of arms of Osnabrück. At that time, the business in Lower Saxony employed eight staff. Karmann built his first car body in 1902, on a Dürkopp chassis. Before the First World War, the company built bodies on chassis such as Daimler and Opel, but its big break came in 1924 with an order for 1000 bodies on AGA chassis. Karmann also built the cabriolet bodies for the 1928 Dixi 9/40PS.

In the 1930s, the company built some Ford Eifel roadsters and worked with Hanomag. Its closest co-operation was with Adler, for whom it created a number of attractive convertible bodies. Those for the 1937 Adler Autobahn

Karmann: Dating from 1926 but looking much newer, this cabriolet body on an Adler 6/25 chassis was a Karmann product. *(Author's Collection)*

model represented an important step for Karmann towards production of all-steel bodywork that would be built on the company's own tooling.

The major post-war body contracts began in May 1949 with one for the four-seater cabriolet body of the Volkswagen Beetle. Between then and 1980, a total of 331,847 left the Karmann works – an average of well over 10,000 examples every year. The link with Volkswagen remained strong throughout the 1950s, and Karmann also picked up the assembly contract for the new coupé design on the Beetle "platform". This had been designed by Ghia in Italy, and emerged in 1955 with the name of Volkswagen Karmann Ghia coupé; a much lower-volume cabriolet version followed two years later, and a total of around 445,000 examples of both types had been built in Germany

Karmann: The 2000CS coupé was an early contract for BMW, beginning in 1964. *(BMW)*

Karmann: BMW also took the revised bodies for its six-cylinder coupés from Karmann, this 1969 3.0 CS being an example. *(BMW)*

Karmann: The VW-Porsche 914 was a modern-looking sports roadster for the 1970s, and Karmann built its bodies from 1973. *(David Hodges Collection)*

by the time production ended in 1974; Karmann's Brazilian factory built more than 41,000 more, including some of a unique design. Throughout the 1950s, Karmann were also building the bodies for some versions of the Porsche 356.

Karmann added BMW to their list of customers in 1965, although the first contract was small by their standards, and called for rather less than 3000 bodies a year for the new 2000C and 2000CS coupés. Porsche returned for more, taking coupé bodies from 1966 for both the 911 and 912 models, and then from 1969 rewarding Karmann with the body contract for their new 914 model, which brought assembly volumes of more than 17,000 a year. There was design consultancy work in this period, too, one of the best known examples being the Triumph TR6 sports car for British Leyland.

Karmann also got into the CKD assembly business in the 1960s, when they picked up the contract for European assembly of the American Motors (AMC) Javelin coupé. The company opened a second factory at Rheine to build

this from 1968, but the car was not a big success in Europe and Karmann built only 300 in all.

The contracts with Volkswagen for the Beetle cabriolet and the Karmann Ghia models continued into the 1970s, and from 1974 were supplemented by body work for motorhomes based on the Beetle van, of which around 1000 were built before the end of the decade. Much larger volumes came from the contract for Volkswagen's first-generation Scirocco coupé, which also made its debut in 1974 and of which Karmann built 504,153 before production ended in 1981.

BMW remained a good customer in the 1970s, with the bodies for its 2800CS and 3.0 CS E9 coupés between 1971 and 1975, and then a contract for the 6 Series or E24 replacement model from 1976, of which 86,314 were built before 1989.

There were contracts for Ford in the 1980s, with the Escort convertible that averaged just under 14,000 a year from 1983 to 1990, and the American-market version of the

Karmann: Mercedes' "small" sports car, the SLK roadster, was another Karmann production. *(Daimler-Benz)*

Ford Sierra, the Merkur XR4Ti that was built at a rate of just over 10,000 a year between 1984 and 1989.

The Volkswagen business continued with the Mk1 Golf Cabriolet (around 27,750 a year from 1979-1993), the second-generation Scirocco coupé (around 26,500 a year between 1981 and 1992), and the Corrado coupé (around 16,250 a year from 1988 to 1995). From 1979, motorhome production switched to the new T3 model, and the Rheine factory built a total of 891 examples of various types between then and 1992. In addition, 3103 motorhomes based on the LT van were built between 1978 and 1996.

The 1990s brought more work for the Volkswagen Group, and Karmann assembled the Audi 80 Convertible (1997-2000), the Volkswagen Golf Mk3 Convertible (1993-1997) and Mk3 Variant (1997-1999), the Golf Mk4 Convertible (1997-2001) and the T4-based camper from (1996-2003). Between 1998 and 2003, Karmann assembled 115,264 examples of the Mercedes-Benz CLK Cabriolet. For Ford, there were the Escort Cabriolet (1990–1997) and the Escort RS Cosworth (1992–1996).

In some cases Karmann carried out only part of the construction. This was the case with the Porsche 968 (1991–1994), for which Karmann only built the body-in-white. The arrangement with Renault was similar, although Karmann built both the body-in-white and the soft tops for the 19 Convertible (1990-1996) and the Mégane I Convertible (1996-2003).

It was a natural progression from traditional convertibles to the folding-roof systems that were beginning to appear at the close of the 20th century, and during the 2000s,

Karmann became a leading specialist in the field. Typically, it would build the convertible or retractable roof as a module that would then be fitted to a car on its manufacturers' production lines. Karmann's Roof Systems division in Osnabrück supplied roof modules to manufacturers that included Audi, Bentley, BMW, Ford (USA), Mercedes-Benz, Nissan, Pontiac, Renault and Volkswagen (New Mexico). More traditional Karmann work was the construction of the complete body for the Mercedes-Benz SLK and the Spyker C8 Spyder, and the company carried out much of the development of the Chrysler Crossfire, which was based on a Mercedes-Benz platform. It also built versions of the car at both Osnabrück and Rheine. Conversions included the VW T5 motorhome from 2003.

From 2002, Karmann also had an assembly plant at São Bernardo do Campo in Brazil. However, the company's sheer size eventually made it vulnerable. The sharp decline in the car market that followed the 2008 financial crisis forced Karmann to seek bankruptcy protection in April 2009. The situation was resolved later that year, when Volkswagen agreed to buy the Osnabrück factory for around 39 million Euros; it renamed the plant Volkswagen Osnabrück GmbH in December 2009, and in 2011 began production of the next-generation Golf Cabriolet there. Within the VW group, the Osnabrück factory has now become the primary location for cabriolet bodies and for small-series production. In 2012, VAG also began building the Porsche Boxster there.

In 2010, Karmann's Roof Systems division and its expertise, plus its satellite factory in the Polish town of Zary, were sold to Valmet Automotive in Sweden, while Karmann's North American operations were sold to the Webasto Group.

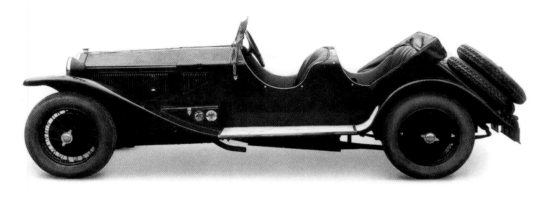

Kässbohrer: Two views of an intriguing and rakish 1928 Lancia Lambda with bodywork by Kässbohrer, doorless and with a neat arrangement for the folded hood. (*Erik Eckermann Archive*)

Kässbohrer (D)
1920s, Ulm
The Kässbohrer name has always been primarily associated with bus bodywork, and in fact the company built its first bus body on a Saurer chassis in 1911. However, during the 1920s it was also noted as a builder of car bodies.

Karl Kässbohrer established Wagenfabrik Kässbohrer to build horse-drawn carriages in Ulm in 1893, and before the First World War had begun to build bodies for motor vehicles. There were, for example, car bodies on Adler, Opel and Stoewer chasis. When the company's founder died in 1922, his sons Otto and Karl junior took over the business. Although car bodywork was always secondary to bus and truck bodies, the company built some interesting bodies on chassis such as Brennabor, Lancia, Mercedes-Benz and Opel before switching entirely to PSV and commercial work.

Kastenhofer (A)
1940s, Wien-Margareten
Kastenhofer was one of the three Viennese companies that constructed aluminium bodies for early Porsche models. (The others were Keibl and Austro-Tatra, qqv.)

Kathe (D)
1833–1948, Halle
Ludwig Kathe set up in business as a wagon maker in 1833, taking on his son Adolf as a partner in 1865. but it was not until the start of the new century that his descendants began to build bodies for passenger cars. Ludwig Kathe & Sohn passed into the hands of Ludwig (junior) and Alfred Kathe, the former handling the business side and the latter taking responsibility for design and the workshop. The company had links with Horch and became a pioneer of torpedo-type bodies, one of which was on a car driven by Alfred in one of the Prince Henry trials.

Kathe built on a variety of chassis in the 1920s, including Dixi, Horch and Opel. In the first half of the decade, a second workshop was opened in Chemnitz, and this worked closely with Audi, DKW, Horch and Wanderer (who became Auto Union in 1932). While retaining conventional lines, the company developed new roof designs, among which were the 1924 roll-top "Limusette" and the 1928 "Landauline" with its folding rear roof section.

However, the 1930s saw the focus of production shift towards bodywork for delivery vehicles and buses. In 1935, the company name changed to Kathe & Co KG, and in 1948 Kathe was absorbed into the Saxony division of the nationalised East German motor industry. Its former works were used for the assembly of Wartburg cars.

Keibl (A)
1930s–1940s, Vienna-Landstrasse
The Austrian coachbuilder Keibl is known for bodywork on Mercedes-Benz SS chassis in the early 1930s. In the post-1945 era, it was one of the companies that completed bodies for the early Porsche models, and was also responsible for the VW-based Denzel sports cars that were short-lived alternatives to the Porsche.

Keibl: Porsche had its first cars bodied by local coachbuilders in Austria, of which Keibl was one. This cabriolet dates from 1949 and has many differences from the later 356 models. (*Porsche*)

Keinath (D)
1980s, Reutlingen

In the early 1980s, Keinath brought to market a cabriolet based on the Opel Ascona that was known as the Keinath C3. The model is often confused with the similar cabriolet produced in greater numbers by Voll and by Hammond & Thiede (qqv). The C3 was built in much smaller numbers, a total of 434 having been built.

Kellner (F)
1894–1940, Boulogne-Billancourt; later Paris

Kellner was one of France's most important coachbuilders before World War II. The company was one of the first to build a car body (in 1894) and is credited with the invention of the torpedo body style in about 1910. During the 1920s, the company was known for the very high quality of its bodywork, and in the inter-war years took on a number of royal commissions. There were orders for the King of Spain, the Swedish court, for Indian royalty (one Maharaja ordered six Kellner bodies on Hispano-Suiza chassis). Kellner also bodied a Renault for the French President.

Best known for its work on Hispano-Suiza chassis, for which there were more than 300 bodies, Kellner built on most of the top-quality chassis of its day. From the late 1920s, the company also had a volume-production subsidiary called Janer (qv). However, Kellner did not survive the 1939-1945 war. All coachbuilding activity ceased when France was occupied in 1940, and two years later the company's head, Jacques Kellner, grandson of the founder, was shot as a member of the French Resistance.

Kellner: Somewhat haughty and typical of the firm's bodies, this cabriolet roadster is on a 1929 Hispano-Suiza chassis. (*David Hodges Collection*)

Kellner: A "Torpédo Scaphandrier" on a Renault Reinastella. The word "scaphandrier" is used to describe a diving bell. *(David Burgess-Wise)*

Kellner: More conventional is this "Double Cabriolet" on a 40CV Renault. *(David Burgess-Wise)*

The Kellner company was founded in 1860 when George Kellner set up in Paris to build custom bodies for horse-drawn carriages. He was an Austrian who had learned the saddle-making trade with Proust & Cammaerts in Brussels, and had finished his apprenticeship with Barker in London. After working his way up the trade in Paris, he established his own business, finally settling in the Avenue Malakoff in 1873, where the company would become a neighbour of Labourdette (qv).

Kellner was joined in the business by his two sons. Paul became the commercial director and Georges (his name was spelled the French way) was responsible for manufacturing. It was these two who steered the company into the emergent motor car business, building their first car body in 1894. In 1902, Kellner built the streamlined body on a steam-driven Serpollet that went on to take the world speed record at over 120km/h, and from 1903 it was clear that car bodies were the future. Kellner soon acquired a reputation for innovation as well as quality, and from 1906, demand prompted the construction of a new and larger factory at Billancourt where the company employed 600 staff. The two brothers took an increasing role in the

business until their father retired in 1910, and Georges Kellner deserves credit for popularizing the torpedo body style; some authorities have even suggested that he was its inventor, although that claim is hotly disputed.

From March 1910, the company was renamed Kellner Frères, Successeurs (Kellner Brothers, Successors). During the Great War, it built military vehicles, including ambulances and gun carriages, and from 1917 became involved in the manufacture of the Spad fighter aircraft; by June 1918 it had a workforce of 1600 and was building 10 aircraft a day.

In 1924, Georges Kellner was joined by his son Jacques and the company was renamed Kellner & Fils (Kellner and Son); Paul Kellner remained involved as their attorney. Kellner opened a showroom in the Champs-Elysées and the company returned to its pre-war focus on luxury bodywork, going on to become France's most important luxury coachbuilder in the 1920s. At the 1924 Paris Salon, for example, the company was able to boast no fewer than 30 exhibits, some on its own stand and some on the stands of the chassis-makers. Recipients of Kellner bodywork in the

Kellner: Few Bugatti Royale chassis were made, but Kellner was one of the coachbuilders to whom a chassis was entrusted. This was the Kellner "coach" (two-door saloon) of 1931. *(David Hodges Collection)*

1920s included Ariès, Ballot, Cadillac, Delage, Delaunay-Belleville, Farman, Lorraine, Mercedes-Benz SS, Peugeot, Renault, Rochet-Schneider and Rolls-Royce.

Meanwhile, in 1923 the company had created the "scaphandrier" (diving-bell) style of body, essentially a torpedo with a three-piece windscreen and fabric roof to enclose the rear compartment. Among the first examples was one on a Renault 40CV chassis for that company's founder Louis Renault. It was a style that would remain popular for many years, being seen on Duesenberg, Hispano-Suiza, Renault and Rolls-Royce chassis. Among the last was one for a Packard Twelve chassis in 1938.

Although Kellner was riding high by the turn of the decade, Jacques Kellner realized that the business needed to diversify in order to guarantee its survival. So he created two subsidiary companies. One was Janer (qv), which handled small runs of saloons and cabriolets for the volume car builders. designed by the Kellner stylists for the chassis makers. The second subsidiary attempted to break into the aviation business by building aircraft from pre-fabricated metal sections. Known as Kellner-Bécherau, this company was a joint effort with aviation pioneer Louis Bécherau, but was not a success.

Jacques Kellner's foresight had been wise, as the 1930s turned out to be a difficult time for the parent company. Not only did the Depression lead to a downturn in demand for the high-quality luxury bodies that were its speciality, but its conservative styling was overshadowed by the more glamorous creations from Fernandez & Darrin, Figoni & Falaschi, and Saoutchik (qqv). Although output dropped, the company did secure notable orders such as a "coach" body for one of the Bugatti Royale chassis in 1932. Kellner was not tempted to flirt with modern fashions, but continued to produce conservative, elegant bodywork. Most of its bodies in this period were built on the traditional luxury chassis such as Bentley, Hispano-Suiza and Rolls-Royce. The company continued working until the outbreak of war in 1939, still one of the most respected and well-known French coachbuilders of the old school.

Kellner (D)
1910–1935, Berlin

The German coachbuilder Alexis Kellner had no connection with the French coachbuilder of the same name. The company first made its name in 1912 with unusual bodywork on NAG chassis, although it also bodied Adler, Benz, Mercedes and others. By 1920 the firm was well established and had registered patents for a number of cabriolet designs that were then licensed to other coachbuilders.

The 1920s brought bodywork for top-quality chassis such as La Salle and Rolls-Royce as well as domestic chassis builders like Maybach and Mercedes. However, Kellner saw the value of an alliance with the newly established Ford assembly plant in Berlin, and by the end of the decade had secured a contract to build luxury bodies on the Model A chassis.

However, the downturn in bespoke coachbuilding in the early 1930s affected Kellner, and Ford's decision to move from Berlin to Cologne may also have had an effect. A relationship with the Cologne coachbuilder Drauz (qv) – who were already one of Ford's major body suppliers – had been established by 1933, when the two companies shared a stand at that year's Berlin Motor Show. By 1935, Kellner had become insolvent and sold out to Drauz. Alexis Kellner himself moved to Switzerland, where he worked for a time with Gygax (as Gygax and Kellner) and later on with Langenthal.

Kelsch (F)
1893–1936, Levallois-Perret

The Kelsch coachworks were best known for sporting and lightweight bodywork and for an innovative system of body mounting.

Clément Kelsch was apprenticed for a time to Kellner in Paris, and in 1893 set up his own business in the suburb of Levallois. Before the Great War, the company had become known for its sporting bodywork on cars, and during the war it was diverted to build military aircraft.

Kelsch became a limited company in 1921 and moved to premises opposite those of Chenard & Walcker, which

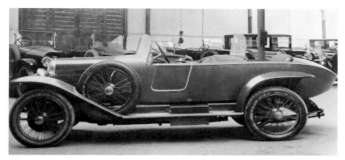

Kelsch: The coachworks was closely associated with Chenard & Walcker for a time, and this open dual-cowl body dated from 1924. (Unknown copyright)

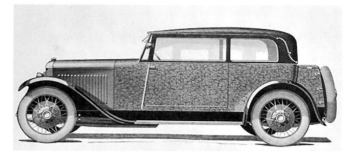

Kelsch: This faux-cabriolet body for a Delage chassis dates from 1926 and its panels appear to be covered with some kind of patterned fabric. (Unknown copyright)

Kelsch: The key element of the company's bodies on Rolland-Pilain chassis, according to this 1920s advertisement, was their light weight. (Author's Collection)

company also bought some shares in the coachbuilder. The 1920s saw Kelsch's business expand, most of its work being on French chassis. In addition to Chenard & Walcker, there were examples on Bignan, Delage, Lorraine-Dietrich, Roland-Pilain, and Sizaire Frères. Still specialising in sporting bodies, Kelsch patented a form of ultra-light coachwork in which the doors and roof were made from mesh covered in leather. He also developed a mounting system where the body was mounted to the chassis at three points and was thus in effect independent of it.

From 1928, he switched from leather to aluminium paneling, and that year also introduced his all-weather body, mounting the first one on a Lorraine-Dietrich chassis. By 1929, the Kelsch business was booming. The next step was a move into aerodynamics, and from 1930 Kelsch built some pontoon bodies using the Guillaume Busson (qv) patents. By the time of the 1933 Paris Salon, Kelsch had his own aerodynamic design ready, and a year later he introduced what he called the Clairtoutemps Universelle (the name translates roughly as Light in all weathers). This combined streamlined elements with a roof that was partially made of glass as an extension of the windscreen, and partially convertible. A similar line of thinking was displayed in his

Kelsch: A handsome "skiff ponté" (decked skiff) on a 1926 Delage DISS. (David Burgess-Wise)

1934 Rapidtoutemps (Rapid all-weather) on a Unic chassis, which incorporated an electrically-operated cabriolet top.

At the same time, Kelsch was working with Henri Pigozzi on adapting the Fiat 6CV and 11CV models for production in France under the Simca name. However, Kelsch himself died in 1934 and his company survived only a couple of years longer.

Klein (D)
Dates not known, Altona
Nothing is known about the Bernhard Klein Wagen- und Karosseriefabrik except that it was based in Altona, in the state of Hamburg.

Kleye (D)
1920s?, Altenburg
The Karosseriefabrik Albert Kleye appears to have been based in Altenburg, Saxony, during the 1920s, but nothing else is known.

Kölz (CH)
1920s, Basle
The Basle coachworks of Julius Kölz was established as early as 1875 and in the early years of the 20th century was mainly concerned with bodywork for commercial vehicles, buses and coaches, and ambulances. Although it advertised a willingness to construct car bodywork as well in 1929, no traces of such bodies have yet been found.

Köng (CH)
1935–1999, Basle
Alfred Köng set up as a cartwright in Basle in 1878, and in 1918 became a founding member of the Swiss Coachbuilders' Association (VSCI). His son Walter joined the business as an apprentice when he left school and subsequently spent a year working for Cesare Sala in Milan. He moved to Gallé in Paris where he rose to become chief designer, still aged only 20. By 1929, he was working in the design office at Chrysler and subsequently spent some time with Packard in the USA.

Köng: Undoubtedly the Basle coachbuilder's best-known work was this extraordinary bodywork for a Riley RMB chassis in 1948. *(Salon Privé)*

When his father died in 1935, Walter returned to Switzerland to take charge of the family business, which that year was renamed Walter Köng Carrosserie. In the second half of the '30s, like several other Swiss coachbuilders, the company built mainly cabriolet bodies on a variety of upmarket British and French chassis.

After the Second World War, Köng returned to coachbuilding, and an early example of his work was a sedanca coupé on Bentley Mk VI chassis in 1947. His best-known product from this period was a daring "transformable coupé" that he built on a Riley 2.5-litre RMB chassis in 1948. The body featured a silk roof lining and mahogany running-boards and door handles, and had in fact originally been intended for a Bentley. Köng showed it at Geneva in 1949, and when its high price deterred buyers, he took the Riley on as his own car.

Like many other coachbuilders, Köng encountered a lack of custom in the post-war period. He re-focussed his business on the restoration of classic cars, notably working on several cars in the Mercedes-Benz Museum collection. Walter Köng died in 1989, but his business survived for a further ten years in the hands of shareholders. In 1999, it was sold to the Basle coachbuilding company Rudi Wenger.

Königstadt (D)
1922–1925, Berlin
Karosserie- und Wagenbau Königstadt was active in Berlin from 1922-1925, but no further information is available.

Kraemer (F)
1940s, Boulogne-sur-Seine
The Kraemer business (R Kraemer Carrossier) was at 20 Rue de la Belle-Feuille in Boulogne-sur-Seine. It specialised in utility bodies and vans but also built some wooden-bodied shooting brakes (called Touristes Commerciales) on the Simca Huit between 1947 and 1949. These were strictly conversions; the Simca-approved shooting brake was built by SIOP (the Société Industrielle de l'Ouest Parisien) from 1948.

Kruck (D)
1838–1930, Frankfurt-am-Main and Wiesbaden
Heinrich Kruck founded his wagon works in 1838, and the business eventually passed to his grandson Georg. By the turn of the century, Kruck was building passenger car bodies, and turned to French examples for inspiration. The company specialised early on in the Roi-des-Belges style, and expanded: in 1905 it opened a branch in Wiesbaden and in 1906 a second one in Berlin. The company was a pioneer of metal body pillars as early as 1906.

After the Great War, Kruck returned to business, and in 1921 introduced bodywork with a luggage boot accessible from inside the passenger compartment. There were bodies on Benz and Dux chassis, among others. In 1925, Kruck was one of a number of German companies that took on a Weymann licence. However, the company was liquidated in 1930.

Kühlstein (D)
1833–1926, Berlin

Established in the Charlottenburg district of Berlin, the Kühlstein wagon-building business became closely involved with Joseph Vollmer's pioneering vehicles after he joined the company in 1887. In 1906 it was absorbed by the Ludwig Rühe wagon building company, which was owned by Max Leuschner, a former Kühlstein employee.

Kühlstein Wagenbau built bodies on a variety of chassis, including Adler, Dinos and NAG, but its output was predominantly on Protos chassis. It was a supplier to the Kaiser and to other members of the German royal family. The company closed down in 1926.

Kühn (D)
1920s–1945, Halle

Karosseriewerke Otto Kühn was based in Halle, Saxony, and was the primary supplier of special bodywork for Opel during the 1920s. The company produced estate, taxi and cabriolet types among others, and held a Weymann licence. In 1928-1929 it produced its own version of the Opel 8/40PS that was marketed as a Kühn 8/40PS. By 1931 the

Kühn: Good customer Opel took bodywork by Kühn on its 7PS model. The car is an Erika cabriolet and dates from around 1928. *(David Hodges Collection)*

company was in financial difficulties but managed to survive by restructuring. In 1945 it fell into state ownership and became part of the East German IFA coachworks in Halle.

Kunz (CH)
1924–1934, Wauwil

Kunz was primarily responsible for commercial bodywork and for trailers, but the company also did some roll-top body conversions for saloon cars.

L

Labourdette (F)

1858–1952, Paris; later Courbevoie

The Parisian coachbuilder Labourdette is particularly noted for two inventions. One was the boat-tailed or skiff body, made from wood and introduced in 1912. The second is the Vutotal system, introduced in 1936 and essentially a frameless windscreen.

Labourdette: The company made an early name for itself with the striking torpedo body for sportsman Chevalier René de Knyff in 1912. (Author's Collection)

Labourdette: The body on the celebrated Bugatti "Black Bess" is by Labourdette. (David Burgess-Wise)

The first Labourdette car body was built in 1896 when the company was in the hands of Henri Labourdette, son of the founder Jean-Baptiste Labourdette who had moved from Bearn to establish a carriage-building workshop in Paris. The car was a Georges Richard with dos-à-dos seating. In 1899, Labourdette constructed a closed body on a Type B Renault for Louis Renault, founder of the car company, and this is believed to be the first car body of its type built anywhere in the world. In the early years of the 20th century, Labourdette's reputation for quality and elegance was such that the company was able to build bodies for numerous royal customers and other VIPs. One of the first French Presidential cars was a Panhard et Levassor with a Labourdette body.

Henri Labourdette died in 1910, and his son Jean-Henri took over the company at the age of 22. Two years later, the Labourdette company made coachbuilding history with a dramatic, doorless four-seat body on a Panhard 20 CV chassis for Chevalier René de Knyff, a leading figure in French motorsport at the time. Supposedly inspired by the canoes at a Monaco boating event, this was made of wood and used traditional boat-building methods. The body was built by the Depujols shipyard and was notable for its light weight of just 180kg. This distinctive design remained

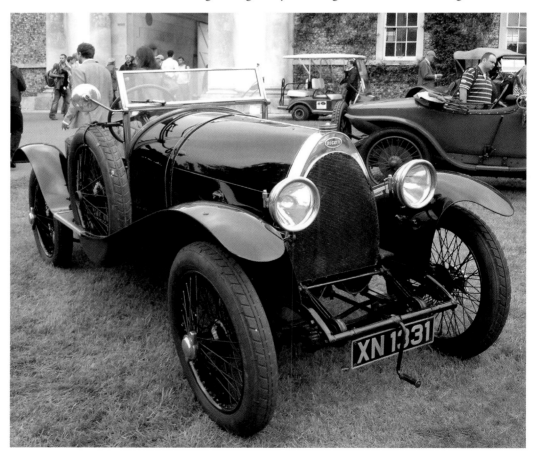

Labourdette: A tourer body on a Delage chassis around 1920. *(David Burgess-Wise)*

Labourdette: The pillarless windscreen of this 1938 cabriolet body on a Chenard & Walcker chassis marks it out as a Vutotal design. *(David Hodges Collection/Cannes Auto Museum)*

Labourdette: Barely recognisable as a V12-engined Rolls-Royce Phantom III, this 1939 car carries Vutotal bodywork. Some of the details are remarkable: note the pop-out door handles and the chromed ornamentation on the wings. *(WikiMedia Commons/ Rex Grey)*

popular until the mid-1920s, and was ordered on chassis by Hispano-Suiza, Peugeot, Renault and Rolls-Royce, among others. Labourdette developed the theme further in the 1920s, producing a version for the small Citroën B2 chassis; this became the prototype of the Caddy, which went on to be built in series by Currus *(qv)*.

The 1920s were a golden age for Labourdette. The company was turning out 15 bodies a month on average, building on chassis such as Delage, Farman, Hispano-Suiza, Isotta-Fraschini, Panhard and Rolls-Royce. However, the 1930s saw Labourdette's customer base thin out, and the company compensated for this fall in demand by adding delivery vans, buses and other commercial bodywork to its repertoire.

What was needed was something new to attract public attention, and at the 1936 Paris Salon Labourdette showed its new Vutotal (total view) design on a Delage D6-70 chassis. Essentially, the Vutotal eliminated the side and top frames of the windscreen, so providing better visibility for the driver. The show car had a "coach" body; on convertibles, the hood was attached directly to the thick glass of the screen. Labourdette also used the design on some bus bodies. Although the design was fashionable for a time, it was not a great success and the results were not always very attractive.

In the mid-1930s, Labourdette also explored aerodynamic designs, and one especially notable example was a 1937 aerodynamic "berlinette" on Delage V12 Grand Sport chassis, which incorporated the Vutotal principles as well. Designed by aerodynamicist Jean Andreau for Louis Delage, this circuit racer was intended to counter German dominance of motor sport and its body was constructed by Labourdette.

After the 1939-1945 war, Labourdette made a slow start back in business. There were some bodies on Delahaye chassis, and a Vutotal cabriolet for an American customer on a 1930s Rolls-Royce Phantom III chassis. Like other coachbuilders at the time, Labourdette also began working with the major chassis-makers, building a small batch of cabriolet bodies on Renault 4CV chassis. In 1950, Labourdette also built a strange-looking experimental streamlined body on Renault 4CV chassis, incorporating both his Vutotal windscreen and headlamps mounted under a glass cover near the centre-line of the car. However, this was one of the company's last efforts at coachbuilding. Labourdette became involved with theoretical research and the creation of concept mock-ups, and closed around 1952.

Labourdette (2) (F)
Late 1920s, Puteaux
There may have been a second and unconnected French coachbuilder called Labourdette at Puteaux. This company supposedly built the bodies for a 1929 Bucciali show car and a Bucciali roadster shown at the 1930 Paris Salon. The design of the latter was by Paul-Albert Bucciali.

Lacanu (F)
1930s
Lacanu is known only for building the bodies on some competition models from Delahaye. The company was owned by Olivier Lacanu-Deschamps and was favoured by Delahaye for the speed with which it could construct special bodies. Known examples are 15 of the 16 short-chassis Delahaye 135s built for American heiress Lucy

O'Reilly Schell, and the four Type 145 racing cars, three of them with a design by Jean Francois.

Lacroix (F)
1920s

Lacroix was a small French coachbuilder that was active in 1920s, but nothing else of substance is known about the company.

Lagache Glaszmann (F)
1920s, Montrouge

The Lagache-Glaszmann company is best known for the sporting bodywork it created during the 1920s. It was founded in 1922 by André Lagache of the Chenard & Walcker company and the Glaszmann brothers. Although the company retained links with Chenard & Walcker, it also made bodies on other French chassis, building saloons using the Weymann patents as well as sporting types. Some of the saloon bodies were characterized by sloping glass side windows and a roof that was narrower than the main body. Among the other makes of chassis that received bodies by Lagache-Glaszmann were Ballot, Bugatti, Delage and Peugeot.

Notable sporting bodies included those on the 1923 Le Mans-winning Chenard & Walcker and the 1925 Peugeot 174S models created for that year's ACF Grand Prix at Montlhéry.

After the 1939-1945 war, the company became a builder of articulated trailers.

Langenthal (CH)
Since 1929, Zürich

The Swiss coachbuilder Langenthal was established in 1929 at the small Swiss town of the same name in the canton of Berne. It was set up as a collective in 1926, and grew out of the wagon works that had been run since the late 19th century by Fritz Grogg, a master coachbuilder who had become a local worthy by the time of his death in 1924. The Grogg company had already moved into building bodies for motorised vehicles, among its first being a van in 1922 on a Ley chassis for the local porcelain business.

Fritz Grogg junior took over the business shortly before his father's death, and was joined in it by his brother Ernst and his brother-in-law Robert Sommer-Grogg, who had useful experience in the coachbuilding trade from time spent at Gygax in Biel and with a Parisian coachbuilder. During the 1920s, the Langenthal company mainly built delivery vehicles and trucks on chassis by Martini, Saurer and some foreign makers, as well as travelling salesmen's cars on chassis such as Fiat.

In 1929, the Langenthal business moved to new premises in Zürich-Bern-Strasse, and soon began to build car bodywork. Initially, there were tourers and saloons on light chassis, but when Swiss import taxes on foreign chassis were reduced in 1931 to aid local coachbuilders, the business rapidly expanded to encompass luxury cabriolets on chassis such as Hispano-Suiza, and on other French and American chassis. There was a licensing agreement with the Alexis Kellner coachworks in Berlin, and in fact Alexis Kellner joined the Langenthal company some time around 1936 after a period working for Gygax in Switzerland. Cabriolet bodies became the company's speciality, invariably elegant and usually revealing German influence in the form of the comvertible tops with their external "landau irons".

Langenthal: There were no fewer than 52 Langenthal cabriolets on the Citroën Traction Avant. Just two were six-cylinder models, and one of them – with modified front wings – was pictured here outside the Langenthal works. (Citroën)

Langenthal: Dating from the late 1940s, this cabriolet was on a Jaguar 3 ½-litre chassis and presented a much more modern appearance than the "factory" offering. *(Author's Collection)*

From 1937, Langenthal also took over the former Geissberger coachworks in Zürich, which became a branch of the main company and was managed by Ernst Grogg and one of his relations by marriage. It was around this time that Langenthal also switched from wooden to alloy frames for the bodies. Unfortunately, the Langenthal records were all lost in a fire, but research has revealed that in the period to 1939, there were bodies on chassis from Austin, Buick, Cadillac, Chevrolet, Citroën, Daimler, Delahaye, Ford, Hupmobile, Jaguar, Lancia, Mercedes-Benz, Peugeot, Plymouth, Rolls-Royce and Studebaker.

Demand for coachbuilt bodies collapsed during the Second World War, and the Langenthal works were given over to building such things as producer-gas trailers, converting delivery vans to electric power and, towards the end of the war, building and repairing railway wagons. When peace returned, Langenthal's return to coachbuilding was slow and difficult, but from 1947 there were small series of bodies on Citroën Traction Avant and Lancia Aprilia chassis. In fact, Langenthal became Switzerland's most prolific converter of the Traction Avant to a cabriolet, and made as many as 52, the peak year being 1951. The Langenthal speciality was to offer a five-seat configuration.

In this period, there were also one-off cabriolets on British chassis from Alvis, Armstrong-Siddeley, Daimler, Healey and Jaguar, some embracing the latest fashion for pontoon styles with an elegance notably lacking from other coachbuilders' efforts. Langenthal also modified factory-built bodies by Austin, Buick, Citroën, Ford and Wolseley, in particular creating rolltop saloons with fabric roofs. However, as car manufacture around the world returned to normal and manufacturers began to produce their own cabriolet models, Langenthal were priced out of the market. The company re-focussed its business on bus and commercial bodies and on repair work, and still survives as a well-known player in this market.

Langutt (F)
1920s, Besançon

Almost nothing is known about this French provincial coachbuilder of the 1920s. A picture of a half-deck torpedo body on a Ravel 12hp chassis dating from about 1923 has survived.

Lavocat et Marsaud (F)
1920s, Boulogne-Billancourt

The heyday of Lavocat & Marsaud was the 1920s, although the company had actually been established before the Great War. Established in a new factory after the war, they specialized in sporting bodywork, and were noted for their torpedo styles on Ballot, Bugatti and Peugeot chassis. In the later 1930s, Lavocat & Marsaud also built saloon bodies on Delage and Itala chassis, among others. The company seems to have made its last appearance at the Paris Salon in 1930, and the partners split up soon afterwards. Marsaud attempted to keep the business going as Marsaud & Cie *(qv)*.

Le Bastard (F)
1940s and 1950s, Rouen

Le Bastard was originally a builder of railway coaches but also built a number of special publicity vehicles. The company called on the services of noted designers such as Philippe Charbonneaux and Carlo Delaisse. Among the company's work on cars was a special body on a Delahaye 135 in 1953, used as a publicity vehicle by the magazine *L'Action Automobile et Touristique.*

Lebranchu (F)
Since 1923, Courbevoie

René Lebranchu did his apprenticeship as an upholsterer with Lavocat & Marsaud *(qv)* before setting up on his own as a repairer of upholstery and coachwork in 1923. His first premises were at Neuilly-sur-Seine, but he later moved to Courbevoie.

Lebranchu carried out sub-contract work for some of the big names in French coachbuilding, such as Chapron, Franay, and Labourdette. After the 1939-1945 war, the company became involved in prototype construction for some of the major car manufacturers, including Citroën, Panhard and Renault. From 1956, the business was run by the founder's three sons, and during the 1980s they became involved with the European arm of Russian carmaker Lada. Lefranchu created the Lada Niva Plein Soleil convertible for

Lebranchu: Among this coachbuilder's efforts was a small-volume conversion of the Lada Niva into a cabriolet. *(Author's Collection)*

the French market in 1983 and also a prototype for Lada France to run in the Paris-Dakar Rally.

Lecanu-Deschamps (F)
1930s and 1940s, Levallois-Perret

Oliver Lecanu-Deschamps is mainly known for the creation of racing bodywork. Known examples include a 3-litre Delage in 1937 and some racing Delahayes in the 1940s. The company subsequently moved into the aviation industry.

Lecoq (F)
From 1963, Bezons

André Lecoq established his business in 1963 to repair cars, but subsequently became well-known as a top-quality restorer of classic cars. The company made occasional forays into custom coachwork conversions, one example being a custom-modified Renault Twingo in 1995. The company was sold on shortly after Lecoq himself retired.

Lehmann & Lindenheim (D)
1920s, Berlin

Almost nothing is known about this Berlin coachbuilder, which is believed to have built the limousine body for a Maybach chassis in 1924.

Lemoine (F)
c1930, Levallois

Henri Lemoine's business in Levallois was primarily engaged in providing such things as axles, springs and other hardware to coachbuilders in the area. However, he also built a few bodies himself, of which a notable survivor is a low-slung two-door coupé on a 1930 Tracta E six-cylinder chassis.

Lepoix (F)
See FTI Design

Leroy (F)
1920s and earlier, Courbevoie

Eugène Leroy was working both in the aviation industry and as a coachbuilder before the Great War. Transformable coachwork was a speciality of this company, which closed during the 1920s.

L'Etoile (B)
1985–1992, Oudenberg

This Belgian firm was also known as the Ronny Coach Building Company, and specialised in conversions of Mercedes S-Class models of the time, mainly selling to clients in the Middle East.

Typically, L'Etoile would lengthen an S-Class saloon by up to 130cm to provide accommodation for seven passengers. Interior upgrades were also on the menu, and such luxury items as fridges, bars, top-quality audio systems and rear-compartment air conditioning were available.

From 1988, L'Etoile applied the same principles to Rolls-Royce and Bentley models, using a 60cm wheelbase extension to provide room for an array of luxury equipment inside. As the appetite for such conversions in the Middle East dried up, so did orders, and L'Etoile closed down in 1992.

Letourneur et Marchand (F)
1905–1959, Neuilly-sur-Seine

Jean-Marie Letourneur and Jean-Arthur Marchand were former employees of the Henri Binder coachworks who set up in business together in 1905. On 1 April that year, they established Letourneur et Marchand on the Ile de la Jatte at Neuilly-sur-Seine, taking over the premises of a bankrupt coachworks called Wehrle Godard Desmaret.

They started out somewhat cautiously with contract work for other coachbuilders, including their former employer Binder and the established carrossiers Franay and Labourdette. Nevertheless, there were also a few complete bodies for car manufacturers such as Darracq. By 1907, the business was firmly established and was turning out bodies for private customers; Marchand knew the aviator Léon Morane, and the company also secured a contract to build wings and fuselages for his Morane-Saulnier aircraft company. By the time the First World War put a temporary halt to proceedings, they had built a total of 1228 car bodies.

Letourneur et Marchand: This 1929 landaulet body was on a Minerva AK chassis. The Rowe Sisters, a Parisian dance act, were roped in for some additional publicity. (Author's Collection)

Letourneur et Marchand: There was strong Art Deco influence on the bodywork for this 1934 Delage D8. *(Author's Collection)*

Letourneur et Marchand: Wheel spat ornamentation and those interesting bonnet vents appeared again on this 1934 Delage D8-15. *(David Hodges Collection)*

The 1920s saw the company becoming more ambitious, and in 1923 they took showroom space at the Hotel Claridge on the prestigious Champs-Elysées in Paris. Some of their later formal bodies took on the Claridge name. Over the next few years, Letourneur et Marchand catered for high-class French makes including Panhard and Voisin, and the French subsidiary of Hispano-Suiza. Bodies were typically grand, elegant and formal. Yet batch-building under contract was still on the agenda to balance the books: it was simply done under another name, and Letourneur et Marchand set up the Autobineau company to handle it.

Letourneur's son Marcel joined the business in 1928 after serving an apprenticeship with an English coachbuilder, and proved to be a great asset as a designer. In 1932 he was responsible for the famous JELM "panoramic coupé" with pillarless design and wraparound glass that was also known as the Yo-Yo coupé after its Art Deco accent line. Several more aerodynamic "coaches profilés" followed along similar lines, and their 1936 Aérosport design (also

Letourneur et Marchand: Not every Delage bodied by the company had the Art Deco style. This D8-S model was more conventional, and yet still beautifully proportioned. *(David Hodges Collection)*

Letourneur et Marchand: Superb lines characterise this late creation, a two-door sports saloon on a Delage D6-70 chassis dating from 1947. *(WikiMedia Commons/ Akelea NDE (talk))*

by Marcel Letourneur) became a small batch run for the Delage D8-120 chassis. It was with Delage chassis that the company was primarily associated in this period, but there were also bodies on Bugatti (a total of 19), Buick, Delahaye, Panhard, Renault, and Rolls-Royce.

When war came, Letourneur et Marchand moved production away from Paris, but their output was necessarily different, and they built ambulances and cabs for lorries. Letourneur senior died in September 1944, just days after the liberation of France, and Marchand died in June 1946. The company made a slow return to its pre-war business, but it was both under new management and in a very different set of circumstances from the one it had known in the 1930s. Letourneur et Marchand built just 67 bodies between 1947 and 1952, the last being for a Hotchkiss 20CV.

Nevertheless, the company was not quite finished yet. Marcel Letourneur drew up an attractive cabriolet design for the Renault Frégate which the company adopted as a catalogued model. However, it was always rare, and just 69 were built between 1954 and 1959, when Letourneur et Marchand withdrew from the car bodying business. Turning to commercial bodywork and especially to building lorry cabs, they continued until 1973, when they closed down for good.

Lindner (D)
1908–1928, Ammendorf

The Lindner business was founded as a saddlery in 1823 at Halle in the Saale region of Germany. By 1830 it had moved into the construction and repair of carriages. From 1883 there were horse-drawn buses and then electric trams. Expansion prompted a move to new premises in nearby Ammendorf, and in 1903 the family-owned business had

became a limited company. By 1905 it was known as the Gottfried Lindner Wagen- und Waggonfabrik, and from 1908 it also constructed individual bodies bodies for motor cars and motor buses.

Rationalisation followed the 1914-1918 war, and the company abandoned individual commissions for car bodies in favour of series production, offering three basic designs with mixed wood and steel construction. The daily output of bodies was claimed to be as high as 88, mainly open touring types and limousines and principally on Adler, AGA, Horch and Protos chassis.

From 1926, the company began to build all-steel bodywork to Ambi-Budd designs, but this led to a sharp decline in orders and in 1928 the Lindner car body business was sold to Ambi-Budd Presswerk GmbH. The company's other activities – in the railway, bus and tram, and commercial vehicle spheres – nevertheless continued for many years.

Lombardi (I)
1947–1973, Vercelli

Carrozzeria Francis Lombardi name is primarily associated with special bodies for Fiats, although the company has also worked on Lancia and NSU models.

Francis Lombardi was a highly decorated First World War fighter ace, who set up a company called Avia Spa in Vercelli to construct light planes in 1938. In 1947, he turned to car bodywork, although the aviation activity continued alongside this until 1950.

Lombardi: The wooden-framed Giardinetta body on this 1948 Lancia Aprilia has extraordinary charm, even if it lacks grace. (WikiMedia Commons/Buch-t)

The first bodies by the Lombardi firm were wooden-framed Giardiniera types for the Fiat 1100. There were similar conversions for Lancia. These were followed in the 1950s by conversions of Fiat 1400 models into seven-seaters, and then by similar conversions of the Fiat 1800 and 2300. These had a lengthened wheelbase and an additional row of folding seats in the middle. Vercelli's work for Fiat continued with a four-door version of the 600, called the Firefly. All these models were built in low volumes.

In 1960, the Lombardi company moved into a new factory at Trino Vercelli. The decade that followed saw more Fiat conversions: eight-seater versions of the 1400, 1800 and 2300 models, as well as a four-door 850 Firefly and a Grand Prix coupé version of the 850 Special.

The 1970s brought more of the same, with coupé bodies for the Fiat 1300 and 1500, a four-door 127 Firefly and a special Fiat 500. Lombardi built the Fiat 128 My Car Star and Smart and Special versions of the 128, as well as vans and other commercial bodies for Fiat. Other products included bodies for the NSU 1000 TTS and the FL1 coupé that used Lancia 2000 IE running-gear. The company closed in 1973.

Lond & Weigold (D)
1920s, Berlin
Little is known about the activities of the Berlin coachbuilder Lond & Weigold, although the company was clearly active in the 1920s and among its identified bodies was a striking limousine with angular lines dating from 1923 on a Mercedes 28/60PS chassis.

Lorenz & Rankl (D)
1980s, Wolfratshausen
Lorenz & Rankl was one of the coachwork conversion companies that sprang up in the 1980s to cater for the custom-building market of the time. Its speciality was Mercedes-Benz 126-series S-Class models, and its work included convertible bodywork.

Lourdel (F)
1920s, Saint-Omer
The Lourdel coachworks is known for a faux-cabriolet body constructed on a 1928 Amilcar chassis, apparently with fabric panelling.

Ludewig (D)
1930s, Essen
Gebrüder Ludewig (Ludewig Brothers) was always best known for its bus bodywork, and remained active in that field at the time of writing. However, during the 1930s the company diversified into car body manufacture as well for a time, and built bodies for Ford on the German-built Model A and other chassis.

Ludwig (CH)
1940s, Zollikon
This Swiss coachbuilder carried out some individual rebuilds of Citroën Traction Avant models in the years immediately after the Second World War.

Lueg (D)
Bochum, 1868–1954
As a coachbuilder, Lueg of Bochum, in the Ruhr district, is best known for its special bodywork on the Mercedes-Benz 170V chassis. However, the Friedrich Lueg Wagenfabrik was founded as a wagon-builder as early as 1868. From early in the 20th century, the company also began to build bodies for motor cars; its first on a Mercedes chassis was built in 1904, and by 1910 the company was a supplier of the Spanish court. From 1914, a link was forged with the Benz company, and this relationship remained intact when Benz and Daimler merged in 1926.

Lueg's distinctive body for the Mercedes-Benz 170V was adaptable as an ambulance, as a hearse, or as a "Kombi" (estate car). As many as 800 were built during the 1939-1945 war before 170V production was halted, and around 1000 more when production resumed in 1947. The last examples were built in 1954, at which point Lueg withdrew from the bodywork business. Today, the company still exists, as a large chain of dealers with a Mercedes-Benz franchise.

Lueg: The firm's body for Mercedes-Benz 170 chassis was adaptable to a variety of uses. With the rear side windows filled in to create a van body, it was used by the Mercedes-Benz Service Department. This example may be a petrol-engined 170Vb or a diesel-engined 170Db, in either case dating from 1952-53. *(Daimler-Benz)*

M

Macquet Galvier (F)
1920s, Courbevoie

Although the company owned by Maurice Macquet and Jean Galvier was usually known as Macquet & Galvier, its emblem showed it as Macquet Galvier. Most of the bodies from this company were for French domestic chassis, such as Amilcar, Deauville, De Dion-Bouton, Chaigneau-Brasier, Chenard & Walcker, Delaunay-Belleville, Renault and Sizaire. There were some aluminium bodies for Rosengart L4 and L6 chassis.

Foreign chassis were not ignored, however. There is evidence of saloon bodywork for an Isotta-Fraschini chassis, and Macquet & Galvier built a remarkable transformable body on a Mercedes-Benz chassis in 1928. The company had a stand at the 1930 Paris Salon, where it exhibited a cabriolet body on a Rolland-Pillain HL Huit chassis, but probably did not survive in business much longer.

Maggiora (I)
1925–2003, Moncalieri

Arturo Maggiora established Martelleria Maggiora as a producer of body panels in 1925, at Moncalieri near Turin. The company supplied panels to several local coachbuilders, but came to greater prominence in its own right after 1945, after which date it worked primarily for Fiat and Lancia on the assembly of complete bodies.

Early work appears to have included some Fiat 1100 Giardiniettas for Viotti. As the company grew, so it also produced bodies for Abarth and Cisitalia models, and then in 1951 it moved to Borgo San Pietro, Moncalieri. The 1950s also brought some bodies for the Lancia Aurelia B20 under contract to Pinin Farina. From 1963 Maggiora built bodies for the Maserati Mistral, and then from 1964 the Frua-designed bodies for the German Glas GT, which later became the BMW 1600 GT. There was work for De Tomaso as well, on the Mangusta from the late 1960s and the Pantera in the early 1970s, and for Alfa Romeo on the 2000 Touring and 2000 Spider. Bitter had Maggiora make the bodies for its SC model from 1979.

In 1991, Maggiora merged with Sanmarco & Lamier to form IRMA SpA, which later became a major components supplier for the Fiat Ducato light commercial range. In 1992, Maggiora SRL took over the old Lancia factory in Chivasso, north of Turin, and there it built the Lancia Delta Integrale and Fiat Barchetta on behalf of their makers, the latter at a rate of around 50 a day. Maggiora also constructed the complete Lancia Kappa Coupé, a low-volume model designed by Gianna Maggiora and introduced in 1994.

In addition, Maggiora produced a number of design studies, prototypes, and special-order models for both Fiat and Lancia. The Fiats included cabriolet versions of the Uno and Cinquecento, some Barchetta Coupés, and a Puntograle (four-wheel drive Fiat Punto). Among the Lancias were some

Maggiora: The 1994 Lancia Kappa Coupé was both designed and built by Maggiora. (*WikiMedia Commons/Christian Campe*)

special Integrales and the prototype of the Thesis Coupé that was shown at Bologna in 2002. However, this Lancia was the company's swansong, and ILCA Maggiora, still owned by the family that had founded it, closed down in 2003.

Maleval & Vacher (F)
1818–1930, Paris
Founded in the 19th century to build horse-drawn vehicles, Maleval & Vacher took advantage of its proximity to the Delahaye factory to build bodies on that maker's chassis in the years before the First World War. After the war, Paul Vacher, grandson of the founder, took on a licence to build Baehr transformable bodies. However, the company's most celebrated design was a saloon for the hair stylist Antoine on a Panhard & Levassor chassis; described as Art Nouveau but clearly Cubist in inspiration with rectangular shapes even for the mudguards, this was shown at the 1923 Paris Salon. In 1930, Paul Vacher became a Renault dealer and the coachworks closed at about the same time.

Mamy (F)
1920s, Besançon
This French provincial coachbuilder constructed a number of bodies on the Ravel chassis that were built in the same town of Besançon up to 1929. Mamy is also known to have bodied Lorraine-Dietrich chassis. The company probably did not survive the Depression.

Manessius (F)
1919–1934, Puteaux; Levallois-Perret from 1922
Carrosserie Manessius was a pioneer of metal-framed bodies in the 1920s and also held a licence to build Baehr transformable bodies; Albert and Gustave Baehr figured for a time among the company's directors. Manessius also pioneered new forms of body mounting and methods of painting, and was among the first to create a luggage boot that was integral with the bodywork.

The company was founded in 1919 by Manes Levy in the Parisian suburb of Puteaux, and its name was a derivation of his first name. The business quickly became successful, and in 1922 moved to larger premises in Levallois-Perret,

selling its Puteaux works to Mühlbacher (*qv*). The company also set up a subsidiary in the Belgian city of Brussels.

Manessius was one of the few coachbuilders to enjoy a link with Voisin, and a saloon on the C7 chassis was listed in that company's catalogue. There were also custom bodies for Chenard & Walcker, Chrysler, Delage, Hispano-Suiza, Panhard & Levassor, Rolls-Royce and Talbot chassis. In the later 1920s, the company moved into volume construction. Manessius first helped Henri Pigozzi to establish himself as the Fiat importer in France, and then became involved in constructing bodies for the French-built Fiats. At the same time, Manessius established close links with Citroën, for whom it built a range of elegant "coach" and cabriolet bodies before the arrival of the Traction Avant in 1934. The company then disappeared from view.

Marazzi (I)
Since 1967, Milan
Although Carrozzeria Marazzi has been involved with the series production of a number of exotic Italian cars and has constructed a number of prototypes for Italian manufacturers, the company has also diversified into other areas, taking on the manufacture of armoured passenger cars in the 1970s and of hearses in the 1980s.

Company founder Carlo Marazzi had worked in the sheet metal department of Zagato as well as at Touring. When Touring closed down in 1967, Marazzi set up in business with his sons Serafino and Mario in Caronno Pertusella, near Milan and not far from his former employer's premises. The new company took on a number of former Touring employees and began to specialise in the same type of small-run production work as Touring, although it had its own design capability as well. Through Carrozzeria Marazzi, Touring's former chief Carlo Felice Bianchi Anderloni was able to preserve the "Touring Superleggera" trademark and to use it on several occasions to support his old company's heritage.

Touring had been building the bodies for the Lamborghini 400 GT 2+2 at the time of its bankruptcy, and Marazzi stepped in to complete the final examples. Other work soon followed: in 1967 the company was

Marazzi: Bodies for the Lamborghini Islero were constructed by Marazzi, who had also stepped in to complete Touring's work on the 400GT when that company went under. This is a 1969 car. (*David Hodges Collection*)

commissioned to construct the bodies for 18 Alfa Romeo Tipo 33 Stradale cars. That year also saw the start of a longer-term relationship with Lamborghini. Among the former Touring staff who had gone to Marazzi was Federico Formenti, and he drew up the Lamborghini Islero that succeeded the 400 GT in 1967; 125 examples were then built at the Marazzi coachworks. Formenti also designed the Jarama for Lamborghini, and Marazzi built the first few examples of that in 1970.

Recognising the risk in focussing on prototype and small-run work alone, during the 1970s Marazzi began to cater for the growing demand for armoured versions of standard production cars that arose from socio-political tensions in Italy. Nevertheless, the company continued to build small runs of bodies for other Italian makers. For Alfa Romeo there were a few Giulia Nuova Promiscua family estates from 1973, as well as a number of replica Tipo 33 Stradale to special order. In the 1980s, notable commissions included the two Alfa Romeo 90 Sportswagon estates to a design by & *Auto Capital* magazine; sadly, this did not enter production. The demand for prototype work continued into the 1990s with such cars as the Fiat Punto Cabrio Wagon Bricò in 1994. In 2008, it was Marazzi who built the prototype of the Alfa Romeo 8C Competizione Spider

In the early 1970s, Marazzi had been one of the first Italian companies to provide armoured conversions of standard production cars. It worked first with Alfa Romeo, and then with Fiat. The Italian police and other civil authorities became regular customers, and Marazzi's work has extended beyond the products of Italian manufacturers to include armoured versions of such vehicles as the Mercedes-Benz G-Wagen and the Land Rover Discovery.

Marbeuf (F)
Late 1920s

The Marbeuf coachworks constructed the first body to use the all-aluminium ("Toutalu") design patented by former aviator Jean de Vizcaya and displayed it at the 1928 Paris Salon. These principles were later more fully exploited by Million-Guiet (qv).

Maron-Pot, Oeters & Cie (F)
1920s, Levallois-Perret

Louis Maron-Pot established his small coachwork business at the start of the 1920s in Levallois-Perret. Shortly afterwards, he joined forces with a blacksmith whose name has variously been reported as Oester, Oeters, and Oters, and the company was renamed as L Maron-Pot, Oeters & Cie (the spelling here being the generally accepted one).

The company built mainly sporting bodies for a number of French chassis, including Bugatti, Delage, Delahaye and Mathis, and also for foreign chassis such as Alfa-Romeo. Maron-Pot also took out several patents, not all of them relating to cars. The company appears not to have survived into the 1930s.

Marsaud (F)
1930s, Boulogne-Billancourt

After the demise of Lavocat & Marsaud (qv), Marsaud made a brief attempt to continue in business alone at the same premises in Boulogne-Billancourt. His known work includes the body on an eight-cylinder Mathis chassis, but the business does not appear to have survived for long.

Matthys (B)
1920–1928, Etterbeek

Matthys was the primary builder of bodies for the Belgian Imperia chassis before that company took its body building in-house in 1928. The coachbuilder also made bodies for other chassis at its premises near Brussels, notably sporting types on French Bignan and Belgian Minerva chassis.

The prime mover in the business was Eugène Matthys, who set up in business again in 1937 with new partners as Automobiles Dematy.

Mauguy
1927, Paris

The coachbuilder Mauguy is claimed to have been responsible for the coupé body on a 1927 Renault type RY.

Merville & Garnier (F)
Early 1900s–c1930, Levallois-Perret; later Paris

The Parisian coachbuilder Merville & Garnier was formed at the start of the 20th century when Garnier joined the established business of Merville Fils. The company is best known for its "Berceuse" (cradle) design of bodywork in the 1920s.

The Berceuse design was first shown in 1924, and was kept independent of the chassis frame by means of spring mountings. It allowed Merville & Garnier coachwork to combine the quietness of fabric bodies with the rigidity of metal-panelled types, and the company used it for both closed and open bodywork. At the 1928 Paris Salon, an improved type called the Mergar was shown, this time using Repusseau Silentbloc mountings. Despite their inventiveness, Merville & Garnier did not survive into the 1930s.

Mesnier & Laforge (F)
1920s, Courbevoie

Although Mesnier & Laforge were based in the heart of the French automotive industry at Courbevoie, the company's bodywork products in the 1920s appear to have been quite ordinary.

Meulemeester (F)
c1927–1930s, Clichy-sur-Seine; from 1936 St Affrique

Meulemeester bodies were primarily associated with Peugeot chassis in the later 1920s and the 1930s. The Meulemeester brothers came from Alsace and had set up their coachbuilding business in Clichy by 1927. That year, they had a stand at the Paris Salon, and over the next few years they bodied a variety of chassis that included Delahaye and Panhard. A close association with Peugeot began around 1930.

Meulemeester: The close association with Peugeot led to the creation of this cabriolet body for the 201 BR3 model, dating from around 1933.

Early work for Peugeot was on the more popular chassis, examples being a coupé on the 5CV in 1930 and a cabriolet on the 201 in 1931. At the 1933 Paris Salon, the company showed an Aerodynamic Convertible body on the 301 chassis, and that inspired the design of the production car for the rest of the decade. Peugeot entrusted the construction of bodies for the 301 cabriolet and the 401D coach and *décapotable* to Meulemeester, and the company built broadly similar bodies for Chenard & Walcker on that company's Aiglon and Aigle 4 chassis in the mid-1930s. The company also built some individual commissions on Delahaye, Lancia and Unic chassis, and in 1935 was responsible for an English-style four-seat tourer body on a Peugeot 601 chassis.

In 1936, Meulemeester moved from Paris to St Affrique in the Aveyron department. Their work that year included a torpédo-cabriolet body on the long-wheelbase Peugeot 601 chassis (which went out of production in late 1935), but it is not clear how much longer the company survived.

Mialle (F)
1954
Mialle is known only for a two-door pillarless hardtop version of the Renault 4CV with wrap-around rear window

that the coachbuilder announced during spring 1954. The car seems to have remained a one-off.

Michel (F)
Late 1940s, Nice
The Michel company in southern France designed a convertible saloon conversion for the Citroën Traction Avant in the years immediately after the Second World War. The company converted some cars itself, and also sold an unknown quantity of conversion kits to the motor trade. The kits included body reinforcements that had to be welded in place. The Belgian firm Carrosserie Franco-Belge is known to have converted five cars with the kit, and the Belgian branch of Citroën appears to have used some, so conferring quasi-official status on the kits.

Michelotti (I)
1955–1980, Turin
Giovanni Michelotti was one of the 20th century's most prolific and most gifted designers of sports cars. Born in Turin, he joined Stabilimenti Farina as an apprentice at the age of 14 in 1935. He subsequently worked with other Torinese coachbuilders, notably Vignale, Bertone, Ghia,

Michelotti: This one-off body on the BMW 507 chassis dates from 1959, and was an early show car that helped get the company noticed. (BMW)

Michelotti: BMW did take notice, and Michelotti played a major part in the design of the 1500 saloon that went on to save the company. (BMW)

Michelotti: This was the 1960 design for the Osca 1500, created at a time when the designer was trying to establish his own company. (David Hodges Collection)

Michelotti: This rather attractive body was done in 1961 for Prince in Japan, and was built on their Skyline chassis. (David Hodges Collection)

Michelotti: The Italian designer bought the remains of a damaged racing D-type Jaguar and created a new body for it. The car was displayed at the 1963 Geneva Motor Show. *(David Hodges Collection)*

Michelotti: This was the 1963 Triumph Spitfire, smaller and more delicate than the TR4. The characteristic Michelotti kick-up to the rear wing is evident here. *(Author's Collection)*

Michelotti: A strong link with Triumph led to multiple designs for that company's production cars. This is the Triumph TR4, introduced in 1961. The car pictured was used by a UK police force. *(Author's Collection)*

and Allemano, and became chief designer for Ghia-Aigle. He also worked as a freelance, notably working on racing bodies for Ferrari from his own workshops after 1955.

Michelotti's obvious skill and his legendary speed in creating new bodies soon led foreign car makers to his door. Among his first clients were Standard-Triumph, for whom he did the 1958 Standard Vanguard Vignale, a rather half-hearted facelift contracted through the coachbuilder whose name it carried. He formed a strong friendship with Triumph's chief engineer Harry Webster, and for that company he designed first the Italia coupé on the TR3, then the TR4 and TR5, the Herald, the Spitfire and Stag, as well as the 1300 saloon and the six-cylinder 2000/2500 saloons. Another early client was BMW, for whom he did the little 700, which entered production in 1959 almost unchanged

from his July 1958 prototype. The 1800, 2000, 2002 and 2800 followed in the 1960s and 1970s.

From 1959, Michelotti ran his own independent design studio, and in 1960 he announced his own first car as a constructor, the Osca 1600 coupé with Pagoda-style roof. At Geneva in 1963 he showed a coupé on the Jaguar D-type done for a French client. As commissions became more numerous, he moved his business to Orbassano, and here he worked on cars for DAF (the 1967 55 saloon and the Siluro based on it that was shown at Geneva in 1968), Fiat

Michelotti: Dating from 1968 is this concept car for DAF. The car was one of the first designs with a true wedge shape and was known as the Siluro. The mechanical elements were from the DAF 55 coupé. *(WikiMedia Commons)*

Michelotti: Still working with the Fiat group on safety concepts, the company designed the Mizar in 1974, based on a Lancia Beta and featuring four gullwing doors. *(Michelotti)*

Michelotti: The 1971 Pulsar was built to investigate safety features and lightweight construction. Underneath was a Fiat 128 Rallye model. *(Michelotti)*

Michelotti: Demountable panels were a key feature of the 1978 Every 4R, based on a Fiat 127. *(Michelotti)*

and Matra. BMW came back for more in 1972, requesting a design for their turbocharged special. That same year, the Michelotti Pulsar, built on a Fiat 128 platform, demonstrated that the shock-absorbing bumpers demanded by US regulations did not have to make a car look ungainly. The 1974 Lancia Beta Mizar saloon had no fewer than four gullwing doors, and that year Michelotti also produced the Lem (Laboratorio Elettrico Mobile or mobile electrical test-bed) electric city-car.

The link with Triumph was broken when Harry Webster moved to the volume cars division of British Leyland, but Michelotti continued to work for the British group, designing truck cabs and working on the Leyland National bus as well.

A notable 1978 design was the Every 4R, based on a Fiat 127 and designed as a project for Italian motoring magazine *Quattroruote*. This concept used demountable panels that allowed the car to be changed from an all-metal city car to a country car with fabric doors and tailgate, and ultimately into a roofless and doorless car for the beach. Michelotti's brilliant career was cut short by his premature death in January 1980.

Miesen (D)
1870 to present, Bonn

The Miesen company is best known for its ambulance and other bodies, many of which have been based on for private car platforms, and the basic ambulance designs have in some cases been adapted both as hearses and as estate cars. Over the years, Miesen bodies have been particularly associated with Mercedes-Benz and BMW car platforms.

The company was founded as a wagon works in Bonn by Christian Miesen in 1870. Its early work on individual commissions earned a reputation for high quality, and in 1901 the company moved to larger premises. That same year saw the first horse-drawn Miesen ambulance; it built its first motor ambulance in 1905.

After the First World War, Miesen specialised in ambulance and medical vehicles, building Europe's first motorised dental clinic in 1926. The 1930s added bus luggage trailers to the range, although most Miesen products were still standardised medical vehicles for the Red Cross. The company held a number of patents and was an acknowledged specialist in its field.

Miesen: Here seen in ambulance guise, the body for the Mercedes-Benz 180 of the early 1950s could have a number of uses. *(Daimler-Benz)*

From 1945, Christian Miesen Fahrzeug- und Karosseriewerken capitalised on a big demand for new ambulances. Orders from Germany were supplemented by orders from overseas, and build totals sometimes reached 1000 vehicles a year. Some of these were special orders to suit specific customer requirements.

Miesen developed designs specifically for Mercedes-Benz saloon chassis in this period, and also did similar work (although in smaller volumes) on other makers' chassis. So, for example, between 1956 and 1959 they built at least four BMW V8 ambulances to two different designs, and one V8 hearse. However, the primary supplier of private-car platforms for Miesen ambulances remained Mercedes-Benz, and the company has continued to build such vehicles on successive versions of the company's mid-sized saloon platform.

The company ran into financial difficulties in 2004 but was restructured and re-established early the following year as C. Miesen GmbH & Co. KG. Production moved temporarily from Bonn to larger premises at Andernach am Rhein, but later returned to Bonn, in different premises.

Mignot & Billebault (F)
1930s–1950s, Boulogne-Billancourt

In the 1920s and 1930s, Carrosserie Mignot & Billebault earned its reputation by building mainly cabriolet bodies. Its work was principally associated with Chenard & Walcker chassis, although there were also examples on the Delahaye 138 and the Renault Viva Grand Sport.

After the Second World War, Mignot & Billebault built a number of "woody" estate cars on the French-built Ford F472 and Vedette chassis; there was a notable example of this type of body on a Hotchkiss 864 chassis at the 1950 Paris Salon, too. At the 1953 Paris Salon, Mignot & Billebault introduced their cabriolet body for the Ford Vedette, but this did not last long as the French arm of Ford merged with Simca in 1954. The company's last major new project was a neat cabriolet version of the Renault Frégate that retained the essential lines of the saloon original from which it was converted. However, just three cars were built,

and the contract for Frégate Cabriolet production went to Letourneur & Marchand (*qv*).

Million-Guiet (F)
1854–1930s, Levallois-Perret; later Argenteuil

Founded as early as 1854 in the Levallois district to build horse-drawn carriages, Million Guiet began building car bodies at the start of the 20th century and by 1908 was successful enough to open a London branch. By the time of the First World War, this had 100 employees, and there were 1500 working for the company in France.

After the war, Million-Guiet became one of the many French coachbuilders who took out a licence to build Baehr transformable bodies. They specialised in luxury bodies for prestige makes, and built on chassis such as Ballot, Hispano-Suiza, Panhard, the more expensive Peugeots, Rolls-Royce

Million-Guiet: The company's formal style is evident on this 1928 cabriolet, built on a Marmon chassis. *(David Hodges Collection)*

Million-Guiet: Also dating from the late 1920s is this elegant saloon on a Mercedes-Benz chassis. *(David Hodges Collection)*

Million-Guiet: The Renault Reinastella was an eight-cylinder chassis intended to compete with existing luxury models, and it attracted coachwork by some of the finest makers. (Renault)

Million-Guiet: This neat all-aluminium saloon body on a Bugatti T46 dates from 1933. (David Hodges Collection)

and a good number of Voisins. In 1928, the company developed an extendible cabriolet design which could be converted from saloon to coupé de ville and then to torpedo. Million-Guiet bodied a Renault 40CV for the French President (Gaston Doumergue), and built an impressive coupé-chauffeur on a Mercedes-Benz chassis in 1930.

From 1928, the company was directed by two young men called Sanz and Mosser, who wanted to create a more dynamic image for the business. Seeking to create lighter bodies, they fell in with former aviator Jean de Vizcaya, initially taking out a patent for his all-aluminium "Toutalu" bodywork designs and from January 1930 acquiring exclusive rights. Million-Guiet developed the ideas further, adding side windows shaped like those of a railway carriage, enveloping wings, tubular bumpers, upturned leading ends to the running-boards and some novel side mountings for the spare wheel.

From 1931, Million-Guiet granted the Belgian coachbuilder d'Ieteren (qv) a Toutalu licence, which was known as Supra-légère in Belgium.

In France, meanwhile, the Toutalu bodies were built on a great variety of domestic chassis, including Bugatti, Chenard & Walcker, Citroën, Delage, Farman, Harris-Léon Laisne, Lorraine-Dietrich, Panhard, Renault, Talbot and Voisin. A few foreign chassis had them, too, including a Lancia Dilambda and a Cord L-29. For a time, a variety of Million-Guiet Toutalu bodies were catalogued as options on Citroën C6 and 15A chassis.

A disadvantage of the Toutalu construction proved to be its inability to adapt to the fashion for aerodynamic designs. There was a Renault Nervastella in February 1934 with a patented trunk which could accommodate the roof, but the aerodynamic saloon on Unic chassis that Million-Guiet showed at the 1934 Paris Salon was its last major creation. The company switched to manufacturing tubular car seats under the Tubauto name, and by the 1950s was building service buses, notably for Somua.

Molier & Muller (NL)

1920s, s'Gravenhage; later The Hague

This Dutch coachbuilder advertised both luxury car bodies and commercial types during 1923. By September that year, it gave its address as The Hague, and the company name was shown as Molier Muller.

Monjardet (F)

Early 1900s–1920s, Besançon

Monjardet is considered to have been the earliest coachbuilder in eastern France. The company was established at the start of the 20th century and became closely associated with chassis maker Rochet-Schneider, based in the same town of Besançon. During the 1920s, the company held a Clairalpax licence. It was still in business at the end of 1931, but appears not to have survived the demise of Rochet-Schneider in 1932.

Montpellier Automobile (F)

1920s–1930s, Montpellier

Before the First World War, this business was known as Faulquier & Jamme, and Gaston Jamme remained at its head in the inter-war years. Renamed Montpellier Automobile (sometimes abbreviated to Monpauto), the company held a Clairalpax licence and built a number of bodies on Voisin chassis. From 1920, it also held a Citroën franchise, and during the 1930s fitted opening roofs to Traction Avant models.

Moratille (F)

Early 1900s–1920s, Levallois-Perret

This company specialised in building luxury bodywork at the start of the 20th century, but by the 1920s was best known for making the utility bodies known as "normandes" – essentially torpedo bodies with a wooden pick-up section at the rear.

Moret (CH)

1918–c1950, Geneva

Ami-Louis Moret set up his blacksmith's business in Geneva in 1918 but the business rapidly developed into a coachworks and in 1929 moved into new and larger premises. The company became known as A Moret & Fils, presumably when the founder's son joined the business. It is known to have built on a variety of chassis during the 1930s, but sadly no pictures have yet been found.

In 1937 the company built a batch of ambulance bodies on Renault chassis for Spain, and in 1945 there was a special one-off cabriolet on a Peugeot 402 chassis, which won a prize at a concours d'élégance event held in Cannes in 1947.

Morelli (I)

1950s–1960s, Ferrara

Morelli is best known for its close association with Osca, for which it built aluminium bodywork. The coachbuilder constructed 40 Spiders on the Osca MT4 chassis. It is also known for the body on a 1953 Ferrari 250MM and for a small number of other sporting bodies in the 1950s.

Moretti (I)

Turin, 1926–1989

Giovanni Moretti started out as a motor cycle maker in 1926, moving on to cars by 1930. After the Second World War, the company continued to make a variety of small and miniature cars mainly for the Italian market, although a few were exported to the USA. Although sales were good in the beginning, in later years Moretti struggled to survive in the face of competition from cars like the Fiat 500 and 600, and in the late 1950s began to produce alternative bodywork for Fiat models. By 1960 it had abandoned production of its slow-selling own-brand cars.

From 1962, it regarded itself primarily as a coachbuilder, and that year changed its name to suit, becoming Moretti Fabbrica Automobili e Stabilimenti Carrozzeria SAS. There were special versions of cars by Alfa Romeo and Maserati as well as Fiat. The company became completely committed to coachbuilding from 1970, and its products were subsequently sold through the Fiat network. As well as

Moretti: By 1957, the company had begun to build special bodywork on Fiat chassis. This coupé design was available on the 1100 and 1200 chassis. *(David Hodges Collection)*

Moretti: There was a complementary spider design for the Fiat 1100 and 1200 as well. *(David Hodges Collection)*

Moretti: This is their "Speciale" edition of the 1958 Alfa Romeo Giulietta 1300 Berlina.

Moretti: By the start of the 1980s, the company was building bodywork like this Midimaxi on the basis of the Fiat 127. *(Luc106/Wikimedia)*

coupé versions of more mundane Fiats, Moretti built beach-buggy conversions of the 126 and 127, and a custom version of the Campagnola 4x4 call the Sporting. In the 1980s came the Fiat Uno Moretti Folk and the Fiat Panda Moretti Rock, but the company closed down for good in December 1989.

Morlet (F)
1920s, Courbevoie
Carrosserie H Morlet was a French coachbuilder responsible for the body on a 1923 Georges Irat 2-litre chassis.

Motto (I)
1932–1965, Turin
Carrozzeria Rocco Motto was best known for building lightweight competition cars and one-off specials. The company worked mainly with chassis from Italy and France, but also had links with some of the major American makers in the early 1950s. Motto bodies often carried a badge incorporating the letters CA-MO, which was in fact the company's telegraphic address.

Rocco Motta was born at Rivarossa in 1904, and was orphaned during the First World War. He became a metalworker and began working for some of the coachbuilders near his home, eventually becoming a team

Motto: Pictured with Raymond Loewy himself, this is the 1960 Loraymo coupé built on a Lancia Flaminia. *(David Hodges Collection)*

leader with Martelleria Maggiora of Turin in 1925. In 1932 he set up his own workshop in the Via Orta in Turin, where he constructed bodies for some of the major makers of the period, including Lancia and the coachbuilders Ghia and Pininfarina. In this period, he developed a distinctive style that depended on clean, simple and smoothly flowing lines and was generally devoid of ornamentation.

After the end of the Second World War, Carrozzeria Rocco Motto moved to the Via Bardonecchia. The company now began to specialise in aluminium bodies for racing cars, and between 1946 and 1949 its name was associated with competition machinery from Alfa Romeo, Bandini, Cisitalia, Ermini and Fiat. The success of the Cisitalia D46 and 204 models helped to spread Motto's reputation, as did a small number of special bodies for the Lancia Aprilia Sport, built to a design by Gianni Basso and constructed at the Motto workshops.

In the early 1950s, Motto also worked on bodies for Renault and Talbot-Lago in France, and bodied a few Delahaye chassis, including a 150, the 175 that won the 1951 Monte Carlo Rally, and the prototype 235 chassis. There were some Jaguars and three special racing bodies using MG TD components for American racing events in 1953. For Italian makers, there were bodies on some racing Lancia Aurelias, bodies for the Siata Daina and 208S, and some work for Ferrari.

When US car makers took an interest in Italian carrozzeria in the early 1950s, Motto secured a commission from Cadillac, and the 1953 Cadillac LaSalle show car was the result. US designers Virgil Exner and Raymond Loewy supposedly became admirers of Motto's work, and it was at Loewy's request that Motto turned his design into the 1960 Lancia Flaminia Loraymo coupé after many other coachbuilders had refused the job because of the complexity of the work.

The 1960s brought some work for Porsche, who commissioned Motto to build the streamlined bodies for the competition special Porsche 356B Abarth GTL cars. However, Motto decided on a change of tack in 1965, and with his son Francesco, Rocco Motto turned to the production of caravans and commercial vehicle bodies. Rocco Motto died in 1996, aged 92.

Mouche (F)
1913–1925, Lyons
Mouche & Catenot was formed in June 1913, but in July 1914 became E Mouche & Cie when one of the partners withdrew. The company specialised in luxury bodies, and was sufficiently confident to exhibit a torpedo style on Rochet-Schneider 12CV chassis at Lyons in 1922. However, by the end of 1924 the company was in financial trouble, and it was declared bankrupt in April 1925.

Mühlbacher (F)
1780–c1930, Paris; from 1922, Puteaux
Mühlbacher can claim to be one of the very oldest French builders of car bodywork, having bodied an Amédée Bollée

steam-powered stage coach in 1887. The company itself had already been in business for over a century, and had been founded at the Rue de Varennes in Paris in 1780 by a German expatriate. Mühlbacher was known as one of the greatest Parisian carriage-makers, and its clientele had included royalty, aristocracy and celebrities in several European countries.

In the years before the First World War, the company is known to have built bodies on Lorraine-Dietrich chassis (in 1908) and a town car with elegant wickerwork panelling survives on a 1913 Renault 22/24CV chassis. Mühlbacher also picked up on the skiff style pioneered by Labourdette in 1912. After the war, there was a body for a Rolls-Royce Silver Ghost in 1919. In 1922, Mühlbacher moved into the Puteaux workshops vacated by Manessius (*qv*), but in 1925 was bought out by Belvalette (*qv*).

The new owners continued to use the prestigious Mühlbacher name alongside their own throughout the 1920s, and Mühlbacher bodies appeared on top quality chassis like Hispano-Suiza, Isotta-Fraschini and Voisin. Mühlbacher also created bodywork for celebrities such as Rudolph Valentino, but the company went down with Belvalette in 1933.

Muling (F)
1920s
This company built the torpedo body on a Panhard & Levassor 20CV chassis in 1924, but nothing else is known about it.

Müller (NL)
1920s–1930s, Rotterdam
Established in 1921 as specialists in leatherwork for cars, Carrosseriefabriek A Muller & Zoon seem to have specialised in open bodywork by 1924.

The company had become sunroof specialists by 1931 and remained active until at least 1960 in that business.

Musigk & Haas (D)
1930s, Berlin
Karosserie Musigk & Haas is known for a special two-seater sports cabriolet body on a BMW 3/20PS chassis in 1933, of which just 10 were built, and for similar bodywork on Hanomag chassis of the same period.

Musigk & Haas: Special two-seater bodywork was available for BMW and Hanomag chassis. This is a BMW 3/20PS from 1933. *(BMW)*

N

Nederlandsche Carrosseriefabrieken (NL)
1920s, Voorschoten

The Nederlandsche Carrosseriefabrieken had its main works in a former saddle-maker's property in the Voorstraat at Voorschoten (close to The Hague), but also used the former steam tram depot at Wijngaardenlaan in the same town. A 1922 magazine report notes that it was then directed by PC Moret and had a staff of 35 people. Bodies in build at that time included a limousine on a Steyr chassis, a landaulet on a Phänomen chassis, and a number of taxi bodies.

Née (F)
1912–1987, Levallois-Perret

Paul Née is best remembered for his work with the French branch of Lancia at Bonneuil in the 1930s. From 1950, he handed over the business to his son, and most subsequent work was with reclining seats and opening roofs. The company also undertook restoration work in the 1980s, but closed down in 1987.

Neé: This rather grand four-seater cabriolet body was mounted on a Hispano-Suiza chassis. *(Author's Collection)*

Née himself was born in Orléans, and opened his workshop in the Levallois-Perret district of Paris in 1912. He soon specialized in pillarless and opening roof bodies, typically with a sporting flavour. From the early 1930s, the company did a lot of work with Lancia's French branch, and this included the two-seat Belna cabriolet that was derived from the French version of the Augusta. Demand for cabriolets also brought in regular work from Lancia. However, Née bodies were never noted for any real originality.

After the Second World War, coachbuilding activity was more desultory. In 1947, the company rebodied a 1936 Bugatti T57 (originally bodied by Fernandez & Darrin) as a pillarless coupé, giving it a large sunroof, chrome wing flashes, and a central spine on the boot lid. From 1950 to 1957, Née's son ran the business, and took it in a different direction. The company specialized in sunroofs, importing proprietary types from Britain, Holland and Germany, and offering both rolltop and sliding roofs for the Citroën Traction Avant and later DS models.

Nembo (I)
See Neri & Bonacini.

Neri & Bonacini (I)
1960–1967, Modena

Neri & Bonacini was a short-lived Italian carrozzeria based in Modena whose designs often carried the Nembo name. They built the bodies for a handful of sports cars in the 1960s and planned their own model, but closed before this entered production.

Giorgio Neri and Luciano Bonacini were both employees of Maserati, and left to establish their own business in 1960. In the beginning, their focus was on making mechanical components, and they also built a few chassis for Ferrari. They established links with Piero Drogo's Carrozzeria Sports Cars, and became involved with the mechanical side of the legendary Ferrari Breadvan, designed by Giotto Bizzarrini for Scuderia Serenissima and panelled by Drogo.

Neri & Bonacini also built the bodywork on four Ferraris in the early 1960s, using a design by the young Californian Tom Meade. One was a coupé on a 250GT; the other three were spyders, one on a 250GT Cabriolet Series 2 chassis, one on a shortened 250GT SWB chassis, and the last in 1964 on a RHD 330GT 2+2. These bodies all had plexiglass headlight covers and a deep, elliptical air intake. All had very noticeably hipped rear wings.

In 1966, the company also built a unique fastback coupé for the Lamborghini 400 GT Monza. In 1967 came the Nembo 7 Litri, another unique fastback coupé based on a Bizzarrini GT Corsa and fitted with a Ford engine.

The next move was to design and build a complete vehicle. Once again, they called on Tom Meade as designer. The car appeared in 1967 as the Studio GT 2 Litri, incorporating a Lancia Flavia engine within a specially designed chassis. It was a small fastback sports car with pop-up lights and a low belt-line with a slight curve that blended into the rear pillars. Although series production was planned, only three examples were built because Luciano Bonacini left the business to work for De Tomaso in 1967, and the Neri & Bonacini business closed down.

Neuer & Thieme (D)
1925–1928, Ulm

Hans Neuer gained his experience with the Austrian body builder Öffag in Vienna before moving to Ulm in Germany to run the body department for chassis-maker Steiger in 1921. After three years, Neuer fell out with Steiger and set up his own business in January 1925 with Karl Thieme (some say Ernst Thieme), a native of Ulm.

The new business promised a wide variety of bodies that included bus and commercial types as well as cars. There were a few more bodies on Steiger chassis, but that company

Neri & Bonacini: This unique fastback coupé was built on a Lamborghini 400GT in 1966. (WikiMedia Commons/Brian Snelson)

went bankrupt in 1926. By 1928, Neuer & Thieme had a contract to build 120 bodies for Hansa-Lloyd in Bremen, but the full quantity was never built because the coachbuilder folded in 1929. It was bought out by Kässbohrer, whose focus was on bus bodywork.

Neuss (D)
1857–1933, Berlin-Halensee

Joseph Neuss set up in business as a carriage maker in 1857 in the Halensee district of Berlin, and rapidly became

Neuss: Just 145 of Audi's eight-cylinder Imperator chassis were built between 1927 and 1929. This one was bodied by Neuss in 1927. (VW-Audi)

the largest such business in Germany. In the 1870s, Neuss senior handed over the business to his son, also called Joseph. Then on 1 January 1898, Nicholas Trutz of the Coburg carriage maker bought the company for his eldest son, Karl Trutz.

Cars entered the picture that year, when the Neuss company seems to have been capable of building complete vehicles to order. At the start of the new century, Karl Trutz gave up carriage building altogether and switched to car bodywork. Among his early work was the Protos 40PS run by a works team in the 1908 New York-Paris event.

In the 1920s, Jospeh Neuss was among the most highly regarded coachbuilders in Germany. There were luxury bodies for Audi, Bugatti, Hansa-Lloyd, Maybach and Mercedes-Benz chassis, and Neuss held the German licence to import Bugattis. From about 1930, the company began to work on less glamorous chassis, probably out of necessity after the Depression, and there were bodies for middle-class makes such as German-built Fords, Steyr and Wanderer.

In 1933, Karl Trutz decided to retire and sold the Neuss business to Erdmann & Rossi, who retained the Neuss name until 1935 alongside their own on the builder's plates they applied to coachwork. Notable among the Neuss employees was Johannes Beeskow, who was the company's general manager and retained that position after the change of ownership. Beeskow went on to become chief designer for Rometsch (qv).

Neuss: Elegant and stylish all at once with its creative use of two-tone paintwork, this sedan de ville was built on a Mercedes 770 chassis in 1932. (Daimler-Benz)

Nieuport (F)
1924, Issy-les-Moulineaux
Nieuport was a major French aircraft maker that was persuaded to build a single car body using aircraft principles. The car was a Hispano-Suiza H6C, which was given a lightweight torpedo body made of tulipwood in 1924 for André Dubonnet, who finished sixth with it at that year's Targa Florio.

Nieveler (D)
1980s, Hamburg
Gerd Nieveler's company was involved in the 1980s Mercedes-Benz custom conversion business, although it is not clear whether it created any cars of its own or merely sold the products of others.

Nowack (D)
1863–1949, Bautzen
August Nowack founded his carriage works at Bautzen in 1863. In February 1922, the company became August Nowack Karosseriewerk AG, and from that year the company became the exclusive provider of bodywork for Phänomen, who were based in Zittau. A new factory was established, where the Nowack workforce of around 500 built 30 different varieties of body for cars, lorries and delivery vans.

In June 1924 the company changed its name to August Nowack AG. The final Phänomen cars were built in 1927, and Nowack then restricted its activities to commercial bodywork.

At the end of the Second World War, the Nowack factory found itself in the Soviet-controlled eastern sector of Germany, and in 1949 it was incorporated into the state-owned Robur truck company, the successor to Phänomen.

Oblin: The influence of Touring's Ferrari 166 Inter is unmistakeable on this 1951 Jaguar XK120.

Oblin (B)

1950–1955, Brussels

Martial Oblin was a Belgian coachbuilder whose premises were in Brussels. He may have had an association with Driesen & Oblin, who built a coupé-chauffeur on a Minerva chassis in 1927, but had clearly set up on his own by the start of the 1950s.

Just three Oblin-bodied cars are known from the 1950s. The earliest was a 1951 Jaguar XK120 coupé that was heavily inspired by the Touring-bodied Ferrari Inter 166. In 1955, Oblin displayed two cars at the Brussels Salon. One was a lightweight aluminium barchetta rebody on a Ferrari 166MM/53, and the other a roadster on the Talbot T26 Grand Sport chassis. Nothing further was heard from the Oblin company after that.

Oertig (CH)

1912–1929, Geneva

Louis Oertig's coachworks was active from 1912 according to some sources, and had a stand at an exhibition in Berne in 1914. It was known for its touring bodies before the First World War and between 1919 and 1929 was a member of the Swiss Coachbuilders' Guild (VSCI). It appears not to have remained in business after 1929. However, further information has so far proved elusive.

OSI (I)

1960–1968, Turin

OSI was founded in Turin in 1960 by Luigi Segre, the former president of Ghia, and Arrigo Olivetti from the Fergat company, a Turin maker of automotive components. The initial letters stood for Officine Stampaggi Industriali (Industrial Pressings Workshops).

Originally known as Ghia-OSI, it aimed to build models designed by Ghia and also to take on special bodywork commissions. Other business included panel pressing and making geartrain and engine parts for the agricultural industry.

OSI established the first independent bodywork plant in Italy, oriented towards series production in batches; this was a method later adopted by both Bertone and Pininfarina.

Right from the start, OSI took on production of the Fiat 1300-1500 Familiale estate cars, the 2300S coupé and the Innocenti 950 spider, all designed by Ghia. By 1962 the company was building 50 cars a day. Sadly, Luigi Segre died in 1962, thus severing the direct link with Ghia. In management terms, his successor was Giacomo Bianco, from Fergat, and in due course OSI was absorbed by Fergat.

In the beginning, the company had no design studio of its own, relying heavily on Michelotti (qv) as a consultant. However, OSI did establish its own styling department in 1962 at Borgaro Torinese. From 1963 this was headed by Sergio Sartorelli , who had come from Ghia, where he had designed the VW Karmann Ghia coupé; other staff included Werner Holbl and Tom Tjaarda.

Michelotti was responsible for the OSI coachwork shown on a Fiat 1600S at the Turin Motor Show in 1963, and also

OSI: The 1967 Silver Fox concept car was inspired by aircraft design. (Author's Collection)

designed the Ford Anglia Torino, which was introduced in Turin a year later and of which OSI built 10,007 examples, all for the Italian market. In addition, there were a Fiat 850 coupé (worked on by Siata) and a coupé version of the Fiat 1200S, again designed by Michelotti.

Several more designs appeared in 1965, including the Alfa Romeo 2600 De Luxe, a four-door prestige saloon; a Ford Mustang; an Alpine berlinetta and an early example of an armoured passenger car, based on a Fiat 1500 and born from an idea by Quattroruote magazine that was developed by OSI.

Geneva 1966 brought a prototype Fiat 1100 R spider and the Ford Taunus 20M TS coupé. This was based on the German-built Ford Taunus 20M and was probably the best known of its models outside Italy. Around 2200 of these cars were built, to a design by Sergio Sartorelli. The same year at Paris, OSI showed the original Scarabeo sporting saloon, a one-off concept with a four-carburettor Alfa Romeo Giulia 1600 engine mounted transversely at the rear; the body was made of reinforced polyester.

There was another collaboration with Quattroruote magazine in 1966, this time the DAF City, a city car that used a 746cc DAF engine. OSI also looked at an all-terrain vehicle, presenting the Cross Country that combined elements of the Fiat 124 with drivetrain elements of the Fiat Campagnola. This was followed at the 1967 Geneva show by another all-terrain prototype called the WeekEnd, this time using the running-gear of the Fiat 850.

However, concept cars were not paying the bills. New contracts had been thin on the ground since the link with Ghia had been severed, and 1966 proved a turning point, when 2000 employees were laid off as neither Ford nor Fiat renewed their contracts. The 1967 Turin Motor Show marked OSI's last appearance at a car show. The company showed three cars: the Silver Fox, a strikingly original aircraft-like twin-boom design with a 1-litre Alpine engine, a cabriolet version of the Ford Taunus 20M TS, and a Fiat 125, called the Estate Car.

The design studio closed its doors later that year and its remains became the Future Studies department at Centro Stile Fiat, with Sergio Sartortrelli still at its head. OSI ended car production at the end of 1968, but remained active as a manufacturer of steel pressings and industrial equipment until the end of the century.

Ottin (F)
1863–1933, Lyons

The Ottin company existed as early as 1863, but first turned to building car bodywork in 1904. It is known for its close links with Cottin-Desgouttes, the Lyon chassis maker, and was proud of becoming the first provincial coachbuilder to have an official exhibit at the Paris Salon, in 1926.

Claude Joseph Ottin of the family that owned the company was killed on active service during the First World War, and in January 1926 the company was re-structured with Méry-François Ottin at its head. By that time, the company held a licence to build Baehr transformable coachwork. Not long afterwards, it began to construct bodies with fabric paneling, using the Weymann principles adapted to incorporate aluminium elements. From 1928, Ottin also offered a folding roof called the Plein Azur, to a design patented by the coachbuilder Dubos (qv).

Ottin built bodies on several types of chassis, examples being Hispano-Suiza H6 and Voisin C16 saloons, and a Bugatti Type 46 roadster. However, its close links with Cottin-Desgouttes ultimately proved fatal, and when the chassis-maker failed in 1933, Ottin went with it.

Ottin: A pretty tourer on a 1922 Cottin-Desgouttes. *(David Burgess-Wise)*

P

Papler (D)
1868–1955, Cologne

Papler was an important German coachbuilder in the 1920s and 1930s, but after the Second World War it turned to series production of bodies for major car manufacturers. The company was established as early as 1868 in Cologne by Franz Papler to build carriages under the name of Papler und Sohn GmbH, and built its first car bodies in 1908.

Nevertheless, its reputation was mainly established in the 1920s. By 1923 the company was building individual bodies on Benz and Opel chassis, and later added to the list Adler, Maybach, Mercedes-Benz, Minerva, Röhr, Rolls-Royce and Selve as well. In the 1930s it began to build series of bodies for the neighbouring Ford works in Cologne as well as for Adler in Frankfurt. There were some bodies for Opel, and from 1933, Papler had a contract to make bodies for German-built Citroëns. Then from 1936 there were emergency-vehicle bodies and special military bodywork on Ford V8 chassis.

After the Second World War, Papler began by building open troop carriers for the West German police on Ford Taunus and (from 1952) Volkswagen chassis, and moved on to do the estate and pick-up versions of the German-built Ford Taunus 12M as well as some bodies for the Ford FK1000 van. In January 1955, the company sold out to specialist truck maker Faun and became a repair shop for Faun products. Papler continued as a panel press shop for Ford and Magirus-Deutz, and survives today as a repair business and panel-maker associated with Ford and Iveco.

Papler: The sport cabriolet body on this Mercedes-Benz SSK dates from 1931. *(Daimler-Benz)*

Paquette (F)
1920s

Carrosserie Paquette was really a commercial body builder, but also constructed a few car bodies. One known example was a four-door saloon on the Peugeot 12CV Six Type 183 chassis in 1928.

Passerat & Radiguet (F)
1920s, Paris

Carrosserie de Luxe H Passerat was established in Paris probably in 1909, and became involved in the aircraft industry. By 1910 it was also involved in coachbuilding, and a known early example was on Pierron 12/14hp chassis. By this time, the company had become Passerat & Radiguet, and by 1913 it was building on better-established makes such as Delahaye. The company was still active in the 1920s, when it held a licence for the Baehr transformable patents. Its address was 127 Rue Michel-Bizot in the 12th arondissement.

Pavesi (I)
1919–present, Milan

Carrozzeria Pavesi was founded in Milan initially to construct hearses and security vehicles. The company moved on to build armoured vehicles as well, and is thought to have armoured some presidential limousines.

From the 1960s, the company also built special conversions of cars by De Tomaso, Ferrari and Maserati. From 1981, it built the small-run Spyder version of the De Tomaso Longchamp for its manufacturer. The 1980s also brought targa models of the De Tomaso Pantera to customer order, and a small number of cabriolet conversions of the Ferrari 400i.

The company remains in business, primarily working on armouring models such as the Maserati Quattroporte.

Pennock (NL)
1900–1953, The Hague

Pennock was one of the largest and best-known Dutch coachbuilders of the inter-war years. It was established in The Hague by Johannes Jacobus Leonarduszoon Pennock in 1898 as Carrosseriefabriek P.J. Pennock & Zonen.

The company constructed bus and lorry bodies as well as cars, and built both to individual commission and in batches. Among the latter were convertible styles on some of the more expensive chassis from France and the USA. Individual Pennock bodies are known to have been constructed on Lagonda and Minerva chassis, too.

In the late 1940s, Pennock became closely associated with bodies on Delahaye chassis, when the company built a number for the marque's Dutch importer. Many were intended for export, but one went to Prince Bernard of The Netherlands. For these cars, Pennock developed a flamboyant style with clearly-defined front wings that to some eyes suggests Chapron. He used minimal timber framing and provided a remarkably rigid structure by welding his coachwork to the chassis.

Pennock: Looking more like a big Humber than the Austin Sheerline it really was, this was the special town car built for Queen Juliana in 1952. (*Author's Collection*)

There were also several Pennock bodies on British chassis in this period. At least four drophead coupés were built on Armstrong-Siddeley 18hp chassis, and one source suggests that there were as many as 26, most intended for export to South America. A special stretched Austin Sheerline Double Convertible Town Car was built for Queen Juliana in 1952. However, the inexorable move towards monocoque construction spelled the end for Pennock. The company's last body was a special coupé on a Talbot-Lago T26 chassis in 1952, and Pennock closed down the following year.

Pezous (F)
1950s, Albi

Maurice Pezous held the Citroën franchise at Albi in the Tarn region of France, and he joined forces with bodywork specialist Albert Mazel to design a sporting coupé around Citroën Traction Avant running-gear. The prototype of the Daphné was completed in 1952 and a further five followed, together with a single cabriolet version. In 1955 Pezous signed a contract with Citroën for the supply of mechanical elements, but for reasons which are unclear, no further production resulted. Later, Pezous also built some bodies for single-seater racers in the Formula Bleue series, known as MEP types after his initials (Maurice Emile Pezous).

Phlups (B)
1949–1950, Ixelles

Théophile Phlups was briefly in business at Ixelles near Brussels in Belgium as a producer of rolltop cabriolet conversions for the Citroën Traction Avant. Typical features of the Phlups conversions were two-tone paintwork, aluminium hubcaps, leather upholstery and a Girard column gearchange conversion.

Pichon-Parat (F)
1947–1983, Sens

Pichon-Parat was a small French coachbuilder best known during the 1950s and 1960s for its conversions of volume-produced cars and for its lightweight bodywork for sporting and competition cars. Bernard Pichon and André Parat set up in business at the Rue Mocquesouris in Sens in 1947. Pichon was the designer and the businessman who looked after the sales side, and Parat was the craftsman who turned their ideas into metal.

Pichon-Parat began by converting American saloon cars into estates to meet a need for dual-purpose vehicles. However, more serious design work began in 1950, with a restyled rear end for the Ford Vedette saloon and an estate conversion of the same car. There would be several more Vedette variants over the next few years.

In 1953, the company began working on the Panhard Junior, turning the standard cabriolet into an attractive

Pichon-Parat: As the 1950s opened, the firm was working closely with Ford's French branch. This was the restyled rear end it produced for the Vedette model. (*Author's Collection*)

Pichon-Parat: Lightweight aluminium coachwork was a feature of this attractive little coupé, here mounted on a DB (Deutsch Bonnet) chassis but also available for the Panhard Junior in the early 1950s. (*Author's Collection*)

Pichon-Parat: This estate conversion of the Panhard PL17 was on the Pichon-Parat stand at the 1958 Paris Salon. (*Author's Collection*)

coupé. A sporting Panhard model called the Dolomites followed, intended for rallying. The Renault 4CV was next for attention, initially only with an enlarged rear window but soon also as a two-door sports coupé, and then from 1955 as the striking Izoard coupé with its gullwing doors and lightweight Duralumin panels on a tubular frame. Some experts suggest as many as 25 were built, but others argue for only three or four.

Pichon-Parat soon acquired a reputation for their ability to create lightweight bodies, and notable successes were with a short-wheelbase coupé on the Salmson 2300 Sport from 1955 and a pair of open Talbot-Lago cars that ran in the 1956 Le Mans 24 Hours race. There were also lightweight conversions of otherwise standard cars, notably the Peugeot 203, for which the company developed Duralumin panels for non-structural areas of the body.

However, Pichon-Parat was never able to attract a volume contract from a major manufacturer, despite several attempts. The company's 1953 Renault Frégate cabriolet lost out to a rival design from Letourneur et Marchand, and a 1956 Dauphine cabriolet again failed to impress Renault. The same year saw a Simca Aronde coupé with a panoramic roof, but Simca declined to take an interest. Peugeot, too, declined to follow up on a two-door pillarless "hardtop" 403 in 1957.

The company's reputation for light weight, a speedy turnaround and reasonable cost nevertheless did attract

the attention of Raymond Loewy, who then ran styling for Studebaker in the USA. In 1957, he had Pichon-Parat build the futuristic coupé body on a BMW 507 to a design that hinted at his later Studebaker Avanti. Two years later, the Sens workshop constructed the body for a Cadillac coupé for Loewy's personal use, and subsequently also remodeled Loewy's own personal Jaguar E-type.

An estate conversion of the Panhard Dyna announced in 1957 lasted for a few years in production and went through several evolutions. A cabriolet conversion of the same model called the "Bordeaux" was licensed to the coachbuilder Vivez in Bordeaux, but few were made. By 1959, Pichon-Parat also had an extraordinary sports body design that could be adapted to suit either Renault Dauphine or Panhard mechanical elements, but even this ploy did not bring in major business.

Still chasing a model that could be produced in volume, Pichon-Parat showed a beach car conversion of the Vespa 400 in 1959, but this did not attract the anticipated interest. Demand for custom-built competition and sports bodies was waning, and in 1960 Bernard Pichon left the business to work for Anthony Lago; Lago died in late 1960 and Pichon moved to Fiat.

André Parat continued alone, initially retaining the Pichon-Parat name but later as Carrosserie Parat, and now turned to the Citroën ID and DS models. First came a short-wheelbase two-door model in 1960, which attracted an order from the Citroën competitions department; the works team subsequently entered several in rallies, and from 1963, Pichon-Parat was building DS coupés to order for private buyers. Their design evolved over the years: from late 1964 came a distinctive front end featuring headlamps from the Panhard 24, and most had a lowered roof with a more steeply raked windscreen and completely redesigned rear end.

Sadly, the DS coupés were too expensive to become numerous, and from 1962 André Parat began to seek business elsewhere, turning increasingly to repair work and to building prototypes for the big manufacturers. There were special cars for films, too. Yet whenever the

Pichon-Parat: The Renault 4CV became a base for many special-bodied cars, and this remarkable gullwing coupé came from Pichon-Parat in 1955. (*Author's Collection*)

Pichon-Parat: American designer Raymond Loewy is seen here with the body he designed for BMW 507 chassis, constructed in 1957. (Author's Collection)

Pichon-Parat: Loewy used the company to build a second of his designs, this time on a 1959 Cadillac chassis. (Author's Collection)

Pichon-Parat: The 1960s brought a small number of these neat estate conversions on the BMW 1800 and 2000. (Author's Collection)

opportunity arose, Parat went back to what he did best. In 1966, for example, he built the lightweight Matra 620 car for Le Mans, and also forged a link with the French BMW importer that led to an order for small numbers of expensive estate conversions based on the 1800 and 2000 saloons.

Still relying on repair and prototype work for his bread and butter, Parat had a hand in the design of the Ligier JS2

in 1970, retouching the original JS1 design by Pietro Frua. In the late 1970s, he was doggedly producing attractive estate conversions of volume saloons as well, although his Peugeot 604, Renault 30 and BMW 7 Series models were made only in tiny numbers. The last appear to have been made around 1980, and in 1983 André Parat finally closed the Sens workshop.

Pingret & Bretau (F)
1914–1927, Puteaux
This French coachbuilder was founded in the early years of the 20th century as Pingret, Guion & Breteau, but by 1918 was trading as Pingret & Breteau. Little is known about their products, which included a limousine on a Hispano-Suiza H6B chassis in 1919 and a coupé-chauffeur body on a Voisin chassis in the mid-1920s. The company is believed to have closed down in 1927.

Pininfarina (I)
1930–present, Turin
Pininfarina was and remains perhaps the greatest of the Italian designer-coachbuilders. Originally known as Pinin Farina – "Pinin" was the nickname of its founder, and is a Torinese dialect word meaning the youngest of the family – it became Pininfarina (one word) in 1961. At the same time, the family name was changed by Presidential decree to Pininfarina. When Battista "Pinin" Farina died in 1966, the company passed into the hands of his son Sergio, who retired in 2001 in favour of his son, Andrea. Andrea died in a traffic accident in 2008, when his brother Paolo became CEO and Chairman of the company. Today, the Pininfarina Group employs over 3000 staff in subsidiary offices throughout Europe, as well as in Morocco and China.

Battista Farina was still a teenager when he joined his older brother Giovanni's coachbuilding firm, Stabilimenti Industriali Farina SA. He did his first coachwork design in 1912. A visit to the USA in 1922 resulted in him being offered a job by Henry Ford, and by the time he returned to Italy he had learned new techniques which helped to give his designs a modernity lacking in most of his contemporaries. Friends encouraged him to strike out on his own, and among them was Vincenzo Lancia, who promised him work as long as the Lancia company existed. So in May 1930, Battista Farina set up his own coachbuilding workshop in Turin as Carrozzeria Pinin Farina.

Among the new company's first jobs was detailing of the Lancia Dilambda, the big V8-engined model announced in 1929. Pinin Farina developed a reputation as the most progressive of the Italian coachbuilders during the 1930s, and grew rapidly, displaying its wares at motor shows and concours events all over Europe. Most of its work in this period was for Lancia or Alfa Romeo, but the company also diversified to build on grand imported chassis such as Cadillac and Mercedes.

Among the Pinin Farina characteristics in these years were angled radiators and windscreens that gave

Pininfarina: The lines of the coupé body on this 1935 six-cylinder Alfa Romeo chassis were bold and advanced for the time. *(David Hodges Collection)*

Pininfarina: Assured and powerful lines characterise this cabriolet on a 1938 V8-engined Lancia Astura chassis. *(David Hodges Collection)*

better aerodynamics; its 1937 aerodynamic coupé on the Lancia Aprilia chassis was capable of 100mph thanks to its streamlined shape, whereas the equivalent saloon could manage no more than 80mph. The company also introduced new painting techniques and borrowed from André Citroën the idea of using bright and light colours.

Preliminary discussions with Renault about contract work were cut short by the Second World War, and Pinin Farina spent the years between 1939 and 1945 turning out items for the Italian army. However, a meeting with Pietro Dusio after the war led to Pinin Farina doing the coupé body for his Cisitalia 202GT of 1946, and this body with

its horizontal grille and low bonnet line was profoundly influential in the development of coachbuilding in the late 1940s. In this period, the company's reputation grew even further, with bodywork for chassis by Alfa Romeo, Bentley and Cadillac, among others. Carrozzeria Pinin Farina also built bodies on Bristol chassis, and in 1951 did a four-door saloon prototype for BMW, although this was rejected because it looked too much like the contemporary Alfa Romeo 1900. The company built most of the bodies on the Lancia Aurelia B20 GT, although the design was in fact done by Ghia.

In the early 1950s, Pinin Farina also forged links with Nash in the USA, designing the Nash Healey sports roadster and contributing to the design of the 1952 Nash Ambassador. Meanwhile, the coachbuilder's work had caught the attention of Enzo Ferrari, and the first Pinin Farina-bodied Ferrari was built in 1952. Although many other styling houses created bodywork for Ferrari, by 1954 it was clear that Pinin Farina was the favoured company. Indeed, a gentlemen's agreement between Ferrari and Farina – no contract was ever signed – saw Pinin Farina becoming the Ferrari house stylist. The Ferrari work was entrusted to Sergio Farina, a businessman rather than a designer like his father, and he oversaw the forging of an alliance that has endured to the present day.

The mid-1950s also saw Pinin Farina break away from the post-war "pontoon" style with its slab sides and rounded themes (typified by the company's 403 saloon for Peugeot) to create a hugely influential new style for closed cars, with sharper and more clearly defined lines. The new Farina ideas were pioneered on a series of three concept coupés between 1955 and 1957, all built on Lancia Aurelia saloon chassis. The distinctive shapes of these three "Florida" cars first saw production in the small-volume Lancia Flaminia coupé of late 1957, and would be echoed in designs for BMC (from 1958) and Peugeot (from 1960), all of them built in large volumes.

The BMC cars were perversely always known as "Farina" types, and included the Austin A40 of 1958 as well as the long-running and badge-engineered 1.5-litre and 3-litre saloons. Their success encouraged BMC to ask Pinin Farina to design the body for their new 1100 models, which would be released in 1962.

Pininfarina: This was the stunning Cisitalia coupé that brought Pinin Farina to international attention in 1947. *(David Hodges Collection)*

Pininfarina: Also dating from 1947, this body on a Maserati A6 1500 was more experimental – and perhaps not wholly successful.

Pininfarina: The company pursued its early post-war style on cars such as this Lancia. (David Hodges Collection)

The mid-1950s also saw Pinin Farina expanding, and the company built a new and larger factory at the Via Lesna in the Grugliasco district of Turin which opened in 1958. At the same time, Pinin Farina relinquished management of the business to his son Sergio Farina and to his son-in-law Renzo Carli. Three years later, he would formally retire and give them full control. In the mean time, the company had

Pininfarina: The early 1950s brought a new and softer style, with more clearly defined wing lines. This one-off for Rover in 1953 had similarities to contemporary bodies for Lancia. (David Hodges Collection)

been pursuing a relationship with Cadillac, and among the first cars to be built at the new factory were the 200 examples of the 1959- and 1960-model Eldorado Brougham.

Under its new name, Pininfarina did a number of superb volume-production designs for Fiat and Lancia in the 1960s, the 124 Spider and 130 coupé for Fiat being particularly notable. Experimental concepts included the 1963 Sigma, a four-seater with sliding doors shown in Turin which embodied safety concepts and was not deliberately based on any existing model. The Sigma name recurred on a 1969 Formula 1 concept car, again incorporating a number of safety features and based on a Ferrari 312 single-seater. Aerodynamic concerns were reflected on a pair of Berlina Aerodinamica design studies based on the BMC 1800 in 1967 and then the BMC 1100 a year later.

From 1968, Paolo Martin, who had earlier worked for Michelotti and Bertone, became head of the styling department. Specials and one-offs continued to come from the Turin studios: Paolo Martin's Pininfarina Modulo, shown at Geneva in 1970 and based on a Ferrari 512S, remained

Pininfarina: From the same period is this Nash Healey, one of the company's earliest American collaborations. *(David Hodges Collection)*

Pininfarina: The firm's association with Ferrari would be an important and enduring one. This delightful design on a 1951 212 chassis was a portent of things to come.

a concept, but the one-off fastback coupé on a Bentley in 1968 led to the design of the 1975 Rolls-Royce Camargue. In 1972, Pininfarina opened its own wind tunnel to aid its pursuit of aerodynamic shapes, and in 1978 it produced the famous "Banana Car", an idealised aerodynamic shape whose development had been sponsored by the Italian government. The 1970s were also notable for work on Maserati saloons and Pininfarina was never afraid to work with countries whose car industries were still developing; in China, the company worked with China Brilliance, and in Korea it worked on the Matrix MPV for Hyundai.

During the 1980s, Pininfarina re-oriented itself as a design and engineering consultancy for the motor industry at large. In that role it not only designed new shapes or variants of existing designs (such as estates, coupés or convertibles) but was also able to advise on body engineering issues and to build both large and small special series of cars, and prototypes as well. Among the designs to which it had input was the Jaguar XJ-S convertible. Pininfarina continued to produce concept cars, one example being the 1989 Ferrari Mythos.

Pininfarina: This coupé on a Ferrari 250GT was created for racing driver Alfonso de Portago. *(Author's Collection)*

The last two decades of the 20th century also saw the company expand rapidly, and it opened several new plants. The one at San Giorgio opened in 1986 for the assembly of bodies for the Cadillac Allanté; another was opened in 1999 at Bairo Canavese near Turin specifically to assemble a new small off-road vehicle for Mitsubishi. This was called the

Pininfarina: Lightness of touch made the spider body for the Alfa Romeo Giulietta Veloce 1300 an all-time classic. *(David Hodges Collection)*

Pininfarina: Exquisite lines created this Ferrari 250GT berlinetta on the short-wheelbase chassis. *(David Hodges Collection)*

Pininfarina: The gently "hipped" waistline seen on the Alfa Romeo above reappeared on this superb Ferrari cabriolet. *(Author)*

Pininfarina: A series of designs on Lancia chassis ushered in a new squared-up style with a hint of American-style tail fins. This was a production Lancia, the Series II Appia coupé from 1957.

Pininfarina: Those new lines began to appear on other chassis, too. This is the Sestrières coupé on an Alfa Romeo 1900 . . .

Pininfarina: . . . and this Buick Lido with similar lines was done as a concept for the Paris Salon in 1957.

Pininfarina: Never afraid to experiment, the company came up with this astonishing "X car" concept in 1960; although it looks like a three-wheeler here, there are actually four wheels in a diamond pattern. The primary aim was to improve aerodynamics, although the odd fins at the rear betray the US influence to which some of the company's designs were subject at the time. (David Hodges Collection)

Pininfarina: Based on the Lancia Flaminia, this is one of a small group of state parade cars built in 1960-1961. (David Hodges Collection)

Pininfarina: Volume contracts included the cabriolet (and later, coupé) bodies for the Peugeot 404, beginning in 1961. (David Hodges Collection)

Pininfarina: Sleeker lines characterised the designs of the 1960s, like this Lancia Flavia Coupé, introduced in 1962. *(David Hodges Collection)*

Pininfarina: For the 1963 Paris Motor Show Pininfarina built this unique coupé body on a Chevrolet Corvette. It was known as the Corvette Rondine. *(Unknown copyright)*

Pininfarina: This was the coupé body for the 1965 Ferrari 500 Superfast. *(Author)*

Pininfarina: Recognised as Ferrari's "house" stylist, Pininfarina produced one superb design after another on the chassis from Maranello. This is the 2+2 body on the 330GT model, introduced in 1965. *(David Hodges Collection)*

Pininfarina: The proportions of the Ferrari 275GTB were controversial when it was released in 1964, the ultra-long nose coming in for criticism. *(David Hodges Collection)*

Pininfarina: There was no such controversy over the 365GTB4 or Daytona of 1968. The car is still recognised as an all-time classic shape. *(Silverstone Auctions)*

Pininfarina: Contracts for mainstream manufacturers remained important. This is the Peugeot 504 coupé of 1969. *(David Hodges Collection)*

Pininfarina: Show cars were also important in keeping the company in the public eye. The Ferrari Modulo was a striking wedge-shaped design by chief designer Paolo Martin that was shown at Geneva in 1970. *(WikiMedia Commons/Morio)*

Pininfarina: Another striking wedge-shaped concept was the 1971 Alfa Romeo Cuneo, based on a P33 chassis used earlier for another concept car. *(David Hodges Collection)*

Pininfarina: The classic Ferrari GT lines continued with the 1972 365GTC4. *(David Hodges Collection)*

Pininfarina: Less glamorous work sometimes had to pay the bills. This was the Talbot Samba cabrio of 1982. (*Author's Collection*)

Pininfarina: The 1988 HIT (High Italian Technology) concept car used light-weight materials and was based on a Lancia Delta HF Integrale.

iO in Italy, but the Shogun Pinin in Britain and the Pajero Pinin in other European markets. Then in 2003, Pininfarina established Pininfarina Sverige AB in Uddevalla, Sweden, as a joint venture with Volvo. The first car built here was the Volvo C70, a coupé-convertible with retractable metal roof.

Renewed global interest in convertibles was reflected in Pininfarina's contract with Ford to build the folding-roof Focus Coupé-Cabriolet from 2007, and there were further contracts to provide folding-roof modules for other manufacturers. Nevertheless, as car makers reined in production during the 2000s, it became clear that Pininfarina's expansion had been made at the wrong time. Mitsubishi assembly ended in 2004 and the factory was leased out, and although the San Giorgio plant would take on assembly of the Brera and Spider models for Alfa Romeo, Pininfarina became unprofitable after 2004.

In the meantime, the company had also designed city trams for France and Greece, high-speed trains for the Netherlands, and trolleybuses for the USA. It continued to design and build one-offs to special order, such as a rebody for a private customer of a Ferrari P4/5 in 2006. It also became involved with the design of electric vehicles, notably working with the French Bolloré Group on a solar-electric concept called the Pininfarina B0 (B Zero) that was shown at Paris in 2008. This four-seat hatchback had a solar panel integrated with the roof to recharge its on-board batteries.

Despite the promise of these additional activities, there were no bidders to buy Pininfarina as a going concern. So the company shut down its manufacturing operations in 2011 to focus once again on design. Then in 2012 creditor banks agreed to an extension of its debt restructuring plan. The same banks rejected a takeover bid by Mahindra & Mahindra in India in 2015.

Piot & Barbary (F)
1921–1923, Lyons
This short-lived French coachbuilder took over the business of Cognat & Piot (*qv*) but lasted for only two more years. Nothing is known about its products. It was later revived by Jean Rozier under his own name.

Plasswilm (D)
1940s and 1950s, Cologne
When Ford of Germany re-introduced its somewhat inelegant 1939 Taunus G73A model in 1948, the car came only as a two-door saloon. However, Ford expanded the range as soon as it was able by supplying chassis with only front end panelling to a variety of coachbuilders. Among these coachbuilders was Plasswilm in Cologne, who from 1950 offered a wooden-bodied estate car or Kombi.

Plasswilm: More functional than attractive, this was the Plasswilm Kombi on Ford chassis. (*Author's Collection*)

Plüss (CH)
1950s? Bern
Plüss was a little-known minor Swiss coachbuilder responsible for some rolltop saloon conversions of the Citroën Traction Avant.

Poberejsky (F)
1949, Paris
Little is known about Jacques Poberejsky except that he appears to have been involved in the motor trade in Paris and to have had some relationship with Mercedes-Benz in France. He acquired a Rolls-Royce Silver Wraith chassis which had been on the maker's stand at the Earls Court Motor Show in 1948, and built for this a rounded, streamlined sedanca de ville body. Poberejsky's

Poberejsky: This extraordinary sedanca de ville body reflected some design trends of the late 1940s, but was not much admired. Its Rolls-Royce chassis was later rebodied more conventionally. (Author's Collection)

Pollmann: Among the host cars for Pollman conversions was the Ford Sierra. (Author's Collection)

design dispensed with the traditional radiator grille and was generally judged to be strikingly ugly. The car was exhibited at the Geneva Show in 1949, but its body was later removed and the chassis was bodied more conventionally by Franay.

Pollmann (D)
1926 to present, Bremen
Conrad Pollmann GmbH was founded as a commercial body builder in 1926 and focussed on small bus bodywork until the 1950s, when it moved into the hearse business. The company developed an enviable reputation for its conversions of saloon cars, predominantly Mercedes-Benz models, but was sold to an investment company in 2006. In summer 2008, the former parent company was declared bankrupt, but the name survives as the Pollmann-Service-Center, which has taken the hearse side of the business forward, for a while using Volvo V70 saloons as the base models alongside Mercedes-Benz saloons.

Pourtout (F)
1925–1939; Bougival, later Rueil-Malmaison
Marcel Pourtout had been the workshop foreman at the Aubertin (qv) coachworks, and bought that business in 1925. However, he chose to sell off the old Aubertin premises and established his business at Bougival. Initially he survived mainly on contract work for other coachbuilders. However, when Italian chassis maker Lancia established a factory nearby in the early 1930s, Pourtout secured a contract to build cabriolet bodies for the Belna chassis. The work for Lancia continued until 1939, and was a key factor behind the company's expansion into larger premises at Rueil-Malmaison in April 1936.

Pourtout: This 1937 Le Mans entry on Peugeot 302 chassis was the result of collaboration between Pourtout and Georges Paulin. (David Hodges Collection)

Pourtout: Pourtout and Paulin again, this time collaborating on the coupé body for a 1938 Peugeot 402DS. (*David Hodges Collection*)

Pourtout: Possibly the most famous Paulin-Pourtout collaboration was the Embiricos Bentley, whose streamlined saloon body inspired the pre-war Bentley Corniche prototype. (*David Hodges Collection*)

Pourtout: The 135MS was the high-performance version of the Delahaye chassis, and is seen here with a cabriolet body that shows all the characteristics of Pourtout's late 1930s style. (*WikiMedia/Kévin Pourtout*)

Pourtout Carrossier (as the company was known) also accepted individual commissions, and during the 1930s worked on chassis from some of the top makers of the day. French chassis included Ballot, Bugatti, Delage, Delahaye, Delaunay-Belleville, Hispano-Suiza, Peugeot, Talbot-Lago and Voisin. From further afield there were Minervas from Belgium, and Pourtout also worked on American Buick chassis.

Nevertheless, Pourtout is probably best remembered for a series of aerodynamic designs drawn up with the aid of Georges Paulin, an amateur stylist who lived near the coachworks. Paulin was a dental technician by trade, who had met Marcel Pourtout in 1933. In collaboration with the Parisian Peugeot dealer Emile Darl'Mat, they designed

and built the revolutionary Peugeot 601 Eclipse of 1934 with its retractable hardtop. In 1937 came the Peugeot 402 Darl'Mat, whose Paulin-designed sporting bodies anticipated stunning series of streamlined bodies on Delage and Talbot-Lago chassis built by Pourtout to Paulin designs.

These designs attracted the attention of Walter Sleator, the Rolls-Royce and Bentley representative at Franco-Britannic in Paris. Sleator wanted to see Bentley models adapted to suit the long straight roads of the European continent, and he encouraged shipping magnate, racing driver and serial Bentley owner Nicky Embiricos to commission a special streamlined coupé body on the 4¼-litre Bentley chassis, with aerodynamic design by Paulin and lightweight aluminium construction by Pourtout. The "Embiricos Bentley" went on to inspire the streamlined Bentley Corniche prototype of 1939 as well as the post-war Bentley R-type Continental.

Pourtout built ambulances during the 1939-1945 war, and in 1945 the founder's sons Marcel and Claude took over the business. A pair of magnificent coupés on Delahaye 135 chassis in 1946-1947 showed great promise, but not all Pourtout's post-war bodies shared their elegance. The 1945 Peugeot 202 record coupé looked clumsy and heavy, and Pourtout's coupé design for the 1947 Bugatti Type 73 prototype was no better, despite its streamlined pontoon wings and spatted rear wheels. The company last exhibited at the Paris Salon in 1951, turning thereafter to building special utility models, particularly for Peugeot.

In the 1990s, Guillaume Pourtout, grandson of the founder, constructed a Ford Fiesta cabriolet designed by Loic Peroïs, but Ford awarded its volume contract elsewhere. Although the Pourtout company still exists today, its focus is on the repair of classic coachwork.

Pozzi (CH)
1920s, Lausanne
Very little is known about Pozzi & Cie, a coachbuilder active in the Renens suburb of Lausanne during the 1920s. The company is believed to have started in 1924 and among its bodies was a limousine on an extended 1928 Cadillac chassis.

Pralavorio (F)
1923–c1930, Lyons

Simon Pralavorio's first car body appears to have been a saloon on a Cottin-Desgouttes chassis that was shown at the Lyons Fair in 1923. He claimed that his construction system depended on two parts, and that it eliminated the creaks and squeaks usually associated with coachbuilt bodies. Pralavorio was still advertising a range of body styles for 1927 that included a cabriolet, a two-door sports saloon, and four-seat saloons with either two or four doors. Little is known about the chassis that received these bodies, although a two-door saloon is known to have been mounted on a 1927 Sizaire Frères 4 RI model.

Pritchard & Demolin (B)
1920s–1930s, Liège

The name of this coachbuilder is sometimes shown as Pritchard-Dumoulin or Demoulin, but the spelling shown above appears to be the correct one. The company was based at Angleur, near Liège, and was certainly active by 1928, when it constructed a neat roadster body on a Bugatti Type 43 chassis. Later known bodies include a three-position cabriolet on a 1930 Bugatti Type 49, and a streamlined saloon on the FN Type 42A Prince Albert chassis of 1934-1935.

Pritchard & Demolin: No great beauty unfortunately, this streamlined body on an FN chassis paid lip service to contemporary ideas about aerodynamics.

Privat (F)
Dijon, 1920s

Albert Privat owned a small coachworks in Dijon which seems to have focused mainly on repairs but also built its own complete light commercial and car bodywork. The company seems to have specialised in torpedo bodies, and examples are known to have been built on Ariès, Delage 11hp and Ford 9hp chassis.

Proux (F)
1920s–c1930, Courbevoie

Maurice Proux had workshops at Courbevoie and a showroom on the Champs-Elysées in Paris. His conservative and classical designs won a number of concours d'élégance events right through into 1930, not least because Proux was an ardent and persistent follower of the concours vogue and entered many cars himself.

The Proux coachworks favoured prestigious chassis, and examples are known to have been built on Bugatti, Cord, Delage, Delahaye, Hispano-Suiza, Minerva, Packard and Panhard. However, Proux was perhaps too closely aligned with the wealthy whose spending power was affected by the 1929 Wall Street Crash, and the company appears not to have survived beyond 1930.

Pruneville (F)
1920s, Lyons

In the days of horse-drawn carriages in the 19th century, Pruneville & Cie started up as a Lyons coachbuilder. In the early part of the 20th century, it bodied chassis built locally, such as Luc Court and Cottin-Desgouttes, and also those built in Paris, such as Delage and Delaunay-Belleville. During the 1920s it held a licence to build transformable bodies using the Baehr patents.

R

Ramseier (CH)
Please see the entry for Worblaufen.

Rappold (D)
1948 to date, Wülfrath
Rappold Karosseriewerk GmbH is best known for its hearses and funeral cars, mostly built from Mercedes-Benz models. It has also built armoured and other specialist vehicles.

Rappold: Built in 1986, this Rappold hearse conversion was based on a Mercedes-Benz 230E. *(Daimler-Benz)*

The company was founded in 1948 in Wülfrath, and in its early years constructed a number of specialist vehicles, including racing cars. However, its first hearse was also made in 1948 for a leading undertaker in Düsseldorf, and the company has always specialised in this market.

Ravistre & Martel (F)
1923–1940, Annonay
Carrosserie Ravistre & Martel grew out of the Grange & Martel business in 1923 when Charles Martel recruited his brother-in-law, Auguste Ravistre, to replace the Grange brothers.

Between 1923 and 1940, this company was extremely active, building large numbers of bus and light commercial bodies as well as no fewer than 575 car bodies. Most of these, a claimed 107, were on Peugeot chassis, but there were also 83 on Delage. Of the others, known examples include some Amilcars, a Bugatti Type 46 and a Hispano-Suiza H6C. The company still existed as late as 1944, but seems not to have built any car bodies after 1940.

Rayton Fissore (I)
1976–c2003, Chevasco
The Rayton Fissore company was set up in 1976 by Fernanda Fissore, daughter of Fissore coachworks owner Bernardo Fissore, with her husband Giulio Malvino. At the time, the Fissore coachworks was becoming heavily dependent on its links with Swiss car maker Monteverdi, and the new company may have been established as a way of retaining some independence for the Fissore family.

Rayton Fissore designed a convertible version of the Fiat Ritmo at the same time as the main Fissore coachworks did, but both versions lost out to the proposal by Bertone. In 1985, Rayton Fissore introduced the Magnum, an off-road vehicle that used an Iveco chassis and was marketed as the Laforza in the USA. The body design was by Tom Tjaarda, who had also done the De Tomaso Pantera.

At the 1986 Turin Salon, Rayton Fissore showed a prototype Alfa Romeo 75 estate car, called the 75 Turbo Wagon. The same car appeared at the 1987 Geneva Show, accompanied by a 2.0-litre naturally aspirated version called the 75 Sportwagon. Some seven or eight prototypes of this design were constructed, but the project was then cancelled when Fiat took over at Alfa Romeo.

Rayton Fissore continued to produce the Magnum, primarily for the US market, until 2003.

Reinbolt & Christé (CH)
1900–1959, Basle
J Reinbolt and JM Christé were long-standing employees of Josef Kauffmann's wagon and carriage building company, and took over his business in 1900. Kauffmann had set it up some time around 1830 in Elsaß, near the Swiss border, and had moved it to Basle in 1855.

Renamed Carrosserie Reinbolt & Christé, the workshop soon began to construct bodywork for cars, and the horse-drawn vehicle business gradually petered out. Early chassis bodied by Reinbolt & Christé included the Swiss-built Martini. After another change of ownership, the company became Reinbolt & Christé SA, Basel in 1929.

When the Swiss government reduced import duty on foreign-built chassis in 1931, Reinbolt & Christé seized their opportunity. The company now became one of the country's leading carrossiers, with a focus especially on cabriolet types. Flowing lines were a Reinbolt & Christé characteristic, and particularly attractive were a series of nine cabriolets built in 1937 on the MG SA chassis.

The wholesale switch to monocoque construction after the Second World War made life as difficult for Reinbolt & Christé as for other carrossiers. Notable designs continued to appear, however, especially on British chassis, and the late 1940s and early 1950s saw some cabriolets on Jaguar 3½-litre, Riley RM and MG YA chassis. There was business to be made from rolltop conversions, too, and Reinbolt & Christé made a number out of Citroën Traction Avant saloons to meet demand.

Nevertheless, business was not easy, and from 1947 the company was obliged to supplement its income through the construction of trolleybus bodies for the Basle municipal network. Sadly, it was not enough, and in 1959 Reinbolt & Christé closed down. The company had built an estimated total of 300 bodies in its 60 years as a carrossier.

Reinbolt & Christé: A Roadster body, with flamboyantly styled wings, on a 1934 Horch 710 chassis. (Nikolaus Scheerbarth-Clasen)

Reinbolt & Christé: The firm was known for its cabriolets, this one being on a 1938 Chevrolet Imperial. The front end looks pure Chevrolet, but the flowing tail is evidently the work of the coachbuilder. (Nikolaus Scheerbarth-Clasen)

Reinbolt & Christé: Cabriolets on British chassis in the 1940s included this one on a Riley 2.5-litre from approximately 1949. (Author's Collection)

Renard (F)
Puteaux, late 1930s

Carrosseries Marius Renard produced conversions of the Ctiroën Traction Avant in the late 1930s, building cabriolets from saloons and modifying elements of the coachwork to give a more modern appearance.

Renard & Bec (F)
1948

Renard & Bec was an obscure French coachbuilder whose sole claim to fame appears to have been a cabriolet conversion based on a Citroën Traction Avant. The coachwork was designed by the well-known motoring artist and amateur stylist Géo Ham and incorporated a number of special touches including a Delahaye-like front end. The car was shown at the 1948 Paris Salon, and it appears that a second example was also built.

Repusseau & Cie (F)
1907–c1930 , Levallois-Perret

François Repusseau was designing and building bodies for Delage before the Great War, and after the war he developed and patented the Silentbloc system of body mounting which was licensed to a number of coachbuilders during the 1920s and 1930s.

Reutter (D)
1906–1963, Stuttgart

The Reutter coachworks was founded in 1906 by Wilhelm Reutter, who was joined in 1909 by his brother Albert as partner and business manager. From 1910, the company was formally established as the Stuttgarter Karosseriewerk Reutter & Co.

The company took out a number of patents, notably for a form of folding roof, and the complete body to this design introduced in 1912 was rather quaintly known as Reutter's Reform Coachwork. During the 1920s, the company

Reutter: The four-door cabriolet conversion of the Citroën DS is a rare car. All were built in 1960. (*David Hodges Collection*)

Reutter: This 1932 Wanderer was Ferdinand Porsche's private car. It was an 8-cylinder of 3250cc, supercharged. (*Erik Eckermann Archive*)

Reutter: The 1949 prototype body for BMW's upcoming 501 saloon. (*Erik Eckermann Archive*)

developed a composite method of body construction using both wood and steel, and attracted business from almost all the major German chassis makers. There were Reutter bodies for Adler, Benz, BMW, Dixi, Horch, Maybach, Mercedes, NSU and Opel, some for volume-produced models and others for low-volume types. An interesting sideline was special bodies for German post office vehicles.

From the end of the 1920s, it was Wanderer who became Reutter's largest client, and in 1937 the coachbuilder opened a new factory in the Zuffenhausen suburb of Stuttgart to build the all-metal bodies for the new Wanderer W24 model. Production rate was as high as 33 bodies a day, and the plant employed 900 workers. Reutter also became involved with Ferdinand Porsche in the Volkswagen project from 1935, and was responsible for the first Volkswagen 30 prototypes and for the VW 38 series cars in 1938.

Nevertheless, Reutter did not confine itself to German-built chassis, and in the inter-war years it also built on chassis that included Ansaldo, Austro-Daimler, Bugatti, Buick, Cadillac, Chrysler, Fiat and La Salle. It also exported widely, one notable contract being for armoured cars delivered to the Chinese government.

After the war, Reutter's main source of business was the new Porsche company. The coachbuilder constructed more than 60,000 coupé and cabriolet bodies for the 356 range between 1950 and 1963. Nevertheless, there were forays into other areas as well. In 1949-1951, for example, Reutter built the prototype and pre-production bodies for the BMW 501, and in 1960 produced a small number of four-door cabriolet conversions on the Citroën DS19 for the marque's German importer.

Reutter built its last bodies in 1963, selling the Zuffenhausen factory to Porsche. The company then moved into the production of seats and seat components at its original Stuttgart premises, changing its trading name to Recaro, a name produced by combining the words Reutter and Carosserie (coachwork). The first Recaro sports seat reached the market in 1965, and the brand has gone from strength to strength ever since, despite several changes of ownership.

Rhéda (F)
Early 1900s–mid-1920s, Levallois-Perret and, later, Ivry
The Rhéda coachwork company was active between the early 1900s and the mid-1920s, and a body is known on a 1912 Brasier chassis. However, almost nothing is known of the bodies it built after 1919.

Rheims & Auscher (F)
See Rothschild.

Riegel-Bérioux (F)
1920s, Clermont-Ferrand
This small French coachbuilder existed before the Great War and is known to have bodied some Panhard chassis in the 1920s.

Rieucros (F)
Late 1920s or early 1930s, Cognac
Nothing substantial is known about this French provincial coachbuilder except a body it built on a Citroën AC4 chassis.

Rochat (CH)
1930s, Morges

Very little is known about the Rochat coachworks that was based in the town of Morges on Lake Geneva. The company is known to have built a coupé body on a Hispano-Suiza chassis in 1935.

Rometsch (D)
1924–2000, Berlin

Karosserie Friedrich Rometsch was established in the Halensee district of Berlin in 1924. The company made its name as a builder of taxis, mainly on Opel chassis, but also built some individual bodies to customer order. During the Second World War, Rometsch turned out mobile field kitchens for the German army.

At the end of the war, Rometsch was fortunate to secure as its chief designer Johannes Beeskow, who had been with Erdmann & Rossi in the 1930s. Few chassis were now available for new bodywork, and it was perhaps inevitable that Rometsch should turn to the VW Beetle. Its first new body arrived in 1949 and was a widely acclaimed two-door drophead coupé for that model; by 1951, some 500 had been built, with several design variations. Rometsch also lengthened the VW Beetle by 30cm (11.8in) to produce a four-door taxi variant, and Beeskow designed some very attractive coupé and cabriolet bodies for the Volkswagen as well. Their curvaceous shape earned these models the nickname of the Rometsch Banana.

All these Volkswagen bodies were hand-built, using a steel frame with wooden pillars covered by lightweight aluminum panels. In the first half of the 1950s, Rometsch added other car makers to its list of clients, building some 200-250 bodies in small series of coupés and some cabriolets for Borgward, Fiat and Goliath. However, the VW Beetle remained a staple product, and in 1957 the company updated its coupé and cabriolet designs to

Rometsch: This is a late example of the Beeskow-designed Volkswagen coupé, dating from 1956. (*WikiMedia Commons/Palauenc05*)

Rometsch: The later Lawrence-designed bodies on VW chassis were often finished in two-tone paint. This is a 1959 example. (*WikiMedia Commons/ Stahlkocher*)

Rometsch: East German leader Erich Honecker had the firm turn a number of Range Rovers into extended-wheelbase hunting vehicles. *(Stefan Thiele)*

reflect contemporary American trends. The new models were designed by Bert Lawrence, Beeskow having left to join Karmann in 1956, and their production continued until 1961, although only around 85 were made. Panoramic windscreens and two-tone colour schemes reflected the fashion of the time, and the car's striking lines earned it the Golden Rose coachwork award at the Geneva Show in 1957. There were also a few Fiat coupés in this period.

Problems arose after the erection of the Berlin Wall in 1961, which separated many of the company's employees from their place of work. So the coachworks effectively closed its doors in 1962 and became a body repair shop, specialising in taxi repairs. Nevertheless, in the 1980s it did create a series of at least three extended Range Rover hunting vehicles for East German leader Erich Honecker, beginning probably in 1984. Its subsequent focus was on manufacturing ambulances and bus bodywork, and on carrying out accident repair work. The company finally closed down in 2000.

Ronny (B)

Ronny Coach Building Company was a trading name of L'Etoile (qv).

Roos (NL)

1927–1955, The Hague

Christianus Albertus Roos set up in the commercial bodywork business in 1927, initially calling his company the 's-Gravenhaagsche Fabriek van Carrosseriebewerking (the 's-Gravenhaag Coachworks). His major activity was the construction of vans and trailers, but the company – later known by the snappier name of Carrosseriefabriek Chris A Roos – also turned its hand to the occasional car body.

The earlier of the two known examples was built in 1948 on a Bentley Mk VI chassis for HRH Prince Bernhard, and was a four-seat drophead coupé to the prince's own design.

This earned the Roos coachworks the title of Hofleverancier – supplier to the Royal Family. The later car was a drophead coupé built in 1949 on an Alfa Romeo 6C-2500 chassis that had apparently been imported to Holland in 1943. There was also a further commission for the Dutch Royal Family, when the Roos coachworks converted a 1947 Daimler DE36 saloon into a landaulet.

Rosenberger (CH)

1920s, Biel

Very little is known about the business of F Rosenberger in Biel. The company had a stand at the Geneva Show in 1928 and is known to have built the saloon body on a Delage DIS chassis some time in the mid-1920s.

Rothschild (Rheims & Auscher successeurs) (F)

1894–1930, Levallois-Perret

Joseph Rothschild was an Austrian who set up his carriage works at Levallois-Perret near Paris in 1838. Some years later, he took on two engineering graduates called Edmond Rheims and Léon Auscher, and by 1896 had passed the business on to them. They retained the original name, and the company's full title became J Rothschild & Fils, Rheims & Auscher Successeurs. Note that there may have been two separate coachbuilders called Rothschild operating in Paris in the early years of the 20th century, the other being associated with the Clement Rothschild car. Neither seems to have had any links with the Rothschild banking family, although the association of the name cannot have done them any harm.

The business was soon breaking new ground in the use of sheet metal for coachwork, and from 1896 was using aluminium for competition vehicles such as Camille Jenatzy's cigar-shaped 1899 La Jamais Contente record-breaker. The innovative side of the company shone through again at the 1908 Paris Salon, when Rothschild showed a Mercedes chassis wearing a "racing phaeton" body that had all the essentials of the skiff or torpedo style which would later become popular and whose origins are still hotly disputed.

Generally, however, Rothschild bodies were elegant and formal, and appealed to a conservative clientele who mostly ordered them on quality chassis such as Delaunay-Belleville and Rolls-Royce. The company quickly became one of the most prestigious French coachbuilders, and from 1906 set up a branch in Turin as well. This Italian branch was later acquired by Fiat, who turned it into their coachwork division.

During the 1920s, Rothschild held a licence to build Baehr bodywork, but towards the end of that decade the company began to suffer from a downturn in business and did not survive beyond 1930.

Rousset (F)

1920–c1931, Lyons

Founded in September 1920 as Rousset Frères, this coachbuilder became A Rousset & Cie two years later. Its geographical proximity to the Rochet-Schneider works at Lyons ensured that many of its bodies would be on chassis by that maker. Rochet-Schneider ceased building car chassis in 1931, and it appears that the Rousset coachbuilding firm closed down at about the same time.

Roze (F)
1920s, Neuilly-sur-Seine
André Roze is known to have been in the coachwork business during the 1920s, and among his creations were an open body for a Ballot 2-litre and a saloon body for a 1925 Sizaire Frères chassis.

Rozier (F)
Lyons, 1930–1960s
In 1930, Jean Rozier revived the Piot & Barbary coachworks business that had closed down in 1923. In its early years, Rozier focused on coachwork repairs, but also built a number of its own luxury bodies. By the 1960s, the company was specializing in caravans.

Ruckstuhl (CH)
c1925–1938, Lucerne
The Albert Ruckstuhl coachworks is known for building balloon hardtops for open tourers in the 1920s, and for constructing cabriolet and limousine bodies on a variety of chassis.

Among the company's creations were a pair of four-door saloons on the Bugatti Type 49 chassis in 1932 and a cabriolet on a Triumph Gloria chassis in 1937. Ruckstuhl was renamed Carrosserie-Werke AG and appears not to have built any complete bodies after that.

Rudy (D)
1945–1976, Delmenhorst
The Rudy coachworks was best known for its involvement with some of the small cars that were popular in Germany during the 1940s and 1950s. Founder Johannes Rudy had worked for the Rembrandt coachworks and for Borgward and Horch before the 1939-1945 war.

Rudy founded his own business at Delmenhorst in 1945, and early on built some special bodies for the Borgward group, including the aluminium body for the three-wheeler Goliath that took 19 world records at Montlhéry in 1951. There were Rudy bodies for two of the 50 Goliath sports coupés with injected engines, but Borgward had the rest built by Rometsch in Berlin. By way of compensation, the Rudy works was given the contract for various body elements for Lloyd and for the three-wheel Goliath truck.

Meanwhile, Rudy also built the bodies for the unsuccessful single-cylinder Pinguin three-wheeler from 1954, various body elements for the Heinkel bubble-cars in the mid-1950s, and also built a one-off Lloyd Arabella coupé for Borgward. In later years, the company moved into aerospace work, and was finally sold in 1976.

Rungette (F)
c1910–c1930, Levallois-Perret
Jules-Victor Rungette opened his coachworks in Levallois-Perret some time before the Great War. Little is known about the company except that it held a licence for the Baehr patents in the early 1920s and was still active at the time of the Paris Salon in 1930.

Rupflin (D)
1909–1969, Munich
The Rupflin business was founded in 1906 by Eugen Rupflin, initially as a wheelwright. However, in 1909 Eugen handed over control to his son, also Eugen, who had worked at Opel, learned the carriage-building trade in Hamburg and had also spent time with coachbuilder Neuss in Berlin. Some sources claim that another wagon-building business was taken over at the same time. The Rupflin company probably spent most of the period between then and the Great War focussing on repair work.

During the 1920s, the business was renamed Karosserie-Fabrik Eugen Rupflin jr. The inter-war period saw Rupflin building many commercial bodies, especially for the Reichspost (German post office) and the police. However, there were also many individual commissions for passenger car bodywork. The company had 35-40 staff by the end of the 1930s.

Rupflin specialised in lightweight aluminium construction, and made most of the fairings for BMW's racing and record-breaking motor cycles. In 1938, it built some early bodies for the Mercedes-Benz G5 four-wheel-drive models, and was noted for a streamlined bus body on Büssing chassis. In 1939 it constructed the streamlined bodies for the three Type 64 Volkswagen record-breakers (although their construction has also been attributed to Reutter).

After the 1939-1945 war, Rupflin continued to build commercial bodies, but its best years were past. It also made small body elements for BMW and for MAN buses. In 1961, Rolf Rupflin took over the business from his father, but soon fell ill and died. A planned takeover by the coachbuilder Leonhard Dreier in Munich fell through, and Eugen Rupflin finally closed the business in 1969.

Rupflin: Three special record cars based on Volkswagen components were built in 1939. Their streamlined aluminium bodies were made by Rupflin… although some sources claim they were made by Reutter. (WikiMedia Commons/MPW57)

S

Saliot (F)
1920s–1930s, Levallois-Perret

Very little indeed is known about the coachworks owned by Francois Saliot. In the 1920s, it was one of the many licence-holders for the Baehr patents, and in 1935 it constructed a stunningly attractive cabriolet on a Voisin C28 chassis. A second cabriolet body, on a modified Voisin chassis of unidentified type dating from 1933-1934, is also attributed to Saliot.

Santschi (CH)
c1924–1928, Berne

The coachworks owned by J Santschi constructed a pair of touring bodies on Alfa Romeo and Salmson chassis in the mid-1920s, and a saloon on a Bugatti. Production was carried out in collaboration with the Fehler coachworks in Berne, but nothing more is known about the company itself.

Sanwald (CH)
c1910–c1927, St Gallen

Research has so far produced very little information about the Sanwald coachworks that existed in St Gallen. The company probably built its first car bodywork around 1910, and from 1919 became a member of the Swiss Coachbuilders' Guild (VSCI). Bodies are known on Fiat and Renault chassis, and on Laurin & Klement and Steyr. They ranged from closed coupé and sport-torpedo types to grander limousines. From the early 1920s, Sanwald advertisements also claimed that the company could build commercial bodywork, and there was certainly at least one tour bus on a Saurer chassis. The company ceased to be a member of the VSCI in 1927, although whether that coincided with its closure is simply not known.

Saoutchik (F)
1906–1955, Paris

Saoutchik was one of France's most important coachbuilders in the mid-20th century, known for its high quality and above all for its flamboyant designs which made great but tasteful use of ornamentation. Jacques Saoutchik was a Russian (or possibly Ukrainian) expatriate, born Iakov Saoutchik, who had emigrated to France with his family at the end of the 19th century. A cabinet maker by trade, he quickly moved into coachbuilding, gaining experience with a number of existing companies before founding his own coachworks in Neuilly-sur-Seine, an industrial suburb of Paris, in 1906.

Saoutchik's ambition was always to cater only for top-class chassis, and his first body was on an Isotta-Fraschini. Within a few years, attractive designs, meticulous craftsmanship and high quality had established his reputation, and he was working on makes such as Delaunay-Belleville, Mercedes, and Rolls-Royce.

The Great War saw the Saoutchik company building ambulances, ammunition trailers, and the like, but by the early 1920s it was ranked as one of the top Parisian coachbuilders. Transformable bodies had been part of the company's repertoire before the Great War, and during the 1920s these became a Saoutchik speciality; a particular feature was that the Saoutchik convertible top could be managed by one person. From 1922 another speciality was a torpedo design that could be transformed into a saloon with a fixed roof.

Saoutchik: Unmistakably grand and luxurious, this was a Mercedes-Benz 630 chassis of the late 1920s with the Kompressor (supercharged) engine. The shapes of the doors, the door handles and the trunk are all typical Saoutchik features. *(Daimler-Benz)*

The company also specialised in convertibles and town cars, gaining multiple commissions from royal families outside France. At home, Saoutchik designs represented the essence of Parisian chic. The company established a distinctive modernistic style; it featured brightwork to highlight the key lines of the designs, creative use of colour, and beautifully finished interiors which often contained marquetry work and exotic upholstery materials as well as exuberant designs. Chassis clothed by Saoutchik in this period included Bentley, Bucciali, Bugatti, Cadillac, Delage, Hispano-Suiza, Isotta-Fraschini, Maybach and Rolls-Royce. By the end of the 1920s, Saoutchik had become one of the French coachbuilders favoured by Mercedes-Benz, and the company constructed several transformable bodies on the Model K chassis and some spectacular cabriolets on the S and SS types at the turn of the decade.

Saoutchik survived the Depression, and retained its leading position among French coachbuilders throughout

Saoutchik: The eye-catching nature of that body on Mercedes-Benz 630 chassis was reflected in the interior treatment as well. *(Daimler-Benz)*

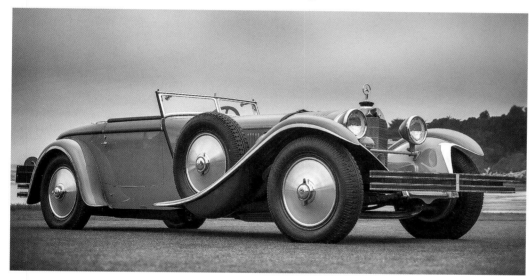

Saoutchik: Careful use of colour sets off the bodywork on this 1928 Mercedes-Benz S, ordered new by a customer in New York. *(Author's Collection)*

Saoutchik: On Mercedes-Benz chassis again, this time a supercharged Model K, this elegant torpedo cabriolet has body mouldings, bumpers and other details typical of Saoutchik creations. *(Daimler-Benz)*

Saoutchik: André Dubonnet modified a Hispano-Suiza H6C chassis to show off his new suspension design in 1938, and had its body designed by Saoutchik. The car is sometimes called the Dubonnet Xenia coupé. *(Concours of Elegance)*

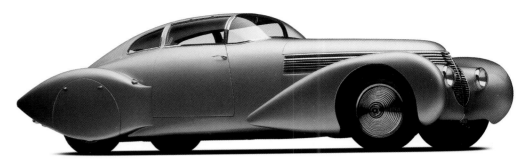

Saoutchik: Unusually restrained, this pillarless two-door body was built on a Delage chassis in the late 1940s. Only the chrome highlights give a hint of its origins. *(David Hodges Collection)*

Saoutchik constructed several bodies for Delahaye chassis in the late 1940s. Though less flamboyant than earlier creations, they were no less distinctive among the austere products of the day. *(David Hodges Collection)*

Saoutchik: Nevertheless, the flamboyance had by no means disappeared. This is a faithful recreation of the original body on a 1949 Talbot-Lago T26 chassis. *(RM Sothebys)*

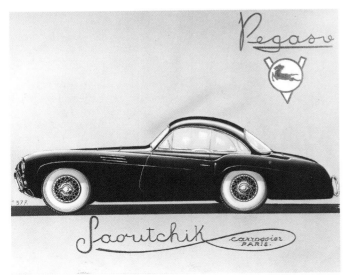

the following decade. Its designs regularly won awards at the fashionable concours d'élégance held in Paris and on the Riviera in the period, but Saoutchik was never a devotee of streamlining, preferring a combination of conservatism with sometimes exuberant ornamentation.

As before, the company preferred to work only on the top-quality chassis of the day. Another novelty arrived in 1939 with parallel opening doors on pantograph linkages, based on a design patented by James Young in Britain. Some were done for cabriolets, including a Delage D8-120 for the 1939 Paris Salon and a number on the Renault Suprastella chassis.

Saoutchik: A small number of bodies for Pegaso Z-102 chassis helped keep Saoutchik alive in 1953-1954, but there was no scope for the company's traditional flamboyance in the coupé design, shown here, with slight variations, as an illustration and in the flesh. *(David Hodges Collection)*

After the 1939-1945 war, Saoutchik suffered like its contemporaries from a decline in the number of commissions. Influence of US designs became apparent, as generous shapes and Saoutchik's traditional use of chrome ornamentation combined; some commentators have argued that these designs bordered on the excessive, and were symbolic of the decline of French coachbuilding in the post-war period. Saoutchik continued to work only with top-quality chassis, which included Cadillac, Daimler, Delahaye and Talbot Lago. The company specialised in building vehicles for heads of state both at home and abroad, and in 1951 a Saoutchik saloon on a Talbot-Lago Record T26 chassis became the world's most expensive car ever made.

Times were certainly changing: in 1952, Jacques Saoutchik handed over control of the company to his son Pierre. The elegance and flamboyance remained undimmed, and Saoutchik took on exclusive rights to import Pegaso cars into France, building a small series of coupé and cabriolet bodies for the company's Z-102 chassis in 1953-1954. However, it was clear that the market had changed and that Saoutchik could not survive on its traditional business. The company closed down in 1955.

Savary (F)

c1912–c1955, Paris, later Aubervillers

Robert Savary bought the body building business that had been founded in 1871 by a widow named Peters, and most of the bodies the new company built were commercial types. However, it also built some lightweight passenger car bodies, notably on the Harris Léon-Laisne chassis for which it had become a distributor.

The company moved to Aubervillers in 1931, and in 1933 exhibited a two-door saloon at the Paris Salon. It remained in business until 1955.

Savio (I)

1919–present, Turin and Moncalieri

The brothers Antonio and Giuseppe Savio served their apprenticeship at the Alessio coachworks in Turin which was responsible for many early bodies on Fiat chassis. In April 1919, they established their own business as Carrozzeria Savio, and were given a helping hand by their former employer who passed on to them a major contract to build 900 bodies for Itala. The Itala contract gained them attention, and other work followed; an example was a silentbloc saloon on an early Ceirano chassis.

The brothers went on to build on many Italian makes, including Ansaldo, Chiribiri, Fiat, Isotta-Fraschini, Lancia and OM. The relationship with Fiat blossomed, and the 1930s saw Savio building bodies for the Fiat 508 and 1100 models.

During the 1939-1945 war, the company began building ambulance bodies. Their Turin workshop was severely damaged and Antonio, discouraged, left the business. Giuseppe carried on, changing the company name to Stabilimento Savio Giuseppe – Carrozzeria Automobili.

Savio: This 1956 body for the Fiat 1100 offered a neat combination of open-air motoring and body rigidity. *(Author's Collection)*

Savio: This neat coupé body for the Fiat 124 had little affinity with the square-rigged parent saloon of the late 1960s and early 1970s. *(Author's Collection)*

Savio: The 1965 Jungla was based on a Fiat 600 and was built in quantity. *(Author's Collection)*

When Giuseppe died in 1954, his son Alfredo Caracciolo took over the business.

Ambulance bodies were still on the agenda when the company moved to new premises in Moncalieri during 1959. The relationship with Fiat remained strong, and there were Savio coupés on the Fiat 1500 in 1961 and 1963, and in 1963 bodies for the 2300 and the 1600S. In 1965 the company introduced its Fiat 600 Savio Jungla, an open leisure car of which 3200 were eventually built. In the later 1960s, Savio built a coupé and a station wagon-cum-coupé on the Fiat 125. Their long-term relationship with Fiat paid off again when the company asked them to build its Campagnola light 4x4 vehicle, and they also developed a coupé in conjunction with the OTAS car company on the Fiat 124.

The 1960s saw Savio building bus bodies in quantity alongside their car and ambulance work, and this gradually came to dominate the business. Car bodies have nevertheless continued to figure in Savio's repertoire from time to time.

In the mid-1980s, the company built the bodies for the Lancia Delta S4 rally car, and from 1987 constructed the Fiat Freely, a Jungla-like model based on the Fiat Panda.

In 1995, Savio took over Boneschi through its holding company Omnia Spa, and the Savio Group was formed; this was subsequently sold to Germantex Srl. Today, Savio's main business is bodywork for trucks and buses, medical care and commercial vehicles – but it also undertakes prototype build for car companies as required.

Sbarro (F)

1968–present, Yverdon, later Pontarlier, later Montbéliard

Sbarro today is a builder of high-performance and replica sports cars, but in the 1980s it was best known for its extravagant – some would say outrageous – conversions of high-quality cars for predominantly Middle Eastern clients. Many of these were based on Mercedes-Benz models. The company has also built a series of exuberant prototypes over the years, a notable example being the spectacular Challenge prototype of 1985, done with the aid of Camille Diebold.

Franco Sbarro himself was an Italian who moved to Switzerland as a teenager. Between 1963 and 1967 he was chief mechanic of Swiss racing team Scuderia Filipinetti, but in April 1968 he set up his own workshop to build cars near Yverdon in France. The current company was established in 1971 and, despite its French base, is often considered to be Swiss.

The legendary Sbarro Mercedes-Benz conversions began in 1983 with the Sbarro Shahin 1000, based on a 500SEC coupé and exhibited at that year's Geneva Show. This was followed at Geneva in 1984 by another gullwing-door car, this time based on a 500SE saloon and made largely from GRP. The car was known as the Sbarro Al-Ajda BiTurbo. Another notable Sbarro conversion was shown at Geneva in

Sbarro: The company favoured an extreme wedge shape for the 1985 Challenge. *(David Hodges Collection)*

Sbarro: Franco Sbarro liked nothing better than to shock, and this one-off conversion of a Rolls-Royce Camargue certainly achieved that end. *(Unknown copyright)*

Sbarro: There were just six examples of the Shahin gullwing coupé, based on a Mercedes-Benz 500SEC. This was the first, built in 1983. *(Author's Collection)*

Sbarro: The shape of the 1978 Sbarro Stash was typically extravagant. *(David Hodges Collection)*

1986, this time based on a 500SEL and featuring four gullwing doors; the car was called the Sbarro Berlina Gullwing 4, was built for the Sultan of Brunei and remained unique.

In the 1990s, Sbarro opened two design colleges, one in 1994 called Crea and located in Casablanca, and the other in 1996 called Espera Sbarro and located in the French town of Pontarlier. In 2006, the Pontarlier school moved to Montbéliard under the leadership of Denis Suau. Retaining his links with the Geneva Show, Sbarro continued to use it to showcase his latest concepts, many of them created with the aid of his students at the Espera training centre.

Scaglietti (I)
1951–1977, Maranello

Carrozzeria Scaglietti became Ferrari's favoured maker of racing bodywork during the 1950s, and the company designed and manufactured the bodies for many sports and racing prototypes. Scaglietti's ability to produce lightweight bodywork also persuaded Ferrari to have it build designs for other coachbuilders. Bodies produced in this way did not carry the Scaglietti badge, but those built to their own designs did.

Sergio Scaglietti had founded his company as a repair shop at Maranello in 1951, together with his brother and a former colleague. The business was across the road from the Ferrari works, and it was not long before links developed between the two companies. Enzo Ferrari came to respect Scaglietti's design and coachwork skills, and his son Dino Ferrari often visited the Scaglietti works in his youth.

Scaglietti is said to have worked entirely by eye, building his bodies directly onto their chassis without creating drawings first. He is credited with the streamlined "headrest" fairing that became characteristic of most racing Ferraris in the 1950s and 1960s; although Enzo Ferrari initially disliked it, he was eventually won over when his son Dino championed it. One of the most famous Scaglietti designs is the 1958 250 Testa Rossa model, with its pontoon wings inspired by Formula 1 practice. Ferrari also had Scaglietti build the bodies for a number of roadgoing cars,

Scaglietti: Although the design was by Pinin Farina, it was Scaglietti who built the bodywork for the elegant Ferrari 250GT "Tour de France" models, of which this is a 1957 example. *(David Hodges Collection)*

notably the Pinin Farina-designed 250 GT Tour de France (1955) and the 250 California Spider (1957).

The close relationship with Ferrari worked to Scaglietti's advantage. When he wanted to expand his business in the late 1950s, Enzo Ferrari found him a bank prepared to make the loan and even co-signed the agreement. Yet the arrangement did not prevent Scaglietti from building a number of bespoke bodies for individual clients on Ferrari chassis, or from creating a special coupé on a Chevrolet Corvette in 1958.

At the end of the 1960s, Scaglietti sold his coachworks to Fiat, although he continued to manage the company until he retired in the mid-1980s. Scaglietti-built Ferraris from this later period included the Dino 246 GT, the 365 GTB/4 "Daytona" (designed by Pininfarina) and the 308 GT4 (designed by Bertone).

The Scaglietti company became Ferrari property in 1977, but the name has not been forgotten. The former Scaglietti premises have been used to build the aluminium-bodied F430 and the 612 Scaglietti Coupé of 2004, the latter actually designed by Pininfarina. A special version of the 456, the 456M GT Scaglietti, was also named in the company's honour.

Scaglietti: The lightweight construction for which the company was renowned earned many commissions for sports-racing cars, like this Ferrari 250GT SWB. *(David Hodges Collection)*

SCAR (D)
1980s, Hamburg(?)
When the Hamburg Styling-Garage coachworks went bankrupt in 1986, an unfinished SGS Arrow C1 Gullwing was purchased by the SCAR company, also known as Michael Hoffberger Styling Car. The car remained unfinished in the late 1980s and it seems likely that SCAR never did complete it, or undertake any other coachwork projects.

Schebera (D)
1911–1926, Berlin
Ernst Schebera founded Carrosserie Schebera GmbH in 1911 in the Tempelhof district of Berlin. From early on, the company gained favour with some of the leading chassis manufacturers, and was able to create high-quality coachwork on expensive chassis such as Rolls-Royce. By the time of the First World War, Schebera had established a sound reputation, and this attracted contracts to build staff cars and ambulances for the German army.

From December 1919, the company was led by the wealthy businessman Jakob Schapiro, who was a shareholder in several major chassis manufacturers, such as Benz, Dixi, Hansa-Lloyd, and NSU. In 1921, Schebera took over the Heilbronner Fahrzeug-Fabrik, which had run into difficulties, and the companies were merged as the Süddeutsche Karosseriewerke Schebera Heilbronn AG. There were bodies for Model T Ford chassis and also on Dixi chassis, the latter including taxi-cabs.

From 1922, the Berlin branch began to build bodies for local chassis maker Cyklon, another company in which Schapiro had an interest. However, business was slow, and some 1000 cars were sold directly to Schapiro's Berlin taxi business, Kandelhardt AG. The Heilbronn branch meanwhile continued to build for Benz. In November 1926, Schapiro arranged for NSU to take over the Schebera coachworks in Berlin, and later the Heilbronn business as well. Schebera ceased to exist as a separate company at this point.

Problems set in during 1928, when NSU failed to take a planned order for 500 bodies. Drastic staff reductions followed, and the 120 staff employed by the coachworks at the start of 1929 had fallen to 25 just five months later.

Schebera: A 1922 advertisement offering luxury and sports bodies for cars as well as bodies for buses and lorries. *(Immo Mikloweit)*

Matters came to a head in 1930, when the Schapiro group of companies was broken up. The Heilbronn coachworks was taken over by Drauz (qv) that year.

Scheiwiller (CH)
1930s, Zurich
Scheiwiller AG has been a body repair shop since it was founded in 1928 by Josef Scheiwiller, but has also been involved with bodywork modifications and in 1939 built a new roadster body for a 1933 Alfa Romeo 8C 2300. This was known as the "saxophone" after the shape of the bonnet side vents, which resemble the valves on the instrument.

The company's work on bodywork modifications in the 1930s focussed on such things as adding external luggage trunks to cars which had none. Legend has it that Scheiwiller also modified a Packard ambulance for the local hospital when the body was found to be too small. The company remains a body shop today and is owned by the third generation of the Scheiwiller family.

Schlechte (D)
1920s, Altona
Little is known about the coachworks owned by L Schlechte in Altona, although some sources suggest it existed between 1873 and 1949. The company was certainly active as a builder of car bodies in the 1920s, and among others built on a Brennabor chassis in 1922.

Schulz-Tuning (D)
1968 to present, Leonberg, later Hildesheim,
Schulz-Tuning is best known for its custom bodywork built during the 1980s boom, most commonly on the basis of Mercedes-Benz or BMW models.

Eberhard Schulz began his career by thinking big, and in 1968 he designed a replica of the Ford GT40 that was powered by a Mercedes-Benz V8 engine and was known as the Isdera Erator. He was next taken on by Mercedes themselves and given the job of designing a successor to the Wankel-engined C111 experimental car. Schulz's design became the CW311 in 1978, but Mercedes decided not to take the project any further. Nevertheless, they allowed Schulz to retain the rights to his CW311 design, and by 1984 he had turned it into the Mercedes-powered Isdera Imperator.

Meanwhile, the great customising boom had begun, and Schulz turned his hand to this. His conversions were predominantly on Mercedes models, and included both stretched limousines and cabriolets, with ornamentation and equipment to suit the customer's taste. Schulz was also responsible for a shortened Mercedes 190, called the Compakt, and for an estate conversion of the mid-range BMW 5 Series saloon. There was also a cabriolet conversion of the BMW 635 coupé, using a design by the Piet Oldenhof company in the Netherlands.

Since those days, Schulz has focused on building highly individual supercars, retaining the Isdera name and working out of premises in Hildesheim.

Schulz-Tuning: The six-door treatment was available for the 124-series estates as well, again under the name of Pullman. *(Author's Collection)*

Schulz-Tuning: Much more practical was this neat estate conversion of the BMW E28 5 Series in the 1980s. *(Author's Collection)*

Schulz-Tuning: This cabriolet conversion of the Mercedes-Benz 190 range was a particularly neat piece of work. Schulz gave it additional appeal by replacing the original engine with a Mercedes-Benz V8. *(Author's Collection)*

Schutter & Van Bakel (NL)
1829–1954, Amsterdam

Schutter & van Bakel took on that name in 1873, although the company could trace its origins as a wagon and saddle maker back as far as 1829. After Hendrik Schutter's death in 1876, the Van Bakel family took over the business, retaining its earlier name.

Willem Johannes van Bakel produced his first car body in 1901. Schutter & Van Bakel worked mainly to individual commissions, but also built a few small-run series. On the death of Willem Van Bakel in 1908, his sons Jan and Jacob took over the business; Jacob had been apprenticed to the

Van den Plas works in Brussels, had been trained in design in Paris, and had also worked as a junior designer with Saoutchik in France.

The 1920s were Schutter & Van Bakel's best years, and the company built up a reputation for elegant luxury bodies, also winning awards regularly at concours d'élégance events in the Netherlands. Jacob's practice was to invite his customers to visit the annual Paris Salon with him, where they would select their chassis of choice. It appears that he would always order the chassis in batches of six, and that his favourites were Lancia, Lincoln and Renault types. However, these were by no means the only ones bodied by Schutter & Van Bakel. The 1920s also saw bodywork on chassis by Ballot, Bentley, Bugatti, Cadillac, Hispano Suiza, Packard, Rolls-Royce and Voisin. At the Amsterdam Motor Show in 1929, the most expensive vehicle on display was 6½-litre Bentley with a limousine body by Schutter & Van Bakel.

However, the recession which followed the Wall Street Crash later that year led to several orders being cancelled. Despite a contract to build a run of 35 convertibles on Ford chassis for that company's Amsterdam dealer, Schutter & Van Bakel entered on a period of decline. By 1938, the company employed no more than six people.

After the 1939-1945 war, demand for special coachwork was very limited indeed, so the company kept going with repair and maintenance work. However, when one of Jacob Van Bakel's two sons died in 1953, it provoked a decision, and a year later the family closed down its business.

Schweizerische Wagonfabrik (CH)
1920s, Schlieren

The Schweizerische Wagons- und Aufzügefabrik AG, also known as SWS, was formed in 1895 as a subsidiary of the Geissberger *(qv)* coachworks to build railway rolling stock. This company is also thought to have built some passenger car bodywork in the 1920s, but nothing is known about them.

SEBS (F)
1920s, Paris

The initials SEBS stood for the Société d'exploitation des brevets Seurin (Company using the Seurin patents). It exhibited a sports saloon with low lines on a Peugeot chassis at the 1922 Paris Salon, but is not otherwise known.

SECA-CD (later SERA-CD) (F)
1962–2007, Fresnes

After parting company with René Bonnet and the DB (Deutsch-Bonnet) concern, Charles Deutsch set up SECA-CD (Société d'études et de constructions automobiles, or Car Design and Construction Company; the CD were Deutsch's initials). When Robert Choulet became technical director in the mid-1960s, the name changed to SERA-CD, which stood for Société d'études et de réalisation automobiles, a title that meant more or less the same as the earlier company name.

In its early years, this company designed a number of aerodynamic bodies for the Le Mans 24 Hours events, using Panhard, Peugeot or DKW running-gear. Matra then commissioned SERA for its 1969 24 Hours contender, the 640 model. During the 1970s, SERA became involved in aerodynamic studies for Porsche, Alfa Romeo and Ligier, and worked with Lola in 1980. SERA-CD was eventually sold to the Sogeclair Group in 2007 and now works to a much wider design brief.

Sécheron (CH)
1936–1963, Geneva
Former Gangloff employees Robert Grau and Edouard Fischer formed Carrosserie de Sécheron in 1936 when the Gangloff business went bankrupt. The company took over the old Gangloff premises in Geneva.

Sécheron is best known for some cabriolets built on Delahaye chassis in the late 1940s, but also worked on other chassis including Armstrong-Siddeley. In 1954, the company pioneered GRP bodywork in Switzerland with its sports coupé design for the unsuccessful Agea de Toledo. Sécheron finally closed in 1963.

Seitz (CH)
c1905–c1930, Emmishofen
Baptist Seitz set up on his own as a wagon builder at Frauenfeld as early as 1850, but business became tougher with the coming of the railways and he returned to his native Emmishofen where he set up another business building horse-drawn vehicles. Around 1905, the Seitz business was passed on by Baptist to his sons and began building car bodywork.

Seitz was most active in the period after 1918, joining the Swiss Coachbuilders' Guild in 1924. For the rest of the 1920s, the company built mainly touring and town bodies, many of them on chassis of German origin although there were also examples on Nash and Studebaker. Bus bodywork was also added the Seitz repertoire in this period, and there were examples for both Swiss and German customers on a variety of chassis.

From 1929, a third generation of the Seitz family took over the business, and from this point onwards all its bodywork seems to have been for buses and coaches. The company had already expanded to open a second branch at Konstanz, and was employing around 150 people. There was work on electric vehicles during the Second World War years, but from 1948 Seitz & Ruf (commercial vehicle engineer Walter Ruf had now joined) was absorbed into the Mowag specialist vehicle business.

Serra (E)
1951–1970s, Barcelona
The Barcelona coachbuilding business of Pedro Serra came to international notice when it became associated with the Pegaso sports car project. Serra built just a handful of bodies for the car, perhaps the most notable being a Spyder in 1956. The company also carried out modifications to some Pegasos that had been bodied by other coachbuilders.

Serra continued to build and modify cars for wealthy clients until the 1970s, and is said to have worked on cars that included Aston Martin DB2, Bentley, Bugatti, Maserati and Rolls-Royce.

Many years later, Thomas "Rocco" Serra of the original family resurrected the family coachbuilding business

Serra: Similar bodywork, with different front end details, was constructed for the Z-103, Pegaso's attempt to improve sales by reducing the cost of its cars. (*David Hodges Collection*)

at Huntingdon Beach, California. In 2014 Serra was offering roadster conversions of the Bentley Continental GT and Rolls-Royce Wraith, and a two-door convertible reconstruction of the Tesla S saloon.

Sibona-Basano (I)
1960s, Turin
The brothers Elio and Emilio Basano set up a small prototype body building works in Turin some time around 1960, and in 1962 they were joined by Pietro Sibona, who had been a panel beater at the Ghia coachworks.

The new company took on the name of Carrozzeria Sibona-Basano, and in 1964 displayed a beach-car conversion of the Fiat 500 called the Decathlon. The car used a moulded plastic body, but nothing further seems to have come of it, and nothing more is known about the Sibona-Basano coachworks.

Sical (F)
1930s, Levallois-Perret,
The Société Industrielle de Carrosserie (Industrial Coachwork Company), or Sical, was established in the early 1930s to provide bodies in volume for French motor manufacturers. In the early years of the decade, the company worked predominantly for Citroën and Delahaye, building special bodies for the former's pre-Traction Avant ranges and producing saloon, faux-cabriolet and limousine bodies for the latter.

There were also some bodies for other companies, such as Chenard & Walcker.

SIG (CH)
1928–1930, Neuhausen
The SIG company was primarily a maker of railway rolling stock, and also built bus bodywork. In 1919 it was responsible for the Fischer cyclecar with its tandem seating arrangement, but this failed to make an impact. Towards the end of the 1920s it began to build car bodies, primarily closed types for the Swiss-built Martini Six chassis, but this business did not last.

Snutsel (B)
1913–1930, Brussels
Active mainly in the 1920s, this coachbuilder is known to have constructed bodywork for Belgian-built chassis by FN and Minerva. It is known to have built torpedo-type bodies and to have constructed a four-door convertible on a Minerva M6.

SPC, later SPCA (F)
c1913–early 1930s, Paris; later Gennevilliers
Just before the Great War, the Société parisienne de carrosserie (Parisian Coachwork Company) took over from the old Bargin & Beckerich company. Its products included saloons and cabriolets that were favoured by doctors and commercial travellers.

After the war, the company became SPCA (Société parisienne de carrosseries pour automobiles, or Parisian Car Coachwork Company) and moved to Gennevilliers. Mostly working on the less expensive chassis, the company was one of many to hold a licence for the Baehr patents. The company soon developed links with Chenard & Walcker and became one of its subsidiaries, with the result that most of the Chenard & Walcker saloons carried SPCA bodies.

It was SPCA who designed the extraordinary "tank" bodies for Chenard & Walcker, first seen at the 1927 Paris Salon. The company also built a number of conventional bodies for Delahaye, but from the early 1930s SPCA dropped out of the car bodywork business and, retaining its existing initials, became the Société parisienne de carrosseries et d'accessoires (Parisian Coachwork and Accessory Company), which built truck cabs.

Spinnewyn (F)
1920s–1930s, Tourcoing
This northern French coachwork business appears not to have been very well known. Nevertheless, it is known to have bodied a Hispano-Suiza H6B chassis in the early 1930s, a Voisin and a Bugatti Type 46.

Splendilux (F)
See Esclassan

Spohn (D)
1920–1957, Ravensburg
Hermann Spohn established his coachwork business in Ravensburg in 1920. Carosseriebau Hermann Spohn (note the French spelling of the word) built some of its early bodies on Benz, NAG and Steyr chassis, but the newly-established Maybach company was only 20km away in Friedrichshafen, and the two fledgling companies soon established close links. There were links with the Zeppelin factory in Friedrichshafen as well, and these led to the construction of a streamlined body to a Jaray design on a Ley chassis.

Hermann Spohn died in 1923, but his company remained active, led by Theodor Spohn and Josef Eiwanger, who had been Spohn's business partner from the beginning. The close association with Maybach continued, and the

Spohn: Streamlining became an important element in Spohn's work, as the tail of this Maybach Zepplein DS8 at the 1932 Berlin Show shows. (*Author's Collection*)

Spohn: The Veritas Nurburgring model of 1951-1952 was a sports cabriolet with lines fairly typical of the era. There was a coupé version, too, also built by Spohn. *(WikiMedia Commons/Stahlkocher)*

Spohn: Some early 1950s designs were a little awkward, but this 1952 Veritas Meteor K3 coupé was neatly resolved. *(David Hodges Collection)*

focus of each company on bespoke commissions and hand construction led to some highly individual creations. Although the majority of Maybach chassis in this period had bodywork by Spohn, the coachbuilder also worked on other chassis, and there were bodies for other great marques such as Cadillac and Hispano-Suiza. The Spohn name was always associated with high quality work and, from 1935, streamlined cars to Jaray designs also gave the company an avant-garde image.

In the difficult period of the later 1940s, Spohn managed to secure a contract to build most of the bodies for the Veritas sports cars, although that work came to an end

when Veritas closed in 1953. There were also a few special bodies on the Mercedes-Benz 170 chassis, and in the early 1950s Spohn kept going by re-bodying around two dozen American chassis owned by officers of the US occupation force, following contemporary US design themes apparently willy-nilly to meet the whims of the customers. There were some "Americanised" Veritas rebuilds, too, best described as very much of their time. From 1950, the company was being run by Josef Eiwanger junior, son of Hermann Spohn's original business partner, and it became involved in some design projects that included the Gaylord and the 1955 Cadillac Valkyrie.

As work remained elusive, so the company's workforce shrank, from 130 in September 1949 to 66 in September 1951 and then 55 in August 1956. Eiwanger nevertheless did his best to keep the business afloat, building Germany's first plastic bodywork from a material called Leguval in early 1954, which he fitted to a VW Beetle. No series production followed. Spohn took on other work, making parabolic antennae and large loudspeakers, but the end came in 1957.

Sports Cars (I)
1961–1973. Modena

Piero Drogo was born in Italy but emigrated to Venezuela with his family, and in the 1950s he earned himself a reputation in South America as a racing driver. At the end of the decade, he returned to Italy and became a mechanic at Stanguellini in Modena. He then established Carrozzeria Sports Cars in the city, where he began building sports and racing bodies for the local manufacturers.

Most notably, Carrozzeria Sports Cars bodies were found on Bizzarrini cars and were used by Scuderia Serenissima.

Drogo attracted occasional work from Ferrari as well, and this brought him some fame. His work was seen on the 206 SP, the 330 P4 and the 250 GT SWB "Breadvan". Drogo himself died in a car accident in 1973, and Carrozzeria Sports Cars closed down.

Sprengers (B)
1914–1930, Antwerp

Théo Sprengers was an Antwerp body builder whose main work was with commercial and industrial vehicles. However, his company also built private car bodies to individual commission, and in the 1920s constructed a number on Belgian-made FN and Minerva chassis. There were also bodies for a number of foreign chassis – Cadillac, Elcar, Essex, Hudson and Lincoln from the USA, Hispano-Suiza from Spain, Fiat from Italy, and Talbot from France. Sprengers exhibited at the Brussels Salon, and in 1929 displayed an interesting extendible body with removable roof that changed the car from a two-seater to a four-seater.

Steinmann (CH)
1950s, Buchs

Little is known about the Steinmann company that was active at Buchs in the Aargau region of Switzerland in the early 1950s. The company is known to have rebodied a 1930s six-cylinder Talbot-Lago chassis as a cabriolet some time around 1951, and to have built a two-seat cabriolet body on a Fiat 1100 in 1952.

Stirling Design (F)
1976–1980s, Couéron

Stirling Design was a design agency established by Joel Brétécher in Turin in 1976. A French branch was established two years later.

Among its clients were Arola (who made city runabouts) and Chausson, with whom it worked on the Peugeot 504 African of 1980. Stirling Design was later closed down, to re-emerge as Euro Design.

Stola (I)
c1990–present, Turin

The Stola business has focussed on building prototype and concept cars, of which some have been exhibited under its own name and some have been for major makers such as Mercedes-Benz. The latter have included the F200 Imagination concept of 1996 and the Maybach Exelero of 2005. Stola probably also built the Vision SLA concept of 2000.

Stolle (D)
1928–present, Hanover

The Stolle company was founded in 1928 and focussed on building commercial vehicles and hearses. Many of its hearses were conversions of Mercedes-Benz saloons or estates, and the company also built a single hearse on a BMW 501. In 1998, the two divisions of the company were separated, the hearse business continuing under the leadership of Hermann Stolle.

Styling-Garage (D)
1979–1986, Pinneberg, later Schenefeld

Peter Engel and Chris Hahn founded Styling-Garage in Pinneberg as a repair shop, but Engel soon left the business and from 1981 Hahn steered it in a different direction, to capitalise on the new fashion for heavily modified cars. The business was so successful that by 1984, Styling-Garage had 100 employees and was having to sub-contract much of its work to other local specialist body building companies. Prominent among these was Wille Body KG, a truck and trailer manufacturer in Seevetal.

Styling-Garage: Most SGS conversions were of Mercedes-Benz models. This estate conversion of the 126-series S-Class saloon was less flamboyant than most. (Author's Collection)

Styling-Garage, also known as SGS, made a speciality of modifying Mercedes-Benz and, less commonly, BMW models to meet the often extravagant tastes of Middle Eastern customers, although it also found many customers in the USA and even in Europe. Several hundred were built, and at the wedding of the Crown Price of Abu Dhabi the guests were conveyed in a total of 40 SGS-modified Mercedes saloons.

Core conversions were based on the Mercedes-Benz W126 S-Class saloon and C126 SEC coupé models. Styling-Garage created long-wheelbase saloons and extensively re-worked the interiors; one version was known as the 1000 SEL (supposedly twice as good as the host 500 SEL) but had to be renamed the 1000 SGS after Mercedes objected. There were convertible versions of the SEC (known as the 500 SGS Marbella) and a gullwing-door version (the 500 SGS Gullwing) is said to have sold as many as 57 examples.

By spring 1986, SGS had run into financial difficulties and was declared insolvent. Mercedes had also publicly

Styling-Garage: The SEC coupé's lines lent themselves well to a cabriolet conversion, and SGS exploited the fact. (Author's Collection)

Styling-Garage: Like Sbarro, SGS offered a gullwing conversion of the Mercedes SEC coupé.
(Author's Collection)

distanced itself from Styling-Garage conversions, suggesting that some elements did not meet their standards. A year later, Hahn founded Design+Engineering, which also specialised in conversions and seems occasionally to have built some cars under the SGS name. Design + Engineering closed down in 2005.

Surirey (F)
1950s, Fers
In the early 1950s, the Surirey business produced an estate version of the Ford Vedette with a horizontally split tailgate.

Szawe (D)
1919–1924, Berlin
Karl Szabo and Erich Wechselmann founded their coachworks in the Reinickendorf district of Berlin during 1919, combining elements of their names to brand it as Szawe. From the start, coachwork designs were by Ernst Neumann, who had his own workshop in Berlin and had been experimenting with coachwork styles before joining forces with the other two. His mingling of French and German design trends produced individual bodies that were not always attractive, but Szabo traded on their individuality to suggest exclusivity.

From 1920, the company worked with the Berlin carmaker NAG to build its own model that was marketed under the Szawe name and, emboldened, the company then enlisted the help of engineer Georg Bergmann to design a new six-cylinder car. Engine and chassis were constructed by Heinrich Ehrhardt in Thuringen while bodies came from Szawe's Berlin works, and from 1922 the two companies merged as Ehrhardt-Szawe. However, the car was designed without regard to cost and was not a success, so the company went under in 1924.

T

Taromo (F)
1928

Taromo, about whom nothing substantial is known, built a coupé on Citroën C6 chassis in 1928, drawing inspiration from horse-drawn taxis.

Taubes (F)
1920s, Paris

This Parisian coachbuilder had its workshops at Vincennes. Little is known about its activities except that it advertised both car and commercial bodywork, and also undertook repair work.

Thiétart (F)
1925–1930, La Garenne Colombe

Carrosserie Thiétart is known mainly for some luxuriously appointed faux-cabriolet bodies. There was at least one on a Talbot chassis in 1928, and two are known on Delahaye chassis from 1930. Thiétart also built the roadster body on a Bugatti Type 44 chassis.

Tissier (F)
1970s–1990s, Villeneuve-le-Roi

Pierre Tissier was the Citroën dealer at Villeneuve-le-Roi, and in 1972 he had the idea of converting a DS saloon into a low-loader for transporting cars. With three rear axles on small wheels, the vehicle was a success, and Tissier took orders for more. Several conversions with twin rear axles were built as vans for long-distance delivery of newspapers in bulk.

The Tissier principle was extended to the new Citroën CX from 1975, and there were ambulances and estate cars as well as more vans and low-loaders. In 1981, Tissier announced a 14-seater CX estate with a total length of 6.92 metres (27ft 3in). There was a single low-loader conversion of the Citroën SM coupé, too. In the 1980s, Tissier carried

out similar conversions on the XM, and added a limousine conversion called the Altesse that was stretched by 55cm (21½in) over the standard saloon. The company continued to build these conversions to order into the 1990s.

Tizot et Viguier (F)
1920s, Marseilles

Very little is known about this Marseilles coachbuilder, who built the body on a Turcat-Méry chassis in 1922.

Touring (I)
1926–1967 & 2008-present, Milan

Carrozzeria Touring was one of Italy's most respected coachbuilders in the middle of the 20th century, known for its elegant lightweight bodies and in particular for its patented Superleggera method of construction.

The company was founded on 25 March 1926 from the ashes of Carrozzeria Falco, a Milanese concern owned by Vittorio Ascari, brother of racing driver Alberto Ascari. Falco had specialised in the production of lightweight airframes, but had run into financial trouble. Its buyers were Felice Bianchi Anderloni and Gaetano Ponzoni. Ponzoni was a banker who provided the administrative expertise; Anderloni had been educated as a lawyer but began his career as a test driver for Isotta-Fraschini in Milan, as well as the Italian operations of Peugeot. After rising to become head of the Isotta-Fraschini test department, he decided to use the contacts he had already made throughout the motor industry to help him set up his own business.

The newly renamed Carrozzeria Touring with its workshop at 65 Via Ludovico da Breme was ideally placed close to Alfa Romeo, the Italian Citroën operation, and Isotta Fraschini. These three chassis-makers quickly made use of the services that Touring offered. For the 1927 Flying Star design on Isotta-Fraschini 8B chassis, Touring hired Giuseppe Seregni, and subsequently took him on as

Tissier: The three-axle conversions included estate cars as well as vans and low-loaders. This was a delivery van based on the Citroën CX. (WikiMedia Commons/ Joost J Bakker)

Touring: The superb sporting lines of this Le Mans Spider on an Alfa Romeo 8C-2300 chassis date from 1932. *(David Hodges Collection)*

Touring: Neat lines once again characterise this saloon body on a 1934 Alfa Romeo 2300GT. *(David Hodges Collection)*

Touring: Rear wings are not allowed to intrude on the body width in this coupé on a mid-1930s Alfa Romeo 8C-2900 chassis. Note the folding sunroof as well. *(David Hodges Collection)*

their first full-time professional designer. The elegant and flamboyant Flying Star roadster design with its dipped waistline was also adapted for Alfa Romeo 6C 1750 and Fiat 522C chassis in the early 1930s.

Anderloni focussed on bespoke coachwork which blended sporting elegance and light weight, and to help achieve the latter, he obtained a Weymann licence. However, the well-known weaknesses of fabric construction persuaded Anderloni to seek light weight elsewhere.

Two factors came into play. One was Anderloni's interest in streamlining, and the other was the experience that Carrozzeria Falco had gained in making lightweight airframes – which were still on the agenda under Carrozzeria Touring. Anderloni developed a system of construction which depended on unstressed aluminium panels attached to a rigid framework made from small-diameter chrome-molybdenum steel tubes. Not only was this light in weight, but it also allowed considerable flexibility of shape and was

Touring: A body for the Mille Miglia, on a 1937 Alfa Romeo 6C-2300B Pescara chassis. *(David Hodges Collection)*

Touring: Streamlining is in evidence on this Alfa Romeo 8C-2900B berlinetta from 1938. *(David Hodges Collection)*

Touring: Dating from 1938 is this Alfa Romeo 6C 2500. *(David Hodges Collection)*

Touring: First introduced in 1939, this sporty-looking berlinetta was on an Alfa Romeo 6C-2500 Super Sport chassis. *(David Hodges Collection)*

therefore ideally suited to aerodynamic designs. Touring patented it in 1936 under the name of Superleggera.

With Superleggera construction came lightweight seats with tubular frames, and Plexiglass windows instead of real glass. Touring improved the aerodynamics of their designs by using wind tunnels at the Milan aircraft maker Breda and at the Polytechnic University of Milan; they subsequently built their own rudimentary wind tunnel. Although some Superleggera bodies were built at Touring's

Milan works, the company also licensed the system to allow other companies, especially outside Italy, to build their own bodies. Among those built in Milan were the BMW 328 models for the 1939 Le Mans 24-hour race.

In 1945, Anderloni's son Carlo Felice Bianchi Anderloni (known as Chi Chi) joined the company, taking over his father's role on the latter's death in 1948. New customers in this period included Bristol, for whom Touring did the 401 body from 1948, and Ferrari. The 1950 Ferrari 166

Touring: Aerodynamic testing with the Touring-built body on a 1940 BMW 328 for that year's Mille Miglia. *(David Hodges Collection)*

Touring: The company built the majority of bodies on the Ferrari 166 Inter, the first road-going model from the chassis maker. *(David Hodges Collection)*

Touring: The post-war berlinetta on Alfa Romeo 6C-2500 Super Sport chassis had beautifully flowing lines. *(David Hodges Collection)*

Touring: Lightweight construction was valuable for sports racers, too. The minimalistic barchetta body seen here was on a Ferrari chassis. *(David Hodges Collection)*

Touring: Tasked with designing bodywork for the Pegaso Z-102, Touring branched out with some new ideas. *(David Hodges Collection)*

Touring: Maserati's 3500GT appeared in 1957, and it was Touring who built its closed bodies. *(David Hodges Collection)*

Touring: This delightful spider body for the Alfa-Romeo 2000 dates from 1957. *(David Hodges Collection)*

Touring: The authorship of this 1959 spider on a smaller-engined Alfa Romeo chassis is not hard to determine. *(Barons)*

barchetta by Touring was a landmark design by the younger Anderloni that combined elegance and light weight on a competition chassis. Superleggera bodies graced Alfa Romeo 6C 2500 chassis, notably the Freccia d'Oro in 1947 and the Villa d'Este in 1949. Touring built some bodies for the Spanish maker Pegaso, and there were several niche models on chassis such as the Alfa Romeo 1900. There was a Touring contribution to the design of the 1954 Hudson Italia, too. Strikingly attractive in the later 1950s was the Touring body for the Lancia Flaminia coupé, while some Touring cabriolet bodies on Aston Martin DB2 models in that decade led to a long-term Superleggera licensing contract that covered the DB4, DB5 and DB6 models right through into the early 1970s.

Touring: The firm got the job of producing bodywork once again when Maserati moved to a V8-engined 5000GT in 1959. *(David Hodges Collection)*

Touring also bodied the Maserati 3500GT from 1957 and the 1959 5000GT, and was chosen to build the production design for the new Lamborghini marque in 1963. Other 1960s designs included the 1962 Alfa Romeo 2600 Spider, the Iso Grifo of 1963, and the 1966 Lamborghini 400GT. However, Touring was also looking for a long-term contract, and in 1961 agreed to undertake assembly of cars for the British Rootes Group, including the Sunbeam Alpine and Hillman Super Minx. The company built a large new factory for the purpose in Nova Milanese, a municipality some eight miles north of Milan. There was some Touring influence on mainstream Rootes Group models in the first half of the decade, and from 1963 there was also a small-volume Superleggera-bodied Sunbeam Venezia.

Touring: Only two Lamborghini 350 GTS convertibles were ever built (although Touring later converted a standard coupé to make a third). The car was introduced at the 1965 Turin Show but no production followed. *(David Hodges Collection)*

Touring: The original shape of the Lamborghini 350GT was by Scaglione, but was reworked for production by Touring. This is an early 400GT, essentially the same car with a larger engine. *(David Hodges Collection)*

Touring: The company went through a difficult period in the mid-1960s, and was keen to get a contract to build cabriolet derivatives of the Fiat 124. However, the prototype car, built in 1966, remained unique. *(David Hodges Collection)*

However, this was not a happy period for Touring. By the time its cabriolet derivative of the Alfa Romeo Giulia Sprint GT entered production in 1964, the company was already in financial difficulty. An attractive four-seat cabriolet derivative of the Fiat 124 was shown at Turin in 1966, but was turned down for production. The Rootes Group was meanwhile in trouble as well, and was gradually slipping into the hands of Chrysler, leaving Touring with massive debts on its Nova Milanese assembly plant. So Carrozzeria Touring closed down on 31 December 1966. Many of its staff went to Carrozzeria Marazzi, set up by a former Touring employee, which continued to build bodies for Lamborghini. Anderloni junior, meanwhile, became a consultant to the Alfa Romeo design department, and eventually became its head.

Touring had lasted for 40 years, and 40 years later it was revived again. On 21 April 2006, the exclusive rights for the Touring Superleggera brand were acquired by the Zeta Europe BV group, a Dutch company whose other branches in the Milan area included Carrozzeria Granturismo near Arese and Borrani Wheels in Rozzano. Now using the name of Carrozzeria Touring Superleggera s.r.l., the company remains in Milan and is headed by Dutchman Paul VJ Koot, with Louis de Fabribeckers as Head of Design. Its focus is on design, models, prototypes and limited production of niche vehicles for the automotive industry internationally. Notable designs have included the Bentley Continental GT Flying Star shooting-brake in 2010, which revived a Touring designation from the 1920s and became a low-volume production model.

Trasco (D)
Early 1980s, Bremen
Sachsenring Fahrzeugbau GmbH was a German vehicle armouring specialist that operated under the trading name of Trasco from premises in Bremen. The company was also a dealer in Mercedes-Benz cars and put its name to a number of conversions of that maker's W126 S-Class and C126 SEC coupés in the first half of the 1980s. Some, and possibly all, of these were actually constructed by Styling-Garage and modified by Trasco.

Trasco was bought out in 2002 by US company Armor Holdings of Jacksonville, Florida.

Tropic (D)
1981–1983, Crailsheim
Tropic Automobildesign GmbH was based in the town of Crailsheim in Baden-Württemberg and was run by Jürgen Weber. Weber had learned the art of converting closed cars into cabriolets during a stay in the USA, and in the early 1980s he converted several hundred cars for the German market. Those known were Toyotas, Hondas, Opel Asconas and, from February 1983, BMW E24s.

The cost of an E24 cabriolet started at 83,100DM, and these cars were made to order rather than in batches. No information about numbers actually built is available, although Tropic envisaged building 400 a year. Some cars had already been built for export when the design's failure to gain approval from the German TÜV vehicle authority put an end to sales in Germany. It is said that BMW took an interest, but that discussions about a co-operative venture broke down when Tropic were unwilling to incorporate design changes that BMW wanted.

In the wake of some quality problems with its Honda Prelude conversions, Tropic closed down, probably in 1983.

TTT (B)
Late 1940s–early 1950s
TTT was a small Belgian coachbuilder established in the late 1940s that was known for its conversions of the Citroën Traction Avant. The initials of the company are said to have stood for Tôle et du Travail de la Triplex, which translates roughly as Panelwork, Hard Work and Triplex Glass.

From 1948, TTT offered a pontoon-style cabriolet body for the Traction Avant, but its real claim to fame was a retractable-roof conversion, also with a modern-looking

TTT: This extraordinary pontoon-style cabriolet body was built in 1948 on a Citroën Traction Avant. *(Unknown copyright)*

pontoon-style body, that was patented in 1950 and was the work of the Belgian inventor Georges Plackle. Just two of these cars are thought to have been converted, using a roof system not dissimilar to that of the Peugeot Eclipse models from the 1930s.

Tunesi (F)
Early 1950s, Vienne
Roger Tunesi specialised in competition bodywork, and is known to have built that on a Talbot Lago T26 GS which ran in the 1951 Le Mans 24-hour race. Tunesi also rebodied a 1936 Bugatti chassis in 1952, in an all-enveloping style that matched the taste of the early 1950s.

Tüscher (CH)
1909–present, Zurich
The coachwork firm of Gebrüder Tüscher (Tüscher Brothers) is known today for its bus bodywork, but from the 1930s to the early 1950s the company also built car bodies. There were around 280 of these, and all except for two were cabriolet types.

The company was founded in 1917 when the wagon works owned by Adolf Tüscher and the "coachworks owned by his younger brother Fritz were merged. The new business focused at first on horse-drawn vehicles, then built some bodywork for motor buses and commercial vehicles. However, the first car bodies followed soon after, and Tüscher created some sports torpedos, of which the most notable was on a 2-litre Diatto chassis in 1925. There were touring and town car bodies, too, on chassis that included Benz, Bugatti, Delage, Delahaye, Fiat and Isotta-Fraschini. and Rolls-Royce.

Commercial and bus bodywork remained Tüscher's primary activity as the 1930s opened, but the company also expanded its car bodywork business. In 1933 it opened a new workshop where it was able to build convertible bodies in small series. Most of these were on American chassis such as Chrysler and Plymouth, which were now more

Tüscher: This 1922 advertisement is from the early days of Tüscher's involvement in coachbuilding. *(Author's Collection)*

freely available in Switzerland, and in fact Tüscher became known for working on predominantly American chassis in this period. There were examples on Auburn, Buick, Cadillac, De Soto, Dodge, Imperial and Studebaker, as well as those already listed.

Nevertheless, Tüscher continued to build bodies to individual order. Links with the importer Emil Frey led to some bodies on SS and later Jaguar chassis, and the

Tüscher: A three-position drophead coupé body on a 1938 Delahaye 135 Coupe des Alpes. *(Nikolaus Scheerbarth-Clasen)*

Tüscher: The firm bodied this 1937 SS Jaguar drophead coupé. In the contemporary German fashion, no attempt has been made to accommodate the folded hood in the bodywork. (Nikolaus Scheerbarth-Clasen)

later 1930s brought individual commissions on Delahaye 135 and Bugatti Type 57C chassis. All these Tüscher cabriolets were known for their elegant styling and quality construction, for the neat and tight fit of their fabric roofs, and for their restrained, almost conservative styling. There was also a Rolls-Royce limousine – one of the only closed Tüscher bodies – in this period.

Like other Swiss coachbuilders, Tüscher saw lean times during the Second World War. Among its activities was the manufacture of producer-gas installations. The late 1940s were also a difficult period, although Tüscher also built at least one body for a Jaguar (in 1945) and probably also at least one for an MG. There were some individual rebuilds of Citroën Traction Avant models to meet demand, and in 1948 Tüscher built a number of rolltop conversions on Volkswagen chassis for the Swiss Army. However, strong demand for commercial and bus bodies soon took over, and car body building ceased.

V

Valéry (F)
Early 1900s to late 1920s, Neuilly-sur-Seine
The Valéry coachworks was originally known as Pasdeloup & Valéry and was best known for its patented transformable bodies. It was taken over by Carrosserie Universelle (*qv*) at the end of the 1920s.

Van den Plas (B)
1870–1935, Brussels, later Antwerp
Van den Plas was one of the great Belgian coachbuilders of the early 20th century. Founded in Brussels 1870 as a wheelwright's business, the company moved to Antwerp in 1884 and added carriage making to its repertoire. As business increased, so a new Brussels branch was opened in 1890, and in 1898 the coachwork company Carrosserie Van den Plas was formed by Guillaume van den Plas and his three sons, Antoine, Henri and Willy.

The business rapidly grew, and by 1908 Van den Plas was building some 300 individual bodies a year, a figure which would later more than double. Meanwhile, the company had moved into the UK market, where in 1912 the car dealer Warwick Wright bought the UK rights to the Van den Plas name and established Vanden Plas (England) Ltd. This initially built bodies to the designs of the Belgian parent company. In 1924, Willy Van den Plas went to Paris to establish a French branch of the company, which traded as Willy Van den Plas et Salomon & Cie, and again used designs by the parent company. The French branch went on to build a number of bodies on Delage chassis but despite successes at concours d'élégance events never gained the reputation of the British or Belgian branches. Its last body appears to have been a cabriolet on Ford chassis that was shown on the stand of Louis Dubos at the 1934 Paris Salon, and it was Dubos who had completed it.

Early Van den Plas bodies were remarkable for the quality of their construction, but they had never showed much originality in design. Determined to rectify this shortcoming, Antoine Van den Plas, who was running the

Van den Plas: Built in 1933 on a Minerva chassis, this cabriolet body has an interesting design of luggage boot – large by the standards of the day. *(David Hodges Collection)*

Antwerp branch, engaged the stylist Alexis de Sakhnoffski in 1924. Some superbly proportioned bodies followed for chassis such as Delage, Excelsior, Hispano-Suiza, Mercedes-Benz, Packard and Rolls-Royce.

Meanwhile, during the Great War, the UK branch of the company had become involved in aircraft production, and was subsequently bought by the Aircraft Manufacturing Company that was based at Hendon on the northern outskirts of London. Re-organisation followed financial difficulties in the early 1920s, and the renamed Vanden Plas (1923) Ltd went on to achieve an outstanding reputation – greater, in fact, than that of the Belgian parent company.

In Belgium, Van den Plas forged a close relationship with Belgian chassis maker Minerva, which invested in the coachbuilder. However, when Minerva went to the wall in 1934, it meant the end for Van den Plas as well, and the company's last body was a torpedo roadster built on a Duesenberg chassis in 1935.

The British Vanden Plas company nevertheless survived longer, being bought by Austin in 1946 and eventually becoming no more than a nameplate from 1967.

Van den Plas: The Cadillac V16 chassis of the 1930s was a notably grand piece of engineering, and demanded equally grand bodywork. Van den Plas rose to the occasion with this well-proportioned saloon, apparently with folding rear roof section. *(David Hodges Collection)*

Van Leersum (NL)
1919–1951, Hilversum

In June 1919, Jan van Leersum set up his body shop in Hilversum. Little is known about his earliest work, but it appears that he became best known for commercial and bus bodywork. Nevertheless, by the 1930s he was building streamlined designs for both cars and coaches; some of the design principles were carried over into fire engines as well. The Van Leersum company was also known for modifying existing car bodywork, fitting more streamlined wings, removable luggage boots, and folding roofs.

After the 1939-1945 war, Van Leersum focused on building coaches, hearses, and commercial bodies. However, during 1946 the company was one of three Dutch coachbuilders that bodied 100 Delahaye chassis imported by the Lagerwij company in The Hague. (The other two companies were Pennock, who bodied the majority, and Van Rijswijk.) Nevertheless, it was bus and coach bodywork that were now the primary sources of income for Van Leersum, and the market in the Netherlands was hotly contested. When it became clear that the company could no longer compete with the larger builders of coach bodywork, it closed down. The end came in December 1951.

Van Rijswijk (NL)
1903–1950, The Hague

BT van Rijswijk was a Dutch coachbuilder whose work focussed on luxury chassis. The company was founded at Voorburg, near The Hague, and at the start of the 20th century made leather goods for the horse and wagon trades. However, they also repaired horse-drawn vehicles and from 1903 were drawn into the newly emergent business of building car bodies. In this early period, they bodied a Minerva chassis for Prince Hendrik of Holland, and earned themselves the title of Hofleverancier (Royal Warrant Holder).

In the 1920s, Van Rijswijk built bodies on top-quality luxury chassis such as Bugatti, Excelsior, Isotta-Fraschini and Rolls-Royce, and their work won several prizes at the concours d'élégance of the time. By the end of that decade, the company was known for its use of Triplex safety glass.

When American chassis became more readily available in Europe, Van Rijswijk turned their attentions to them, and

Van Rijswijk: This splendid example of formal coachwork was on a 1930s Packard chassis. It was clearly a town car design, as the roof section above the chauffeur is removable. It looks as if the rear roof section folds back as well. (Author's Collection)

the company built a number of bodies on Buick, Chevrolet, Ford, Nash and Packard types. However, European chassis still figured in their repertoire, and the last car body the company built before World War II was on a Lancia Aprilia chassis. The plan had been to show this at the 1939 Paris Salon, which was cancelled because of the war.

After 1945, Van Rijswijk kept afloat mainly by undertaking bodywork repairs. It built its last car body in 1950, a roadster on the Panhard Dyna X86 chassis. The plan had been to build a limited run of such cars, but the cost was too high and this prototype therefore remained unique.

W.J. van Trigt & Zoon (NL)
1927–1934, Scheveningen

The Van Trigt business was founded in 1878, and was quite distinct from Van Trigt of s'Gravenzande, an old-established commercial body maker.

Its main period of activity in the car body business was the late 1920s and early 1930s, during which time it was being run by AI Monsantofils. Van Trigt is known to have built on Hispano-Suiza H6B chassis, to have constructed an advertising vehicle for Electrolux, and to have undertaken coachwork repairs.

Vanvooren (F)
1910–1950, Courbevoie

Achille Vanvooren set up his coachwork business in the Courbevoie suburb of Paris in 1910, to build bodies for both horse-drawn carriages and cars. In these early years, the car output was quite small. In 1919, Vanvooren retired from the business, handing over control to his technical director, Marius Daste, and to his son-in-law.

Under this new management, the Vanvooren business expanded. A Paris showroom was established at 33 Rue Marbeuf. From 1923, Vanvooren held a Weymann licence, and built bodies with this construction on several different chassis, including Ballot, Bugatti, Delage, Hispano-Suiza and Panhard. By the late 1920s, it was also working on foreign chassis, a notable example being a Rolls-Royce Phantom in 1927.

The new decade brought innovation. Working with Robert de Prandières, Marius Daste developed a flexible body mounting system that depended on rubber bushes manufactured by a neighbouring company, Repusseau. This system was quickly patented under the Silentbloc name, and from 1930 it was licensed to many other coachbuilders and chassis manufacturers in Europe. It also allowed Vanvooren to introduce a pillarless saloon body, which became one of the company's characteristic designs from 1931. Delage and Hispano-Suiza chassis were among the beneficiaries; Vanvooren also supposedly had some involvement with the establishment of the company that became Simca in the early 1930s, and pillarless construction was seen on some Simca-Fiat 11CV models.

Yet despite such advances in construction methods, Vanvooren remained a fundamentally conservative coach-

Vanvooren: This mid-1930s design was prepared for the aviator Marcel Doret, to be mounted on a Hispano-Suiza 30CV chassis. *(David Hodges Collection)*

Vanvooren: With somewhat less rounded lines than the Doret car, this is a four-seater "coach", or two-door saloon body, on a Hispano-Suiza chassis. *(Author's Collection)*

builder, preferring restraint and elegance to the flamboyance embraced by many of its contemporaries. This period was to be the company's golden age, although some sources mention a little-known project with Citroën to produce a volume car that collapsed after just a few prototypes had been constructed.

The 1930s saw Carrosserie Vanvooren working on grand chassis from both French and foreign car makers, the

Vanvooren: Links with the French Rolls-Royce and Bentley importers were strong, and Vanvooren were given the job of creating the streamlined body for the 1939 Bentley Corniche, built on a modified Mk V chassis. *(David Hodges Collection)*

domestic marques including Delage and Delahaye, while there were also notable creations on Cadillac V8 chassis, on the Alfa Romeo 8C 2300 (in 1933), Mercedes-Benz 500K (in 1934), and Alvis Speed 20, the latter being a drophead coupé which introduced Alvis to the French market at the 1935 Paris Salon.

The company forged strong links with Bugatti, with Hispano-Suiza, and with the related Bentley and Rolls-Royce marques in Britain. The link with Bugatti was furthered by the friendship between Robert de Prandières and a director of the Bugatti agency in Paris, and there were multiple Vanvooren bodies on the Type 43, 44, 46, 49, 50, 55 and 57 chassis. The Hispano-Suiza factory was close to the Vanvooren works and the two companies had already collaborated on some products, but in 1932 Marius Daste left Vanvooren to become Hispano's production director. From then on, Vanvooren would build a large proportion of the bodies for the Hispano HS26, J12 and K6 chassis.

The Rolls-Royce and Bentley link also depended on personal relationships: Walter Sleator, who ran the company's French importer Franco-Britannic in Paris, had been Vanvooren's sales director in the 1920s. Impressed by Vanvooren's work, Rolls-Royce ordered a pillarless saloon body on a Bentley 3½-litre chassis and brought it to the UK for some of the leading British coachbuilders to study. Vanvooren subsequently bodied a large proportion of the Rolls-Royce and Bentley chassis sold in France, and was chosen to build the lightweight bodies for the streamlined Corniche model that was abandoned when war broke out in 1939. A co-operative arrangement with Park Ward, Rolls-Royce's favoured British coachbuilder, had also been planned.

Among Vanvooren's last creations before it closed down on the outbreak of war in 1939 was a Bugatti 57C roadster for the Shah of Persia. This had a flamboyant design that was wholly uncharacteristic of the company, but did not indicate a change of design direction. The car was in fact built to a Figoni & Falaschi design.

All coachbuilding at Vanvooren ceased for the duration of the war, and the Courbevoie workshops were badly damaged by bombing in 1943. The first post-war Vanvooren bodies were not built until 1947, but the company's output never reached its pre-war levels again. It survived by rebuilding pre-war cars and constructing a handful of bodies to special order, including some on Bentley and Delahaye chassis and a Presidential limousine, but the market that had once existed was no longer there. In 1950, Vanvooren closed for good.

Varesina (I)
1930s, Varese
Carrozzeria Varesina was established as early as 1845, but in the automotive world was primarily known for its bus and coach bodywork during the 1930s. Its involvement with the car bodywork business has been confined to the construction of prototype bodywork for Lancia, and it has also done some prototype body construction for the coachbuilder Zagato *(qv)*.

Verheul (NL)
1900–1970, Waddinxveen
Verheul is best known as a Dutch builder of bus and truck bodies, but the company also built a handful of bodies for cars as well. The company was established by Dirk Verheul

Verheul: This 1950 advertisement is for the special pontoon-bodied Rileys built by Verheul. *(Author's Collection)*

at Waddinxveen, near Rotterdam, in 1900 as a carriage and wagon works, but began building car bodies after the First World War. Verheul began building bus bodies in 1920, and subsequently became a major builder of bus and truck bodies until its factory was destroyed by fire in 1970; the site then became the Dutch headquarters of British Leyland.

Known car bodies are a small number of pontoon-bodied Riley RM four-seat cabriolets in 1950 (there were either two or three), and a single MG TD two-seater sports from the same period. The Rileys were commissioned by Dirk Van der Mark, the Amsterdam dealer, and their body design is thought to have been by Cees Akkermans of the Akkermans coachbuilding company at Oud Gastel.

Vereinigte Werkstätten für Karosserie- und Wagenbau (D)
1911–1950, Munich
The name of Vereinigte Werkstätten für Karosserie- und Wagenbau translates as "United workshops for bodywork and vehicle building", and this was an unusual co-operative that centred on the workshops of Georg Engelhard in the Munich suburb of Au.

From 1911, Engelhard was the guiding light and, apparently, manager of the co-operative. As a result, its products are often known by his name. In its first few years, the company built on Daimler, Protos and several other chassis, but immediately after the 1914-1918 war, the VWKW (the full name was a deterrent to its own use) initially focussed on conversion or modernisation of older vehicles. There were taxicabs on NSU chassis and then a number of delivery vans on Ford Model A, Ford Eifel and Opel P4 chassis.

However, VWKW also returned to passenger car bodywork, and is known to have built such bodies on chassis by Benz, Buick, Bugatti, Mercedes, NSU and Opel. In the 1930s, there were hardtop coupés and cabriolets on the smaller BMW chassis. Some of the VWKW bodies on all chassis were individual commissions, but others (like the 1937-1941 BMW 328 Sport-Cabriolet) were built in small series.

During the 1939-1945 war, VWKW built bodywork for the military, in particular open Kubelwagen types on Hanomag, Mercedes-Benz 170 or Steyr chassis. When the war ended, the company gravitated towards building commercial and bus bodywork, but finally closed in 1950.

Verplancke (F)
1920s
Very little is known about this French coachbuilder, more formally known as Verplancke Père & Fils and clearly involving two generations of the same family. It is known to have shown a saloon body on Panhard et Levassor chassis at the 1927 Paris Salon.

Vesters & Neirinck (B)
1923–1956, Brussels
The Brussels coachbuilder Vesters & Neirinck is mostly remembered today for its bodywork on Derby Bentley

Vesters & Neirinck: Well-proportioned coachwork on a 1937 Rolls-Royce Phantom III. *(WikiMedia Commons/Stephen Foskett)*

Vesters & Neirinck: Dating from 1932, this cabriolet body was on a Minerva chassis. *(David Hodges Collection)*

chassis in the late 1930s, although the company also built on many other types of chassis. Examples are known on Delage, Delahaye, Graham (unusually), Minerva and Rolls-Royce.

The early years of the company are obscure, although a Brussels coachbuilder called Vesters Inc was recorded in the press around 1914 and may be the same company. Vesters & Neirinck appeared as an exhibitor at the 1923 Brussels Auto Salon and would continue to exhibit regularly at the major European shows.

Even so, Vesters & Neirinck built relatively small numbers of bespoke bodies. The Bentleys, of which there were 11, began in the mid-1930s and ended in 1938, and are considered some of the most attractive of their period.

Vesters & Neirinck was one of the few Belgian coachbuilders to remain active after the Second World War. Few bodies are known, but among them was an interesting four-door drophead on a 1949 Austin Sheerline A125 chassis, clearly inspired by Saoutchik. However, the company clearly suffered as demand for coachbuilt bodies shrank, and by 1955 its stand at the Brussels Auto Salon could only showcase custom sunroofs in plexiglass and steel for volume-produced Alfa Romeo and Fiat models. This seems to have been a last gesture, and Vesters & Neirinck closed for business in 1956.

Veth (NL)
1840–present, Arnhem

Carrosseriefabriek Veth & Zoon (the name means Veth and Son) was established in the Dutch town of Arnhem in 1840. Like many other firms, it built its reputation in the horse-drawn carriage trade before turning to car bodies.

Although Veth became an official supplier to the Dutch Royal Family in 1914, it was never one of Holland's better-known coachbuilders. In the inter-war years, its known bodies were on chassis by Bentley, Bugatti, Hotchkiss, Maybach, MG, Packard, Spyker, and Rolls Royce. At the start of the 1950s, Talbot Lago was added to the list.

As the opportunities for car bodybuilding declined with the move to monocoque construction, Veth turned to the commercial vehicle market. Carrosseriefabriek Veth still exists in Arnhem, as a builder of truck and van bodies.

Vetter (D)
1922–1945, Cannstatt; later Fellbach

Walter Vetter founded his company in 1922 in the Stuttgart suburb of Cannstatt as the Walter Vetter Karosserie- und Fahrzeugbau. His early bodywork was built on Benz and Daimler chassis, among others, and of course on Mercedes-Benz as well after the 1926 merger of the two companies. In the 1930s, the company moved to nearby Fellbach, and responded to commercial demand by beginning construction of bus bodywork.

Vetter had meanwhile gained a reputation for producing very special bodies, and during the 1930s he became closely involved with all the leading German aerodynamic experts – Paul Jaray, Reinhard Freiherr Koenig-Fachsenfeld, and Professor Wunibald Kamm. Most notably, in 1932 the Vetter workshops constructed the streamlined body for the Mercedes-Benz SSKL with which Manfred von Brauchitsch won that year's international Avus race. This sealed the

Veth: This stylish sports saloon body was built on a 1939 Bugatti Type 57 chassis. (*Christie's Auctioneers*)

Vetter: In 1932 the firm constructed a pair of streamlined single-seater bodies on Mercedes-Benz SSKL chassis. This one was the short-tailed version; in the driving seat is Otto Merz, who was killed at the wheel during practice for the Avus race that year. (*Daimler-Benz*)

Vetter: The second car, for Manfred von Brauchitsch, won the Avus race and led to more commissions for special bodywork. (*Daimler-Benz*)

company's reputation in the specialist bodywork field, and Vetter went on to build the bodies for numerous record cars from BMW, DKW, Mercedes-Benz and Standard, as well as single-seater racing bodies for Imperia and Maserati. The company even held a licence from Paul Jaray for the construction of streamlined bus bodies.

However, there would be no more car bodies after 1939. During the 1939-1945 war, Vetter's workshops focussed on repairing and rebuilding bus bodies for the German Army and the German Post Office, and after the war it focussed entirely on bus bodywork, becoming one of West Germany's largest companies in that field during the 1960s.

Veuillet (F)
1920s, Fleurieu-sur Sâone
Veuillet Carrossier was a small coachbuilder from Fleurieu-sur Sâone in the Rhône department. In the 1920s it offered mahogany coachwork that was supposedly constructed like a boat, although that seems to have referred more to the method of construction than to the shape.

Vignale (I)
1948–1969, Turin
Carrozzeria Alfredo Vignale was one of Italy's best-known coachbuilders in the 1950s and 1960s, building individual commissions, small-run batches and derivatives of mainstream models to which it applied its own name.

Alfredo Vignale had worked for Stabilimenti Farina before founding his coachworks in Turin in October 1948. His first body was built on a second-hand Fiat Topolino, and there was a special Fiat 1100, but Vignale quickly attracted an order from Cisitalia for coupés and cabriolets. These established the early Cisitalia style, with aerodynamic shapes, a low roofline and quite bold chrome ornamentation.

From 1950, Vignale replaced Touring as Ferrari's coachbuilder of choice and, although Ferrari would later settle on Pininfarina as his favourite, this period saw Vignale working with the freelance Giovanni Michelotti as designer. The pair of them went on to create original shapes for endurance racers like the 340 Mexico and luxurious GTs like the 212 Inter or 375 America.

Most of Vignale's work in the 1950s was on Italian cars, by makers including Alfa Romeo, Ferrari, Lancia, Maserati and Osca. However, there were rare collaborations with others: Vignale worked with the American Briggs Cunningham on the Continental C-3 in 1952, for example, lent his name to a disappointing titivation of the British Standard Vanguard in 1958, and built a one-off BMW 507 that was shown at Turin in 1959. In the late 1960s, Vignale also worked with Tatra in Czechoslovakia to design their 613 saloon, which did not enter production until 1975.

Vignale: This 1951 barchetta bodywork on a Ferrari 212 Export chassis is a good illustration of Vignale's ability to create a pleasing shape within tight dimensions. *(Unknown copyright)*

Vignale: A similar shape worked well as a berlinetta on the Ferrari 212 chassis. *(David Hodges Collection)*

Vignale: Once again on Ferrari 212 Inter chassis and dating from around 1951, this is one of half a dozen "Geneva coupés". The low roofline, two-tone paintwork and trim strip running around the car are typical Vignale design traits – although the appeal of the high-mounted trim doubling as quarter-bumpers at the front is questionable. (Author)

Vignale: 1953 Cunningham C3 Continental.

Vignale: Designed by Michelotti, this 1958 show car was called the Raggio Azzurro II (Blue Ray II) and was based on a Lancia Aurelia B24 chassis modified by Nardi. (Author's Collection)

Vignale: Svelte lines anticipate the tastes of the new decade on this 1960 Lancia Appia cabriolet. (Bonhams Auctioneers)

Vignale: Trying to attract a contract from Opel, Vignale prepared this pretty cabriolet on the Kadett for the 1965 Geneva Show. He turned the car into a coupé for the Turin Show later that year, but Opel did not bite. (Author's Collection)

Vignale: This extraordinary one-off shooting brake body was constructed on a Ferrari 300GT in 1967. *(Author)*

Vignale: Between 1967 and 1970, the company built 100 of these smart coupés on the Fiat 125S. They were known by the name of Samantha. *(Author's Collection)*

Vignale: The Maserati Indy arrived in 1969 as a four-seat fastback tourer. Pictured is a 1972 example. *(David Hodges Collection)*

Although Vignale's glamorous low-volume cars caught the headlines, the company's volume business lay elsewhere in the 1960s. The collaboration with Michelotti ended in 1959 when the designer set up his own coachbuilding company, and in 1961 Vignale opened a new factory close to Fiat's Mirafiori plant in Turin, where he built cars under his own name in greater quantities. Most of these were low-volume derivatives of mainstream Fiats, such as the 1500, 850, the Eveline and the pretty Samantha coupé, the latter based on a Fiat 125S.

In 1967, Vignale introduced the retro-styled Vignale Gamine open buggy, based on the 500, but sales proved disappointingly slow. The company ran into economic difficulties, and in 1969 Vignale sold his coachworks to De Tomaso, which by this stage was already owned by Ford. Alfredo Vignale himself was sadly killed in a car accident just three days after the sale was concluded.

De Tomaso made use of the Vignale factory to build its Pantera sports cars, but the Vignale company itself was doing little beyond early prototype work for Maserati and a few others, and the whole business was closed down in 1974 when the Pantera was discontinued as a result of the energy crisis.

Since then, the Vignale name has reappeared on a Lagonda concept car shown at Geneva in 1993 (Lagonda's parent brand, Aston Martin, was owned by Ford at the time). Ford used it again on a Ford Focus concept car at the 2004 Paris Motor Show, and from 2013 made it the badge of top models in Europe.

Viguier (F)
1950s, Levallois-Perret
Viguier was responsible for estate bodywork on the Ford Vedette in the early 1950s. There is no further hard information about the company.

Ville et Sport (F)
1926, Puteaux
Almost nothing is known about this coachbuilder, which in 1926 put its name to a low-built, lightweight drophead coupé with fabric-covered wooden panels.

Viotti (I)
1921–1964, Turin
Vittorino Viotti set up in business with a man named Tolfo near the Fiat factory in Turin in 1921. Initially known as Viotti & Tolfo, the business became well known in its sector, building on luxury chassis to individual commission. In the mid-1920s, it took out a licence from the French Audineau company for their Clairalpax body construction that used slim metal pillars to increase the window area and light available in the passenger compartment.

Viotti: This lovely streamlined coupé by Viotti was a 1935 re-body of an earlier Alfa Romeo 6C 2300. (Concours of elegance, above. David Burgess-Wise, below)

Viotti: American influence is discernible in the styling of this handsome 1947 Fiat 1500 cabriolet body.
(*Giles Chapman*)

Viotti: A 1950 Alfa Romeo 6C 2500 in the rather unexpected form of a "woody" station wagon.

In 1930, the company was liquidated and re-emerged as Carrozzeria Viotti SA, with Viotti as director and new, larger, premises. The company moved into small-batch production, working primarily on Italian chassis, and is reputed to have been the first Italian coachbuilder to set up a proper production line. First came the Fiat 525 SS sports, then bodies for the 508 Balilla which became catalogued models. There were cabriolets and spiders on the 508C and 1100 chassis throughout the 1930s. Viotti also built bodies for the Lancia Augusta, Aprilia and Artena, and for some Alfa Romeos; and alongside the batch builds were individual custom bodies as well. Notable were designs for the 6C 2300 and 8C 2300 Alfa Romeo chassis by Mario

Revelli di Beaumont, who may also have been responsible for the 1935 re-body of an earlier 8C 2300 as a striking streamlined coupé.

During the 1939-1945 war, the Viotti workshops focussed on Lancia Artena bodies for the military. When British bombing destroyed their workshops, they moved temporarily into a building owned by Fiat, but after the war moved again to new premises in Turin.

In 1946, again working with Mario Revelli di Beaumont as designer, Viotti began production of a wooden-framed station wagon body, initially for the Fiat 1100 Giardinetta. The basic design was then replicated on Alfa Romeo and Lancia chassis. From 1951, the company had the contract for the first 100 Lancia Aurelia B20 GT bodies. Further Viotti work for Lancia included a 2+2 derivative of the Appia to a design by Pinin Farina from 1957, and a three-door Giardinetta to their own design from 1958.

Vittorio Viotti died in 1956, and his cousin Francesco Viotti took over the company. Viotti bodywork now began to appear on other chassis, such as the Fiat 600 (in Granluce form) and GT derivatives of the 1100 and 1200. The late 1950s also brought special bodies for the Fiat 500 (the Viotti Sport coupé), the 1800 and 2100, and for the Osca-engined 1500. There were show specials in this period, too, notably a four-seat cabriolet on the Bristol 407 that appeared at the 1962 Turin Show.

Viotti's final batch contract was a Giardinetta estate body for the Fiat 1300 and 1500 models, introduced in 1961. This remained in production until 1964, but after that Viotti changed its business focus to become an engineering and prototype build company. The brand later passed into the ownership of a Piedmontese business group.

Visse & Haf (F)
1920s, Levallois-Perret

This small company was active in the 1920s and was noted for its use of stainless steel for car bodywork. At least one of the company's advertisements suggested it was active at concours d'élégance events of the time.

Vogt (D)
1960s, Bad Neuenahr

Vogt Autotechnik was responsible for a number of conversions of the Opel Kapitän, Admiral and Diplomat saloons in the 1960s. There were estate cars and hearses, fastback models with hatchback-like tailgates built specially for a German TV station, plus some ambulances on an extended wheelbase.

Vogt & Demeuse (B)
1900–1930, Liège

There is little information about the activities of this Belgian coachbuilder, founded at the start of the 20th century in Liège. Raoul Demeuse became a senior figure in a local coachbuilders' organisation from 1919, and the company was active during the 1920s, but did not survive the stock market crash of 1929.

Voll & Ruhrbeck (D)
1920–1945, Berlin & Essen

Voll & Ruhrbeck were based in the Charlottenburg district of Berlin and also had a branch in Essen. They made their public debut at the 1921 German Motor Show, the first to be held after the war. They initially became known for their elegant torpedo bodies, which were found on many higher-quality chassis, often by Benz or Protos.

The company built both to individual commission and in small batches for various chassis manufacturers. The 1930s saw a wide variety of commissions, ranging from sporty roadsters on Adler Trumpf chassis through grander cabriolets for the larger Mercedes-Benz chassis such as the Nürburg and the 620K, and on to the 12-cylinder Maybach. American chassis also attracted the company's business, and there were cabriolets on both Cadillac and Hudson chassis. Also notable was a striking streamlined pontoon-type cabriolet body on a Bugatti Type 57C.

In the later 1930s, Voll & Ruhrbeck also built a number of unattractive aerodynamic bodies on Mercedes 170 chassis to the designs of Professor Eberling, using aluminium construction. The coachbuilder constructed its last passenger car bodies in 1939 before devoting its resources to military requirements. It finally closed down in 1945 without returning to its former business.

W

Walch (B)
1921–1925, Liège

The Belgian coachbuilder M Walch operated from two addresses in Liège in the first half of the 1920s – 49 rue de Fétinne and 15 rue des Houblonnières. The company is best known for its "transformables", fully closed four-seater bodies that could be swiftly converted into open torpedos; Walch applied for a patent for his system. Advertisements claimed that the conversion could be achieved without tools in two minutes. Examples (with dual windshields) are known on Belgian FN 3800 chassis, and Walch produced two designs, which he called the T3800 and the 3800F.

Wandrès (F)
1920s, Belfort

Maison Ch Wandrès was a French provincial coachbuilder active in the 1920s.

Weinberger (1) (D)
1908–1927, Munich

The less well-known of the two German Weinberger firms was set up by Karl Weinberger senior in 1865 as a wagon works. His sons, Karl junior, Hans and Heinrich, took over the business from 1908 and added car bodywork to their repertoire. The company became the Bavarian franchisee for Protos chassis, and it was no surprise that many of its bodies were on this make; many were bodied as taxis in the 1920s. There were commercial bodies as well in this period.

Protos closed in 1927, and the Weinberger brothers turned to building bus and commercial bodywork. The company survived until 1944, when it was closed for good after its premises had been severely damaged by bombing.

Weinberger (2) (D)
1898–1953, Munich

Ludwig Weinberger was a cousin of Karl Weinberger (qv), and established his wagon-building business on the same street in Munich in 1898. Nevertheless, the two companies had no direct business links. In the beginning, Weinberger built only horse-drawn vehicles, but from 1904 he diversified into motor cars, taking individual commissions for bodies on a wide variety of chassis.

The business took a major step forward in 1931, when Ludwig Weinberger junior joined his father and they took on a BMW franchise. A particularly notable commission that year was for the bodywork on a Bugatti Type 41 Royale, for a German doctor who had emigrated to the USA. However, for the rest of the decade the Weinberger coachbuilding business focussed almost exclusively on BMW chassis, specialising in roadsters, open two-seaters and open four-seaters which had something of the style of British tourers. There were more typically German cabriolets, too, particularly in the later 1930s. In all, Weinberger is thought to have built around 300 special bodies on BMW chassis before being obliged to suspend operations when war broke out.

After the 1939-1945 war, the Weinberger company continued to tick over but the heart had already gone from the conversions business. Its work in this period included wood and steel bodies for de-mobbed US Jeeps. Ludwig Weinberger retired in 1953 and closed his business down at the same time.

Weinsberg (D)
1912–present, Weinsberg, near Heilbronn

The Weinsberg company began by building both horse-drawn vehicles and motor car bodies, specialising in leather panelling over wooden framework. In 1913 it was bought by Fritz Eisenlohr, who came to own it jointly with Georg Authenrieth. However, Authenrieth left the business in 1922 to establish a new coachworks under his own name in Darmstadt.

The company's first batch contract came from NSU in 1925, by which time it was working with metal panelling. Weinsberg came to work with many major manufacturers in the 1920s, including Auto Union, BMW, Citroën,

Weinberger: One of the Bugatti Type 41 Royale chassis was entrusted to Weinberger in 1932 to be fitted with this cabriolet body. Getting the proportions right on such a large car was no easy task. *(Author's Collection)*

Weinberger: This 1938 cabriolet on a BMW 326 chassis is notable for its lack of running-boards: in their place is a small side step. (BMW)

Daimler-Benz, Ford, Magirus, Opel and Wanderer. After 1931, it developed close ties with the German branch of Fiat, building 1500 taxis for Berlin and becoming the largest employer in Weinsberg.

In 1938, Eislenlohr sold the company to Fiat. During the 1939-1945 war, Weinsberg built military runabouts and aircraft sections. After the war, it turned to truck cabs for Büssing, and from 1950 to 1954 built the bodies for the small two-seater Gutbrod Superior. The company built its last wooden-framed body for the Fiat 500C in 1950, and painted many bodies for Porsche in the early 1950s. By 1955 Weinsberg was turning to accessories such as sunroofs, and in more recent years it has been known for campers and accident rescue trucks.

Weinsberg: This roadster body dates from 1940 and was built on a German-made Fiat chassis, badged as an NSU-Fiat. (WikiMedia Commons/Lother Spurzem)

Wendler: The firm became known for its streamlined bodies in the later 1930s. This one, using the Kamm aerodynamic principles, was on a 1938 Mercedes-Benz 170V chassis. *(Daimler-Benz)*

Wendler: There were some streamlined bodies on BMW 328 chassis, too. *(WikiMedia Commons/ Marco 56)*

Wendler: Dating from 1952, this cabriolet design was for the Gutbrod Superior Sport. *(WikiMedia Commons/Buch-t)*

Wendler (D)

1840–2000, Reutlingen

The Wendler coachworks was at its height in the 1920s and the 1930s, and in the latter decade was particularly well known for the experimental streamlined bodies it built, using Jaray, Kamm and Koenig-Fachsenfeld patents. It also had a resurgence in the 1950s through work for Porsche.

Erhard Wendler set himself up in business as a builder of horse-drawn carriages in 1840 at Reutlingen. Under the

talented designer Helmut Schwandner, the company began building car bodies in the 1920s, and before the end of the decade Wendler had a staff of around 100 and was using the Weymann patents. Known examples were on chassis by Bugatti, Ford, Mercedes-Benz, NAG and Wanderer.

Although these 1920s confections were elegant, they were not particularly distinctive. Wendler became far more individual during the 1930s, making a speciality of two-seater and 2+2 sport-cabriolet bodies. Adler, BMW,

Mercedes-Benz and Wanderer figured among the chassis to benefit from Wendler's attentions. The streamliners included a Ford V8, a small group on BMW 327/28 chassis in 1937-1938, one on a Mercedes 170V in 1938, and a diesel-powered Hanomag record car in 1939.

Wendler was drawn into military work as early as 1937, when it built a small series of Kübelwagen on the Opel Super 6 chassis. Inevitably, car body activities were suspended for the duration, but once the war was over Wendler resumed its former activities. The late 1940s and early 1950s brought a number of one-off bodies, some as prototypes for companies such as Adler and BMW while others were to the individual order of private customers.

Wendler swiftly embraced the post-war fashion for pontoon styling, and became involved in series production for Porsche, constructing more than 80 of the racing 550 models in the mid-1950s. By 1960, it was still working with Porsche, and built the bodies for the special racing RS60 models. The company was still building to individual order in the early 1960s, a notable example being a special coupé based on a BMW 3200 Super. However, before long Wendler's primary focus had become repair and restoration work, along with special bodywork for armoured limousines.

By the close of the 20th century, Wendler was heading for bankruptcy. The company continued for a while under the name of PGAM AG, but closed down in 2000.

Wenger (CH)
1919–present, Basle

Carrosserie A. Wenger & Cie has always been primarily involved in the commercial vehicle market, but at various periods in its existence it has also built car bodywork.

The company was founded at Basle in 1919 by Dominique Wenger, who had worked for the bodywork department of Saurer in Arbon since 1914. The early years were devoted to repair and rebuild work, but around 1923 the first car bodies appeared – a Sizaire and a sporty two-seater on Salmson chassis. A move into larger premises in 1924 allowed new work to be taken on, and before long the company was building saloon car bodies as well as sporting bodywork on French, German and Italian chassis. Among its other specialities was converting older cars into light commercial vehicles.

The company has not built complete car bodies under its own name since about 1930, focusing instead on activities such as making cabriolet hoods, fitting sunroofs of its own design and interior trim work. Between 1947 and 1984, the Wenger company also created more than 1000 closed bodies for open military vehicles (such as Jeeps) that were being sold on the civilian market. In the 1970s, the company also did some work for Basle car maker Monteverdi, building some of its 375 models and then making about 20 examples of the Sierra between 1977 and 1982. In 1999, Wenger bought the former Köng coachworks in Basle.

Today, the company is still in the ownership of the Wenger family and still carries out bodywork repairs and refurbishment alongside the construction of new bodies for light commercial vehicles.

Westfalia (D)
1950s, Wiedenbrück

The Westfalia-Werke in Wiedenbrück is best known for its camper and motorhome conversions, the former particularly based on Volkswagen light commercial models. The first of these was built in 1951 and its successors have made the company into a household name. However, while the company was still finding a market niche in the early 1950s, it also built the four-seat "Kombi" (estate car) derivative of the two-seater Gutbrod Superior car between 1950 and 1954.

Weymann (F)
1922–1930, Levallois-Perret

In the years immediately after the Great War, former aviator Charles Terres Weymann developed a new system of body construction in tandem with fellow former aviator Maurice Tabuteau. This depended on metal joints which allowed the wooden framework to flex, so reducing rattles and squeaks; it was covered with fabric, which in turn reduced weight. Seats were attached directly to the chassis rather than to the bodywork.

Weymann set up in business in 1922, and introduced several body designs that were adaptable to multiple chassis. The idea caught on rapidly. By 1923, the company was already employing 300 staff, and that year built 600 bodies; five years later, the Weymann works turned out no fewer than 13,000.

The Weymann patents were licensed to multiple coachbuilders and motor manufacturers in Europe. Weymann established branches in Britain (at Addlestone) and the USA (Indianapolis). But this massive success was followed by a backlash as it became clear that Weymann-patent bodies had poor durability. By the time of the 1929 Paris Salon, Weymann was looking at alternative construction methods, and had developed a semi-rigid method of construction using aluminium. The company did not survive the economic crisis of 1930.

Winter (D)
1920s–1930s, Zittau

The Karosserie-und-Wagenbau Gustav Winter was active in the 1920s and 1930s, and an example of its work has survived on an Audi 18/70PS Typ M model from 1925 in the Audi historical collection. The company continued to build car bodies in the 1930s but appears to have diversified into commercial bodywork as well.

Worblaufen (CH)
1929–1958, Worblaufen

Fritz Ramseier-Scheidiger opened his wagon works in the small village of Worblaufen near Berne in 1900, but it was his sons – Fritz, Hans and Ernst – who would turn

Worblaufen: The cabriolet body on this Jaguar Mk VII chassis completely alters the character of Jaguar's big saloon. The car dates from around 1951. *(Author's Collection)*

the company into one of Switzerland's most respected coachbuilders after taking over in 1929. In its 30 years of existence, interrupted by World War II, the company built more than 800 bodies.

The younger Fritz Ramseier is said to have worked for the coachbuilder Gangloff in Geneva before returning to the family business, although other sources say that he had spent time with truck builder Saurer. One way or the other, he took the lead in the new company, which was now re-named Fritz Ramseier & Cie, Carrosserie Worblaufen. Although the coachbuilder's plate gave prominence to the Worblaufen name, the Ramseier sub-title was always included and the company has always been known by both the Ramseier and Worblaufen names.

Like so many of their Swiss contemporaries, Worblaufen specialised in elegant cabriolet bodies, and by 1932, the company was exhibiting at the Geneva Show. Their 1930s output was mainly on French, Italian and German chassis – Alfa-Romeo, Bugatti, Isotta-Fraschini, Lancia, Mercedes-Benz, Opel and Panhard-Levassor. There were also some special bodies on Peugeot 402 chassis, built in small series from 1936, and at least one cabriolet was built on an SS (Jaguar) 100 chassis in 1939.

Work resumed slowly after 1945, and there were Worblaufen cabriolets on Delahaye chassis, on the Jowett Jupiter, Ford Vedette, Hotchkiss Grand Sport and, this time in small series, on the Lancia Aprilia. By the close of the decade, the company had bodied at least one Talbot Lago Record, an MG YA, a Jaguar Mk IV, a 2.4-litre Healey (as a coupé) and a 1948 Bentley that was displayed at that year's Geneva Show. To supplement its core business, Worblaufen had also begun in 1948 to produce cabriolet conversions of the Citroën Traction Avant, focussing particularly on the 15/Six model.

The most numerous Worblaufen cabriolets at the start of the 1950s were conversions of the Peugeot 203, of which there were supposedly 20. Both cabriolet and coupé designs were built on the Lancia Aurelia B12, and between 1952 and 1957, Worblaufen created several different designs for the Alfa Romeo 1900. There was a special cabriolet body for a Jaguar Mk VII some time around 1951, and in the middle of the decade there were several (some claim eight) cabriolets and coupés on BMW 502 chassis.

However, demand for Worblaufen's traditional work was shrinking, and the company's final creation was a magnificent new body for a 1930s Rolls-Royce Phantom III in 1958. After that, the company focussed on coachwork repairs and on utility bodywork, and finally closed down in 1983.

Worblaufen: A four-door cabriolet by Worblaufen/Ramseier on a 1949 Hotchkiss.

Worblaufen: This neat two-door saloon was built around 1953 on the basis of a Lancia Aurelia B52. (Author's Collection)

Worblaufen: Built around the middle of the 1950s, this coupé was one of several on the BMW 502 chassis. *(Author's Collection)*

Z

Zagato (I)
1919–present, Milan

Carrozzeria Zagato has consistently been one of the outstanding design houses in Italy since the 1920s, and for a period from the 1960s also assembled small-volume specialist derivatives of mainstream production cars. The company has always been particularly noted for its sporting bodywork, although more recently it has diversified into areas such as trams and industrial design.

Like many others who would make their name in the coachbuilding trade of the 1920s, Ugo Zagato had been struck by the possibilities of transferring aircraft construction techniques to car bodywork. Before the Great War, he had spent time with the coachbuilder Varesina, and had studied technical drawing before joining the aircraft manufacturer Pomilio in Turin. In March 1919 he left Pomilio and set up his own business in Milan with five employees, with the intention of building and repairing both car bodies and aircraft.

Carrozzeria Zagato focussed largely on sporting and racing bodywork in the 1920s, and its lightweight, aerodynamic constructions quickly attracted the attention of Alfa Romeo. As early as 1921, Zagato built its first bodies for the Milanese manufacturer, on the unsuccessful G1 luxury chassis. Much more important was Alfa Romeo's recognition that Zagato's lightweight bodies would improve its sports and racing models, and with bodies for the 6C 1500 and 6C 1750 SS, Zagato had established a sound reputation by the end of the decade.

Even so, the Depression of the early 1930s caused a blip in the Zagato fortunes; the company briefly went into liquidation and Ugo Zagato acted as a consultant for the coachbuilder Brianza, set up in his old works by former employees. But the customers soon returned, and there

Zagato: The firm's early reputation was founded on lightweight sporting bodywork like that on this 1931 Alfa Romeo 8C-2300 MM. (*Author*)

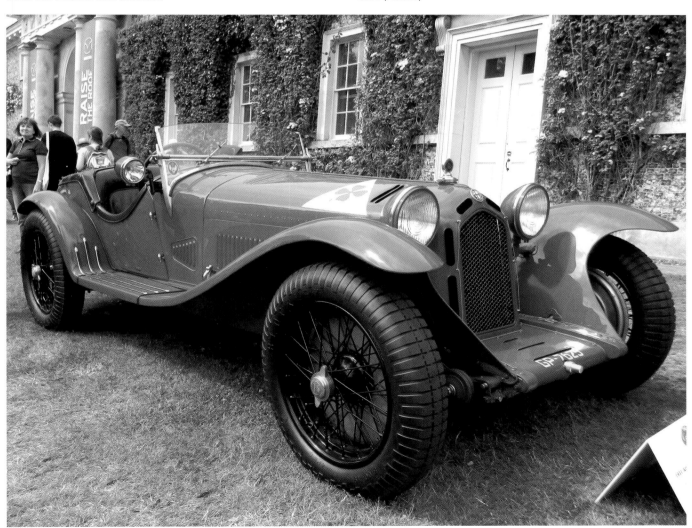

Zagato: Early bodies carried this coachbuilder's plate; later ones had a stylised Z. *(Author)*

Zagato: A late 1940s feature was the Panoramica roof, seen here on an MG Y-type chassis from 1948. *(Author's Collection)*

Zagato: On this unique 1949 Maserati A6-1500, the Panoramica roof is less noticeable from the side . . .

. . . but very clear in this close-up. *(Author's Collection)*

was work on chassis by Bugatti, Diatto, Maserati, OM and even Rolls-Royce; Zagato also bodied some Fiat 501, 503 and 509 chassis. Alfa Romeo remained the core of Zagato's business during the 1930s, with bodies for the 8C 2300 and others from 1931, but there were also bodies for Fiat and Lancia. Zagato bodies were light and aerodynamic, gradually adopting such features as raked windscreens and faired-in headlights. The company's association with racing bodywork was such that no fewer than 36 Zagato-bodied cars lined up at the start of the 1938 Mille Miglia.

During the 1939-1945 war, the Zagato works were given over to military production. The original premises were destroyed in a bombing raid during 1943, and Zagato moved to new workshops close to the Isotta Fraschini works, where the company constructed truck cabs and military vehicles. Zagato also worked in secret on the four-door saloon body for the Isotta Fraschini 8C Monterosa, which was officially announced in 1947 but did not enter production.

The post-war era saw Zagato set up in new workshops near the Alfa Romeo plant in Portello, north of Milan. Zagato's main innovation in this period was the "panoramica" body design, with Plexiglass windows that curved into the roof to create a light and airy passenger cabin. The proportions of some bodies were rather strange, but from 1947 Zagato offered such bodywork on all the main Fiat models from 500 to 1400, and examples were also built on Lancia, Maserati, and MG chassis. A panoramica body built on a Ferrari 166 Mille Miglia in 1949 became the first-ever Ferrari coupé. The year 1949 was also important because it was the year that Zagato's two sons, Elio and Gianni, joined the business.

By this time, Zagato's primary focus was on GT models, to fit the requirements of the new racing category conceived in 1949 by Count Giovanni Lurani and others. GTs had to be cars that had a production chassis, were capable of everyday use, but were also suitable for weekend racing. Nevertheless, Zagato remained involved with monoposto cars as well, building the body for Fangio's world championship-winning Alfa 159.

In the early 1950s, Zagato also built 30 coupé bodies for the short-lived Fiat 8V, and Elio Zagato (who was now managing the company) drove one of these to victory at the Avus circuit in 1955. Notable designs in this decade included the Alfa Romeo Giulietta Sprint SZ (the letters stood for Sprint Zagato), the Giulia TZ sports-racing coupé

Zagato: A much-liked feature from the 1950s and 1960s was the "double-bubble" roof, seen here on a 1957 Ferrari 250GT LWB model. *(Author)*

and the Fiat-Abarth 750. Zagato also built the tubular-framed coupé version of the Maserati 450S sports racer to a design by Frank Costin. Outside Italy, there were bodies for makers such as Bristol (on the 406 chassis), AC (on the Bristol-engined Ace) and Jaguar (on the XK sports car chassis). Characteristic of many 1950s Zagato coupés (and some later ones as well) was the so-called "double-bubble" roof design, featuring a bump or "bubble" to provide headroom for each front seat occupant.

As the GT vogue took hold, so demand for Zagato bodies escalated, and by the turn of the decade the company had geared up for small-volume production with a new factory at Terrazzano (north-west of Milan) that had a capacity of around 3000 cars a year. Ercole Spada was engaged as chief designer and was responsible for some instantly recognisable Zagato designs in the 1960s.

The Zagato name remained closely allied with Italian makers, for whom the company built small-volume specials that used essentially standard mechanical units. The principal links were with Alfa Romeo (the Giulia SZ, the TZ, TZ2, 2600 SZ, the 1750 4R and the Junior Zagato) and Lancia (the Appia Sport, Flaminia Sport and Super Sport, Flavia Sport and Supersport and the Fulvia Sport and Sport Spider). Another notable design was the 1600

GTZ for Osca, but there were several commissions from beyond Italy. Aston Martin requested a special lightweight DB4GT body for racing, and even Rover investigated a fastback coupé based on its 2000TC model. Zagato also experimented with bodies for small cars, doing a coupé on the BMC Mini (actually a long-wheelbase van chassis) in 1961 and making three prototype Zimps based on the Hillman Imp in 1964.

Ugo Zagato died in 1968 and his sons took over the business, but the 1970s would prove more challenging for the company. Zagato was now effectively divided into two elements, Zagato Car (the manufacturing side) and Zagato Design. Zagato designs in this period moved away from the curvaceous style of the 1960s towards a squarer, more geometric style. Typical examples were the Alfa Romeo Junior Z and the Lancia Fulvia Sport. Meanwhile, the Terrazzano factory assembled more than 9000 examples of the targa-top Lancia Beta Sport Spyder to a Pininfarina design and, from 1975, the Bristol 412 targa as well. Zagato built (but did not design) the extraordinary Cadillac NART

Zagato: The same "double-bubble" roof is seen on this Abarth 750 coupé from around 1958. *(David Hodges Collection)*

Zagato: Just 200 of these delightful short-tail: Alfa Romeo Giulietta SZ 1300 models were built; this one dates from around 1960. *(David Hodges Collection)*

Zagato: This rather attractive 1961 coupé was based on the long-wheelbase floorpan of a Mini van. *(Author's Collection)*

of 1970, and there were projects for Ferrari, for Fiat and even for Volvo in this period. A far less well known project was the Zagato Zele, an electric microcar with GRP bodywork of which around 500 were built.

Concept cars and limited production models characterised Zagato's output during the 1980s. Returning to work for Maserati after a gap of 30 years, Zagato built the Biturbo Spider from 1984 and then the Karif coupé from 1988. From 1986 there was the V8 Zagato for Aston Martin, of which 52 Vantage coupés and 37 Volante convertibles were made. Then from 1989 Zagato assembled the limited-volume Alfa Romeo SZ coupé, the related RZ roadster following in 1992; both were actually designed by Robert Opron in the Fiat studio.

Zagato: Elements of earlier Panoramica designs seem to have crept into the coupé body for the Lancia Flavia Zagato Sport. This is a 1964 car. (David Hodges Collection)

Zagato: Also dating from 1964 is this Lancia Flaminia Supersport coupé. (David Hodges Collection)

Zagato: The bodyside crease distinguishes this design for the Lancia Fulvia Coupé, a 1968 1.3S Rallye model. (David Hodges Collection)

Zagato: A cut-off tail features on this 1972 Alfa Romeo Junior Z coupé, the Z of course standing for Zagato. (David Hodges Collection)

However, during the 1990s Zagato turned away from production to focus on design and prototype build work. Its last production car was the Lancia Hyena, based on the Delta Integrale and penned by Zagato designer Marco Pedracini; production was halted in 1995 after just 24 had been built because of difficulties with Fiat, who supplied the running-gear.

The design studio also worked on projects for Mercedes-Benz, Nissan and Toyota among others. It also changed its name twice, first to SZ Design and then to Zagato Centrostile. There were design projects for railways and industrial vehicles, as well as better-known projects such as a pair of Ferrari show cars that anticipated the later F355, 360 Modena and Enzo models. For Lamborghini there were the Raptor and the Superdiablo Vmax concept,

the former produced with great speed thanks to the use of new integrated technology applied to the CAD/CAM system that allowed the intermediate styling buck phase to be eliminated. At the other end of the performance scale, Zagato was commissioned in 1998 by Fiat to produce prototypes with ultra-low fuel consumption, and of these the Ecobasic won a prize at the 2000 Geneva Motor Show.

Zagato rekindled its relationship with Aston Martin in 2003 with the 99-strong DB7 Zagato edition and related DBAR-1 roadster. In 2009, Zagato passed to the third generation of the family when Elio Zagato died and passed the succession to his son Andrea. The company continued to work on special projects for a multiplicity of car makers, and from time to time the results of its work have been made public. In 2008, for example, Zagato worked on the

Spyker C12 supercar, in 2012 it produced the BMW Zagato roadster and coupé (both based on the E89 Z4), and a more recent example has been the Maserati Mostro concept, revealed in 2015.

Meanwhile, economic reality intervened and the company was bought in 2011 by CPP (Coventry Prototype Panels), which itself was acquired in 2012 by Evisage Group, a consulting-service company in the automotive engineering field based on Coventry. Zagato continues to major on design consultancy work, but is also capable of building initial models, producing prototypes, and of limited-volume production.

Zander (D)
1883–1929, Döbeln
Karosseriewerk Emil Zander in Döbeln was active in the car bodywork business during the 1920s, and is known among others for its work on Elite chassis in the early years of that decade. The company folded in 1929 and two of its former staff established a new company, Döbelner Karosseriewerk, which became established as a builder of commercial vehicle bodies.

Zanolo (CH)
c1930, Lausanne
The only known body by Carrosserie Zanolo is a two-door coupé on the Delage D8 chassis, dating from 1929-1930.

Zietz (CH)
1930s, Geneva
Almost nothing is known about this Geneva coachbuilder which was responsible for an attractive tourer body on a Mercedes S Chassis in 1931.

Zimmerli (CH)
1940s, Reiden
The brothers Werner and Fritz Zimmerli owned the Vauxhall and Chevrolet dealership at Reiden. In 1948, Fritz's son was serving an apprenticeship in the business,

and he put forward the idea of a two-seat roadster based on the latest six-cylinder Velox model. Zimmerli built a special tubular chassis for the car, and the alloy body was constructed by an Italian who had been a PoW during the Second World War. Vauxhall declined to take an interest in the project, and just a single prototype was built.

Zschau (D)
1878–1939, Leipzig
Karosseriewerke Friedrich August Zschau was founded in Leipzig in 1878 by Friedrich August Zschau. Construction of car bodywork began in the early 1920s and by the middle of the decade Zschau had begun to specialise in building small series of special tourer and cabriolet bodies. All were for German marques, including Dux, Elite, Horch, Mercedes-Benz, Presto and Wanderer, and this work continued through the 1930s. The company had around 350 employees in this period, but did not undertake individual commissions.

During the 1939-1945 war, the company was obliged to undertake work for the military. When peace came, Zschau found itself in the Soviet-controlled Eastern sector of Germany after the Second World War, and became a producer of body panels within the state-owned IFA (Industrieverband Fahrzeugbau, or Industrial Association for Vehicle Construction).

Zschau: This four-seater cabriolet body is on a 1927-1928 Mercedes-Benz 8/38PS chassis. *(Daimler-Benz)*